State and
Local Government
Administration

PUBLIC ADMINISTRATION AND PUBLIC POLICY

A Comprehensive Publication Program

Executive Editor

JACK RABIN
Graduate Program in
Public Affairs and
Human Services
Administration
Rider College
Lawrenceville, New Jersey

Other volumes in preparation

State and Local Government Administration

edited by

Jack Rabin
Graduate Program in Public Affairs
and Human Services Administration
Rider College
Lawrenceville, New Jersey

Don Dodd
History Department
Auburn University at Montgomery
Montgomery, Alabama

[handwritten note:] To the Alabama authors' (UNA graduates') section of the UNA Library. For several years at AUM in the 1970s, I had a joint appointment in History & Government and taught State & Local Gov't (survey course) & graduate course). This book is a product of that tenure and is still used (1997) as a textbook in the same name graduate course by the same name as the text.
D D Dodd (Florence) Class of 1961 UNA

MARCEL DEKKER, INC.   New York and Basel

Library of Congress Cataloging in Publication Data

Main entry under title:

State and local government administration.

(Public administration and public policy ; 28)
Includes index.
1. State governments. 2. Local government--United
States. I. Rabin, Jack, [date]. II. Dodd, Don.
III. Series.
JK2408.S78 1985   353.9   85-12873
ISBN 0-8247-7355-1

MARCEL DEKKER, INC.
270 Madison Avenue, New York, New York   10016

Current printing (last digit):
10 9 8 7 6 5 4 3 2 1

PRINTED IN THE UNITED STATES OF AMERICA

Preface

This introduction to the administration of state and local government focuses on four crucial areas of public administration:

1. Organization and management
2. Budgeting, decision-making, and financial management
3. Policy-making and policy implementation
4. Personnel administration and labor relations

These areas consume most of the resources, both human and financial, that states and localities use in their operation and management. Unit One on organization and management includes the management structures of states, counties, and cities, and the leadership functions of chief executives, administrative officers, and court administrators.

James L. Garnett, Division of Business and Public Management, West Virginia College of Graduate Studies, introduces management structures with a survey of the organization and reorganization of state and local governments in the United States. He begins with Herbert Kaufman's explanation of the values traditionally sought by state and local governments and then breaks down the organizational forms and reorganization efforts by state, county, municipal, township, and special district levels. He notes that the general trend of all reorganization has been to centralize control in the executive and for states to give their agencies and local governments greater organizational and managerial flexibility.

Alan Reed, Division of Public Administration, University of New Mexico, discusses the leadership functions of the mayor, the city manager (CM), and the chief administrative officer (CAO). He distinguishes between the chief executive, who incorporates the symbolic and political facets of the executive branch, and the chief administrator, who incorporates only the organizational facets. Reed illustrates the different roles CAOs play using the examples of San Francisco, New Orleans, Los Angeles, New York, Boston, and his home city of Albuquerque. He compares the CAO to the CM and sees the CAO as an attractive alternative to the CM for many cities.

In the 1960s, massive arrests of civil rights and antiwar demonstrators, combined with increased civil litigation, overburdened the judicial machinery and revealed the need for more efficient court management. The professional responding to this need was the court administrator. Steven W. Hays, Vice-Chairman, Department of Government, University of South Carolina, surveys and assesses the functions and roles of this new government professional. Hays sees a more significant place for court administrators in state and local government, particularly if court systems obtain sufficient administrative authority to manage their own affairs and if court administrators are allowed to evolve naturally toward fulfilling their professional potential.

Unit Two, which covers budgeting, decision-making, and financial management, considers mechanisms and processes as well as internal and external controls. The mechanism and processes section concentrates on the functions that state budgeting serves, the local budget area and its problems, and the nature and extent of state limitations on fiscal authority. The controls section emphasizes productivity and performance measurement, information systems technology, and fiscal stress in state and local government.

Regis L. Chapman, Virginia Department of Planning and Budget, initiates the budgeting part of the mechanisms and processes section by describing state budget processes as complex intersections through which state policies and programs must travel. Each state is different, and not all intersections are identified on current maps. The numerous roads being traveled by actors with diverse perspectives steer innovators toward new road and intersection construction. Thus, the budget process must be custom-built for each state. From this overview, Chapman describes the evolution of the budgeting function; its operational environment; the major budgeting stages; and future initiatives.

Although budgeting suggests to the layperson the drudgery and boredom of ledgers, accounts, and journals, it is the heart of the political and decision-making process. If politics is who gets what, when and how, then budgeting is the essence of politics. The budget is the best statement of public priorities because it allocates money among competing programs. Perry Moore, Dean, College of Liberal Arts, Wright State University, Ohio, explains the various purposes of municipal budgeting and how each purpose is related to a specific budgeting format. He notes that although budget formats may differ, the budget cycle is the same for different formats. This cycle includes revenue estimation, budget formulation, budget approval, budget execution, and audit of expenditures. Moore concludes his explanation with a brief review of capital budgeting.

Patricia S. Florestano, Director of the Institute for Governmental Service at the University of Maryland, concludes the mechanisms and processes section with a discussion of the historical relationship of state and local governments; types of taxes and the fiscal process (including full disclosure requirements); the problems of state-imposed limitations; and recent state-local financial developments. Florestano stresses the importance of the state to localities, pointing out that states bear a significant part of the cost of local operations, assist in improving management, coordinate and supervise local program administration, and contribute to good local government.

Harry P. Hatry, The Urban Institute, Washington, D.C., begins the control section with a definition of productivity and performance measurement, and discusses various types and uses; data collection procedures; how governments can determine if the performance measures are working; and suggested steps for agencies to follow to develop their performance measurement processes. He feels that current procedures can provide a reasonable perspective on the performance of most agencies, although managers and officials are slow to adopt them. Although cost-effectiveness is a valid concern, Hatry sees the potential improvement of performance measurement as meeting a major need for state and local government.

In the post-World War II era, legislative control mechanisms, attempting to achieve accountability in government, faced massive state and local government paperwork. Many public administrators saw automated information systems as a panacea for this paper explosion. As with most simple solutions to complex problems, disillusionment was inevitable. Edward Jackowski, Graduate Program for Administrators, Rider College, New Jersey, summarizes the use of information systems in state and local government and assesses their use in the 1980s. He concludes his survey with a "propositional inventory of future trends."

After an examination of recent changes in state perspectives and policies, David P. Rebovich, Department of Political Science, Rider College, portrays increases in state expenditures and revenue-raising in the 1980s, and focuses on situational factors influencing fiscal policies: changes in managerial factors—particularly resource mixes; differences among the states; and state responses to fiscal stress in 1982-1983. In the future, Rebovich expects increased state taxes (especially personal incomes taxes), decreased federal aid, and increased state assumption of service responsibilities.

A principal thesis of John J. Gargan, Political Science Department, Kent State University, is that the complexity of city fiscal dependency has been understated, and that the public administration community's dominant paradigm of governing capacity is inadequate for dealing with that complexity. In developing his thesis, Gargan distinguishes between fiscal stress and fiscal dependency; lists municipal revenue sources; notes differences in the degree of cities' reliance on external revenue sources; and describes the dominant community paradigm (and its good management focus) and criticizes its neglect of the local political context. He concludes that the establishment of modern management practices requires demonstrated benefits to the local officials who adopt them.

Unit Three, on policy-making, takes two paths. The first focuses on policy-making patterns within the executive and legislative branches, particularly *internal* processes that affect public policy formulation and implementation. Aspects of policy-making included are: chief executive innovation and gubernatorial administration, personal liability, state budgeting and appropriations in the legislature, and the growth of legislative staffs. The second path of policy implementation develops the two fields of alternatives to municipal service delivery and the integration of human services management within delivery systems.

The chief executive plays a major role in the state and local government innovative process. He or she can develop appropriate expectations among staff and constituents, create a supportive organizational climate, and provide adequate resources. Even with chief executive support, however, innovation may fail. The lack of appropriate technologies and legal uncertainties are but two reasons for failure. These are the conclusions of James L. Perry, Graduate School of Management, University of California at Irvine.

In "The Governor as Administrator," Alan J. Wyner, Political Science Department, University of California at Santa Barbara, cautions that the administrative role of a governor cannot be divorced from the other roles of politician, ceremonial head of state, bearer of mandated responsibilities, and policy formulator. With this qualification, he discusses the governor's administrative role with particular attention to the personal staff, appointments to executive branch leadership positions, and executive branch management activities.

The liability of public jurisdictions and their agents reflects the trend towards more accountability of public entities and agents to citizens. While governmental entities face the most threat from state law or common law, the most significant personal liability exposures for officials and employees come from recent interpretations of the Civil Rights Act of 1871. These are major points made by W. Bartley Hildreth, Graduate School of Management, Kent State University, and Gerald J. Miller, Public Administration Department, Rutgers University. Their chapter also introduces relevant legal rules and their consequences and discusses major management policy issues arising from the vulnerability of governments and their agents to tort liability suits.

In a transitional chapter between the policy-making roles of the executive and legislative branches of state government, James E. Skok, Department of Public Administration, Pennsylvania State University, observes that budgeting in the 1980s is the central process through which managers can effect a reduced growth in state government. As a result, the budget process is likely to become more politicized as interest groups mobilize to limit their losses and legislative bodies struggle to maintain some control over state appropriations. Skok discusses recent analytic methods to reform the budget process (Planning-Programming-Budgeting-Systems and Zero-Base Budgeting) and the role of state legislatures in appropriating funds.

Alan P. Balutis, Director of the Office of Systems and Special Projects in the U.S. Department of Commerce, surveys modernization efforts that have produced larger legislative staffs, and examines their functions and speculates on their future use. He notes how the legislative environment molds the behavior and influence of the professional staff and comments on the staff's political role. He adds that the legislature and their professional staffs should be a part of the study and *practice* of public administration.

David R. Morgan, Bureau of Government Research, Department of Political Science, University of Oklahoma, in a chapter focusing on policy implementation, observes that the greatest impetus to the use of alternative service delivery mechanisms is a fiscal crisis; thus, an increasing number of cities are considering this option. The four most commonly used arrangements are contracting, intergovernmental agreements, franchising, and voluntary service, with the first two the most widely used. Morgan notes that many service alternatives save money but that service quality is not always maintained. He concludes that "if studied thoroughly beforehand and entered into cautiously and carefully, such arrangements may indeed provide local management with a useful tool for controlling costs without serious erosion of service quality."

Beaumont R. Hagebak, counseling psychologist and mental health project officer, U.S. Public Health Service, Atlanta, states that the "bottom line" for any human service agency is client gain in such intangibles as health, happiness, productivity, responsibility, and independence. Hagebak believes that the integration of human services management and delivery systems is one way of maintaining excellence in the face of diminishing resources and would be of special value in treating the multiple-problem client.

Unit Four covers personnel administration and labor relations in state and local governments. Part A covers processes and techniques such as performance appraisal, organizational training, and pension systems. Part B surveys the development and extent of public employee unionism and collective bargaining in states and localities.

Where stringent state and local budgets and public outcries for governmental accountability prevail, governmental officials seek cost-effective, operational procedures and the efficient use of available resources, including human ones. A central personnel problem is balancing accountability and merit. Arthur L. Finkle, New Jersey Department of Civil Service, Division of Appellate Practices and Labor Relations, focuses on the problem of balancing accountability and merit in a survey of the performance appraisal system in New Jersey.

Lyle J. Sumek, Sumek Associates, Inc., Boulder, Colorado, discusses the training aspect of personnel management in the 1980s and provides an organizational effectiveness model and a learning model. He also considers the training responsibility of managers, traditional training, and training frontiers for the 1980s and 1990s. Sumek concludes that effective training programs are guided by well-defined managerial values within an organizational philosophy; training activities are individual-directed but should be integrated into the functional organization so as to be organizationally supported; and managers have personal responsibility for training.

State and local government pension systems are important employee fringe benefits which have increased in number and assets in recent years, but they are also a significant public policy concern. A recent Advisory Commission on Intergovernmental Relations report indicated that 56% of 72 public pension systems studied were not funded on an actuarially sound basis. Donald E. Klingner and Randy L. Nutter, Florida International University, identify inadequate disclosure, funding, and management policies as major pension system problems which can be corrected by state or federal laws specifying minimum standards for disclosure and actuarial soundness and by the adoption of strategic investment techniques.

Nor are pension systems the only employee benefit concerns of state and local governmental employees. In 1980, more than one million full-time state employees belonged to employee groups, and forty states had a labor-management policy covering at least a part of their workforce. So notes Arthur Finkle in his chapter on state unionism, which details why unionism exists in state governments; explains its evolution; discusses the inner workings of bilateralism; and assesses the impact of collective bargaining in state government.

Unionism is also a phenomenon of local government. In fact, 52% of all full-time local government employees belong to employee organizations. The three highest percentages were for firefighters (70.6%), teachers (67.9%), and police officers (52.8%). Of the approximately 80,000 local governments in the United States, less than 15,000 (17.9%) reported a labor relations policy in the last census. Ernest Gross, Institute of Management and Labor Relations, Rutgers University, profiles local government employees and then discusses the legal basis for collective bargaining; the parameters of negotiations; state and local civil service systems; the impact of the civil rights laws; grievance procedures; hiring; the right to strike; fact-finding proceedings; and compulsory arbitration.

Since World War II, states and localities have expanded in numbers of employees, services provided, and expenditures. Unfortunately, administrative structures, processes, and techniques have not usually kept pace with this growth.

The original essays in this text address some of the major issues of state and local government administration and should provide a better understanding of where state and local administration has been and where it is going. Both the editors and the chapter authors welcome comments and criticisms.

The editors gratefully acknowledge the helpful editorial assistance provided by Bernice Liput and Eileen K. Abatto, Rider College; Lloyd Cornett, Director, USAF Historical Research Center, Maxwell AFB, Alabama; Dess Sangster, Auburn University at Montgomery; and institutional support from Rider College and Auburn University at Montgomery.

Jack Rabin
Don Dodd

Contributors

ALAN P. BALUTIS* Office of Systems and Special Projects, U.S. Department of Commerce, Washington, D.C.

REGIS L. CHAPMAN Virginia Department of Planning and Budget, Richmond, Virginia

ARTHUR L. FINKLE Division of Appellate Practices and Labor Relations, New Jersey Department of Civil Service, Trenton, New Jersey

PATRICIA S. FLORESTANO Institute for Governmental Service, University of Maryland, College Park, Maryland

JOHN J. GARGAN Department of Political Science, Kent State University, Kent, Ohio

JAMES L. GARNETT Division of Business and Public Management, West Virginia College of Graduate Studies, Institute, West Virginia

ERNEST GROSS Industrial Relations and Human Resources Department, Institute of Management and Labor Relations, Rutgers, The State University of New Jersey, New Brunswick, New Jersey

*Present affiliation: Office of Management Analysis and Control, U.S. Department of Commerce, Washington, D.C.

BEAUMONT R. HAGEBAK U.S. Public Health Service, Region IV, Atlanta, Georgia

HARRY P. HATRY State and Local Government Research Program, The Urban Institute, Washington, D.C.

STEVEN W. HAYS Department of Government and International Studies, University of South Carolina, Columbia, South Carolina

W. BARTLEY HILDRETH Graduate School of Management, Kent State University, Kent, Ohio

EDWARD M. JACKOWSKI Graduate Program for Administrators, Rider College, Lawrenceville, New Jersey

DONALD E. KLINGNER Department of Public Administration, Florida International University, North Miami, Florida

GERALD J. MILLER Institute of Public Administration, Rutgers, The State University of New Jersey, Newark, New Jersey

PERRY MOORE College of Liberal Arts, Wright State University, Dayton, Ohio

DAVID R. MORGAN Bureau of Government Research, Department of Political Science, University of Oklahoma, Norman, Oklahoma

RANDY L. NUTTER* Institute for Public Management and Community Services, School of Public Affairs and Services, Florida International University, North Miami, Florida

JAMES L. PERRY Graduate School of Management, University of California, Irvine, California

DAVID P. REBOVICH Department of Political Science, Rider College, Lawrenceville, New Jersey

ALAN REED Division of Public Administration, University of New Mexico, Albuquerque, New Mexico

JAMES E. SKOK Department of Public Administration, Pennsylvania State University, Middletown, Pennsylvania

LYLE J. SUMEK Sumek Associates, Inc., Boulder, Colorado

ALAN J. WYNER Department of Political Science, University of California, Santa Barbara, California

*Present affiliation: Village of Miami Shores, Miami Shores, Florida

Contents

Unit One

ORGANIZATION AND MANAGEMENT OF STATES AND LOCALITIES

Part A   Management Structures
Chapter 1

Part B   Leadership Functions
Chapters 2-3

1
Organizing and Reorganizing State and Local Government

James L. Garnett   Division of Business and Public Management, West Virginia College of Graduate Studies, Institute, West Virginia

I. THE SEARCH FOR STRUCTURE

A. Relevance of Organizational Structure

Few issues in American state and local government have generated as much controversy and effort as have issues surrounding *structure*. Issues debated at length include the following: Does a strong governor system enable more effective state government than a weak governor system? Which structure is superior for municipal governments: strong mayor-council plan, weak mayor-council model, council-manager plan, or commission form? What are the potentials and risks for counties moving from the plural executive model to a single executive? Charles Hyneman showed how intensely government officials, scholars, and reformers have debated over structure when he wrote: "most of the rationalizers of state reorganization . . . appear to proceed blithely on the assumption that God looks after fools, drunkards, and the liberties of the people" (Hyneman, 1939:73). These controversies over state and local structure were often battlegrounds for political and administrative theory (Hyneman, 1939; Waldo, 1948; Gottlieb, 1976; Garnett, 1980) and the testing grounds for structural reforms later adopted by the federal government (Graves, 1949:140; Garnett, 1980:18,19).

Aside from people's fondness for crusades and controversy, why has so much attention been paid to structural-organizational issues? One reason is that structure affects the pattern of influence and indeed often reflects who has the upper hand. A multimembered county board with both legislative and administrative powers invites a "you scratch my back and I'll scratch yours attitude" (Adrian, 1976:165). Another reason for a preoccupation with structure stems from its effect on government performance. Despite the many attempts to prove the relevance or irrelevance of structure for government effectiveness, the picture is still unclear.[1]

Few would doubt that structure affects performance, but it is difficult to demonstrate how and to what degree this influence takes place. But, the quest to explore this relationship continues.

This chapter first addresses the emphases reflected in government organization and reorganization, then turns to look at the major structures used in state, county, municipal, town, and special district governments and also at the trends in reorganizing those governments.

B. Emphases in Government Organization

State and local government organization and reorganization is a difficult subject to cover. The types of governments involved vary in size, legal status, and political culture. The structural forms differ even among governments of the same type. The motives for reorganizing and the tactics employed also vary considerably.

Because of the scope and complexity of the task, it helps to have a conceptual framework for explaining the patterns of state and local government organization. Herbert Kaufman's classic thesis on public administration doctrine provides such a framework (Kaufman, 1956).

In Kaufman's formulation, state and local (and national) administrative institutions:

> have been organized and operated in pursuit successively of three values . . . representativeness, neutral competency and executive leadership. Each of these values has been dominant (but not to the total suppression of the others) in different periods of our history; the shift from one to another generally appears to have occurred as a consequence of the difficulties encountered in the period preceding the change. (Kaufman, 1956:1057)

These stages in state and local administrative development and some characteristics of each stage are shown in Fig. 1.

1. Representativeness

The first emphasis on the part of the state and local governments after independence was toward representativeness in government. This value had its roots in the colonial period and was, in effect, a reaction to the executive dominance exerted by royal or proprietary governors. Kaufman maintained that frequently during this period elected legislatures were seen as champions of the colonists in competition with governors appointed by the King of England or by a branch of directors of a chartered company (Kaufman, 1963:35).

After the Revolution, legislative bodies held the upper hand in most state and local governments and the executives were reduced to mere figureheads. For example, governors were elected by the legislatures in eleven instances, chosen for one-year terms in most cases, and for the most part had negligible powers of appointment and removal, no veto, no supervisory authority, no role in the budgetary process, no legislative function worth noting, no investigatory powers, and practically no staff aid.

Supremacy of the elected legislative body was one reflection of the emphasis placed on representativeness during this period. An almost unquestioning belief in the electoral principle constituted the other element of the "core value" of representativeness. Kaufman describes how faith in the electoral principle was carried to excess:

> The first half of the Nineteenth Century saw the number of elective offices sharply increased, especially after the Jacksonian Revolution burst upon the country. The ballot grew in length until almost every public official from President down to dogcatcher came to power via the electoral route. (1956:1059)

Carried to this extreme, it became evident about the time of the Civil War that legislative supremacy, the long ballot, and the spoils system did not increase representativeness in state or local government, but indeed had the opposite effect. Voter confusion and resulting apathy plus lack of cohesion provided the opportunity for political machines to achieve power. Whereas these machines did provide some cohesion, corruption often resulted and decision-making was hardly representative.

2. Neutral Competence

Unbridled representativeness had proven to be dysfunctional, and reforms were sought to remedy the excess that had resulted. The direction these reforms generally took was toward neutral competence. In Kaufman's terms this core value involved "the ability to do the work of government expertly, and to do it according to explicit, objective standards rather than to personal or party or other obligations and loyalties. The slogan of the neutral competence school became, 'Take administration out of politics'" (Kaufman, 1956: 1060).

The mechanisms for achieving neutral competence were using independent commissions and boards to conduct state and local government business and installing and expanding the merit system. Bipartisan and staggered appointment to these boards and commissions was intended to make these bodies more

Fig. 1 Emphasis in State and Local Executive Organization: Three Stages of Administrative Development[a]

Characteristics	Representativeness (1787–Civil War)	Neutral competence (Civil War–WWI)	Executive leadership (WWI–Present)
Length of executive's tenure	Executive's tenure short—mostly one-year term	Term of executive increased to two years	Four-year terms with succession allowable
Executive's power of appointment (over administrative officials)	Executive's power negligible—direct election of administrative officers	Appointment power primarily with executive, but appointee tenure staggered and often longer than executive; often protected from removal	Executive has appointment and removal powers over department head
Degree of agency autonomy from executive	No supervisory authority over agencies by governor	Strong legal and administrative autonomy on part of agencies	Reduce autonomy of agencies; consolidate into larger functional departments under executive's leadership
Executive's role in budget	No role in budgetary process	Limited role in budget process	Executive budget

Personnel selection (nonagency heads)	Legislature chooses personnel	Merit apparatus chooses personnel (came to many jurisdictions late)	Opening up merit system to allow more appointees by executive
Executive's involvement in the decision-making process	Virtually all decisions made by legislative enactment	Greater involvement by executive in decision-making but still limited	Strong involvement by executive in decision-making process
Executive's veto power	No veto	Veto	Item veto
Length of ballot	Long ballot	Shorter ballot	Short ballot
Executive's responsibility for administrative action	Low	Moderate	High
Overall power position	Legislative supremacy	Legislative/bureaucratic/executive stalemate	Executive supremacy

[a]Kaufman does not indicate what the governor's budget role was during the phase emphasizing "neutral competence." It could be assumed that the governor's role was primarily greater than that during the representativeness phase and less than that during the predominantly "executive leadership" stage.

Source: From Kaufman (1956, 1963).

resistant to partisan or corrupt influence, but these measures also had the effect of limiting the chief executive's control over these agencies.

Much of state and local administration at this point could be characterized by fragmentation, proliferation, lack of overall direction, virtual capture of many "islands of decision-making" by special interests. Just as excessive stress on representativeness resulted in problems that proponents of that doctrine had not anticipated, so too did inordinate reliance upon neutral competence lead to overcompensation and dysfunction in state and local government.

3. Executive Leadership

Kaufman contended the "centrifugal drives of the representativeness and neutral competence institutions . . . found no important counterforce in the legislature or in the courts" (1956:1063). The executive (governor, county executive, mayor or city manager) was thus turned to as a means of giving overall direction to drifting administrative machinery. The formula for achieving executive leadership was essentially that proposed by the administrative orthodoxists—consolidating a large number of agencies into a smaller number of departments organized along functional lines while being legally and politically responsible to the executive. Other elements included augmenting the executive's control through executive budget, shorter ballot, increased veto power, and additional staff assistance.

This framework adds perspective to the more detailed discussion that follows.

II. STATE GOVERNMENT ORGANIZATION AND REORGANIZATION

A. Forms of State Organization

State government structures are usually classified as weak governor systems or strong governor systems. *Weak governor* systems carry over the colonial suspicion of strong executive rule and emphasize representativeness and neutral competence. Further, these systems are characterized by a long ballot (a number of executive branch officials elected besides the governor), weak power of governor to appoint department heads, a large number of state agencies, heavy reliance on boards and commissions to handle administrative work, and relatively weaker gubernatorial budgetary and other powers.

Strong governor systems emphasize Kaufman's core value of executive leadership reflecting strong appointive and removal powers, fewer, more consolidated administrative agencies, and more power centralized in the governor's hands. According to Charles Adrian, Alaska, California, Idaho, Kentucky, New York, Ohio, Pennsylvania, Rhode Island, Virginia, and Washington use strong governor systems (Adrian, 1976:169). Keep in mind, though, that these classifications refer to *formal organization structure.* A governor in a weak governor system may have tremendous informal power because of strong political party discipline, patronage power, force of personality, or some other reason. Likewise, a governor in a strong governor state may lack the experience, expertise, or backing necessary to take advantage of his considerable formal powers.

B. Reorganizing State Government: Types and Trends

A typology developed by George Bell is useful for tracking structural patterns in state reorganization. According to Bell (1973, 1976) there have been three principal types of state reorganization—traditional, cabinet, and secretary-coordinator. The *traditional* type most closely embodies the core value of neutral competence. This is because most state executive branches reflected the dominance of neutral competence when the modern reorganization movement began around 1910. The traditional reorganization is the least drastic, leaving more of the premovement status quo that the other types. A larger number of state agencies, higher proportion of boards and commissions, lower gubernatorial appointment power, and diffused managerial control are characteristic of the traditional reorganization. This type also contains more representativeness since more elected administrators besides the governor are usually found in this structure. (See Fig. 2 for definitions of the primarily structural dimensions of these three types.)

The *cabinet* type embraces more of the elements of Kaufman's executive leadership value. This includes stronger gubernatorial appointment power, less diffused managerial control, and a lower proportion of agencies run by plural executives.

The *secretary-coordinator* type also is oriented toward the value of executive leadership. This interposes a supercoordinator department-secretary between the governor and the heads of operating departments in an umbrella, super-agency structure. It goes further toward the ideal of executive leadership than does the cabinet form, except for the higher degree of management authority retained by the component operating agencies.

Table 1 shows overall patterns in adoption and structure of state executive reorganization from 1910 to 1981. Of the 154 state executive branch reorganizations attempted during this period, 39 (25%) resulted in no adoption at all, and 115 (75%) resulted in adoption of at least some proposals. Based on these results, it would appear that there were favorable odds (about 3:1) of at least some reorganization provisions being adopted. These odds have shifted over time, increasing from the 42 and 57% adoption rates in the 1910s and 1920s to the 90%+ rate in the 1960s and 1970s.

Part of the explanation for the more receptive climate for adopting executive branch reorganizations is a greater perceived need for modernizing state

Fig. 2 Types of State Reorganization

Dimension 1: number of agencies after reorganization

Traditional: (high) >17
Cabinet: (medium) 9–16
Secretary–coordinator: (low) 1–8

Dimension 2: degree of functional consolidation

Traditional: (low consolidation) over 50% of all
consolidation is into single-function agencies,
narrowly defined (e.g., water supply, highways)

Cabinet: (moderate consolidation) over 50% of all
consolidation is into single-function agencies, broadly
defined (e.g., environmental protection, transportation)

Secretary–coordinator: (high consolidation) over 50% of
all consolidation is into very large multiple-function or
broad single-function agencies (e.g., human resources,
natural resources)

Dimension 3: proportion of postreorganization department
heads appointed by governor

Traditional: (low) <50%
Cabinet: (moderate) 50%–66%
Secretary–coordinator: (high) >67%

Dimension 4: proportion of postreorganization agencies with
plural executives (e.g., boards or commissions)

Traditional: (high) >25%
Cabinet: (moderate) 10%–24%
Secretary–coordinator: (low) ≤9%

Dimension 5: degree of management authority retained by
transplanted agencies

Traditional: (high) most (50%) of the reorganization
transplants involve transplant of agencies into other units,
with the transplanted agencies primarily retaining their
statutory authority, structural identity, and control over
management support services (e.g., budgeting, purchasing)

Cabinet: (low) most (50%) of the reorganization transplants
involve transplants into other units, with the transplanted
agencies primarily relinquishing statutory authority,
structural identity, and control over management support
services

Secretary–coordinator: (moderately high) most (50%) of
reorganization transplants involve the transplant of
agencies into superagencies, with the transplanted agencies
primarily retaining their structural identity and much of
their statutory authority while relinquishing some control
over management support services (e.g., submitting to
budget review by the superagency)

Source: From Garnett (1980).

Table 1 State Executive Branch Reorganization: Adoptions, Failures, and Types, 1910–1981

| Years | Reorganization[a] | | Types[b] | | |
	Adoptions	Failures to adopt	Traditional	Secretary-coordinator	Cabinet
1910–1919	5 (42%)	7 (58%)	4 (40%)	1 (10%)	5 (50%)
1920–1929	21 (57%)	16 (43%)	10 (42%)	0	14 (58%)
1930–1939	25 (76%)	8 (24%)	15 (63%)	0	9 (37%)
1940–1949	12 (75%)	4 (25%)	5 (71%)	0	2 (29%)
1950–1959	8 (89%)	1 (11%)	3 (60%)	0	2 (40%)
1960–1969	24 (92%)	2 (8%)	11 (65%)	3 (18%)	3 (18%)
1970–1979	20 (95%)	1 (5%)	8 (47%)	2 (12%)	7 (41%)
1980–1981	0	0	0	0	0
Totals	115 (75%)	39 (25%)	56 (54%)	6 (6%)	42 (40%)

[a]Adoptions includes those reorganization attempts where at least some restructuring is adopted. Failures includes those attempts where no reorganization was adopted.
[b]Types are defined in Table 2. Not every reorganization could be typed because of missing data.
Source: From Garnett (1980); Bell (1973, 1976); and Beyle (1982).

governmental machinery. The increased demands and problems facing state governments in the post-World War II era have created pressures for states to revamp their administrative apparatus to cope. In the words of Mosher:

> Herein lies a basis rationale, and often the underlying reason, for administrative reorganization: to bring up-to-date, or to permit the bringing up-to-date, of those aspects of organizational operation and relationships that have suffered from "lag"—i.e., that have failed to modify themselves through incremental changes sufficiently to keep up with the changing context within which they operate. (1967:494)

Many executive branch reorganizations in the 1960s and 1970s accompanied an expanded, more active role for states in delivering services to residents and in relating to federal and local governments.

But these administrative adjustments were not always consistent with executive leadership values. The less reform-oriented traditional reorganization has been applied more frequently overall (56 times, 54%) than the more reform-minded secretary–coordinator (6 times, 6%) and cabinet (42 times, 40%) models. In fact, application of the more rigorous cabinet type patterned after the federal executive branch model has been applied more than might have been expected in light of the greater political and legal efforts necessary for thorough-going reform.

Because early reformers like A. E. Buck and Luther Gulick advocated more sweeping reform, and because state machinery then needed more drastic overhaul, states attempted a higher proportion of cabinet reorganizations in the 1910s and 1920s than in later decades. The secretary–coordinator type is a relatively recent phenomenon even though Iowa attempted, but failed to adopt, this type in 1915. California (1961 and 1968), Massachusetts (1969), Virginia (1972), and Kentucky (1972-1973) adopted the secretary-coordinator type patterned after the Department of Health, Education, and Welfare (HEW) model in which many related agencies are clustered in a large umbrella department. But a more recent trend has been away from having so many functions consolidated in so few departments. Such superagencies are usually expensive because extra layers of administration are needed to coordinate many programs and subagencies.

Not only have some types of reorganization been used less in recent years, but states have also relied less on executive branch reorganization itself as a tool for change and reform. After a spurt of executive branch overhauls in the 1960s and early 1970s, no major reorganizations have occurred since 1977 when New Mexico, Connecticut, and West Virginia adopted broad-scale reorganizations. Several reasons exist for this diminished activity in state executive branch reorganization.[2]

1. Most governors and state administrators think structural overhaul is unnecessary in their state and have therefore not pushed for more structural change. According to Eric Herzik, no governors called for overall reorganization in their 1981 "state of the State" addresses compared with fifteen governors announcing reorganization plans in their 1973 addresses (Herzik, 1981). In addition, Deil S. Wright and Ted F. Hebert surveyed 1400 top state agency administrators in 1978 as part of their State Administrators Project (Advisory Commission on Intergovernmental Relations, 1980). They found that 62% of all respondents thought their state did not need major reorganizing. In only five states did a vast majority of respondents think major restructuring needed. Since all but three states—North Dakota, Texas, and South Carolina—have had at least one major executive branch reorganization, the need to bring state governmental machinery up to date is perhaps less keenly felt. And even in these states, incremental restructuring has taken place. As of 1983, South Carolina is strongly considering comprehensive reorganization.

2. That reorganizing that has occurred recently has been more incremental, involving only a few agencies or functions at a time. Consistent with the trend away from comprehensive, all-eggs-in-one-basket tactics, recent reorganizations have been more focused and less sweeping. A study of reorganizations from 1900 to 1975 found that incremental tactics tended to fare better with legislatures and voters than did more ambitious tactics (Garnett, 1979, 1980). This did vary over time and by region, but incremental tactics were typically less risky

politically. Examples of states recently undertaking agency-by-agency functional reorganization are: Arkansas, 1980 (energy); Illinois, 1981 (energy and natural resources); Indiana, 1980 (transportation-highways); Kentucky, 1980 (education, energy, and transportation); Louisiana, 1980 (higher education); Minnesota, 1980 (public utilities); Mississippi, 1980 (planning, housing finance, motor vehicles); Montana, 1981 (commerce); North Dakota, 1981 (higher education and corrections); Rhode Island, 1981 (education); Tennessee, 1981 (transportation); Utah, 1981 (energy and natural resources); Washington, 1981 (corrections); and Wisconsin, 1981 (local affairs and development) (Beyle, 1982).

3. Governors and other state officials have been preoccupied with other concerns, primarily with budget crises and the shape of the newest "new federalism." Recent financial crises brought on by inflation, rising costs, flagging tax revenues, and diminished federal aid have tended to take priority over structural reform. Even some of the reorganizing that has occurred has been of the cost-cutting variety. For example, Tennessee's 1981 reshaping of its Department of Transportation was an economy move (Beyle, 1982). In keeping with the recent economic climate, more emphasis has emerged in economy and productivity reforms than in structural change as such. Economy efforts concentrate on improving procedures and management systems and operations, moves more directly related to saving money. For example, in 1980, Kentucky's Governor John Y. Brown, Jr., established an Executive Management Commission "to introduce business practices into the operation of State Government." A team of state employees and business executives loaned to assist state government reviewed twenty agencies aiming to introduce economy and efficiency reforms. Louisiana's Governor David C. Treen started a similar joint economy drive in 1981. New Jersey, the state that started the reorganization movement in 1915, in 1982 dropped the idea of a general reorganization study. Instead, New Jersey's new Office of Management and Budget will spearhead a study to uncover and eliminate waste, duplication of effort, fraud, and abuse. Indeed, such economy and efficiency drives not only replace structural reorganization, they often accompany or follow it as was the case in Kentucky. For example, Colorado in the late 1960s and Oregon in the early 1970s followed structural reorganization with economy and efficiency campaigns designed to upgrade management practices.

Does all this mean broad-scale executive branch reorganization has gone the way of the saber tooth, that Professor Hyneman's warning is finally being taken seriously? Probably not. State reorganizing has typically occurred in cycles. States not only perceive the need to reorganize based on internal conditions, they also take cues from other states. It is likely then, that changing state responsibilities and changing relationships with federal and local governments will prompt executive branch reorganizations in some states. These reorganizations (and similar conditions in other states) will trigger reorganization elsewhere.

Fiscal austerity and political and economic uncertainty now take priority over state structural issues. But whether this austerity and uncertainty vanish or become more pronounced, reorganization may well follow to adjust to changing conditions and changing state roles.

III. LOCAL GOVERNMENT ORGANIZATION AND REORGANIZATION

A. Types of Local Government

Unlike state governments that are recognized by the U.S. Constitution as full-fledged partners in the federal system, local governments have traditionally been creatures of their state with only the structure and powers their state chooses to allow them. States as architects of local government organization either specify the type of structure local governments may use (e.g., some states require all their counties to use the commission form which is described later) or give their local governments a choice of structures. Greater choice, either through state constitutional provision, statute, or grant of home rule powers to local governments, has been the recent trend.

Diversity in size, political climate, and administrative functions makes it difficult to classify local governments. But the classification shown in Table 2 has become generally accepted.

Table 2 shows that school districts and other special (water, sanitation, housing, fire protection, and so on) districts still comprise the majority of local governments, even though the number of school districts has declined significantly. Yet the number of counties, municipalities, and townships has remained fairly stable in the last two decades. This section focuses primarily on these general-purpose local governments and special districts, discussing each in turn.

1. County Government Organization

Counties, derived from the English "shires" of Anglo-Saxon government, are among the oldest and most widespread forms of local government in the United States. Counties occur in every state except Connecticut, Rhode Island, and parts of Alaska, Montana, and South Dakota. Despite widespread use, patterns of county government vary widely among states and even within states. The major forms of county government include the *commission* plan, featuring a plural executive, and the *council-administrator* and *council-elected executive* forms featuring a single executive.

Commission Form. The most traditional and widely used form of county government is the *commission* form. More than 2398 (79%) out of 3040 counties (county-type governments) use the commission form (National Association of Counties, International City Management, 1978). The commission plan

Table 2　Number of Units of Local Government by Type, 1962–1982

	1962	1967	1972	1977	1982	1962–1982 ±	1962–1982 Change (%)
Counties	3,043	3,049	3,044	3,042	3,041	−2	−0.06%
Municipalities	18,000	18,048	18,517	18,862	19,076	+1076	+6.0%
Townships	17,142	17,105	16,991	16,822	16,734	−408	−2.4%
School districts	34,678	21,782	15,781	15,174	14,851	−19,827	−57.2%
Special districts	18,323	21,264	23,885	25,962	28,588	+10,265	+56.0%
Total	91,186	81,248	78,218	79,864	82,290	−8896	−9.8%

Source:　U.S. Bureau of the Census (1983 and 1979), Table A.

remains the only form permitted in Idaho, Iowa, Massachusetts, Oklahoma, Texas, Vermont, West Virginia, and Wyoming (Duncombe, 1977). Under the commission form an elected board of from 2 to over 100 has legislative powers, such as passing ordinances, adopting budgets, and also administrative powers, such as supervising some or all departments and appointing some administrative employees. A hallmark of the commission form is that "county commissioners share administrative responsibility with a number of independently elected 'row' officers who frequently include: a county clerk, auditor and recorder, assessor, treasurer, prosecuting attorney, sheriff and coroner" (Duncombe, 1977:41). This form embodies Kaufman's principle of representativeness with its emphasis on the long ballot, but it also has facets of the neutral competence value as evidenced by the many administrative boards.

In practice, many variations of the commission plan exist. The most common and important variations include:

1. Strong chairman.   In many counties the chairman of the board, because of seniority, expertise, or willingness, makes daily administrative decisions. Other commissioners rubberstamp those decisions or delegate decisions to the chairman who functions in some ways like a county administrator.
2. Coequal commissioners.   Where no strong chairman of the county board or commission exists, commissioners share leadership and duties, reaching decisions by consensus or vote. As with other commission forms, commissioners have many administrative as well as legislative duties.
3. Supervisor form.   The *supervisor* plan is a special case of the commission form characterized by larger county boards ranging from about 20 to 117 members. Traditionally these boards had town or township supervisors sitting ex officio on the county board. The number of townships determined the number of seats on the board. The U.S. Supreme Court, in its landmark reapportionment case, *Baker v. Carr* (1962), reinforced by later decisions, challenged the unrepresentativeness of many supervisor plans. As a result, Wisconsin and Michigan shifted to other forms of the commission plan in the 1960s, and New York, the primary proponent of the supervisor plan, altered the means of selecting supervisors.
4. Strong supporting official.   Another variation of the commission plan features a strong elected administrative official, typically a county clerk, who performs much of the administration function in addition to supervising elections, keeping records, and carrying out the other duties of his or her own office. This may particularly be the case when the clerk is full time and the commissioners part time and when there is a heritage of leadership from the clerk's office.
5. Strong appointed officer or assistant.   This differs from the preceding variation in that the strong administrative official assisting the commission is

appointed rather than elected. An appointed county clerk, administrative assistant, or other official assists the council in preparing the budget and advises commissioners on managerial matters (Duncombe, 1977).

6. Elected judge as commission chairman. In some states, such as Alabama, Tennessee, and Texas, an elected county judge serves as chairman of the county commission. These judges perform administrative duties in addition to their judicial responsibilities and in some cases have the power of an elected county executive.

Council-Administrator Forms. As with the commission form, a number of variations of the council-administrator plan exist. But two primary types are the *council-manager* and *council-administrator*.

1. Council-manager plan. This form features a professional manager appointed by the county legislative body—the county commission or board—and serving at the board's pleasure. County managers typically prepare the county budget, appoint most or all department heads, advise the board on administrative matters, and make daily decisions on programs and policies. The county board or commission under this plan performs the legislative role—adopting ordinances, approving taxes, and overseeing administrative operations. Iredell County, North Carolina first adopted the council-manager plan in 1927. Dade County, Florida (population 1.2 milion) is the largest user of this form.

2. Council-administrator plan. The council-administrator closely resembles the council-manager form, differing primarily in the powers held by the administrator. County administrators typically hold most of the budget and advisory powers county managers employ, but usually lack the power to appoint and supervise department directors. The council-administrator form predominates in California. Los Angeles County is the largest user of this form of county government. Of the three primary forms, the council-administrator/council-manager most emphasizes Kaufman's value of neutral competence, but includes some aspects of executive leadership.

Council-Elected Executive Form. The *council-elected executive* organization approximates the relationship between legislature and governor, and between council and mayor. The board or commission carries out the legislative functions, and the county executive is elected to preside over the administrative branch.

County executives typically have power to prepare the budget, recommend legislation, and appoint, supervise, and dismiss all or most department heads. But unlike the county managers, elected county executives usually have power to veto bills passed by the county board, although this veto can be overridden by a two-thirds majority (higher in some counties). Another difference lies in the number of independently elected county administrative officials. Council-executive counties typically have fewer elected administrative officers besides the county executive than do commission plan counties. Of the three basic county structures, the council-executive plan emphasize Kaufman's executive leadership value. Westchester and Nassau counties in New York in the 1930s were the first counties to adopt the council-elected executive form, now used by some other populous counties, such as Maryland's Montgomery, Prince Georges, and Baltimore Counties. In fact, Baltimore County's executive appoints a professional administrator to help supervise agencies, thus freeing the executive for more political and community relations functions.

2. County Reorganization

The trend in county reorganization is toward *executive leadership*—centralizing more control in the hands of an elected or appointed executive. The use of council-executive structures has increased from 8 counties in 1950 to 142 counties and city-counties in 1977. The single-executive forms have been particularly employed by larger counties, as Table 3 shows.

Data from the *County Year Book 1978* show counties with administrators (administrators, managers, or executives) comprise only 21% of all counties, but 62% of all counties of 100,000 population or more.

Another trend has been toward expanding the services counties provide. Since counties, like other local governments, are creatures of state government, county services have traditionally reflected this role as local units of the state. These traditional functions are still provided: property tax collection (95.6% of all counties) and assessment (92.5%); election administration (96.8%); police protection via county sheriff's office (93.1%); road maintenance (87%); and, recording of documents (97.2%). But added to these traditional ones are other services modernization and urbanization have forced or stimulated counties to adopt. Examples include: maternal and child health (74%); communicable disease control (79%); fire protection (54.5%); recreational services (45.3%); airports (42.4%); public assistance (45.6%); family social services (64.7%); and, manpower work training (59.7%) (Lawrence and DeGrove, 1976). This expanded role (*local service provider*) supplements the county's traditional role (*unit of state government*) and has accompanied the trend toward executive leadership.

The push for county administrative reform has been limited, however. As the Advisory Commission on Intergovernmental Relations points out:

> While counties have been granted local home rule in 28 states, by
> 1980 only 75 counties had adopted home rule charters, of which 21
> adoptions had occurred since 1972. On the structural front, more-
> over, over three-fourths of the counties still used the plural executive

Table 3 Forms of County Government by Population Size

Classification	All counties	Counties over 2500	Counties over 5000	Counties over 10,000	Counties over 25,000	Counties over 50,000	Counties over 100,000	Counties over 250,000	Counties over 500,000	Counties 1,000,000 and over
Total, all counties	3040	2944	2751	2255	1274	679	343	137	63	19
Form of government										
Without administrator	2398	2306	2118	1673	838	371	150	43	16	4
With administrator	642	638	633	582	436	308	193	94	47	15

Source: National Association of Counties and International City Management Association (1978).

or board form of government including in 1978, 32 of the 137
counties with populations over 250,000. (ACIR, 1982:240)

As with state executive branch reform, county reorganization continues, but at a
slower pace.

3. Municipal Government Organization

The *1982 Census of Governments* defines a municipality as a political subdivision that meets several criteria. (a) Muncipal *incorporation* has been established to provide (b) *general* local governments for (c) *a specific population
concentration* in a (d) *defined area*. A municipality can be called a *city, village,
borough* (except in Alaska, where boroughs are like counties), or *town* (except
in New England states, Minnesota, New York, and Wisconsin). In these states,
"town" relates to an area subdivision that may be incorporated and be a general
government, but that is a geographic area unrelated to a population concentration.

For most citizens, a municipality is the government that most closely
affects them. Of all local governments, municipalities in 1977 spent the most for
direct services in police, fire protection, parks and recreation, housing parking,
libraries, and highways (ACIR, 1982).

Municipal governments take three basic forms: *Mayor-council, commission*, and *council-manager*. These forms parallel their counterparts at the county
level, and also have variations.

Mayor-Council Form. The mayor-council form is used by 54% of all
municipalities, 61% of those over 250,000 population, and 100% over 1 million
population (International City Management Association, 1981).

Three major variations of the mayor-council form exist: weak mayor-
council, strong mayor-council, and strong mayor-council with chief administrative officer.

1. Weak mayor-council. This form predominated in the early and
mid-nineteenth century when cities and other municipalities were primarily
small, rural and suspicious of strong executive control. Also consistent with the
representativeness values of this era, mayors were supplemented with many
other elected administrative officials: auditors, assessors, clerks, treasurers, and
administrative boards and committees. Some weak mayors had veto power over
council actions, but little or no power to develop a budget or coordinate the
work of administrative agencies.

Weak mayor-council systems today are likely to have smaller councils than
in years past, use nonpartisan elections, and allow the mayor to develop the
budget as well as initiate and veto legislation. Weak mayor–council systems exist
today primarily in smaller cities and villages, but some large cities, mostly in the
South, have weak-mayor forms. Chicago, technically, has a weak-mayor system.

But as with weak governor systems, *formal* powers or their lack, are only part of the picture. The late Mayor Richard J. Daley's ability to control administrative machinery via party and personal power has become legend. But current Mayor Harold Washington must attempt to manage a large, complicated, heterogeneous city using limited formal powers.

2. Strong mayor-council.   The strong-mayor form, like its strong governor and county executive counterparts, is an attempt to overcome the centripetal force of numerous elected officials, boards, and agencies pulling in different directions. The strong mayor form embodies Kaufman's executive leadership value—centralization of authority and responsibility in one office. The municipal reform movement beginning in the 1880s strongly promoted the strong mayor-council plan.

Today this form shows variations among municipalities. Typically, it features the veto and budget preparation powers of the weak-mayor form, but gives the mayor few or no other elected administrative officials with whom to compete, fewer boards and commissions, and stronger mayoral appointive and budget administrative powers.

3. Strong mayor-council with chief executive officer.   Emphasis on strengthening mayors to cure the ills of overrepresentativeness and independent bureaucratic fiefdoms left some problems unresolved. As with elected county executives and governors, mayors sometimes have greater interest and ability in campaigning, dealing with councils, and relating to community and interest groups than in overseeing administrative and service delivery operations. One remedy many cities use adds a chief administrative officer (CAO) to relieve the mayor of many managerial functions. Variously called "City Administrator," "Deputy Mayor of Operations," or some other title, these CAOs typically serve at the mayor's pleasure and oversee city administration. In some cities CAOs appoint major department heads subject to the mayor's approval. Cities that use the strong mayor-council with CAO system include Washington, D.C., New York City, Los Angeles, Philadelphia, Boston, and New Orleans.

Commission Plan.   Like the county commission form of government, the municipal commission plan combines legislative and administrative powers within one body. Collectively, city commissioners serve as the legislature; individually, they administer city departments or functions. The mayor is usually one of the commissioners and serves a largely ceremonial role. But unlike the county commission form which predominates, city or village commissions are used by only 6% of all municipal governments and by only 2% of municipalities over 250,000 population.

After a brief period of popularity following its 1903 inception in Galveston, Texas, the municipal commission form has steadily declined in use since 1917. Today, primarily smaller cities use it. North and South Dakota cities show the highest use of the commission plan. Of the large commission cities, such as Portland, Oregon, and Tulsa, Oklahoma, a chief administrative officer is often used to manage the city (Press and Verburg, 1979). This reduces the problems of diffused authority and lack of coordination almost inherent with the commission form.

Council-Manager Plan. Just as the birth of the commission form was dramatic, civic leaders of Galveston banded together to run the city after a flood had killed or injured one-sixth of the population; the council-manager plan was born more of tedium. "In 1908, the city council members of Staunton, Virginia, became frustrated with the welter of 'administrivia' of city government that tends to crop up under any weak executive model. They decided to hire a professional manager—the council could decide policy, the city manager would execute it" (Henry, 1980:156).

The council-manager form, like the strong mayor-council system, spread widely through efforts of municipal reformers in the Short Ballot Organization, the National Municipal League, in universities, and even in the United States Chamber of Commerce (Stillman, 1974:5–53). Business support for the council-manager plan is understandable in light of the plan's emphasis on "businesslike" efficiency. Under the basic plan, voters (stockholders) select council members (directors) who appoint a manager (chief executive) to oversee administrative operations.

The separation of powers strongly contrasts with the commission plan where commissions hold both legislative and administrative powers. In theory, city councils concentrate on making policy through legislation and allow the manager to administer that policy by preparing and executing the budget and appointing and supervising department heads. In practice, councils often delve into administrative details and city managers frequently initiate policy. Variations of the council-manager model itself also bound. For example, some plans include an elected mayor to serve with the council-appointed manager. The mayor's role in such hybrid forms varies from ceremonial figurehead to political leader, depending on the charter, the local political culture, and the mayor's relationship with the manager. Methods for selecting council members also vary. Some elections are partisan, most nonpartisan. Some council members are elected at large; some represent wards. Some cities have both ward and at-large representatives on the council.

Use of council-manager systems is greater in suburbs than in central cities, greater in the South and West than in the North and East, stronger in white-collar communities than in blue-collar ones, and higher in small and medium-sized cities than in larger ones. But some large cities like Dallas, Kansas City, Phoenix, and San Diego use this form. Of all municipalities, 36% use the council-manager form compared with 28% above 250,000 population and only 16% above 500,000. All cities above a 1 million population have mayor-council systems. But as reported earlier, some of those cities also have appointed administrators.

4. Municipal Reorganization

The overall trend in the last 50 years has been toward the strong executive structures—the strong mayor form and council-manager plan. This trend includes an increase in the number of administrative agencies. Although precise data are unavailable, the overall number of agencies has likely risen to accommodate many new municipal functions, such as energy conservation, disaster preparedness, airports, and economic development. Accompanying the addition of new agencies to manage new functions has been a trend toward consolidating more functions into fewer, larger agencies of the former Department of Health, Education, and Welfare (HEW) mold. But some municipalities have joined several states in backing away from so much consolidation. New York City, for example, has dismantled several of its superagencies (e.g., Human Resources Administration and Housing Development Administration) because they were costly and tended to overdo "layering," screening directors of operating agencies from the mayor.

City-county consolidation, another approach to municipal reorganization, has been tried and, with exceptions, has had limited impact on reforming municipal gogvernment. Marando (1974:17-51), Zimmerman (1980), and the Advisory Commission on Intergovernmental Relations (1982:395-405) have thoroughly documented the political, legal, and economic obstacles to city-county consolidation and its limited use.

At the same time centralization has been the overall trend in municipal reorganization, some decentralization to community districts or service delivery districts within cities has also been undertaken (Shalala and Merget, 1974: 153-177).

5. Township Organization

"Township" according to the Census of Governments refers to "16,734 organized governments in 20 states. This category includes governmental units officially designated as towns in the six New England states, New York and Wisconsin and some 'plantations' in Maine and 'locations' in New Hampshire, as well as governments called townships in other areas" (Bureau of the Census, 1983). Townships differ from municipalities in that townships serve inhabitants of areas defined without regard to population concentrations. This reflects their roots as geographic subdivisions of counties. Another difference is that townships, unlike the other types of local government, are found in only twenty northeastern and north central states, rather than all or almost all fifty states.

Townships differ widely in role and powers. Town and township governments administer a wide variety of services, including fire and police protection; rescue services; road and bridge repair and maintenance; social services for the poor, elderly, and youth; and parks and recreation facilities. According to the

U.S. Bureau of the Census, the most frequently reported township-owned and operated services are libraries, sewage disposal and treatment, landfills, and water supply.

Township structures vary as do their powers. The three principal township forms of governance are the town meeting, the representative town meeting, and council-administrator form.

Town Meeting Form. The town meeting, the closest American form to pure democracy, originated in New England and still sees use there and elsewhere. An annual or semiannual meeting where citizens directly discuss their concerns and vote on local policy is characteristic of this form. Budgets are pre-pared, ordinances passed, contracts approved, and other major business trans-acted in open meetings where eligible voters participate. Special meetings can be called by voter petition but most governing takes place in general, scheduled meetings.

Representative Town Meeting. The direct town meeting comes from an earlier, simpler era. Today, larger, urban townships and even many rural town-ships are too populous and too complex to be governed directly by citizens. In these instances, voters elect representatives called selectmen or councilmen, who serve on town boards or councils and act on the voter's behalf. Nonelected citizens may attend meetings but not vote. In some states, resident citizens are permitted to vote on a limited number of issues; some vestiges of the direct democratic form remain. Between meetings, township government is delegated to the board of usually three to seven members.

Council-Administrator Form. This form parallels the municipal council-manager plan and county council-administrator form. Part-time townships councils unable to handle day-to-day administrative routine have increasingly hired a professional administrator who serves at the council's pleasure. This trend has been particularly at work in New England and other strong township states where demands on townships are stronger. Township administrators func-tion like city managers or county administrators, although typically without such broad responsibility.

6. Reorganizing Townships

As just noted, a trend toward council-administrator structures exists. About half the township states use Administrators/CAOs to manage township affairs (Dvorin and Misner, 1970:139). This trend is consistent with Kaufman's execu-tive leadership value and, to a lesser extent, neutral competency's emphasis on professional, apolitical administration. Despite this trend, township structures, especially in rural township states, tend to reflect the continued dominance of representativeness.

A more drastic form of township reorganization involves abolishing the township altogether. Five hundred and nine fewer townships existed in 1982 than in 1942. Most of this decline occurred in the Midwest where rural townships predominate. In fact, all rural township states lost townships between 1972 and 1977 except Indiana, where there was no change, and Illinois, which gained four (ACIR, 1982:248-252). Counties and sometimes municipalities have had to assume the load of abolished townships.

On the other hand, townships have increased in some areas, and the populations they serve have increased. Since 1977, township governments with at least 10,000 population increased by sixty-six and gained 2 million people. Similarly, townships with populations of 1000-10,000 gained in number and population between 1977 and 1982.

Townships, like other forms of local government, reflect tremendous diversity. No single level of powers, services, or structures holds for all townships. They vary because of geography, custom, law, politics, and the particular needs of the areas and people they serve.

7. Special District Organization

Special districts are limited-purpose units created to perform one or at most several functions. Special districts comprise the most numerous and fastest-growing (a 56% increase from 1962-1982) form of local government, as shown in Table 2. These figures likely understate the real number of special districts due to problems with *Census of Governments* definitions (Walsh, 1978: 353-356.

Their narrowness of purpose distinguishes special districts from general-purpose local governments—counties, municipalities, and townships. School districts have traditionally been included in a separate category, although they really constitute a particular case of special district. Most, but not all, public authorities are considered special districts.

All states and the District of Columbia have local special districts. Yet, 64% of all special districts in 1982 were found in thirteen states—Illinois, 2602; California, 2506; Pennsylvania, 2050; Texas, 1681; Kansas, 1370; Missouri, 1195; Nebraska, 1157; Washington, 1130; Colorado, 1030; New York, 923; Oklahoma, 916; Indiana, 897; and Oregon, 825 (*Census of Governments*, 1982: xi). Three of the states relying on special districts most heavily (Illinois, Nebraska, and New York) lost districts between 1977 and 1982. But large increases in other states (especially Oklahoma, California, Texas, Missouri, Kansas, Montana, and North Dakota) offset these declines.

As Table 4 shows, 90.9% of all special districts perform a single function, although this percentage has dropped since 1972. Multiple-function districts, which usually perform no more than several services, are increasing faster than

Table 4 Special Districts by Function: 1972, 1977, and 1982

By function	1972		1977		1982		Change 1972–1982	
	(No.)	(%)	(No.)	(%)	(No.)	(%)	(No.)	(%)
All special districts, total	23,885	100.0	25,962	100.0	28,588	100.0	+4703	+19.7
Single-function districts, total	22,981	96.2	24,242	93.3	25,991	90.9	+3010	+13.1
Cemeteries	1494	6.2	1615	6.2	1577	5.5	+83	+5.5
Education (school building districts)	1085	4.5	1020	3.9	960	3.4	−125	−11.5
Fire protection	3872	16.2	4187	16.1	4560	16.0	+688	+17.7
Highways	698	2.9	652	2.5	598	2.1	−100	−14.3
Health	257	1.1	350	1.3	451	1.6	+194	+75.5
Hospitals	657	2.7	715	2.8	775	2.7	+118	+18.0
Housing and community development	2271	9.5	2408	9.3	3296	11.5	+1025	+45.1
Libraries	498	2.1	586	2.3	638	2.2	+140	+28.1
Natural resources	6639	27.8	6595	25.4	6232	21.8	−407	−6.1
Parks and recreation	750	3.1	829	3.2	924	3.2	+174	+23.2
Sewerage	1411	5.9	1610	6.2	1631	5.7	+220	+15.6
Water supply	2333	9.8	2480	9.5	2637	9.2	+304	+13.0
Other[a]	1016	4.3	1195	4.6	1712	5.9	+696	+68.5
Multiple-function districts,[b] total	904	3.8	1720	6.6	2597	9.1	+1693	+187.2

[a]Includes parking garages and lots; water transport and terminals; airports; transit districts; and gas and electric utilities.
[b]Primarily districts combining sewerage and water supply, and a lesser number combining natural resources and water supply.
Source: U.S. Bureau of the Census, *Census of Governments,* 1972, 1977, 1982, (1973, 1978, 1983), Table 15 (1972), Table 12 (1977), Table G (1982); Advisory Commission on Intergovernmental Relations, (1982), Table 154.

those performing single functions, but still comprise only 9.1% of all special districts.

Table 4 also reflects the wide range of uses special districts serve. Between 1972 and 1982 special-district use increased in all functions except highways, school building, and natural resources, although natural resources and fire protection special districts continue to be the most widely used form. Housing and community development districts (up 45%) and health districts (up 75%) have proliferated since 1972.

Special district boundaries typically do not coincide with those of general-purpose governments. Only one-fourth of all special districts have boundaries that conform to those of counties, townships, or municipalities. And even though most special districts fall entirely within one county, about 9% of all districts extend into two or more counties (Bureau of the Census, 1983).

Critics claim the proliferation of special districts and their failure to coincide with general governments or with each other cause fragmentation and competition among governments. Another common criticism is that special districts, because they typically have their own revenue source and often investors to satisfy, are less accountable to voters (see Smith, 1964; Walsh, 1978).

For all the criticism surrounding special districts, many reasons exist for their widespread usage. First, despite complaints about special district infringement, general-purpose governments' managerial inability or political unwillingness to assume new functions has sometimes created need for special districts. Boundary restrictions have meant local governments are sometimes too small or bounded in the wrong places to handle functions, such as environmental control or water supply, where economic spillovers or economies of scale pertain. Second, fee-for-service financing, the cornerstone of most special districts, tends to be more flexible and more politically expedient than levying taxes. In fact, in this era of public sector retrenchment, general-purpose governments too are utilizing user fees more heavily. Special districts are also a means for circumventing spending restrictions on general-purpose governments. Third, federal government mandates and incentives have triggered some special districts. Districts or authorities for soil conservation, flood control, and housing are prime examples.

Most special districts and especially larger public authorities model their organization after private corporations (see Fig. 3).

Most special districts have a part-time board of directors or commissioners charged with making policy. As with business, these directors usually take their policy cues from the full-time staff. But unlike business, special-district directors are typically appointed by officials of those governments sponsoring the district or authority (e.g., governors, mayors, city councils, county executives) rather than bondholders. Directors are typically appointed for staggered terms, many overlapping those of appointing officials. This insulates directors from some, but

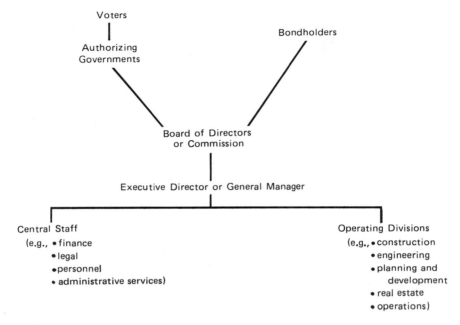

Fig. 3 Typical organization of a special-district public authority. (Adapted from Walsh (1978), chart 3.1.)

not all, political pressures in an attempt to emphasize neutral competence. Directors or commissioners normally reach internal consensus on policy, presenting consensus decisions at open meetings.

Operating control is typically centralized in the hands of a general manager or executive director who holds most budget, appointment, and supervisory powers of city managers/CAOs, with greater autonomy than most city or county managers enjoy. Executive directors oversee central staff and operating units like those shown in Fig. 3.

8. Special-District Reorganization

One form of special-district reorganization involves changing the method for selecting directors. Most directors are now appointed because they represent special economic or social interests in the district's service area. Another method is to appoint public officials who serve by virtue of their office as transportation commissioner or housing administrator, for example. Most districts have directors of the first type. Many combine private citizens and public officials on the board. To help make special districts more responsive to the public interest, constitutions or laws increasingly specify the inclusion of public representatives on the boards. Another trend is to select directors via direct election by voters. Direct election is more common in the Midwest and Far West, with special districts having taxing powers making them more like general-purpose governments (Walsh, 1978:188).

At the administrative level, reorganization often involves decentralizing powers and functions to staff and operating units closer to actual decisions and incorporating business methods. The Port Authority of New York and New Jersey has undergone several reorganizations of this type and serves as a model for many other special districts.

Special districts typically have greater flexibility to reorganize and to manage internal affairs. But modern structures and methods have yet to reach many special districts, especially the smaller ones. In 1976, 93.8% of all special districts had twenty or fewer employees, and 67.6% had no full-time equivalent employees (ACIR, 1982:253). Small districts may well be the grounds for future reorganization.

IV. OBSERVATIONS ON ORGANIZING AND REORGANIZING

Some general observations are in order. First, the general trend for state, county, township, municipal, and special-district organization has been toward executive leadership—greater centralization of power and consolidation of functions under a chief executive. The greater complexity and faster pace of our technocratic society have emphasized single-executive forms and deemphasized slower plural-executive forms. But this trend has not been universal. Some state and local governments have experienced decades of administrative consolidation, finding that executive leadership, as with earlier emphasis on representativeness and neutral competence, is no cure-all for government problems. This partly explains the slowdown in reorganization emphasizing far-reaching administrative centralization. Other governments with little executive leadership may continue to reorganize along those lines.

Second, any discussion of state and local structure leads to an inescapable conclusion: structures and practices are incredibly diverse, making generalizations risky at best. For example, generalizations about the capacity of states, the efficacy of townships, or the professionalism of special districts would appear foolhardy. Administrative and organizational reality is so varied.

Third, a trend exists for states to give their own agencies and their local government creations greater organizational and managerial flexibility (ACIR, 1982:415). This trend is healthy because it allows governments to better design their organization according to task, environment, clientele, and other factors (Garnett, 1981).

NOTES

1. The quest for the effect of structure on state government performance includes Jacobson, 1929; Dye, 1966; Sharkansky and Hofferbert, 1969; Jacob and Lipsky, 1968; Fenton and Chamberlayne, 1969; Garnett, 1980; and Meier, 1980. For studies exploring the impact of structure on local government policy and operations see Lineberry and Fowler, 1967; Cole, 1971; Levy, Meltsner, and Wildavsky, 1974; Ostrom, 1976; Bahl and Burkhead, 1977; and Jones, 1980.
2. This discussion appeared previously in Garnett, 1982.

REFERENCES

Adrian, C. R. (1976). *State and Local Governments*, 4th ed. McGraw-Hill, New York.

Advisory Commission on Intergovernmental Relations (1980). *State Administrators' Opinions on Administrative Change, Federal Aid, Federal Relationships*. U.S. Government Printing Office, Washington, D.C.

Advisory Commission on Intergovernmental Relations (1982). *State and Local Roles in the Federal System*. U.S. Government Printing Office, Washington, D.C.

Bahl, R. and Burkhead, J. (1977). Productivity and the measurement of public output. In Levine, C. L., ed., *Managing Human Resources*. Sage Publications, Beverly Hills, Calif., pp. 253–270.

Bell, G. (1973). State administrative organization activities, 1970–1971. In *The Book of the States, 1972–73*. The Council of State Governments, Lexington, Ky.

Bell, G. (1976). State administrative organization activities, 1974–1975. In *The Book of the States, 1976–77*. The Council of State Governments, Lexington, Ky.

Beyle, T. L. (1982). The governors and the executive branch, 1980–81. In *The Book of the States, 1982–1983*. The Council of State Governments, Lexington, Ky., pp. 141–150.

Cole, R. L. (1971). The urban policy process: A note on structural and regional influences. *Social Science Quarterly* (December): 646–655.

Duncombe, H. S. (1977). *Modern County Government*. National Association of Counties, Washington, D.C.

Dvorin, E. P. and Misner, A. J. (1970). *Governments Within the States*. Addison-Wesley, Reading, Mass.

Dye, T. R. (1966). *Politics, Economics and the Public: Policy Outcomes in the American States*. Rand McNally, Chicago.

Fenton, J. H. and Chamberlayne, D. W. (1969). The literature dealing with the relationships between political processes, socio-economic conditions and public policies in the American states: A bibliographic essay. *Polity 1*: 388–404.

Garnett, J. L. (1979). Strategies for governors who want to reorganize. *State Government 52* (Summer 1979):135–143.

Garnett, J. L. (1980). *Reorganizing State Government: The Executive Branch.* Westview Press, Boulder, Colo.

Garnett, J. L. (1981). Implications of state government organizing for targeting resources to urban areas. *The Urban Interest 3*(Special Issue):97–108.

Garnett, J. L. (1982). State organizations decline. *Public Administration Times* (September 15): 3 and 10.

Gottlieb, A. (1976). State executive reorganization: A study of hallucination supposition and hypothesis. Ph.D. dissertation, The George Washington University, Washington, D.C.

Graves, W. B. (1949). *Reorganization of the Executive Branch of the United States: A Compilation of Basic Information and Significant Documents.* Library of Congress, Washington, D.C.

Henry, N. (1980). *Governing at the Grassroots: State and Local Politics.* Prentice-Hall, Englewood Cliffs, N.J.

Herzik, E. (1981). Governors and issues: A typology of concerns. Paper presented at the Annual Meeting of the Southern Political Science Association.

Hyneman, C. S. (1939). Administrative reorganization: An adventure into science and theology. *The Journal of Politics 1*:62–75.

International City Management Association (1981). *Municipal Yearbook, 1981.* International City Management Association, Washington, D.C.

Jacob, H. and Lipsky, M. (1968). Outputs, structure and power: An assessment of changes in the study of state and local politics. *The Journal of Politics 30*:510–538.

Jacobson, J. M. (1929). Evaluating state administrative structure: The fallacy of the statistical approach. *American Political Science Review 22* (November):928–935.

Jones, B. D. (1980). *Service Delivery in the City: Citizen Demand and Bureaucratic Rules.* Longman, New York.

Kaufman, H. (1956). Emerging conflicts in the doctrines of public administration. *American Political Science Review 50* (December):1057–1073.

Kaufman, H. (1963). *Politics and Policies in State and Local Governments.* Prentice-Hall, Englewood Cliffs, N.J.

Lawrence, C. B. and DeGrove, J. M. (1976). County government services. In *The County Yearbook 1976.* National Association of Counties, International City Management Association, Washington, D.C.

Levy, F., Meltsner, A., and Wildavsky, A. (1974). *Urban Outcomes.* University of California Press, Berkeley, Calif.

Lineberry, R. L. and Fowler, E. P. (1967). Reformism and public policies in American cities. *American Political Science Review* (September):701–716.

Marando, V. L. (1974). An overview of the political feasibility of local government reorganization. In Murphy, T. P. and Warren, C. R. eds. *Organizing Public Services in Metropolitan America.* Lexington Books, Lexington, Mass., pp. 17–51.

Meier, K. J. (1980). Executive reorganization of government: Impact on employment and expenditures. *American Journal of Political Science 24* (August): 396–411.

Mosher, F. C., ed. (1967). *Governmental Reorganization: Cases and Commentary*. Bobbs-Merrill, Indianapolis.

National Association of Counties and International City Management Association (1978). *The County Yearbook 1978*. National Association of Counties and International City Management Association, Washington, D.C.

Ostrom, E. (1976). *The Delivery of Urban Services: Outcomes of Change*. Sage Publications, Beverly Hills, Calif.

Press, C. and Verburg, K. (1979). *State and Community Governments in the Federal System*. Wiley, New York.

Shalala, D. E. and Merget, A. E. (1974). Decentralization Plans. In Murphy, T. P. and Warren, C. R., ed., *Organizing Public Services in Metropolitan America*. Lexington Books, Lexington, Mass.

Stillman, R. J. (1974). *The Rise of the City Manager*. University of New Mexico Press, Albuquerque, N.M.

U.S. Bureau of the Census (1979). *1977 Census of Governments, vol. 1 Governmental Organization*. Government Printing Office, Washington, D.C.

U.S. Bureau of the Census (1983). *1982 Census of Governments, vol. 1 Governmental Organization*. Government Printing Office, Washington, D.C.

Waldo, D. (1948). *The Administrative State: A Study of the Political Theory of American Public Administration*. The Ronald Press Company, New York.

Walsh, Annmarie E. (1978). *The Public's Business*. MIT Press, Cambridge, Mass.

Zimmerman, J. F. (1980). United States In Rowat, D.C., ed., *International Handbook on Local Government Reorganization*. Greenwood Press, Westport, Connecticut.

2

Chief Executives and Administrative Officers

Alan Reed Division of Public Administration, University of New Mexico, Albuquerque, New Mexico

I. INTRODUCTION

Urban local governments must deal with a remarkable range of problems and processes. In addition to the essential requirements for staffing organizations and funding their operation, local governments have major intergovernmental obligations, regulatory requirements, and policy-making demands. The ordinary management of such complex activities is a challenge to the most capable people, but moving beyond maintenance of the status quo, providing initiative, and asserting control over major social problems requires extraordinary effort and ability.

While policy and budget matters are vitally affected by legislative elected officials, many initiatives are normally taken by executive officials. The executive branch of local government is usually organized for leadership and initiative more effectively than a city council or county commission. Therefore, the positions with substantial executive authority should be studied for their attributes and capabilities to understand the operation of local government. This chapter focuses on two kinds of officials who can provide these essential leadership and initiative capabilities. We distinguish here between the chief executive and the chief administrator. The former incorporates the symbolic and political facets of the executive branch, the latter only the organizational facets. They occur in a variety of governmental forms. Some forms distinguish quite clearly between them. Others do not. Several forms of local government are discussed as well as both chief executive and administrator characteristics.

Portions of this chapter were adapted from the author's early work in the *International Journal of Public Administration*.

Much attention (in professional meetings and publications) has been given to issues of finance, organization, policy, or intergovernmental relations. The decline in federal budget support especially has become a central concern of the local government field. All of these issues are certainly worthy of considerable attention. However, they have probably been studied too often without sufficient attention to the local government executive and administrator.

The character of daily administration and the mundane decisions of top executives could contain the keys to whether problems are great or small, understood or baffling, manageable or disastrous. Much more attention must flow to the mayors, city managers, and chief administrators. Their organizations, capabilities, and policy influences could determine to a great extent the outcome of this period of great change that the nation is experiencing. One must balance the national understanding of local government by adding some practical managerial considerations. Concentration on particular problems (i.e., inadequate budgets) or on particular conditions (i.e., urban blight) without a full appreciation of administrative and executive capabilities is comparable to entering a darkened movie theater on a sunny day. One can dimly perceive the big screen directly ahead, but cannot see an empty seat in the crowd.

Once the eyes adjust then one can focus clearly on local government administrators and executives. First, one needs to put his weight into the scales to determine the realistic impact of his actions. For example, it is common to assume that mayors are very important because they are always in the news. They get a great amount of attention and publicity, and have their sycophants who always laud their accomplishments. Some mayors who have been around through three or four elections achieve incredible 90% name recognition among the voters. The question then becomes: Do recognition and publicity equate with power or achievement?

If the current troubles of new mayor Harold Washington in Chicago are any indication, the city councils of the land might have the last word in many circumstances. Certainly the crucial executive-legislative interactions are the most important measure of a mayor's effectiveness.

A second important factor in getting this subject in focus is the historical and theoretical influences on choice of government in a locality. In some forms, the mayor has considerable influence. In others, there is no mayor, and one must look elsewhere for the chief executive office. In others, the role of chief administrator appears as well as a chief executive. The alternatives available for selecting and organizing a chief executive or administrator position must be examined and compared.

Third, the characteristics of the various executives should be covered with consideration of the practical problems they confront daily. Their role in making public policy, especially with their local legislative or governing body, is the point at which the most important problems are handled. It is therefore in that interaction between the policy background and the cast of executive or administrator and council that much light can be cast on the local executive's behavior.

In the following discussion, three offices are discussed. The first is the mayor, which varies considerably from one form of government to another. The second is the city manager, who can be treated as the chief executive in some forms of government, and without question is the highest administrator in any system where one appears. The third is the chief administrative officer (CAO), an office hardly as well known as the other two, but increasing in number and influence. The CAO is distinguished from a chief executive in that it does not have the ultimate political recognition found in budget and appointive powers.

It is useful to distinguish local government from state and federal levels historically. Cities, in particular, have experienced a long period of change that has not affected state and federal government. This period of change has created forms of government found only in cities and has caused cities to diverge markedly from two principles central to the other government levels.

These two principles involve the separation of powers and representation. In the executive branches of state and federal government, the separation of powers (or functions or responsibilities) is understood and carefully guarded, both legally and politically. Cities, as a result of the changes brought by what is commonly labeled the "urban reform movement," have seldom been concerned with a careful delineation of legislative and executive offices. In both mayor-council and council-manager systems, as shall be discussed, executive functions often are difficult to differentiate.

The principle of representation underlies the large legislative bodies at the higher levels. Again, the urban reform movement and simpler ideas governing the organization of local government have produced very small city councils. The purpose of elections for such local governing bodies then is also different, but not without controversy. Analysis of recent trends in "re-reforming" city governments involves this representation issue.

II. URBAN REFORM AND EXECUTIVES

The urban reform movement started in the latter years of the last century as a protest against living and political conditions in large cities. It seemed clear that patronage had become so insidious that the basic functions of urban government themselves were faltering. Money was being wasted and misappropriated. Industrial development proceeded with little planning and regard for the deleterious effects on the quality of urban life.

To get at the problems of management and patronage, the reformers had to concentrate on organization of the urban executive office. The earliest publications of the chief reform organization, the National Municipal League, advocated substantial changes in the organization of city political and administrative agencies. The main purpose aimed to remove politics from administration and patronage from the executive operations.

The result was the city manager position. It began to take form in 1912 in small towns; within a decade it had become the predominant form of executive in the United States. The International City Managers Association (now entitled the International City Management Association, ICMA) soon espoused the virtues of a nonpolitical executive, and the citizens groups and ICMA formed a lasting bond.

In the reform backwash, mayors lost status and recognition. In many cities, the city manager charters included a mayor in a ceremonial capacity only. Many cities appeared to ape the traditional diffuse organization of their state governments, creating numerous city boards and commissions beyond the mayor's control as well as other plural elected executives (such as a city comptroller, attorney, treasurer, or public safety commissioner).

City managers, on their part, quickly emerged as the competent, professional city executives, working closely with the governing bodies to install merit personnel systems and modern engineering. The objectives of these reformed city governments were heavily biased in favor of physical infrastructure, responding to their business leaders' interests. Road building, water and sewer systems, schools, parks, and suburban planning were pushed forward as the agenda for the future. In most cities, these currents predominated for fifty years or more.

In large, traditional cities such as Chicago, Philadelphia, and New York, the urban reformers' influence never equaled their impact in small or new, western cities. Still, the problems of finding consistent modern management troubled all cities and elements of reform thought permeated city government. Some very large cities, such as Dallas, Kansas City, and San Diego, in fact have classic city manager forms of government. These seem to work in the presence of adequate public consensus on their virtues. In Chicago, the mayor has been viewed entirely differently, and it is to the mayor that executive problems come.

Some cities that have not been able to discard their mayor's position as chief executive nevertheless have attempted to upgrade management beyond simple patronage or mayoral politics. In the process they have created a little-known position entitled the chief administrative officer (CAO). All three of these offices (mayor, city manager, and CAO) need to be assessed in light of their different origins and perspectives. In the following section, the city manager and CAO differences are illuminated.

A. The City Manager

The city manager (CM) is the recognized professional, chief executive in council-manager governments. The institution's strengths have been the removal of administration from politics and the embodiment of the reform movement's chief principle of professionalism in the city's executive agency. The reform view that there is no partisan way to build a road, only the right way, led to the conclusion that embodying the executive and administrative powers in the CM would remove political and ideological strife from the city's daily running and bring stability and high-quality performance.

The most significant facet of the CM position is its relation with the council. Those councils that elect a mayor as a ceremonial head seldom infringe on the real control by the CM over the executive functions of the city. The councilors usually consider themselves all equals. They are the board of directors to the city corporation, and the CM is the president and chief executive officer. As chief executive, the CM exercises substantial control over the administration. Only the limited personal influence of the mayor as ceremonial figure or pre-eminent politician sometimes intrudes on the CM's domination of policy. A CM could even defy a mayor in the council-manager form of government, as long as he retains the support of the council majority.[4]

The council theoretically dominates in policy-making, but Nolting points out that very early in the evolution of the CM as an executive institution, it became clear the council needed initiative and suggestion from the CM.[5] Bromage described the CM-council relation as one of partnership, which varies considerably from city to city.[6] It is notable that the 1969 Code of Ethics for professional urban administrators adopted by the International City Management Association deleted the stricture against a CM taking a position in public contrary to the council's.[7]

The city manager institution achieved maturity during a period of nearly seventy years. Nolting itemizes the usual requirements of the council-manager system as follows:

1. The CM is appointed by the council and given full authority over the administrative affairs of the city.
2. The CM has full authority to appoint and remove department heads and other key personnel and to make recommendations regarding appointments to other municipal positions such as boards and task forces.
3. The CM also has the responsibility of preparing and presenting the budget, advising the council on all matters, preparing reports, and enforcing the laws and ordinances of the city.
4. The council deals with administrative officials only through the CM.[8]

In the typical city, the CM position is nonpartisan, professional, and encompasses the functions of chief executive. A delicate balance is managed with the council in policy-making. The CM traditionally concentrates on implementation and avoids active politics. He generally initiates new policies carefully and with the full awareness of the risks involved if he should lose the support of the council majority.

B.   Recent Trends

The urban scene today, especially in large cities, tests the council-manager form of government to the maximum. Major issues of recent times create conditions often incompatible with the best features of the city manager institution. Many issues are politically volatile, and major controversies regarding limitations on growth, environmental quality, mass transit, open government, and popular participation in policy-making are splitting urban power structures and politicizing large numbers of citizens who previously might have accepted professional city management with few questions. The issue is whether professional managers can continue to determine the lifestyle and nature of city government for millions of increasingly sophisticated urban dwellers.

After studying the behavior of CMs in handling federal revenue sharing, Almy concludes:

> The unwillingness of most managers to open up decision-making processes portends serious problems for responsive, representative local governments. Ironically, in a federally sponsored program sold to the American public as a remedy for distant government unresponsive to local needs, there is little in the manner in which city managers have approached revenue sharing that has made it a model of responsiveness. City managers do avoid the public, and the result of that avoidance may be increased administrative and policy-making autonomy.[9]

It might be said further that such avoidance encourages disillusionment with the CM institution. The Aleshires suggest that and advise changes in the style of administration practiced by city managers.[10]

Sayre, Adrian, Lineberry, and Fowler and others have focused on the declining influence of the reform movement on large cities.[11] A few cities such as Kansas City, Dallas, and San Diego have retained the council-manager form of government, but it seems likely that the mayor in such large cities has considerably more influence over the performance of the CM than in smaller cities.

Recent trends in the nature of public issues and the continued rapid growth of many American cities pose difficult questions for the council-manager form of government. Is it nearly impossible for the professional, nonpartisan chief executive to manage the collective policy-making institution of the council in a large city split by major controversies? Do the residents of large cities demand an accountable elected chief executive rather than the reform image of the CM? Can a CM trained in and dedicated to nonpartisan, apolitical, executive decision-making cope with highly political environments found in large American cities in recent times?

Such questions arise in the obvious trend toward alternative forms of government in large American cities. The large majority of cities of more than

250,000 population have adopted the mayor-council form, but in an increasing number of them, the position of the chief administrative officer (CAO) appears. It seems likely that this institution reflects the influence of the reform movement, although we must look closer at the nature and operation of the CAO to determine how the position relates to the concerns here.

III. THE CHIEF ADMINISTRATIVE OFFICER

Recognition of the CAO system has come very gradually. Bollens described such systems among California cities in the early 1950s.[12] Sayre wrote the initial description and defense of the CAO system in larger cities in 1954.[13] Adrian has continued to keep the subject before the urban management profession through his contributions to Banfield's *Urban Government* (1969) and to his coauthorship of *Governing Urban America* (1972, 1977).[14] Nolting has done much to define and critique the CAO institution (1968, 1970).[15] The most important description of the contemporary CAO systems has come from Hogan.[16]

Considerable confusion exists among the various authorities about the number of CAO systems in existence. Nolting identifies 132 cities with some form of CAO in 1968.[17] Hogan says thirteen cities adopted the plan during the 1950s and forty-eight during 1968-1972. He ultimately identifies 205 CAO systems from his survey.[18] Confusion regarding the number of CAOs is understandable at this stage of study, when a position definition is unclear.

It should be noted that many authors have discussed the CAO in different contexts—when appointed by the council, when appointed by the mayor alone, and when appointed by the mayor with the council's consent. An alternative term applied to CAO systems has been mayor-manager systems. In view of the clear definition of the manager within the council-manager system, such a term as mayor-manager seems untenable. In any case, this chapter concerns the CAO position in the strong mayor type of mayor-council government. Detailed consideration of some examples will lead to a clearer position definition as well as comparisons with the city manager.

A. San Francisco

San Francisco seems to have invented the CAO as a distinct role in urban administration in 1931.[19] Today San Francisco has one of the most interesting variants of the CAO system, which could be referred to as the strong CAO form. Of course, the concept of the CAO has evolved into a clearer position in cities that have started it recently.

In San Francisco, the CAO is given many direct powers by the city charter under the board of supervisors. Several departments are placed under the CAO rather than the mayor, and the board of supervisors is responsible for any organizational changes in those departments. The charter states that the board of supervisors "shall deal with the administrative service for which the Chief Administrative Officer is responsible, solely through such officer."[20] The CAO may initiate any matter directly with the board, is primarily responsible for the operating budget, and makes many appointments to boards and commissions and administrative offices, such as voter registrar and recorder. The board is forbidden to interfere with any personnel matter in the departments. The CAO is removable only by a two-thirds board vote and has charter rights to hearing, written charges, and reply.[21]

The mayor is the designated chief executive officer with the power to appoint many important boards and commissions, which control such departments as police and fire, and generally has supervision of the administration under them. He makes a state of the city address to the board of supervisors in October of each year, but has only indirect budget authority.

In the spring of 1977, a considerable effort was made to reduce the autonomy of the CAO in San Francisco, and a charter amendment proposition was presented that would have eliminated the CAO and consolidated all administrative power under the mayor. The mayor intended to appoint a deputy mayor for administration—a position that exists in many large cities. A board committee killed this measure in May. Clearly the mayors of San Francisco have found the CAO an impediment to full exercise of their executive authority.

San Francisco has a unique form of city government, and its experience exposes many of the complexities of the CAO position. San Francisco's CAO is strong in charter rights and direct relations with the board of supervisors, but weak because he has responsibility only for certain specified departments, not including such major ones as police and fire.

B. New Orleans

The oldest CAO position having the most attributes of the genre is in New Orleans, which established its model in 1952. The New Orleans sustem is probably the prototype for cities considering adopting the CAO position. The mayor is the chief executive, elected at large, and the council is districted. The CAO is appointed by the mayor with the consent of the council, and is removable by the mayor. Although the CAO is responsible for the departments and the main administrative activities of the city of New Orleans, there are several assistant CAOs for specific functional areas. The New Orleans model is limited somewhat by state law, which removes the merit system from city control and vests it in the state civil service commission. State law also restricts the city's ability to engage in collective bargaining with state agencies dealing with unions.[22]

C. Los Angeles

Other large cities have created similar CAO positions with different titles. Los Angeles has an "administrative officer" whose strength lies somewhere between the San Francisco and New Orleans CAOs. The Los Angeles administrative officer is removable only with the consent of the council, after proper notice, hearing, and response, as in San Francisco, but without clear autonomy to the mayor, as in New Orleans.[23] The Los Angeles administrative officer also does not have clear operating oversight of the departments. He is given carefully drawn mandates to control financial planning and to research all management operations for efficiency, accountability, and financial control. However, the position does not direct administrative personnel in the departments or set policy. The Los Angeles charter framers were concerned about professionalizing money matters and providing research assistance to the mayor, rather than instituting a theoretically whole administrative position. It is an example of the improvisation and eclecticism common to urban administration in the United States.

D. New York

New York City has struggled with reorganization of the executive branch for years, especially recently, as its financial crisis grew worse. For some time, the deputy mayors were appointed for their administrative experience and ability to augment the political role of the mayor. The CAO position established by Mayor Robert Wagner in 1953 appears to have disappeared. However, in February of 1977, the mayor, by executive order, created the position of director of operations, which looks very much like a CAO.

The director is under the supervision of the first deputy mayor (and has frequent direct contact with the mayor). The executive order charges him with the following functions and responsibilities:

1. Under the supervision of the mayor and first deputy mayor, to plan, coordinate and direct New York City governmental operations
2. To assure a responsive management structure and resource capability to deal effectively with the rapidly changing demands of our socio-economic environment in New York City
3. To ensure the continuity of competent management organization through the development, motivation, appraisal, and review of key personnel
4. To plan, devise and innovate cost effective improvements to reduce operating expenses and minimize the need for additional capital or human resources
5. To provide the leadership, guidance and motivation to the operations management and work forces to ensure maximum productivity within the terms of our labor contracts and resources capabilities

6. To direct the mayor's Management Planning and Reporting system.

In addition, it is made clear that department heads report through the director of operations and are responsible to him.[24] The importance of this post to the city was illustrated when a recent mayor appointed a top-ranking executive from the telephone company to the post and announced the appointment with great ceremony and publicity.

E. Boston

Boston gives the vice mayor the role of director of administrative services with the assistance of the board of administrative services. The principal duty of the vice mayor is very similar to the duty of the administrative officer of Los Angeles and falls short of the board administrative responsibility of the New Orleans CAO. Boston's administrative structure leaves a very ambiguous line of authority between the operating departments and the director of administrative services; apparently the mayor has direct supervision of both.[25]

F. Albuquerque

One city that has adopted the CAO position recently is Albuquerque. With the benefit of information gathered from other cities, charter reformers drafted a new charter in 1974 and clarified the notion of the CAO, probably creating the clearest currently available example.

The 1974 charter creates a strong mayor-council system. The council is composed of nine members elected from districts of approximately equal population. The mayor is elected at large, is the stated chief executive, and has the power to formulate and present the budget.

The provisions of the charter dealing with the CAO are brief and direct:

1. For the purpose of providing professional assistance in the administration of the City, the mayor shall hire, subject to the advice and consent of the council, a chief administrative officer.
2. The chief administrative officer shall be employed for an indefinite term, and shall hold office until a vacancy is created by death, resignation or removal by the mayor.
3. The chief administrative officer shall be chosen solely on the basis of professional administrative qualifications.
4. The chief administrative officer shall:
   a. Exercise administrative control and supervision over the merit system; and
   b. Subject to the authority of the mayor, supervise the operations of all departments; and
   c. Whenever possible, attend all council meetings; and

    d. Perform such other duties not inconsistent with the provisions of this charter as the mayor may prescribe.[26]

G. Main Features of the CAO

Hogan suggests the following working definition for a CAO city:

> . . . a city where the Chief Administrative Officer (CAO) is appointed by the mayor, by the council, or nominated by the mayor and certified by the council. What is unique about the arrangement, however, is that the CAO is, *unlike a city manager*, to aid the mayor in the performance of his administrative and policy responsibilities and only indirectly is he to be responsible to the council.[27]

Adrian's work and examples from such cities as New Orleans and Albuquerque emphasize CAOs appointed by the mayor with the consent of the council and removable by the mayor only. A CAO appointed by the collective body of the council differs so little from a CM that there is little to say about it.

Hogan's survey asked mayors and CAOs to describe and evaluate their positions and formal functional relations. With his information and the aid of the examples above, the CAO position can be summarized as:

1. The CAO is not the chief executive, but is a professional administrator in charge of the city's daily operations and accountable to the mayor. The position brings a strong element of the reform nonpartisan professionalism to the elective executive and is seen by CAOs and mayors alike as an important complement to the mayor's political and policy authority.
2. Most CAOs have personnel and budget powers nearly equal to the CM's; however, they are subject to the final authority of the mayor. Hogan's results indicate this leads to a much closer working relation than can be achieved between the city manager and the council.
3. CAOs are recognized as having policy-making potential, but are reluctant participants in public policy debates and politics. They see administration as their main concern and administrative achievements as their main rewards.
4. The CAO system is a flexible, powerful adaptation of the reform model to large city, strong mayor systems. It works well in many different contexts and the CAO receives considerable personal satisfaction and professional enhancement from the position.
5. The mayor has the ability to adjust the CAO's position to suit his political and personal needs, without abandoning the attributes of a professional administrator role in urban management.

IV. THE CHIEF ADMINISTRATIVE OFFICER AND THE CITY MANAGER

Comparison of the CAO and CM positions reveals several important differences (see Fig. 1). The CAO from the beginning is an integral component in an elective executive agency concerned with executive leadership as well as professional administration. The CM is an appointed executive trying to carry out professional administration with a collective political body. The CAO has appointive powers over the city departments and power to develop a budget, but the policy decisions involved with those activities are predominantly in the hands of the mayor. The CM makes appointments and prepares budgets subject to the potentially shifting council majority. Although in some states such as California, procedural safeguards exist, the CAO can usually be removed by the mayor. On the other hand, the CM can be removed by the majority of the council.

It appears that the urban management profession has underestimated the importance of the CAO type of mayor-council government for the improvement of urban management. Little appears in the literature regarding the implications for the profession or the reform tradition of the emerging position of the CAO, especially in larger cities. Bebout and Nolting have written about CAOs from the viewpoint of career exponents of the council-manager form of government and, therefore, as rather severe critics.[28] In 1969, the International City Manager's Association (ICMA) changed its name to the International City Management Association to recognize the increasing number of city administrators not qualifying as city managers. Nolting produced an unpublished study for the association in 1970, attempting to assess the impact of the CAO on the profession. Oblique references appear in the ICMA publication, *Municipal Yearbook*, usually in a critical style, such as the following:

> . . . their administrative authority is limited—they often do not directly appoint department heads or other key city personnel and their responsibility for budget preparation and administration while significant, is subordinant to that of the elected officials.[29]

Yet no clear distinction is made between the terms *chief administrative officer* and *city manager* in most literature. The ICMA statistics list hundreds of cities with a CAO that clearly have a council-appointed manager, not a CAO as described by Sayre, Hogan, and this chapter. It seems time for the urban management profession to come to grips with the CAO as a professional position, especially its appearance in larger cities.

My primary question concerns the CAO in medium and large cities. However, the existence of the CAO in such small cities as Stillwater, Minnesota (10,000 population), Sharonville, Ohio (11,000), and Clark, New Jersey (19,000), could indicate more sweeping competition for the city manager institution than is expressed here.

Fig. 1 Comparison of the Chief Administrative Officer and City Manager

	CAO	CM
Method of selection	Appointed by mayor with consent of council	Appointed by council
Method of removal	Removed by mayor, sometimes with consent of council	Removed by majority of council
Appointment power	Appoints most department heads and other key personnel Oversight of merit system Competes with mayor's assistants Seldom recommends board appointees	Appoints all key personnel and department heads Oversight of merit system Recommends board appointees
Removal power	May take initiative in removing key personnel, requires mayor's approval Competes with mayor's assistants	May remove key personnel, although subject to override and political influence of department heads
Budget power	Top budget official of city, usually prepares and defends budget, in unity with mayor	Prepares and presents budget Responsible for all aspects of financial management
Policy role	Considerable ability to set priorities for mayor, initiate discussions of policy, defend policies to council and public	Theoretical limits on policy initiative, not always followed in practice Often major policy initiators

Some reasons for a turn toward the CAO position might be suggested by Albuquerque, which made the transition from a classic council-manager system established in 1919, to a strong mayor system with a CAO in 1974. As a rapidly growing city, it faced disruptions and strains of many kinds that the CM could not accommodate. In 1971, a referendum indicated that citizens wanted major new efforts in both environmental planning and management and in human rights. Various citizens' committees demanded stronger initiatives from the city manager's office. However, shifting majorities on the city council created uncertainty and the city hired and discharged three city managers within four years. When the public finally took charge and prepared a new city charter, the CAO was the choice for the professional administrative position rather than the CM.

A. The CAO in Urban Administration

The CAO position in urban administration is increasingly accepted as a legitimate reform professional position when the CM does not seem adequate. In American cities of more than 250,000 population, a definite trend is toward strong mayor systems. When professional administration is desired as an adjunct to the mayor's political and policy-making roles, the CAO can meet the need.

The CAO lacks the complete executive status of the CM, but in most cities, as Hogan and a review of charters confirm, the CAO has considerable appointment, removal, budget, and policy authority. The position can contract or expand with changing mayors, but so can the CM with changing councils. Hogan's results indicate considerable congruence in role perceptions between mayors and CAOs. The close integration of their efforts exceeds the best that can be achieved between the nonpolitical CM and a group of councilors.

If one assumes that growing cities and changing public perceptions require clear, forceful executive leadership by an elected chief executive, the strong mayor system presents itself as the best model. If large cities seem to require different executive-administrative strengths than those offered by the city manager system, the CAO position appears to offer an attractive alternative. The election of the mayor resolves political cleavages temporarily, and the appointment of a CAO brings promise of administrative competence and the reform influence against the spoils system. In major American cities today, there are many pressures for social sensitivity and forceful executive leadership that still call on the best administrative talents available and for policy-making that is open and responsive. It is a strength, not a weakness, of the reform tradition and the city management profession that the position of the CAO has been created and improved to respond to these needs. The profession should recognize the CAO as a great step forward in the constant effort to manage American cities better.

V. EXECUTIVES IN THE POLICY PROCESS

Modern city or local administration involves the most complex policy process in history. The rise of interlocking policy levels has integrated local governments, sometimes against their will, into a network of power centers derived from different bases, in which each government struggles to assert its direction while not losing the benefits of contact with the others.

There is little purpose in holding public office for mayors, councilors, county commissioners, or administrators if no decisions can be made and if no money is available to pay for the organizations to carry out the decisions. The flow of funds from the federal level has colored every aspect of the scene in which local government functions. As fluctuations in that flow sweep through the intergovernmental system, the power of offices changes, the connections among organizations shift, and the influence of one policy or another waxes and wanes. People rise and fall; their offices come and go.

In addition to the rhythmic interference emanating from Washington, local government leaders must contend with a diverse, cantankerous audience. The interests of each small faction compete for attention and predominance with all others. The general interest is increasingly defined in maintenance of the privileges already gained. Planning is still not accepted as a legitimate set of ties on the activities of an interest group when its own preferences are at stake. It is perfectly appropriate to insist on policies limiting the options of the opponents, but to resist vehemently any such policy limiting one's own options.

The contending interests from development to education, from health to transportation, and from housing to conservation are so numerous and organized that the institutions of local government have strained to encompass the demands of making decisions and governing and administering in such an environment.

The central means for dealing with the consequences of this tremendously fragmented and demanding setting is the election. Electoral outcomes must ensconce the leadership at the levels of decision that operate the ponderous machinery of administration, intergovernmental relations, finance, and policy, and determine the behavior of government and the direction of local society.

The elected leadership reaches out for the appointed followers who will execute its policies and the resolution of the many strains inherent in daily management. These appointed officials must have the values, experiences, preferences, priorities, skills, and even personalities, that complement the elected officials and provide the human capabilities essential to the success of this enormously complex system.

Chief among these elected and appointed officials are the legislative figures. It might be heresy to note, but it seems clear that the influence of executives on policy is overrated. Publicity can certainly be equated with influence (and even wealth in most cases). However, the high level of publicity given to mayors or county executives is not indicative of their decision-making role.

City councils probably are the heavyweights in local government. Their predominance in two crucial policy areas, finance and land use, overrides the influence of any other actor. If one adds to this reality the preemptive power of federal programs, one can perhaps understand the high level of limitation on the local executive.

If city councils make the major decisions relating to land use and development and have final authority over budgets, does this indicate a range of postures for local executives? It seems so. City managers are by their very origins integrated with the council's process. The whole history of the urban reform movement subsumes the manager's authority within the integrated executive and legislative roles in the council. This appears to give the manager structured integration into the policy process. He operates almost as a surrogate for the council's majority in initiating or projecting policy.

A council comes to rely on the manager without thought. There is a natural symbiosis of interests. Communication is direct and continuous, with managers meeting regularly at the council table. The source of information for councils in the manager system is normally the manager or his designated speakers. Few councils have council offices and staffs serving only the council.

A major concern for modern city managers is the extent to which they initiate policy issues. The possible consequences of exposing a policy preference are often felt, and the relatively short average tenure for city managers is usually the result of political controversy. For many years, the code of ethics of the ICMA prohibited the city manager's involvement in policy initiation. Only recently has the ICMA revised the code to recognize the desirable reality of the policy role.

However, managers often feel they must bring serious policy questions to the council for resolution if they are to manage the city effectively. It is impossible to ignore the need for expanded subsidy to the bus system, or the need for major revision of the capital financing program in many cases.

The most appropriate summary of the manager's place as the executive in the policy process seems to be that an astute manager with good political judgment cannot only initiate policy but can control the information flow to the council to a great degree and lead the council in policy. There are risks involved, but the idea that a manager is a passive recipient of the judgments of a political process in which he has no role is undoubtedly inaccurate and dated.

A mayor in a mayor-council system must expect to take a policy role much more apparent than the manager's and much more exposed to political risks.

The exaggerated attention given to a mayor's schedule and utterances politicize practically everything done. The public only has a dim perception of what constitutes "policy" and an excessive fondness for what constitutes "politics." The result is that the usual mayor treads daily through a minefield of transitory problems that can blow his administration into oblivion. Policy issues of real significance can get lost in the clamor over minor matters.

The attention paid to mayors and their recognition as a result usually of being elected in a citywide vote gives them the possibility of exerting policy guidance on the strenuous environment in which they operate. A mayor's personal and political judgment and character can dislodge policy concerns from the background clamor and raise them to the top of the agenda of public dispute. The council can be alerted and led by a capable mayor. The articulation of long-range perspectives, the proposal of major initiatives, and the commitment of resources to significant programs, can all be accomplished by a capable mayor.

A mayor who has the personal ability to become policy leader nevertheless must realize that councils control money and land use, the two essential ingredients of urban policy. Therefore, the most important site for evaluating a mayor's administration is in the linkage with the city council.

Cities that seat the mayor with the council, usually as presiding officer, have a decided advantage over those that replicate the so-called separation of powers found in the federal government. A mayor who does not sit in when the council is making major policy decisions is operating with a severe handicap— with one eye closed, and one arm tied behind him.

The necessity for policy to emerge from a widespreading process of debate and information exchange makes it essential for the mayor to be involved in the crucial final stages of policy decision-making in the council. If he sits as presiding officer, he cannot avoid this crucial participation. A mayor of a city with a separated mayor and council should routinely sit through council meetings, answering questions and participating in the discussion, if he is to perform his policy role as expected. The best decision-making is a cooperative process in which gradual achievement of common understanding and consensus as the basis for a policy decision are reached.

The most difficult policy role to assess is that of the CAO. Because this office only appears under the jurisdiction of a mayor, many variables could influence the relations between these two important offices. In a CAO system, the mayor not only has the usual difficult connections with the council to manage, but the additional problem of making connections with the daily administrative work of his CAO and the CAO's connection with the council.

In the Albuquerque system, the CAO is required to attend all council meetings, whereas the mayor is not. Any city executive branch with such an arrangement runs the risk of the CAO becoming closely tied to the council and running ahead of the mayor. Information about the council's deliberations, frame of mind, and decisions is not only an advantage to the CAO in acting apart from the mayor, but also a stimulus to the CAO attempting to respond to the clear intentions of the council. The mayor might not be operating in the same frame of mind.

A strong CAO is surely going to build up a public identity for himself. As administrative crises are handled and public inquiries reach his desk for disposition, the CAO could become a major figure in the public's perception of the city's administration. A close and personal working rapport between mayor and CAO would preempt any problems arising from this situation. However, the cumulative outcome of the CAO's influence as a major executive branch figure is difficult to predict. Probably the best summary of the CAO role as a policy actor is that the CAO and mayor will determine together how the CAO will influence policy. A mayor with a weak personality might allow the CAO to initiate policy. An aggressive mayor might almost totally submerge the CAO, especially in a system in which the mayor sits with the council. A strong CAO can tackle both the mayor and the council in attempting to put forward policy issues that are priorities to him.

VI. CONCLUSIONS

Executive governance in city and local government today involves the dynamics of relations among mayors, councils, and other major administrators such as city managers and CAOs. The designation of the chief executive is not as important as the quality of daily interactions in administration and policy-making.

The large variety of local government forms in existence in the United States today makes generalization difficult. Chief executives are characterized by a political capacity exceeding administrative requirements of their office, and the mayor is the usual chief executive. In a city manager system, the urban reform tradition demands that the manager exercises the full range of chief executive power, but mayors in such systems can often impede the full flowering of this theoretical model. In mayor-council systems with a CAO, the chief administrator's involvement with the top executive functions of budgeting and policy initiative can be great, depending on the personal and political realities of the particular city in question.

Although a clear view of city governance indicates that the city council is the predominant force, especially in the critical areas of finance and land use, chief executives and chief administrators both can influence the council tremendously from their superior position of information and public recognition.

A city desiring strong executive *and* administrative operation would choose a mayor-council system with the mayor presiding over the council. If the city wished to have a healthy dose of professional management as well, as propagated by the urban reform elements in local politics, it would have a chief administrative officer with close linkages to the council also.

If, on the other hand, the city had a consensus that a city manager offered the highest level of professional administration without the unfortunate political demands of a mayor, it could adopt the council-manager system without a mayoral office at all. Then, the majority of the council would exercise the integrated policy and administrative controls of the city government and the manager would be accountable for all aspects of the executive branch.

ACKNOWLEDGMENT

Marcia Lubar, former Assistant to the Chief Administrative Officer, City of Albuquerque, is due special thanks for assistance with this chapter.

NOTES

1. See Boynton, Robert P. (1976). City councils: Their role in the legislative system. *Municipal Yearbook 43*:67–77.
2. Lineberry, Robert L. and Fowler, Edmund P. (1968). Reformism and public policies in American cities. In Wilson, James Q., ed., *City Politics and Public Policy*. Wiley, New York.
3. Winter, William O. (1969). *The Urban Polity*. Dodd, Mead, New York, pp. 76–77, 225–248.
4. Bromage, Arthur W. (1970). *Urban Policy Making: the Council-Manager Partnership*. Public Administration Service, Chicago, pp. 8–18.
5. Nolting, Orin F. (1969). *Progress and Impact of the Council-Manager Plan*. Public Administration Service, Chicago, p. 37.
6. Bromage, Arthur W. Op. cit.
7. Ibid, p. 9.
8. Nolting, Orin F. Op. cit., pp. 32–33.
9. Almy, Timothy A. (January–February, 1977). City managers, public avoidance, and revenue sharing. *Public Administration Review 37*:26–27.
10. Aleshire, Frank and Aleshire, Fran. (May, 1977). The American city manager: New style, new "game." *National Civic Review 66*:235–239.
11. Sayre, Wallace S. (Autumn, 1954). The general manager idea for large cities. *Public Administration Review 14*:258 Adrian, Charles R. (1969). Recent concepts in large city administration. In Banfield, Edward C., ed., *Urban Government*. Free Press, New York. See also Interview with L. P. Cookingham (Winter, 1976). In *Praxis 2*:22–27.
12. Bollens, John C. (1952). *Appointed Executive Local Government: The California Experience*. The Haynes Foundation, Los Angeles.
13. Sayre, Wallace S. Op. cit.
14. Adrian, Charles R. Op. cit. Adrian, Charles R. and Press, Charles. (1972, 1977). *Governing Urban America*, 4th and 5th eds. McGraw-Hill, New York.
15. Nolting, Orin F. Op. cit. Nolting, Orin F. (1970). Mayor-appointed administrators in the United States. Unpublished report for the International City Management Association.

16. Hogan, James B. (1976). *The Chief Administrative Officer: An Alternative to Council-Manager Government.* The University of Arizona, The Institute of Government Research, Tucson.
17. Nolting, Orin F. *Progress and Impact of the Council-Manager Plan*, p. 42.
18. Hogan, James B. Op. cit., p. 13.
19. Ibid., p. 8.
20. Charter of the City and County of San Francisco, Section 2.401.
21. Ibid., Section 3.200.
22. Adrian, Charles R. and Press, Charles. Op. cit., 4th ed., pp. 214, 218.
23. Charter of the City of Los Angeles, Sections 50–52.
24. Executive Order No. 75. (February 4, 1977). See also Mayor's management advisory board. (January, 1977). *Executive Management*, Part II, Section L, Director of operations, and the *New York Times* (February 4 and February 11, 1977).
25. City of Boston (1976–1977). *Municipal Register*, pp. 45–46 and insert following p. 47.
26. City Charter, City of Albuquerque, Article VII (as revised January 1, 1976).
27. Hogan, James B. Op. cit., p. 8.
28. Bebout, John E. (Summer, 1955). Management for large cities. *Public Administration Review 15*:188–195.
29. *Municipal Yearbook 40* (1973):3.

3

Court Administrators

Steven W. Hays Department of Government and International Studies, University of South Carolina, Columbia, South Carolina

I. INTRODUCTION

Court management has traditionally been one of the most neglected facets of state and local management. Whereas management specialties have existed for all but the newest components of public administration for decades, court administrators did not emerge as a credible professional group until the 1970s (Meyer, 1971). The delayed arrival of court administrators to public management is somewhat understandable, given the fact that the administrative failings of the judicial system did not become widely visible until the 1960s. During that decade, the massive arrests of civil rights and antiwar demonstrators, coupled with rapidly increasing rates of civil litigation, so overburdened judicial machinery that the news media began to expose the shortcomings of our nation's court systems to public scrutiny. Shortly thereafter, the academic and professional communities awakened to the perceived "crisis in the courts" (James, 1967) with the publication of such works as Leonard Downie's *Justice Denied* (1972) and Jerome Frank's *Courts on Trial* (1972).

In response to the growing clamor arising from citizens' groups and members of the legal community, a number of reform commissions assembled to investigate the administrative maladies of the courts and to offer suggestions for change (National Advisory Commission, 1973; National Conference on the Judiciary, 1971; President's Commission, 1967). The reports of these commissions detailed administrative inefficiencies sufficiently pronounced to shock and embarrass the judiciary and the legal establishment as a whole. Court systems throughout the country were found to be operating with archaic procedures and equipment, leading several commentators to label the judicial system an "administrative backwater." Most local court systems, for example, maintained their records and dockets in handwritten ledgers, as had been the practice since the 1700s. Similarly, patronage personnel systems, nonroutinized budget practices, inconsistent paper flow procedures, and fragmented administrative authority characterized a majority of the nation's lower courts.

An immediate byproduct of these disturbing revelations was the belief that the traditional managers of courts, the judges, needed professional assistance in dragging their organizations into the twentieth century. To this end, Chief Justice Warren Burger, the American Bar Association (ABA), and dozens of other illustrious individuals and organizations advocated the recruitment, training, and employment of a corps of experts in judicial management. This endeavor was aided by the influx of funds from the Law Enforcement Assistance Administration (LEAA), which provided the requisite financial assistance to enable numerous court systems to employ their first court administrators. Additionally, LEAA funds were instrumental in the establishment of specialized training programs for court managers, most notably the Institute for Court Management in Denver, Colorado (Baar, 1982).

As a direct result of this groundswell of opinion and support, a truly phenomenal increase in the number of practicing court administrators occurred within the past twenty years. As recently as 1971, for example, only twenty-five states employed full-time state court administrators to assist supreme courts in overseeing their states' lower judiciary. Likewise, less than 100 trial court administrators were known to be employed in county and circuit courts within the states. By 1983, conversely, *all* states employed full-time state court administrators, as well as professional staffs ranging in size from 5 to 200 employees. Moreover, the number of trial court administrators had swelled to well over 500.

This chapter aims to survey and assess the functions and roles of court administrators in the context of state and local government. Although court administration is admittedly in an embryonic stage, most authorities agree that it is well on its way to achieving a measure of professional stature and responsibility that befits the significant contribution it can make to the quality of state and local management. Before disucssing their functions and roles, however, it is necessary to review (albeit briefly) various aspects of their professional environments that influence the performance of practicing court administrators.

II. THE COURT ADMINISTRATORS' ENVIRONMENT

Judicial systems are encumbered by more intellectual and administrative baggage than perhaps any other component of state and local government. The heart and soul of American jurisprudence has by definition been tradition, both in terms of adherence to substantive precedent *and* the continued application of time-honored procedures and practices. Because court administrators represent change, their appearance in courthouses has not always been met with laurels and rose blossoms. They have been compelled to carve an administrative niche out of organizations in which existing managerial relationships and practices have been sanctified by time and tradition. Understandably, then, the range and significance of each court administrator's functions depend in part on the peculiarities of the court system in which one is employed. Among the many variables that dictate the character of individual court systems, three stand out in importance: the local political culture; existing organizational arrangements; and, the professional orientations of judges.

A. Local Political Culture

It is a truism that court systems are microcosms of the political and social systems in which they exist. This fact is especially relevant in the United States because courts have been closely tied to city and county government since colonial times. As a consequence, a vast majority of the administrative, financial, and personnel supports to state court systems have been provided by counties and cities (Hays, 1979:10).

For court administrators, the close relationship between courts and local governments presents several institutional realities that largely determine how their jobs are performed. One of the most important of these is that trial courts are usually financed by county and city funds funneled through the relevant councils and commissions. Despite its constitutional status as an "independent" branch of government, the judicial system is thereby dependent upon local politicians for its buildings, operating revenues, and personnel. In addition to depriving the courts of control over their own administrative infrastructures, this situation has occasionally resulted in severe shortages of critical resources, including sufficient numbers of judges and adequate facilities (McLaughlin, 1970:333).

Another factor that complicates the jobs of court administrators is that most of the support personnel on whom the courts rely are city and county employees who belong to organizations located outside of the judicial system. District attorneys and sheriffs, for example, are independently elected officials, whereas probation officers, court reporters, and bailiffs are provided either by separate executive departments or through contractual agreements (probation officers generally belong to a probation department, bailiffs are employees of the sheriff, and court reporters are often independent contractors). Obviously, engineering the coordination of large numbers of employees who do not formally work for the judicial system can be a delicate and painful task.

Of all the local officials who play a significant role in court management, none is as important as the *court clerk*. Prior to the advent of professional court administrators, these officials were almost entirely responsible for supervising the administrative arm of local courts. Court clerks managed the space and equipment of county courthouses, prepared and administered the court's budget, hired and fired deputy clerks (who are responsible for record-keeping, docketing, and other aspects of case flow management), and supervised the selection and assignment of jurors. To a great extent, they continue to exercise these same functions.

An obvious question that arises at this point is, If court clerks are responsible for all of these components of judicial administration, then why do we need court administrators? A flippant yet not altogether inaccurate response would be that the presence of court clerks is precisely *the* reason why we need court administrators. To understand this statement, it is necessary to review very briefly the nature of the court clerk position in county government.

Court clerks, who are also referred to as *prothonotaries* and *registers of probate*, are popularly elected in all but six states.[1] In addition to their responsibilities in court management, they often serve as county treasurers, recorders, auditors, comptrollers, finance officers, and secretary-treasurers to the county commissions (Berkson and Hays, 1976:501–503). Their elected status, coupled with their responsibility over important budgetary functions, gives court clerks a sizable amount of political clout within both the court system and county government in general. This situation would probably be very beneficial for the courts if it were not for the fact that court clerks are notoriously amateurish in their administrative styles. Most clerks use patronage personnel systems to enhance their political security, and many have been known to flagrantly defy judicial authority (Berg, 1972; Hays, 1978; Jensen and Dosal, 1977). Although research on their backgrounds and professional credentials is sparse, there is some evidence that indicates that they generally lack any prior administrative experience and/or academic training in management (Berkson and Hays, 1976). Given these facts, it is not surprising that administrative innovations have been so slowly adopted in our judicial bureaucracies.

B.   Existing Organizational Arrangements

An implicit theme of the preceding discussion is that courts in the United States have a decidedly "local" character. This phenomenon may be attributed both to federalism and to an American affinity for what is referred to as "local responses to local problems." The practical effect of this method of delivering judicial services, however, has been the creation of numerous semiautonomous courts that often operate in a fragmented and inconsistent manner. This is exemplified by the existence of many types of specialized courts (probate, municipal, juvenile, divorce, equity, magistrate's, etc.), the tremendous variety of legal forms and procedures used within and among state court systems, and by wide discrepancies in funding levels, support services, and administrative practices. Although similar traits characterize public administration at all levels of government, the legal community has for nearly sixty years advocated greater uniformity in court administration to ensure that the quality of justice does not vary significantly from jurisdiction to jurisdiction (Pound, 1927).

Proponents of court reform point to three characteristics of state court systems that are perceived as being most detrimental to administrative efficiency and the quality of justice: complicated judicial structures, including the presence of specialized courts, that result in duplication and overlapping jurisdictions; diffused administrative authority that prevents the judiciary from managing its own affairs; and, inappropriate methods of staffing and financing the judicial system. To deal with these dilemmas, the ABA has issued several versions of a model law intended to guide state governments in reforming their judicial systems. The latest and most sophisticated of these reform proposals, *Standards Relating to Court Organization*, calls for the following revisions in court structure and administration:

- *Court unification*: Including the elimination of specialized courts and the creation of a simplified three-tier court structure (supreme court, intermediate appellate court, and trial court of general jurisdiction).[2]
- *Centralized management*: Involves granting the chief justice of the state supreme court direct administrative authority over lower courts; state legislatures are to give the supreme courts rule-making authority; creation of court administrators' offices in all court systems.
- *Centralized budgeting and state financing*: The state supreme court, through its administrative office, is to prepare the budget for the entire court system; the legislature should not be empowered to veto the judicially prepared budget; responsibility for all judicial expenses should be assumed by the state government.
- *Centralized staffing*: Creation of a merit personnel system for the recruitment, training, and assignment of quasi-judicial personnel.

These measures are obviously intended to wrest control of trial courts from city and county government and to create a judicial bureaucracy that will be administered from the state capital. Despite an established professional bias against centralization as a panacea for all administrative ills, most of the ABA proposals have been very positively received by state governments. Presently, at least forty-five states have taken steps to simplify their lower court structures. Such reforms vary from the elimination of special courts to the establishment of the ultimate in unification, a two-tier court system consisting of only a supreme court and a trial court of general jurisdiction. Centralized rule-making has become equally popular, as over forty state legislatures have effectively surrendered that responsibility to their supreme courts. In providing their court systems with centralized financing and personnel systems, however, state legislatures have been less accommodating. Fewer than fifteen state court systems exercise total control (i.e., management of their *own* personnel system) over auxiliary personnel, although an additional sixteen states provide for the merit selection of some or all support employees by including them in the existing state personnel system. Similarly, less than ten states provide 80% or more of their judicial systems' funding, whereas thirty states provide less than 40% of the requisite financing (Berkson, 1977a).

In summary, there is a definite yet incomplete trend toward the centralization of judicial authority in state supreme courts. To date, this has been most thoroughly accomplished in rural or sparsely populated states. The larger and more populous states are generally the least centralized. States of the old confederacy digress from this general trend, as they are primarily both rural and decentralized (Berkson, 1977b).[3]

C. Professional Orientations of Judges

In actuality, judges have been *the* court administrators ever since courts first appeared in the American colonies. Thus, no matter how enthusiastically the judicial system embraces contemporary managerial practices, judges will probably continue to retain ultimate responsibility for court administration. It is difficult to conceive of a scenario in which judges would willingly surrender all administrative authority to professional court managers. As a consequence, judges will be the court administrators' "bosses" for the foreseeable future. This reality is recognized in the ABA *Standards*, which specify that court administrators should "be appointed by the presiding judge of the court in which they serve, with the advice and approval of the judges of the court and should serve at the pleasure of the presiding judge" (ABA, 1974:89).[4]

When the first large wave of court administrators was appointed in the early 1970s, the initial reactions of judges were less than heartening. Many court administrators had few or no duties, and several presiding judges seized the occasion to offer friends and relatives the newly created positions (Berkson and Hays, 1976b,c). A popular expression at the time was that court administrators were "bagmen" (i.e., they carried the luggage of judges while the latter were attending professional conferences).

In fairness to the judges, however, it is easy to understand their reluctance to immediately hand over the judicial establishment to court administrators. For a profession as tradition-bound and independent as the judiciary, the arrival of court administrators must have been very disconcerting. In a sense, the mere presence of court administrators was an admission that the judges were somehow derelict in performing their functions. Moreover, the new managers threatened, at least by implication, to turn the judges into bureaucrats by requiring them to adhere to rules and timetables heretofore unknown in courts. Little in the education or experience of judges had prepared them to be "managed." Most judges lack administrative experience, and a great many have an instinctive distaste for bureaucracy. Administration connotes efficiency and speed, and speed is regarded as being counterproductive to fairness and the proper regard for due process (Hays, 1977:171). According to some authorities, the combined experiences of a legal education, the practice of law, and sitting on the bench actually *teaches* judges to be antibureaucratic (Kandt, 1960; Greene, 1972).

Despite their initial reticence, most judges have learned to accept if not appreciate court administrators. Their attitudes have changed through positive working relationships with other administrators, as well as in response to a concerted educational campaign sponsored by such organizations as the ABA, the American Judicature Society, and the National College of the State Judiciary. At present, almost all presiding judges annually attend at least one training program and/or conference designed to impart understanding of and appreciation for managerial techniques. The fact remains, nevertheless, that the duties and responsibilities of any court administrator are directly dependent upon the good offices of the presiding judge. Although dramatic progress has been made within the past several years, it is still possible to find highly trained court administrators vegetating in a managerial vacuum.

III. MANAGEMENT ROLES AND FUNCTIONS

As should be evident from the preceding discussion, there is no typical court administrator position (Saari, 1970:2). Roles and duties vary according to the presence or absence of traditional court managers (such as court clerks), the degree of centralization or decentralization in the court system, and the professional orientations of the judges who supervise them. Moreover, the authority and responsibility they acquire can contract or expand in response to such variables as their own level of professional competence, the specific nature of the judicial tasks performed by their court system, and the level of managerial sophistication present within their judicial organization. These facts should be kept in mind as the roles and functions of contemporary court administrators are reviewed.

A. Professional Roles: Two Pictures of Reality

Management literature has long recognized that professional organizations are fundamentally different from other types of organizations. Bureaucracies that are dominated by one or more professional groups place a premium on *professional authority*. Indeed, *administrative authority* is perceived as being incompatible with professional authority (Etzioni, 1964:76). Professionals fear that administrative authority will result in inattention to, or subversion of, cherished professional goals and norms of behavior. Usually then, the professional group retains its control over most organizational policy matters, and jealously protects its occupational prerogatives. The manager in such an organization generally lacks power, relative to managers in more traditional bureaucracies. The professionals strive to maintain control over their own work, and "also seek the collective control of the administrative decisions that affect them" (Mintzberg, 1979:358). By these standards, courts are truly professional organizations (Stott, 1982).

Within such an organizational setting, what roles can court administrators be expected to assume? The conventional wisdom of court management depicts the court administrator as an assistant to the judge. This implies that the administrator handles the "housekeeping" functions to free judges from the drudgery of day-to-day management tasks. To distinguish between administrative and judicial functions, the early literature of court management offered extensive lists of *quasi-judicial*, as opposed to *judicial*, functions (Friesen et al., 1971; Saari, 1970). Judges were solely responsible for all judicial functions, such as deciding issues of law and court policy, and retained final authority over the quasi-judicial functions that were delegated to court administrators. Among the quasi-judicial functions that are most commonly mentioned are budget preparation, personnel supervision, space and equipment management, and jury and witness coordination.

Although the conventional perception of court administrators as merely assistants to judges is probably the most accurate picture of contemporary reality, the profession has now matured to the point that many court administrators have begun to assume a wider and more significant array of managerial responsibilities. Instead of simply attending to housekeeping functions, they engage in an administrative partnership with judges. According to E. Keith Stott (1982), the nature of this partnership is best characterized by reference to a continuum of administrative/judicial activities. At one end of the continuum are purely administrative duties that the court administrator performs without consulting the presiding judge. Record-keeping, purchasing, accounting, and most personnel matters involving auxiliary employees are included in this category. On the opposite end of the continuum are the duties, such as deciding cases and assigning judges, for which judicial officers assume sole responsibility. Activities that fall in the center of the continuum are performed as a *joint* venture where judges and court administrators *share* decision-making authority (Stott, 1982: 162). For the most part, these activities blend administrative and judicial functions. Included among the shared responsibilities are public information activities, the drafting of new rules and procedures, probation supervision, and forward planning.

The premise behind this new way of perceiving the court administrator's role is both logical and appealing. By operating as a team in administering these activities, the judge and administrator complement each other's competencies and thereby provide a more effective "product" than otherwise would be the case. Although it is much too premature to suggest that the partnership role will soon become the predominant administrative style in court administration, it *is* reasonable to expect judges and court administrators to share increasing amounts of responsibility as the profession acquires confidence.

B. Leadership Functions

The leadership activities of court administrators at all levels may be roughly categorized according to three broad functions: internal management, relations with external entities, and system improvement. These functions, and the duties attached to each, are briefly discussed next.

1. Internal Management

The court administrator concept originally developed as a method of upgrading the internal efficiency of courts. This is accomplished by relieving judges of direct supervisory responsibility over judicial support activities. In addition to the obvious benefits that accrue from the presence of full-time administrative officers, the introduction of modern management practices is an implicit byproduct of the professionalization of court administration (Malech, 1973).

The duties that are most often associated with the court administrator's internal function include:

- *Calendar and caseflow management*: To reduce court delay[5] by monitoring the assignment of cases to judges and courtrooms; to ensure that the caseload burden is equitably distributed to the various judges; to enforce policies and procedures that inhibit attorneys from acquiring unnecessary postponements[6]
- *Jury and witness management*: Processing of the vast number of citizens who are called for jury duty and testimony; to supervise their selection, payment, and housing
- *Space and equipment supervision*: Procurement and maintenance of adequate inventories of supplies and equipment; courtroom and courthouse management, including the provision of any security measures necessary for the protection of judges and citizens
- *Personnel management*: To supervise the selection, training, evaluation, and coordination of support personnel employed by the court system; to devise and implement procedures providing for the coordination of quasi-judicial personnel employed by independent criminal justice agencies

- *Financial management*: Preparation and execution of the court's budget; establishment of financial accounting, procurement, and auditing procedures
- *Statistician*: To compile and analyze statistics concerning caseloads, dispositions, and judicial workloads; trial court administrators are also required to tabulate statistics for reports required by the state court administrative offices
- *Records management*: Establishment and maintenance of filing systems and paper flow procedures for court records and other legal documents

2. Relations with External Entities

One of the most significant contributions that has been made to date by court administrators is a marked improvement in many court systems' relations with citizens, legislative bodies, and government agencies. Prior to the advent of court administrators, courts were notoriously lax in cultivating positive relationships with external bodies. Most of this oversight was attributable to the judges' lack of time, rather than inclination, to develop outside constituencies. Court administrators, conversely, have focused many of their energies on this task.

Few public agencies are regularly visited by more citizens than the courts. Many of these "visits" are involuntary, as anyone who has been called to testify or to serve on jury duty can attest. In an average year, most urban trial courts call at least 15,000 citizens for jury selection, and an additional 1000 appear as witnesses. Yet, despite the high level of traffic through the courts, they represent one of the most bewildering of government institutions to the average citizen. Part of this bewilderment is a product of the antiquated and ritualistic terminology that they used, as well as strange modes of dress and decorum. Traditionally, however, courts provided citizens with little assistance in understanding the complexities of the judicial system. To compound their error, courts were also incredibly inattentive to the comforts and sentiments of the citizens they depended upon for most of their activities. Prospective jurors and witnesses would be summoned to appear at 8:00 A.M., only to be dismissed at 5:00 P.M. without ever being called for questioning. Creature comforts were virtually absent, and no explanations were offered regarding what to expect and/or *why* the procedures used were necessary. Needless to say, this situation accomplished nothing for public relations for the judicial system.

Court administrators have ameliorated much of this problem. Through the use of queuing theory and other statistical methods, the average size of jury selection pools has been greatly reduced. Once they are called, jurors are regularly provided with handbooks describing the nuances of the jury selection process. Moreover, in most jurisdictions more comfortable facilities have been provided for waiting periods, and care has been taken to improve the quality of dining services and the like.

In addition to upgrading the treatment of jurors and witnesses, court administrators have devised more broad-based programs to enhance the judicial system's image with the general public. Many serve as a type of ombudsman, fielding complaints from citizens and responding to inquiries. Similarly, court administrators often establish *reception centers* designed to refer citizens to the appropriate offices and/or to explain legal technicalities. These activities have also been supplemented with the creation of *public information offices* that prepare press releases and public service advertisements concerning judicial functions.

Court administrators have also proven to be especially useful in improving the flow of communication between and among the courts and other government organs. Most notable among these activities is the assumption of responsibility for keeping legislative bodies informed of judicial needs. State court administrators, for example, devote a sizable portion of their time preparing reports for legislative committees (Doan and Shapiro, 1976). Likewise, trial court administrators often assume a role as legislative liaison, through which they apprise city and county legislative groups of developments in the judicial system that may have financial or other legislative consequences. In a real sense, court administrators are becoming the courts' lobbyists.

3. System Improvement

As has probably been apparent throughout this chapter, court management prior to the arrival of professional administrators was characterized by "crisis management." Judges were, for the most part, so preoccupied with holding down the fort that there was no time for the design and implementation of major policy initiatives.

Many of the functions and duties that have been described in the preceding pages imply major changes in traditional practices that result in greater judicial efficiency. Revisions in jury selection techniques, records management practices, and public relations activities, all represent system improvements that are both necessary and valuable. But they do not tell the entire story. Perhaps the most significant function that court administrators can perform is that of *planning* for future needs (Gallas, 1967).

The planning function in court management consists primarily of juxtaposing current judicial capabilities with expected demands on judicial services. The court administrator must ask such questions as, Is the current record management system sufficient to withstand an expected 15% increase in litigation, and Do we have enough judges and courtrooms to accommodate a 20% increase in population over the next 10 years? Based upon the answers, the court administrator must formulate and oversee the introduction of major improvements in the court's capacity to adapt to changing conditions. This function might include, but is not limited to, the introduction of computer technology, the design and acquisition of additional courthouses, and the employment of greater numbers of judicial and quasi-judicial personnel. If this responsibility is accomplished adequately, then the court administrator will not only have assisted the judicial system, but will have provided a valuable service to the many public agencies required to furnish the requisite funds and personnel.

IV. CONCLUDING OBSERVATIONS

Despite the recency of court administration's development, the profession has made significant inroads into the most traditional organizational setting in American government. This is indeed remarkable, given the institutional and political obstacles that have littered the paths of most court managers.

Yet, although the profession can justly take pride in its accomplishments, it will probably be some time before the typical court administrator exercises the entire range of duties and functions detailed in this chapter. Before that occurs, at least two major changes must transpire. First, the judicial system must be granted its rightful status as a coequal branch of government. Continued dispersion of judicial administrative authority among a plethora of state and local political actors is inconsistent with the need for a properly managed court system. The extent to which court administrators approach the ideal in authority and responsibility is inversely related to the power of local judicial officials. Although most authorities agree that the best way to reduce local influence in court systems is to convert court clerks into appointed rather than elected officials, progress in this area has been very slow. Important progress has been made, however, in providing court systems with sufficient administrative authority (rule-making, budgetary, and personnel) to enable them to manage most of their own affairs. Second, the profession of court management must be allowed to mature naturally, so to speak, in developing its identity. As court administrator positions currently exist, they are often merely collections of assorted duties and responsibilities that the judges simply did not have time for. Through more elaborate training and professional degree programs, continued education of the judiciary, and progressive specialization, the profession should overcome many of the problems that have plagued its early years.

NOTES

1. In Colorado, Connecticut, New Hampshire, and New Jersey, court clerks are appointed and hold office at the pleasure of judges. In Rhode Island, they are appointed by the governor.
2. There is by no means unanimity on the issue of the "best" organizational structure. Some reform groups advocate a four-tier court system (adding a

trial court of limited jurisdiction or a county court), whereas others argue that only two tiers are needed, a supreme court and a trial court of general jurisdiction.

3. One possible explanation for this phenomenon is that larger and more populous states require a greater amount of local flexibility within their judicial systems because they must respond to a more diverse set of demands and constituents. It may also be argued that the southern states have been slower to centralize because local political forces are more deeply embedded in their judicial systems, and suspicion of centralized authority is more prevalent in the South than in other regions.

4. This provision of the ABA *Standards* is challenged by such groups as the Advisory Commission on Intergovernmental Relations and the National Advisory Commission on Criminal Justice Standards and Goals. Both of these reform bodies recommend that trial court administrators be appointed and supervised by the *state court administrator* to provide a true chain of command (see Berkson, 1977a:379).

5. Court delay, which is defined as "undue" time required to bring a case to trial, has been variously reported to range from three to six *years* in many civil cases. Whether or not delay is a product of poor court management practices, inadequate numbers of judges, or simply a society that is much too litigious is a matter of great debate.

6. One practice that is especially troublesome in this regard is "judge shopping," by which attorneys continue to seek postponements until they are scheduled before a judge they regard as being "friendly."

REFERENCES

American Bar Association (1974). *Standards Relating to Court Organization.* American Bar Association, Chicago.

Baar, C. (1982). ICM and court administration: The first decade. *Justice System Journal* 6:176–199.

Berg, J. (1972). Assumption of administrative responsibility by the judiciary. *Suffolk University Law Review* 6:790–815.

Berkson, L. (1977a). The emerging ideal of court unification. *Judicature 60*: 372–382.

Berkson, L. (1977b). Court unification in the fifty states. Paper delivered to the Annual Meeting of ASPA, Atlanta.

Berkson, L. and Hays, S. (1976a). Court clerks: The forgotten politicians. *University of Miami Law Review 30*:499–516.

Berkson, L. and Hays, S. (1976b). Injecting court administrators into an old system: A case of conflict in Florida. *Justice System Journal 2*:57–71.

Berkson, L. and Hays, S. (1976c). The unmaking of a court administrator. *Judicature 60*:134–139.

Doan, R. and Shapiro, R. (1976). *State Court Administrators.* American Judicature Society, Chicago.

Downie, L. (1972). *Justice Denied*. Penguin, Baltimore.

Etzioni, A. (1964). *Modern Organizations*. Prentice-Hall, Englewood Cliffs, N.J.

Frank, J. (1972). *Courts on Trial*. Atheneum, New York.

Friesen, E., Gallas, E., and Gallas, N. (1971). *Managing the Courts*. Bobbs-Merrill, Indianapolis.

Gallas, E. (1967). The planning function of the court administrator. *Judicature 50*:268–271.

Greene, H. (1972). Court reform: What purpose? *American Bar Association Journal 58*:247–250.

Hays, S. (1977). The traditional managers: Judges. In Berkson, L., Hays, S., and Carbon, S., eds., *Managing the State Courts*. West Publishing, St. Paul.

Hays, S. (1978). *Court Reform: Ideal or Illusion?* D.C. Heath, Lexington, Mass.

Hays, S. (1979). The logic of court reform: Is Frederick Taylor gloating? *Criminal Justice Review 4*:7–16.

James, H. (1967). *Crisis in the Courts*. David McKay, New York.

Jensen, L. and Dosal, F. (1977). Circuit clerks' study. *State Court Journal 1*: 17–21.

Kandt, W. (1960). The judge as administrator—Let us look at him. *Kansas Law Review 8*:435–439.

Malech, A. (1973). A glass house: Court administration from the inside. *Judicature 56*:249–251.

McLaughlin, W. (1970). Of men and buildings—Crisis in judicial administration. *Massachusetts Law Quarterly 55*:331–334.

Meyer, B. (1971). Court administration: The newest profession. *Duquesne Law Review 10*:220–235.

Mintzberg, H. (1979). *The Structure of Organizations*. Prentice-Hall, Englewood Cliffs, N.J.

National Advisory Commission on Criminal Justice Standards and Goals (1971). *Courts*. U.S. Government Printing Office, Washington, D.C.

National Conference on the Judiciary (1971). *Report*. American Bar Association, Chicago.

Pound, R. (1927). Organization of the courts. *Judicature 11*:69–76.

President's Commission on Law Enforcement and Administration of Justice (1967). *Report*. U.S. Government Printing Office, Washington, D.C.

Saari, D. (1970). *Modern Court Management: Trends in the Role of Court Executive*. Law Enforcement Assistance Administration, Washington, D.C.

Stott, E. (1982). The judicial executive: Toward greater congruence in an emerging profession. *Justice System Journal 7*:152–179.

Unit Two

STATE AND LOCAL GOVERNMENT BUDGETING, DECISION-MAKING, AND FINANCIAL MANAGEMENT

Part A   Mechanisms and Processes
Chapters 4-6

Part B   Internal and External Controls Over State and Local Government Budgeting, Decision-Making, and Financial Management
Chapters 7-10

4

The Functions and Processes of State Budgeting

Regis L. Chapman   Virginia Department of Planning and Budget, Richmond, Virginia

I. INTRODUCTION

State budget processes are the primary intersections through which virtually all state policies and programs must pass. Generalizations about these intersections are difficult. Each state's budget functions and processes are products of unique historic, economic, legal, administrative, political, and social environments (Howard, 1973:28). Their natures can range from a simple country crossroad to a system of highways, the number and complexity of which can overwhelm decision makers.

A major problem for career executives is that their effectiveness and successes can be diminished by failure to understand and anticipate the various budgetary intersections. Budget experts comprehend quickly through correspondence or conversation whether someone understands the budget environment just as an airline pilot determines whether a visitor to the cockpit understands its environment.

A major problem for political executives is lack of knowledge of the history, functions, and capacities of a state's budget processes so that the processes can be adjusted to meet the needs of a political administration. Governors and appointed officials interested in making substantial changes to the administrative behavior of state government face the possibility of paralysis by bureaucratic discretion and control over the flow of information (Hale and Douglass, 1977:368).

The word "budget" is one of the vaguest words in public administration. It might refer to what a governor proposes to a legislature; to what a legislature passes; to what a governor signs after legislative approval; to what has been adjusted by executive or legislative authority during the budget year; or, even to what has been mentally adjusted by knowledge that expected revenues have not materialized. In order to make state budgeting less vague, this chapter will review the evolution of its functions; describe its environment; discuss major stages of state budgetary processes; and, summarize considerations important to the evolution of executive branch budgeting initiatives.

II. EVOLUTION OF THE FUNCTIONS

Prior to 1911, legislatures dominated state budgeting. Agencies submitted budget requests to legislative committees with minimal central executive review of their requests or subsequent spending. Significant increases in amounts of spending, corruption, and the influence of the scientific management school of thought contributed to a reform movement that included the executive budget as one of its keystones. Public administration theory during this period advocated executive budget reform to enhance chief executive capacities to better perform certain functions. These functions included the following (Schick, 1971:14-43).

- Central control to deter wasteful and unlawful administrative behavior and to coordinate closely with accounting, purchasing, audit, and personnel controls
- Management to standardize and consolidate agency budget estimates and otherwise strengthen central administrative capacities to ensure greater efficiency
- Planning to ensure comprehensive and consistent statements about budget policies and programs

The case for an increase in the chief executive role in budgeting was sufficiently strong that significant reforms were adopted by all of the states by 1926 (Schick, 1971:14). However, legislatures generally agreed to reductions in their authority only to the extent that reforms be primarily directed to a control function that emphasized a budget information structure organized by detailed *objects of expenditure*.

Subsequently, there have been a series of reform movements in state budgeting. Reforms primarily emanated from the executive branch, with each movement being advocated as a panacea for the uncertain decision environment in which public officials operate. Each movement promised chief executives a system of budgetary processes to implement their policies more effectively. The postmortem on each budgetary reform produced a long list of unrealized expectations, suggesting the reforms were more form than substance.

During the control period of budgeting, through the 1930s, substantial improvements in accounting, personnel, audit, and procurement processes reduced the compelling need for budget processes to provide the first line of defense against the misuse of public funds. Increased attention was given to the management function through the review of the efficiency of activities for which resources were consumed. Subsequently, the first Hoover Commission recommended performance budgeting in 1949.

In the 1950s, the performance budgeting movement involved reorganizing budget information structures from objects of expenditure to categories of similar activities that could be assessed on the basis of efficiency. Workload and unit cost measurements were the most common methods of assessing efficiency (Lee and Johnson, 1983:71).

The planning function of budgeting was emphasized during the late 1960s and early 1970s through planning-programming-budgeting systems (PPBSs), whereby planning and budgeting processes are more closely integrated. PPBSs commonly utilize a budget information structure in which units of analysis and decision-making are based on the similarity of objectives. This structure provides a means to consider alternative long-term goals and objectives before actual means to accomplish them are selected. PPBSs also emphasize the need for chief executives to articulate their policies to reverse the flow of budget information and decision-making from a bottom-up method to a more top-down policy-sensitive approach (Schick, 1966:258).

The most recent state budgeting reform to receive general attention has been zero-base budgeting (ZBB). ZBB emphasizes the management function of budgeting; however, it can be installed on any type of budget information structure. The essential element of ZBB is that budget requests are prepared with discrete decision packages at alternative levels of funding with at least one alternative below current levels of service. Decision packages proposed above the reduced level of service are prioritized and allow for tradeoffs between new and existing activities. ZBB is advocated by cutback management experts as the approach best suited for decision-making in the face of revenue reductions because the decision packages are useful for political bargaining and negotiating (Levine, 1978:322). ZBB does not require extensive analysis to support budget proposals, but relies on agency management to prioritize proposals in order to shift resources from lower- to higher-yield activities (Schick, 1977:15). The rapid increase in the use of ZBB techniques through 1979 had apparently subsided, with twenty-one states indicating they were using some ZBB techniques (Schick, 1979:7).

III. ENVIRONMENT

Allen Schick's classic conceptualization of public budgeting as evolving through stages from control, to management, to planning suggests that the evolution is sequential and that state budget entities must have the capacity to perform the earlier function before moving to the next one. A less idealized viewpoint is that state budgeting functions have not changed significantly since the inception of the executive budget movement and that state budget officials have tended to make marginal adjustments, relabel, and advertise certain elements of their processes to reflect each generation of panaceas. The strong influences of the state budgeting environment may preclude substantial changes in state budget office technologies and in their structures.

A. The External Environment

The state budgeting environment can produce very high levels of uncertainty. Multiple entities external to the state budget office generate needs, demands, and expectations for guidance, decisions, recommendations, and actions so that their respective uncertainties about the future will be reduced. These sources include a governor and his staff or cabinet; other elected executive officials; line and central state agencies; federal agencies; regional and local units of government, courts, legislatures, and advocacy organizations; and, the media. Likewise, each of these external entities is responsible for creating uncertainty within the central budget office. Such uncertainty may result from unexpected conditions that require decisions; short deadlines for decisions that preclude thorough analysis; and the intentional and unintentional withholding of available information needed to support analysis and decision-making.

Many state agencies have clients, advocates, and other interests that benefit from their existence. These beneficiaries often attempt to exert budget influence on a governor outside formal budget processes. When they are not successful with a governor, they may become particularly active in lobbying the legislature.

Although most state agency heads serve at the pleasure of a governor and career officials report to them, they sometimes consider the governor a "short-termer," trying to implement policies contrary to the long-term interest of their agency and its mission. State agencies are frequently organized congruent with professions whose norms, values, and ethics may call for policy priorities inconsistent with those of a political administration. For example, engineers dominate transportation departments; physicians dominate health departments; and, social workers dominate welfare agencies. Agency staff may have long-term acquaintances with legislators, legislative staff, and with program beneficiares that provide continuity through numerous governors' terms.

B. The Technology of State Budgeting

The technology of state budgeting includes the processes used by budget offices to convert information inputs into information, decisions, and recommendations to be exported to the external environment. It includes the manner in which the budget office sequences its activities and the knowledge it applies to converting information inputs into outputs.

State budget technology can require the application of high levels of analytic skill because of the high rate of exceptions that occur in the analytic process. The exceptions are encountered due to uncertainty in and the absence of information and policy guidelines necessary to support analysis in the time available for decision-making.

The knowledge of budget staff is one of the most crucial variables affecting the capacity of a state budget office to meet the demands of its environment. Depending on whether emphasis is placed on the control, management, or planning function, its needs for staff knowledge and skill will vary accordingly. Control processes most commonly rely on accounting; management processes rely on administration; planning processes usually rely on social science methods of analysis. State budget offices that change the emphasis of their budget functions may face the prospect of significant proportions of their primary staff knowledge being outmoded. In a survey of state budget directors, the capabilities of budget staff were the most frequently cited impediment to budget innovation (Ramsey and Hackbart, 1979:67). Trends from 1970 to 1980 in the academic credentials of state budget staff indicate a decline in the proportion of staff from the accounting and business administration disciplines and an increase in public administration and other social science disciplines (Lee, 1980).

C. The Structure of State Budget Offices

About 60% of state budget offices are organizationally located either as a part of a governor's office or as a department that reports directly to the governor's office or as a department that reports directly to the governor. The rest are typically subunits within a department of finance or administration: 40% of state budget offices have less than 20 staff members; 35% have between 20 and 40 staff members; 25% of the states have over 40 staff members; two states (California and New York) have over 150 staff (National Association of State Budget Officers, 1981).

State budget organizational structures vary from very flat hierarchies with all budget analysts reporting directly to a budget director, to very tall hierarchies with multiple specialized units. The number of units varies not only with the size of the state but with the number of control, management, and planning functions the budget office performs. For example, a budget office might only be responsible for budget planning, development, and execution, or it could also include processes related to revenue estimating, policy analysis, program evaluation, management analysis, intergovernmental coordination, legislation development and analysis, and economic analysis.

IV. THE BUDGET PROCESSES

State budget processes can be conveniently described in four stages. Each stage occurs relatively sequentially and within an identifiable timeframe. However, there is significant overlap between them, and some activity associated with each is continuous. The stages are as follows:

- Planning and development
- Executive review and submission
- Legislative review and appropriation
- Execution and evaluation

A. Planning and Development

1. Central Budget Office

Most governors choose to provide formal policy guidance to influence agency budget and legislation proposals. Budget offices commonly participate in developing this guidance, but participation can range from primary authorship of formal guidance to a simple review and comment of guidance produced by other staff entities.

A budget office objective is to establish a budget planning and development framework through which accurate information can flow for review, analysis, and decision-making. Thus, it usually controls the content of instructions to agencies for the development of their budget proposals. Control-oriented processes usually emphasize detailed financial information at the object of expenditure level and explanations of proposed changes from prior budget periods. Management-oriented processes focus on information about proposed levels of activity and their costs to facilitate assessments of operating efficiency. Planning-oriented processes are most likely to require multiyear estimates, projections of needs and problems being addressed; information about objectives being pursued; and, descriptions of activities proposed to accomplish objectives.

Because most agencies have a vested interest in making their budget proposals appear to meet a governor's priorities and in manipulating the process when possible, the budget office must also design the framework to neutralize manipulation attempts. Some of the most common manipulation tools employed by agencies and that budget offices try to prevent include the following:

1. Overestimates of the need or demand for a service
2. Overestimates of the need for personnel to provide new services to meet a governor's or a legislature's policy priority
3. Burying new initiatives as current services if a governor is discouraging new initiatives

4. Underestimating federal revenues for programs of high priority to generate support for state funds to replace them
5. Overestimating the probability of long-term federal funding in order to build client/constituent pressure for state funds to replace them when they are reduced
6. Assigning a popular program with a low priority so efforts to reduce overall agency funding can be blocked by client and constituent groups
7. Proposing scheduled changes as new initiatives and requesting additional funding for them if they match with a governor's priorities
8. Circumventing controls on employment levels by changing to contractual services that may be more expensive
9. Proposing legislation that, if approved, will make a subsequent case for additional funding to implement it

2. Agency Proposals

The planning and development of proposals for appropriations are almost universally initiated by agencies seeking funding. State agencies may have many variables to consider in preparing their proposals.

Multiple sources outside the executive branch of state government can affect the priorities and amounts of agency requests. These include beneficiaries, advocates and critics of the agency's services, legislators, and legislative staffs and committees. An agency must consider the status or results of special studies it may be required to submit to the legislature and any studies the legislature is conducting. Frequently, legislatively mandated studies and evaluations are predictions of a legislature's predisposition to take certain budget and statutory actions. Assumptions must be made about economic, demographic, and social trends likely to affect service needs and demands. Projections of likely changes in federal policies and programs must also be developed and updated.

From within the executive branch, agencies must review policy guidance issued by the governor and other elected and appointed officials. An agency must review its patterns of expenditures to ascertain whether or not they are consistent with past appropriations and whether or not they are expected to change. It is also essential for agencies to estimate revenues likely to be generated through charges, fees, special-purpose taxes, and any planned transfers and reimbursements from other agencies. New information resulting from operating experience and from executive branch analyses of the efficiency and effectiveness of programs and policies is often considered.

Requirements established by the central budget office for the content of budget proposals are reviewed, and plans are made for the production of a proposal by a specified deadline. At the same time, an agency may develop its package of legislation proposed for submission to the legislature. Frequently, there are direct relationships between legislation proposals and budget proposals that must be coordinated.

B. Executive Review and Submission

Budget offices analyze agency proposals using their internal knowledge and processes to test the reasonableness of proposals based on the control, management, and planning criteria implicit in the budget preparation instructions. The analyst in a control-oriented environment will typically focus on prior-year appropriations and expenditures in comparison with what is proposed, and spend a major share of time assessing deviations from whatever control criteria have been established as budget policy. For example, a policy control might include no additional funding above that required to cover the cost of inflation or current levels of service. Policy controls might also be in effect for the use of contractual services, personnel, data processing systems, travel, and other major objects of expenditure.

The analyst in a management-oriented process ideally concentrates on examining the extent to which proposed resources appear reasonable in relation to planned levels of activity. If a management-oriented budget process includes zero-base budget features, the analyst's time is primarily spent reviewing those proposed programs and activities for which decision packages were developed for funding above the established base.

In an ideal planning-oriented process, a budget analyst might review economic and demographic descriptions and projections related to, for example, infant mortality problems. If this information appears reasonable, proposed objectives and perhaps alternative objectives may be assessed to determine their reasonableness in relation to the problems. Next, a review of information about what activities are proposed could be undertaken to test a cause and effect hypothesis. For example, an agency might propose to add twenty-five physicians to provide more prenatal care to accomplish the objective of reducing infant mortality. Available analysis might show, however, that this would not have a significant effect because high rates of infant mortality primarily result from a lack of knowledge among pregnant women about the need for prenatal care.

Such analysis is, however, idealized. The truth is that central budget offices are deluged with proposals several months prior to the time when the budget proposal is due to the legislature. The content of submissions is often deficient in terms of what the budget office needs to know to confidently present recommendations to reflect a governor's policies. In addition, the control, management, or planning emphasis of the budget office may be an impediment to the decision-making needs of the governor. Some of the reasons for these conditions are as follows:

1. Executive branch political officials may provide unclear, conflicting, or changing policy guidance during the planning and development stage.
2. Budget officials may not understand policy priorities sufficiently to adjust submission requirements along the control-management-planning continuum to secure and present information organized for the governor's decision-making criteria.
3. Executive branch political officials may be too clear in providing policy guidance. Subsequently, threatened agencies employ some of the manipulation tools discussed previously.
4. Agencies may invest insufficient effort and expertise in developing their proposals because they do not believe the quality of their proposals and the budget office analysis have an effect on their level of appropriations.

In addition to the uncertainties surrounding the content of submissions, a number of events that introduce further uncertainty may take place after budget proposals are submitted for review. The federal government changes laws, regulations, and funding; the courts make rulings that affect programs; the economy changes direction; health-care benefit premiums are increased; state general-fund revenue estimates are revised; the results of studies are announced; proposed high-priority legislation is discovered to have fiscal implications; and, executive officials receive cues on how legislative priorities are evolving.

Agency budget proposals are the official requests for funding; however, most experienced officials know there are other ways to gain approval of their proposals. Agency heads and their advocates commonly lobby with the governor and other political officials. Decisions are sometimes made outside the budget process, and the budget office is directed to reflect them in the budget.

Toward the end of the budget review stage, budget officials, the governor, and other political officials make the final decisions necessary to ensure that a budget proposal with estimated revenues equal to estimated expenditures is sent to a printer at almost precisely the hour necessary to meet the deadline for submission to the legislature.

C. Legislative Review and Appropriation

After the introduction of a governor's budget proposal as one or more budget bills, it is most commonly referred to appropriation committees of the legislature and frequently to their subcommittees. Specific budget issues may also be addressed by other committees with substantive policy responsibilities (e.g., agriculture). The governor's budget and agency officials are often called upon by legislative committees to make presentations and respond to questions about the budget bill(s). Lobbyists representing interest groups may also participate in these forums.

Legislatures have significantly expanded their staff capacities in recent years. Appropriations committee staffs are usually among the largest and most proficient in conducting professional budget analysis. They symbolize a trend of state legislatures toward more effectively asserting themselves as equal partners in state government (Howard, 1973:31).

Most legislatures have the authority to amend a budget bill, thus, the saying, "the executive proposes; the legislature disposes." Legislators feel a compulsion to amend a budget bill regardless of how compatible it may be with their own preferences (Lee and Johnson, 1983:199). The extent to which budget bills are amended varies from marginal adjustments to ignoring executive proposals and the legislature developing its own budget. When the legislature has completed its amendments, the budget is sent to the governor for approval by signature or for veto and reconsideration by the legislature. Most governors have line-item veto power whereby parts of the budget may be selectively vetoed.

D. Budget Execution and Evaluation

The intracacies of the budget execution and evaluation stage place budget officials in potentially powerful positions to control the programs and policies of state government. There has been a distinct trend for central budget offices to increase their control over expenditures in recent years. No clear patterns are identifiable in terms of what types of states exercise the greatest levels of control, but the best indicator of a state's propensity to do so is the number of central budget office staff (Lee, 1981:79).

1. Budget Execution

Most observers of the functions and processes of state budgeting underestimate the effects of budget execution. Budget execution authority may be found in a state constitution, the enabling legislation of the budget entity, an appropriation act, a governor's executive orders, executive branch directives, a budget manual, and in the past practices and traditions of a state's budget process. When an appropriation act goes into effect (usually July 1), a number of budget execution actions are required, particularly in those states whose processes emphasize the control function.

Authority to take certain budget execution actions can lie with the governor, or more commonly, a lower-level official. Budget office staff can have significant effects on programs and policies by offering or withholding advice on alternative ways agencies can accomplish their financial objectives; interpreting whether or not proposed actions are subject to established control criteria; and, interpreting whether or not approval criteria have been met. Some of the most common budget execution processes are as follows:

1. *Allotment*: Budget offices may have authority to allot appropriated funds in increments. The objective of allotment is to control the rate of agency expenditures. Allotments can be made at annual or more frequent intervals and can be used as mechanisms for implementing cutbacks in funding.
2. *Transfers of appropriations*: Most budget offices control approvals for the transfer of funding between appropriation or other control units within an agency. Some states require legislative approval of all appropriation transfers. Executive authority to transfer funding between departments is limited to a few states.
3. *Transfers from prior years*: Under some circumstances appropriations or revenues (not necessarily appropriated) from prior fiscal years may be carried forward as an appropriation to the current year by executive action.
4. *Increases in nonstate fund appropriations*: Agencies may generate more revenue than was appropriated through federal grants and special taxes or charges. Most budget offices have authority to increase certain appropriations to allow agencies to spend additional revenues.
5. *Cash advances/loans*: Many state activities must spend money before revenues are available. Although appropriations may have been made, the revenues from grants, special taxes, charges, or other special revenues may not have been received. Budget offices may control the amounts, duration, and terms of cash advances or loans to cover expenditures until revenue is received.
6. *Encumbrances*: Restrictions on how certain appropriations can be spent may be established through the budget office. A common restriction is to encumber personnel funding to avoid a common agency practice of gaining funds for unnecessary staff positions, or of leaving positions vacant to make excess funds available for other purposes.
7. *Employment controls*: Various mechanisms are used to control personnel. Some appropriation acts establish employment or position limits with certain authority for changes given to the executive branch. Some budget offices review all proposals for new positions and reclassifications.
8. *Grant application approvals*: Some budget offices have authority to approve all applications for federal funding and the transfer of federal grant funds between departments.
9. *Capital outlay projects*: A budget office may control approval of each step in the development of major construction, renovation, or acquisition of capital facilities.
10. *Contingency accounts*: Approval of requests for the expenditure or transfer of appropriations from central contingency accounts almost always involves the budget office. Requests are most commonly approved for agency deficits, natural disasters, or public safety purposes.

11. *Other central accounts*: Central budget accounts are often established for special purposes which may include unanticipated increases in fuel, roof repairs, snow removal, fringe benefit and salary increases, asbestos removal, and so on. Budget offices typically analyze agency requests for these funds and control approvals.

12. *Reduction strategies*: An appropriation act or other law may require that certain reduction strategies be employed when revenue collected is estimated to be less than amounts appropriated. The budget office is usually responsible for implementing the required strategies.

Other common budget execution mechanisms include approval of certain types of travel, equipment purchases, contracts, and initiation of new services. Many unique budget execution mechanisms are found throughout the states as reflections of individual history and character. At least one state maintains a special provision of its appropriation act to ensure that, in the event of major financial disaster, the wives and daughters of confederate veterans are not denied their pensions.

2. Evaluation

The more fundamental budget processes use specific terminology to define their complex elements. These terms include appropriation, allotment, revenue, expenditure, and fund. The term *evaluation* has no precise definition and is often used interchangeably with policy analysis, program analysis, monitoring, assessment, management analysis, and productivity analysis.

For the purpose of budget decision-making, evaluation can be termed as a reexamination of the variables used to make resource allocation decisions. Thus, decision-making processes include evaluation to the extent that information about the past is used in making decisions about the future. A primitive form of evaluation would be to ask administering officials whether things went according to plan. Sophisticated evaluations involve comprehensive reexaminations of needs, objectives, activities, and resources. Such evaluations are undertaken to analyze changes in current and predicted levels of need, the appropriateness of objectives in relation to those needs, analysis of the extent to which activities are effective in achieving their objectives, and the extent to which activities are carried out efficiently.

Budget processes that emphasize control generally place the least emphasis on evaluation; feedback is typically related to reporting on deviations from control criteria. Budget processes that emphasize management are likely to employ analyses of the efficiency or productivity of activities. Budget processes with a planning emphasis normally focus on the effectiveness of activities in accomplishing objectives and on the appropriateness of objectives.

Although only eight state budget offices indicated they were conducting effectiveness analyses in 1970, twenty-five states did in 1980. Similarly, conducting efficiency analyses increased from fourteen to thirty-five states (Lee and Johnson, 1983:177). Whereas analysis is becoming more common in both central budget offices and among line agencies, there is a gap between the conduct of analysis and its actual use in policy deliberations (Lee and Staffeldt, 1977:405).

The organization of state budget office evaluation functions ranges from individual budget analysts conducting or coordinating analysis in time not absorbed by other responsibilities to separate organizational units whose staffs specialize in evaluation. Methods for the selection of evaluation topics range from analyst initiative to formal evaluation assessments that involve top decision-makers, including the governor. Those states that claim the best results in applying formal evaluation methods to budget decision-making appear to have separate evaluation units and involve top-level decision-makers in topic selection and implementation of evaluation results (Polivka and Stryker, 1983).

V. CONCLUSION

State budget processes are complex intersections through which state policies and programs must travel. The intersections are encountered during the stages of budget planning and development; executive review; legislative review; and, execution and evaluation. Each state's map of budget intersections is different, and all intersections are not likely to be identified on available maps. The numerous roads being traveled by multiple actors with different perspectives, needs, and motivations will continue to steer innovators toward the construction of new roads and intersections. To the extent that future evolution of this construction can result in positive effects on a state's capacity to govern, it is appropriate that increased attention be given to accurate mapping of current intersections and developing charts for the future.

Observers, practitioners, and students of state budgeting appear to realize that there are substantial gaps between the theory, practice, and demands of a state budgeting environment. For example, the fiscal austerity common to state governments through 1984 has resulted in an increase in blunt, top-down budgetary decisions, and thus contributes to increases in budget centralization (Bozeman and Straussman, 1982:515). Although such a trend might appear to place governors in firm control of executive decision-making, a paradox may be occurring whereby state agencies are encouraged to hide significant policy and program initiatives within their current budget allocations (Hale, 1977).

Unrealized expectations following each generation of budget reform panacea have contributed to the realization that no single formula is applicable to all state budgeting environments (Caiden, 1981:13). Deliberations on what budget innovations are appropriate for an individual state are best served by the assumption that it is necessary to custom design its functions and processes. In addition, the active support of the governor and his administration is necessary to ensure agency cooperation (Ramsey and Hackbart, 1979:66). Long-term economic, social, physical, and political environments must be projected to estimate resources available and issues generally confronted; existing budget information structures must be compared with the type of information needed to support issues normally encountered; and, the inertia and capacities of a state's current budgetary functions and processes within the control-management-planning continuum must be assessed.

REFERENCES

Bozeman, B. and Straussman, J. D. (1982). Shrinking budgets and the shrinkage of budget theory. *Public Administration Review 42*:509–515.

Caiden, N. (Spring, 1981). Public budgeting amidst uncertainty and instability. *Public Budgeting and Finance 1*:6–19.

Hale, G. E. (1977). Executive leadership versus budgetary behavior. *Administration and Society 9*:169–190.

Hale, G. E. and Douglass, S. R. (1977). The politics of budget execution: Financial manipulation in state and local government. *Administration and Society 9*:367–378.

Howard, S. K. (1973). *Changing State Budgeting.* The Council of State Governments, Lexington, Ky.

Lee, R. D., Jr. (1980). Developments in state budgeting: Selected results from a survey of state budget officers. Survey conducted by the National Association of State Budget Officers and the Institute of Public Administration, The Pennsylvania State University, University Park, Pa.

Lee, R. D., Jr. (Winter, 1981). Centralization/decentralization in state government budgeting. *Public Budgeting and Finance 1*:76–79.

Lee, R. D., Jr. and Johnson, R. W. (1983). *Public Budgeting Systems*, 3rd ed. University Park Press, Baltimore.

Lee, R. D., Jr. and Staffeldt, R. J. (1977). Executive and legislative use of policy analysis in the state budgetary process: Survey results. *Policy Analysis 3*: 395–405.

Levine, C. H. (1978). Organizational decline and cutback management. *Public Administration Review 38*:316–325.

National Association of State Budget Officers. (1981). *Budgetary Processes in the States.* National Association of State Budget Officers, Washington, D.C.

Polivka, L. and Stryker, L. T. (1983). Program evaluation and the policy process in state government: An effective linkage. *Public Administration Review 43*:255–259.

Ramsey, J. R. and Hackbart, M. M. (Spring, 1979). Budgeting: Inducements and impediments to innovations. *State Government 52*:65–69.

Schick, A. (1966). The road to PPB: The stages of budget reform. *Public Administration Review 26*:243–258.

Schick, A. (1971). *Budget Innovation in the States*. The Brookings Institution, Washington, D.C.

Schick, A. (1977). Keynote address: Putting it all together. In *Sunset, Zero-Base Budgeting, Evaluation*. The Virginia General Assembly, Richmond, pp. 9–18.

Schick, A. (1979). *Zero Base '80*. National Association of State Budget Officers and the Urban Institute, Washington, D.C.

5
City Budgeting and Budget Problems

Perry Moore   College of Liberal Arts, Wright State University, Dayton, Ohio

I. INTRODUCTION

Although budgeting suggests the drudgery and boredom of ledgers, accounts and journals, it is the heart of the political and decision-making process. If politics is who gets what, when, and how, then budgeting is the essence of politics. The budget is the best statement of public priorities because it allocates money among competing programs.

This chapter examines various purposes of budgeting and how each purpose is related to a specific budgeting format. The essential elements within most budget formats are described. The budget cycle, which includes revenue estimation, budget formulation, legislative approval, budget execution, and auditing, is discussed. The chapter concludes with a brief description of capital budgeting.

II. PURPOSES OF BUDGETING AND BUDGET FORMATS

Allen Schick (1966) proposed a classic typology of budget purposes: control, management, and planning. Each purpose may produce a particular budget format: line-item, performance, or program budget. The control approach attempts to assure that money is spent according to law and that no resources are spent for illegal activities. When control is the primary concern of budget makers, the line-item budget is generally used. The management approach is more concerned that the money is spent in the most efficient way possible to

achieve stated objectives. When management is the chief concern, the performance budget may be used. The planning approach attempts to use the budgeting
process to answer broad policy questions, such as what should be the long-range
goals and policies of the government and how particular expenditure decisions
are related to these goals. When the planning purpose is the primary concern,
the program, planning budget may be used.

A. Traditional, Line-Item, Incremental Budgeting

The line-item budget as used in United States cities dates only from the late
nineteenth century. Before that time, government agencies were often given
lump-sum appropriations that did not list specific expenditures. When
administrative officials obtained lump-sum appropriations, they were often
tempted to arrange special deals with employees or contractors. Graft and
corruption in the last half of the nineteenth century produced a reform movement that brought about various governmental reforms including the line-item
budget. The reformers were particularly concerned that money was spent for
legitimate purposes; therefore, they called for specification of the expenditures.
The line-item budget itemizes expenditures on a line-by-line basis. Strict line-
item budgets give detailed enumerations of every expenditure, but most
line-item budgets place expenditures into general categories such as personnel,
supplies, equipment, printing, travel, and so on. Moore (1980a) found that most
cities use the line-item budgeting format. An important characteristic of line-
item budgeting is incrementalism. Most budgets do not start from scratch each
year. Rather than start with a zero base and build up, most of the preceding
year's budget is accepted as proper, and budget reviewers focus attention on new
items and requested decreases and increases in the current level of spending. The
increments, not the base, are examined closely.

Critics of line-item budgeting and incrementalism claim that the incremental approach is not "rational." These critics call for a rational budgeting
process in which:

1. The goals of an agency are clarified.
2. Methods for attainment of the goals are listed and the cost-benefit ratio of
    each method is analyzed.
3. The method that *maximizes* the benefits to the costs is selected.

The critics point out that the existing budget base in a traditional, incremental,
line-item budget reflects prior history that may not represent the best way to
allocate resources at the present time.

Critics also note that as long as the budget represents small increments
added to last year's budget, the budget cannot be used as a planning device
whereby decision-makers can look ahead four or five years and determine their
goals and attempt to develop a comprehensive budget to accomplish the goals.

Because incremental budgeting does not emphasize a statement of goals or objectives, but provides only incremental increases in a number of line items, it encourages logrolling tactics. One interest group may agree to support an increase for a second group in return for the second group's support of an increase for the first group. Some contend that these logrolling tactics contribute to an ever-expanding budget without any concern for the collective or higher interest.

Finally, critics object to the line-item object of expenditure format because it provides no method by which the effectiveness or efficiency of an agency can be analyzed. The line-item budget only notes for what money is to be spent. It does not indicate what is to be accomplished or whether the money is being spent in the most efficient way.

Aaron Wildavsky (1974) is perhaps the primary defender of traditional, incremental, line-item budgeting. Wildavsky points to serious deficiencies in the rational approach to decision-making and budgeting. First, the goals of an agency often cannot be stated precisely. Second, there may be insufficient time to pursue the kind of analysis inherent in the rational model. Third, it may be impossible to obtain the information needed to make a rational decision, or the costs of getting the information may outweigh its benefits.

Wildavsky contends that attempting to look at everything in the budget (base plus increments) may mean that everything receives a cursory examination. It may be more rational to assume that past decisions (base) were correct and concentrate limited analytical resources on the increments to the base.

Wildavsky also believes that logrolling is not bad. Indeed, it's simply part of the only process—the political bargaining process—that is capable of weighing the costs and benefits of the very dissimilar things produced by governments. In other words, defenders of incremental budgeting contend that there is no quantitative analysis or mathematical formula as effective as a typical political bargaining session in deciding which department should receive more money.

Although there are numerous criticisms of traditional line-item budgeting, it continues to be used by most American cities (Moore, 1980a). It is the dominant format because: it is relatively simple to do; it consumes little time and paperwork; and, departments and city council members prefer the traditional format.

B. Performance Budgeting

One criticism of traditional line-item budgeting is that it concentrates on items purchased and ignores the activities such items produce. It is difficult to see in line-item budgeting the impact that budget cuts will have on programs and activities. Performance budgets, however, emphasize the use of unit costs and workload measures that allow for comparisons of outputs among units or employees. For example, the activity of "maintenance of motor vehicles" might give unit cost measures such as cost per mile driven. A municipal hospital nursing service might give nursing costs per hours of patient care. The sanitation budget might include projected cost per ton of garbage collected, or cost per number of households served. In each example, the performance budget format allows comparisons of efficiency and enhances the use of the budget as a management tool.

There are a number of problems associated with performance budgeting. Because data are often unavailable for measuring many activities, administrators attempt to invent or adopt workload measures that are not really representative of the activity being measured; or they may be tempted to concentrate on measurable activities. For example, if a training program is evaluated by the number of graduates of the program, it may concentrate on processing students as opposed to imparting skills.

Another problem of performance budgeting is that knowing how much an activity costs per unit of service or product delivered and knowing the impact of the activity are two different things. Most performance measures fail to measure effectiveness. For example, knowledge of the number of miles patrolled by police and the cost per mile provides little if any information concerning the actual impact of the patrols on crime reduction.

Because it is difficult to obtain agreement on the appropriate workload measures for various activities and because of the expense involved in collecting information, comparatively few cities use performance budgeting (Moore, 1980a).

C. Planning, Programming, Budgeting (PPB)

Planning, programming, budgeting is the most ambitious approach to budgeting. PPB moves far beyond the control or management functions of budgeting, and attempts to provide a basis for policy decisions. It combines long-range planning with budgeting. PPB requires government agencies to establish a hierarchy of objectives coupled with an analysis of alternative ways to achieve them. At the heart of PPB is cost-benefit analysis. In many cases, however, the estimates of costs and benefits are quite difficult and time-consuming, and many municipal budget offices do not have the expertise or time to engage in such analysis. In addition, the cost-benefit analysis often concentrates on economic costs and benefits and ignores political costs and benefits—the kind of cost-benefit analysis in which most council members are interested. Moreover, council members often find it difficult to understand PPB and continue to insist on the traditional line-item budgets, which necessitates the translation of planning, programming, budgets into line-item budgets. Given the council's lack of enthusiasm for PPB, agency executives quickly realize PPB may not be important to them; they, therefore, do not concentrate on doing a good job of cost-benefit analysis.

D. Zero-Base Budgeting (ZBB)

ZBB, like performance budgeting, is a results-oriented, management-oriented approach. The three basic elements of ZBB are: (a) identification of *decision units*, which are the lowest-level organizational units for which budgets are prepared; (b) formulation of *decision packages*, which are different combinations of services and spending levels for each decision unit; and, (c) ranking of the decision packages by the higher-level managers. Packages that can be funded within the available total revenue are included in the budget; those that cannot are dropped. Although there are variations of ZBB, most plans include these elements.

Decision packages provide managers with sufficient information about a decision unit to evaluate and rank it with other decision units competing for funds and to decide whether or not to fund it. Decision packages are developed in two steps. First, different methods of accomplishing the unit's objectives are identified and the preferred method is selected. Second, different *levels of effort* to achieve the selected alternative are noted. Levels of effort refer to incremental levels of cost and performance beginning with the minimum level below which it would be foolish to continue the activity followed by one or more increased levels of spending and performance.

Moore (1980b) found that 35 cities or 17% of the 205 cities in his survey used or had used ZBB. The survey of city budget directors revealed general satisfaction with ZBB. The biggest problem was the time and paperwork involved. Despite this problem and others, ZBB was able to reduce some agency budgets and control the rate of increase in others. It encouraged greater line-management participation in budget preparations and proved useful in educating top city officials about the operations of municipal departments.

III. BUDGET CLASSIFICATION STRUCTURE

The budget classification structure provides the framework around which budget requests are prepared and presented. Rosenberg (1978) suggests that a budget classification structure could include the following components:

1. The *fund* from which money is to be appropriated for a particular activity: Cities obtain money from various sources (taxes, user charges, permits, grants, etc.). The city may use money from some sources for any purpose, but in some cases it must be used for only specified purposes. It is therefore essential that the source of appropriations be identified in a city budget. There are eight major types of funds, with the most important one usually the *general fund*, which refers to all unrestricted revenue that can be used for any purpose. The *special revenue funds* are funds earmarked for a special purpose. *Debt service funds* are used to account for the accumulation of interest and principal on long-term debt. *Capital project funds* are used to account for receipts and expenditures

related to projects such as construction of a new park or city hall. *Enterprise funds* are used for businesslike expenditures and are generated by municipal enterprises such as local utilities, golf courses, parking garages, and other businesslike operations of the city. *Intergovernmental service funds* are used to account for transactions within the government such as central duplicating, data processing, and central stores. *Trust* and *agency funds* are used for assets belonging to others such as retirement funds or for donations for specific public purposes such as purchase of playground equipment. *Special assessment funds* are for the financing of public improvements *benefiting* specific property owners. For example, homeowners might be assessed a certain amount to pay for sidewalk improvement.

2. The *organizational unit* which is responsible for a particular budget: In general, the department is the organizational unit. Small cities may need only the department as the lowest budgetary unit, whereas larger cities may use subdivisions within departments.

3. *The object of expenditure*: This refers to the specific category within which money is expended. It could refer to personnel expenses, supplies, equipment, communication, and so forth.

4. *Source of revenue*: This refers to the source of revenue such as taxes, license fees, and sales receipts.

5. *Activity*: Activity refers to the programs or functions on which money is to be spent. A budget should make it relatively easy to identify how much money is being spent on a particular service. In small cities, activities may follow departmental organizations. For example, providing water may be entirely within a water department, or street construction maintenance may be within a street department. In a larger city, a department may involve several activities. For example, a police department could contain at least two activities, patrol and investigation.

6. *Program*: A program includes a broad category of services that may extend across several departments. For example, a public safety program may contain activities from the police and fire departments. The use of programs in budgeting will contribute considerable complexity to the budgeting process because most participants in budgeting (agency administrators, executive officials, and council members) are accustomed to thinking along traditional departmental lines, not along program lines.

IV. THE BUDGET CYCLE

Although local budgetary procedures are diverse, most practices can be subsumed under five broad steps in the budgeting cycle: (a) revenue estimation; (b) budget formulation; (c) council approval of the budget; (d) budget execution; and, (e) audit of expenditures. Although it simplifies discussion to speak of a budget cycle, there is no single budget cycle in operation at any one time. Local governments are involved in several budget cycles simultaneously. For example, agency officials may be preparing estimates for next year's budget while they are carrying out the present budget and undergoing an evaluation of expenditures in last year's budget.

A. Revenue Estimation

Before budgeters can decide how much to place in a budget, they must estimate the revenue for the fiscal year covered. A typical municipality will obtain funds from taxes, user charges, business licenses, fines, and grants. Different estimating techniques are necessary to estimate revenue from various sources. Taxes include sales, property, and income taxes. Property taxes are relatively easy to predict because assessed valuation of present real property exists, and a trend analysis allows one to predict the probable increase in the valuation. The trend analysis will include projections on new property construction and increases in the value of existing property. Sales taxes and income taxes depend on economic conditions in the city, state, and nation. If a recession occurs, both sales and income taxes will decline. Given the inexact nature of the science of economics, it is difficult to predict what the economic conditions will be in a particular city in a specific time period.

User charges refer to charges for water, sewer, recreation, parking, and other goods and services provided by the city. These can be estimated through a historical examination of past demand for such services and the establishment of the average rate of change each year. After such an analysis, one can predict the likely demand for services and goods in the next fiscal year. Of course, any unusual events that may occur in the next fiscal year should be factored into the analysis.

Cities do not always find it easy to predict the income they will receive from grants. Grants based on a formula are relatively easy to predict, but categorical grants such as those of the Law Enforcement Assistance Administration are much less predictable because they are granted on a case-by-case basis.

B. Budget Formulation

In most cities, the chief executive officer (mayor or city manager) has the primary responsibility for developing the budget. The mayor or manager will generally delegate the responsibility to a lower-level executive officer. If the city is large, a full-time budget director and the central budget office have the responsibility. In other cities, the finance director may assume the primary budget responsibility.

To develop some basic policy guidelines for the preparation of the annual budget, the central budget office will examine several variables:

Current revenue estimates for the budget year
The prospects for a deficit or a surplus to carry over to the next budget year
Trends in inflation and local economic conditions
Prospects for new taxes or changes in current tax and fee rates
Any major, unusual costs due to occur in the budget year

The chief executive officer and the central budget office will discuss the demand for services. The chief executive may wish to emphasize a particular service. Based on these discussions and analyses, the central budget office can issue some broad budget policy statements such as:

Guidelines for inflationary increases
A range for cost of living increases for salaried employees
An indication of what areas are to receive any special attention

These guidelines should be approved by the chief executive and the city council, and become the basis for instructions contained in *the call for estimates.*

C. The Call for Estimates

The typical city budget is built by collecting expenditure estimates from the city agencies. The annual call for estimates is usually initiated by a letter from the chief executive to the agency heads. This transmittal letter may contain:

The chief executive's view of the general fiscal situation
A budget calendar of important dates in the budget cycle
General guidelines to be used when computing increases in costs due to
     inflation
Budget forms

With receipt of this letter the budget process formally begins.

D. Preparation of Department Budgets

The chief executive may establish a budget ceiling for the departments in his call for the estimates. If he does, and if history indicates that departments should not submit estimates that exceed the ceiling, the departments will attempt to justify a budget request that equals the ceiling. If no ceiling is given, or if history indicates that there is no penalty or disadvantage in submitting an estimate in excess of the ceiling, the departments must decide how much to request. Variables that department officials will consider when deciding the amount to request include the present budget base, the history of reductions of past departmental estimates by central budget officials, the estimate of average increases for other departments, the perceived degree of support among significant public interest groups and the city council, the visibility of the department's programs to the general public, and the estimate of the demand for the services of the department. The main factor shaping a departmental budget estimate is the present budget or base. Most departments assume their base is secure and that it will never be reduced. They expect an increase; therefore, the present budget total becomes the minimal request. Most department administrators do not expect that they will have to defend their present base, and they will concentrate on defending additions.

Departments also know how much the chief executive has reduced their past requests. This history provides a rough guideline of the increment that they can probably obtain. Of course, this estimate is influenced by the department's best estimate of the average increase likely to occur for all departments in the coming fiscal year. The estimate accuracy is dependent on the adequacy of the department's informal contacts with the central budget office, the city council, and the other departments.

When preparing a budget request, departments will also consider the general level of support for their department's services among interest groups and the general public. This support may change from year to year. For example, if the public is extremely concerned about crime, the police department is more likely to receive greater support. In another year, there may be an unusual number of fires, or a major hotel fire, which generate more than usual public support for the expansion of fire prevention services. An astute department administrator is aware of changing public preferences, and knows how he can benefit from these changes by initiating new services or asking for significant expansion of existing services.

Departments have their own goals, values, and interests. It is only natural that each desires to expand the scope of its activities and to extend its jurisdiction because each believes that its services are more important than those provided by other departments. Therefore, the head of the department views his role as the defender and promotor of his department in the interdepartmental battles for scarce resources. Each department administrator expects all other department heads to fight for budget increases, and concludes that he too must fight for an increase to protect his department.

Although the preceding discussion seems to imply that departments fight for every dollar they can get rather than ask for what they really need, the implication is not accurate. Departments contain many professionals and experts in particular policy areas who believe that their services are very important and that even a very expansive budget could not meet the need for their services. They believe in the importance of what they are doing, and develop budget requests that call for expansion of existing services, or funds for supplemental ones to meet their perception of the demand for their services.

E. Service Goals, Objectives, Performance, and Costs

Because of the antitax militancy of citizens and the resultant necessity to spread scarce resources across many needs, and because of the increased emphasis on results-oriented budgeting, chief executives and central budget offices have increasingly required departments to: state their goals; provide objectives to reach the goals; suggest methods of measuring progress in achieving the objectives; and, detail the costs required to accomplish the different objectives.

The department must first develop goal statements. Good goal statements are stated so that observers can tell if they have been accomplished. In other words, the goal must be susceptible to measurement. After a goal or goals have been stated, objectives to accomplish the goals must be given. Good objectives should be results-oriented, specific, achievable in measurable terms, attainable within a specific time period, and related to the department's goals. For example, the objective for the patrol activity within a police department might be, "The patrol program will protect life and property by responding to (X) number of calls, with (Y) percent of these responses made within (Z) minutes during a specific time period." The objective for the investigative activity of a police department might read, "To achieve and maintain a clearance rate for all crimes equal to or greater than the national clearance rate for like crimes during a specific time period."

After a department has prepared objectives, it should develop quantitative measures of performance. The quantitative measures could include demand or need measures (Rosenberg, 1978). Demand measures indicate the need for a particular public service. Some examples of demand measures are number of miles of streets to be cleaned, number of residences and businesses requiring garbage pickup, and the number of traffic accidents that occurred in the preceding year. Demand measures are important because they indicate why a service is needed. (See Table 1.)

Workload measures indicate the amount of work actually performed. Examples include number of patrol hours, tons of garbage collected, number of streets paved, number of fires responded to, and number of permits processed. When possible, workload measures should be directly related to demand measures to show how the activities of the department are responding to the needs that fostered the service. Although workload measures are relatively easy to develop, they offer limited information about the resources used or the results accomplished.

Efficiency measures establish a relationship between resources used and results obtained. Some efficiency measures are number of garbage pickups per crew, number of patrol hours per policeman, number of fire inspections per unit, and number of beds per nurse.

Table 1   Goals, Objectives, and Performance Measures[a]

Program:	Public safety
Goal:	To protect persons and properties against criminal activities and man-made hazards, enforce animal control, and coordinate the municipal response to disaster situations as a result of natural or human causes
Department:	Police department
Goal:	To protect persons and property against crime, to uphold the legal rights of all persons, to help in providing a secure and orderly environment, and to respond promptly to a citizen's need for assistance
Activity:	Night patrol
Objectives:	To reduce the incidence of burglaries in the downtown business area by 20% during the year
	To reduce response time to 5 minutes for all valid calls for help

Performance measures for activity:

	Prior year	This year	Budget year estimate
Demand measures:			
Number of emergency calls between hours 7 P.M. and 7 A.M.	2910	3150	3300
Number of burglaries in downtown business	47	52	55[b]
Workload measures:			
Patrol hours	9600	10,400	19,200
Patrol teams	4	4	6
Efficiency measures:			
Patrol hours/patrolman	1200	1300	1600
Effectiveness measures:			
Average response time	8 minutes	7 minutes	5 minutes
Number of burglaries	NA	NA	42[c]

[a]This table illustrates how goals, objectives, and performance measures are related to the various levels of the budget structure.
[b]Estimated without increased patrols.
[c]Projected with increased patrols.
Source: Rosenberg, Philip. (1978). *An Operating Budget Handbook for Small Cities and Other Governmental Units*. Municipal Finance Officers Association, Chicago, p. 49.

Effectiveness measures determine how well an activity meets an objective. These measures emphasize program impact or results. Some examples are average response time to a fire alarm, number of accidents reduced per percentage increase in patrol hours, and number of burglaries reported cleared by arrest.

The department must use the goals, objectives, and various measures to develop sound budget requests. The department's request should show: how much service is needed (demand measures); how much work must be performed to meet the need (workload measures); how much personnel, equipment, and other resources are needed to accomplish the work (efficiency measures); what the schedule for accomplishment of the work is; what alternatives exist to the proposed method of servicing the need; and, what the costs of the alternatives are.

Although the preceding discussion appears to be a very rational process of relating budget requests to service demands, one should remember all the obstacles to the criticisms of rational, results-oriented budgeting (PPB, performance and ZBB) noted earlier. It is often very difficult and time-consuming to construct performance measures for many government services, and many department administrators believe that politics, not performance analysis, will determine the final budget allocation. Therefore, they may be less than enthusiastic about developing performance measures for their department's services.

F. Executive Review of Budget Requests

As the departments provide the impetus for increased spending, the chief executive is the economizer who serves as a restraint upon expansion by cutting requests and submitting a budget to the city council that contains smaller annual growth than initially proposed by the departments (Friedman, 1975). The chief executive may pursue the economizer role for two primary reasons. First, he has the primary responsibility for balancing the budget. Revenues must equal expenditures. Second, he may believe the departments include some frills in their budgets and that he must cut the padding.

In all but the smallest cities, the chief executive employs budget reviewers who work in a central budget office or the city finance office and who review all budget requests from the departments. The central budget office really has only one supporter, the chief executive; therefore, budget reviewers purvey the official policies, which often are not what the departments wish to hear. Consequently, they may not have many fans in the departments (Wanat, 1978).

Because there are insufficient funds to give every department all requests, the budget reviewer must insist that departments cut their requests to fall within the guidelines set by the chief executive. Budget reviewers cannot look at everything. They tend to concentrate their attention on expenditures that are discretionary rather than mandatory, large rather than small, and increasing rather than decreasing or stable (Lehan, 1981). A large discretionary increase will receive plenty of attention, whereas a small recurring or mandatory one will not.

Budget reviewers may accept significant portions of budget requests without rigorous reviews because they know the programs have considerable political support and that reviews of such requests would represent poor, perhaps futile, investment of scarce analytical resources. If the reviewer attacked very popular "sacred-cow" programs, he would incur serious opposition to his analytical judgment. Such a loss of analytical credibility is too high a price to pay for a futile attack on a popular program.

According to Lehan (1981), chief executives and budget reviewers who wish to improve the quality of executive budget making should:

1. Master factors such as demographic data, employment and income data, and other information on the community to understand the change in demands made on city services.
2. Acquire operating knowledge of the expenditure details of department budgets.
3. Seek options to the departmental expenditure requests.

If the central budget office has required the departments to submit budget requests that contain good objectives, demand measures, workload measures, and efficiency and effectiveness measures, the budget reviewer should be in a good position to properly evaluate the probable outcome or impact of a particular expenditure.

After the budget office has reviewed the departmental requests and the chief executive's changes are incorporated in the proposed budget, a budget document is sent to the city council. The completed budget document may include:

1. A message from the chief executive that describes the major assumptions behind the budget, the major issues the council must face, and major changes from the current budget
2. A summary of total revenue by sources
3. A summary of total expenditures by department or program
4. Detailed justification of budget recommendations

G. Approval of the Budget by the City Council

The council's budget-making role is primarily responsive. Because the origins of the budget lie with the chief executive and the departments, council members often feel inadequate in their review. This is particularly the case when the council is essentially an elected board of laymen who have full-time jobs in addition to their council duties. They often lack adequate time and expertise to act as full equals in the budgeting process. To say that the council's role is primarily a responsive one is not to say that the council is unimportant or powerless in the budgeting process. The council's main impact is in questioning and reducing the level of expenditures suggested.

Whereas the chief executive acts as an economizer when reviewing departmental budget requests sent to the central budget office, he also acts as a defender of the requests once they have been sent to the council. The executive must assume this role with the council to protect his own legitimacy and power in his negotiations with the departments. One primary reason for the departments' willingness to accept executive cuts is their acknowledgment that they need the executive to defend their requests before the council.

Although departments and agencies at the federal level may contact congressional committees and attempt an "end-run" around the president, such contact between city councils and municipal departments is rare, particularly in city manager cities. Departments do not appear often before the council, and when they do, it is generally to support the chief executive. City managers are particularly opposed to the council's independent contact with departments. They view such action as undermining the professional, managerial role of the city manager. Most city managers also believe that their recommendations will be adopted more rapidly if department heads are not present to comment on their departmental budgets. If department heads are not present, the budget officer and/or chief executive, together with supporting staff, may answer all questions posed by the council.

The council has influence not only when it reviews the requests submitted by the executive, but it also has influence much earlier in the budgetary process. The astute chief executive will discuss the major assumptions behind his call for the estimates with the council. For example, he may discuss likely salary increases, or he may suggest several programs that need particular attention and significantly more resources. The council may suggest modifications or other concerns. The chief executive can see the major council concerns, and part of the chief executive's subsequent behavior in the budgetary process is anticipatory of the council's likely response when the budget requests are submitted. A chief executive will seek to avoid a situation in which the council mandates major changes in his requests by submitting a budget that the council can accept with relatively minor changes.

Most councils provide public budget hearings. Citizen opinions on budgetary decisions may be obtained by allowing interested citizens and groups to appear before the council. Friedman (1975) found, however, that there was little connection between group influence and expenditures. Friedman (1975) also found a low level of organized activity specifically aimed at influencing spending levels. Citizens may be apathetic, or lack the skills and capacity to understand budgeting. On the other hand, citizens may have more influence on the budget by controlling revenue levels. Because budgets must balance revenues and expenditures, citizen opposition or support for taxes has a dramatic impact on the size of municipal budgets.

At the close of the council's budget deliberations, the council adopts an appropriation ordinance that establishes the spending ceiling of the city for the fiscal year and authorizes all municipality financial transactions.

H. Execution of the Budget

A major concern at the start of the execution phase and throughout the fiscal year is cash flow. An overall cash flow plan will be established to balance revenues by expected date of receipt with expected expenditures. Funds not immediately needed will be invested to earn interest. The investments will be scheduled to be available as needed, and they are generally limited to very secure government securities.

The next major concern of the chief executive and the central budget office is the rate of expenditure of authorized funds. In general, funds are apportioned by means of an allotment on a monthly or quarterly basis to control departmental or agency expenditures. The allotment provides authority to the operating officials to incur obligations within prescribed amounts for a specific period of time. Allotments prevent departments spending all of their money in the first part of the fiscal year.

Municipal financial records are maintained by the funds noted in Sec. III. The funds are used to make sure that specific revenue sources will finance specific, newly authorized activities.

Financial records can be kept on a *cash basis* with entries made only when cash is received or payment made. The cash basis will work only in very simple operations. In more complex situations, the cash basis may provide a misleading picture because goods and services may be received in one time period and paid for in another. *Accrual* accounting remedies this problem by recording expenditures as soon as the services or goods are ordered. Accrual accounting also applies to revenues, with revenues being recorded when earned or receivable. Most cities use some version of accrual accounting.

Most cities also use an *encumbrance system* with accrual accounting. Under an encumbrance system, a purchase is recorded as an obligation against an appropriation when the order is placed, not when it is actually paid. Money that is encumbered cannot be used for other purchases.

I. Audit

Auditing seeks to assure the correct operation of the accounting system and checks to see that expenditures follow the provisions of the authorizing legislation.

Audits can be classified as internal versus external and pre- versus postaudits. An internal audit is generally a preaudit; that is, it takes place before the transaction occurs. The internal audit is designed to determine efficiency and compliance with established procedures and is conducted by an official inside the executive branch. An external audit is conducted by an independent outside party and occurs after the transaction. In general, audits are done on a sample basis in which the legality, propriety, and accuracy of a department's financial transactions are determined by examining only a sample of all transactions. If the sample is representative and if no errors are found in the sample, it can be assumed that the remaining transactions are free of errors or illegalities.

V. THE CAPITAL BUDGET

Most cities have two types of budgets—operating and capital. The operating budget concerns the recurring normal expenditures needed each and every year. The capital budget involves unusual, large expenditures for capital items that will be used for more than the current year. The purchase of land, or the building of a road, water supply system, or sewage system are examples of capital projects.

Most cities attempt to plan for the purchase of capital items over a five- or six-year period. As the capital plan for each year becomes the forthcoming fiscal year's capital budget, the capital plan is extended one year.

Capital budgets are carefully reviewed by both budget analysts and planners. Public hearings are often held. Ultimately, the capital budget is approved by the city council or possibly even the electorate if a bond issue is involved. It is vital that executives and the council realize the impact of a capital expenditure on an operating budget. The construction of a new building with funds from a capital budget will also increase the maintenance and energy costs in future operating budgets, for example.

Capital budgets are generally financed by the sale of bonds. *General obligation bonds* are backed by the full faith and credit of the city. Payment on these bonds may come from the general fund. *Special assessment bonds* are sometimes used to finance the construction of streets, storm drains, sewer lines, sidewalks, and other items that improve the value of private property owners. Special assessments are levied against the property owner, and the income is pledged to the repayment of the bonds. *Revenue bonds* are those to which income from a specific enterprise is pledged. For example, revenue bonds may be used to build a toll bridge, and the income from the toll is pledged to bond repayment.

VI. SUMMARY OF THE MAIN POINTS

1. Different budgeting formats reflect different purposes of budgeting. The line-item budget is primarily for control, whereas the performance budget

emphasizes management. Program, planning budgets accentuate long-range planning, whereas zero-base budgets emphasize both management and planning.

2. Traditional, line-item budgeting continues as the typical budgeting format, but it is subject to numerous criticisms from critics who prefer a more rational, comprehensive approach to budgeting.

3. Comprehensive, rational budgeting occurs in performance budgeting and zero-base budgeting, and is most pronounced in planning, programming budgeting. Critics of the rational approach, who defend the incremental nature of most budgeting, contend that rational attempts at budgeting fail to reflect political realities and demand analytical skills, information, and time, which are generally unavailable in city budget offices.

4. Most city budgets should include the fund from which money is to be appropriated, the organizational unit responsible for a particular budget, the object of expenditure, the source of the revenue for the expenditure, the activity on which money is to be spent, and the program or broad category of services for which money is to be expended.

5. A typical budget cycle includes revenue estimation, budget formulation by the departments and the central budget office, council approval of the budget, execution of the budget by the chief executive and the departments, and audit of the expenditures.

6. Different participants in the budget process play different roles. Departments generally attempt to expand their budgets. The chief executive allows some expansion, but attempts to reduce the rate of expansion. The council generally accepts the chief executive's recommendation, but it may also attempt to reduce further requests to expand the departmental budgets.

7. If a city's central budget office seriously intends to gather information on the results of municipal expenditures, it should require departments to submit budgets that include goal statements, objectives, and demand, workload, efficiency, and effectiveness measures.

8. After the chief executive submits the budget to the council for approval, the council's role is primarily responsive. It may attempt to reduce the budget submitted by the chief executive. Municipal departments are not as effective as national departments in making direct appeals to the legislature for more money than the amount approved by the executive.

9. The major concern during execution of the budget is that the budgeted money is not exhausted before the end of the fiscal year. Allotments are used to control the rate of expenditure.

10. Audits are conducted to assure that expenditures match the appropriations as passed by the council.

11. The capital budget is used for large expenditures on capital items that will be used over a number of years and are usually financed by bond sales.

REFERENCES

Friedman, Lewis. (1975). *Budgeting Municipal Expenditures: A Study in Comparative Policy Making*. Praeger, New York.

Lehan, Edward. (1981). *Simplified Governmental Budgeting*. Municipal Finance Officers Association, Chicago.

Moore, Perry. (1980a). Types of budgeting and budgeting problems in American cities. *International Journal of Public Administration* 2:501–514.

Moore, Perry. (1980b). Zero-base budgeting in American cities. *Public Administration Review* 40:253–258.

Rosenberg, Philip. (1978). *An Operating Budget Handbook For Small Cities and Other Governmental Units*. Municipal Finance Officers Association, Chicago.

Schick, Allen. (1966). The road to PPB: The stages of budget reform. *Public Administration Review* 26:243–258.

Wanat, John. (1978). *Introduction to Budgeting*. Duxbury Press, North Scituate, Mass.

Wildavsky, Aaron. (1974). *The Politics of the Budgetary Process*. Little, Brown, Boston.

6
State Limitations on Local Fiscal Authority

Patricia S. Florestano   Institute for Governmental Service, University of Maryland, College Park, Maryland

I. RELATION OF STATE AND LOCAL GOVERNMENTS

Colonists settling in America during the country's early years established boroughs, counties, cities, and towns to satisfy their local needs. Some of the royal charters and grants they used failed to mention local government at all, whereas others expressly provided for these various forms. With American independence, the state legislatures presumed the new states to be the source of local government power, irrespective of whether express legal authority for local government already existed. Over the years, conventional political theory has taught that the state governments can unilaterally make decisions regarding state-local relations and the allocation of functions within their boundaries.[1] The idea that the states are unitary systems and that all local governments are simply their creations has been upheld by the U.S. Supreme Court and lower courts and generally reaffirmed when the issue has been raised.[2]

The Dillon Rule, promulgated in 1872, held that plenary power resided exclusively in the state, that localities possessed only those powers expressly granted or clearly implied, and that "as the state creates, so may it destroy."[3] Constitutionally and legally, the presumption in any state-local conflict is that state powers are preemptive and local powers are limited to the express terms of the state grant.

Meanwhile, localities anxious for the authority to make decisions about local needs initiated the movement for home rule. The concept of home rule rests on the assumption that the local government, not the state legislature, should make policy decisions concerning local structure and responsibilities. Iowa, in 1858, took the first legislative action to grant cities the right to formulate and adopt their own charters. Missouri, in 1875, adopted constitutional home rule first, and since then as other states have enacted similar legislation, municipalities and counties too have been authorized to structure varying degrees of local autonomy. On the whole, however, their freedom to structure local functions is still limited. In many states, local government continues to be restricted in its authority over its own services, personnel, and financial matters.

Almost all fiscal options of local governments are determined at the state level. The states decide what revenue sources can be used by localities, how local funds can be spent, which budgetary procedures must be used, and sometimes salaries and fees. The power to tax is conferred on local governments by state constitutions and legislative enactments; without such authority, no local government can impose any tax. Indeed, as noted previously, in the strictest legal sense no local government exists without the specific or general authority of the state constitution, its legislature, or both. For many years, local power to tax was confined to the property tax, and, based on the general police powers, to various types of business and regulatory license taxes.

II. PROPERTY TAXATION

A. Historical Development

Since colonial times, the taxation of property has been the main source of revenue of American local government, and property taxation is older than the Republic. Property taxation began as a selective tax on enumerated classes of property, but early in American history the principle was adopted that, unless specifically exempt, all property should be part of the tax base and taxed uniformly within each jurisdiction. In eighteenth-century New England, property taxes accounted for about two-thirds of all tax revenue; in the agrarian South, on the other hand, with its politically powerful plantation owners, property taxation was less common, forcing the use of other forms of taxation. By the Civil War period, however, the general property tax dominated American state and, especially, local taxation. Local governments financed their activities in large part by levying an ad valorem property tax, commonly referred to as the general property tax because of its universality and the uniformity requirements characterizing it.

For many years, states and localities shared property tax revenues; state shares only began to decline as they developed new sources of revenues. At the turn of the twentieth century, property taxes still provided the bulk of state revenue, but the figure had declined to approximately 4% by 1982 [Advisory Commission on Intergovernmental Relations (ACIR), 1983]. Nevertheless, state governments continued to play an important role in property taxation because they enacted the laws under which local governments taxed.

B. Traditional Problems and Responses

Because it has been widely used, the property tax has received more scrutiny by fiscal experts than other taxes. Certainly, it has been more criticized. Critics have focused on its regressivity, inequity, and difficulty in administration. Other concerns related to exemptions, equalization problems, and assessor incompetence.

Although largely locally administered, local property taxation has been circumscribed by a variety of controls and restrictions imposed by state constitutions and legislative enactments. Many of these controls stipulated reporting requirements, assessing procedures and standards, and uniform record-keeping methods. Other regulations provided for the review of local assessments by a state agency and for the right of appeal by dissatisfied taxpayers.

State constitutions typically restricted types of taxes and tax rates, but the use of constitutional limits varied over the years. Between 1776 and 1834, state constitutions made little mention of tax limits, but after 1834, and especially after the Civil War, constitutional provisions dealing with tax matters multiplied in number and became more detailed.

State restrictions on local property taxation specified the maximum rate that could be imposed. That rate limit was expressed as a percentage of assessed valuation: a number of dollars per $1000, a number of cents per $100, or a number of mills per $1.00. Rhode Island (1870), Nevada (1895), Oklahoma (1900), and Ohio (1911) were the first to impose property tax rate limits. Rate limits traditionally were supported during times of economic downturn or in periods of rapidly rising expenditures for the construction of public works, all of which allegedly necessitated state restraints on local revenue raising. Other state regulations took the form of levying limits that restricted the total amount of property taxes a government could levy on the taxable property within its boundaries, no matter how much the property's annual value.

Over the years, such restrictions have been blamed for the creation of special districts to avoid them, short-term financing to cover operating deficits, much long-term borrowing, numerous pieces of special legislation, the impaired ability of local officials to administer effectively, and overloaded court dockets.

III. NONPROPERTY TAXATION

A. Historical Development

By contrast with the universal use of property taxation by local governments, nonproperty taxes available to local governments were severely limited in the past. With the exception of the power of cities in most states to levy license taxes, including the authority to base those taxes on gross receipts of business, local governments have commonly not had the power to levy a variety of nonproperty taxes. Either by means of specific statutes or some interpretation of constitutional or statutory provisions as to home rule powers, local governments have imposed nonproperty taxes as revenue-raising measures rather than as regulatory measures. For years, many state constitutions said nothing about specific nonproperty taxes, and a number of local jurisdictions enacting such taxes have been upheld by the courts simply because they were not forbidden by the laws or preempted by the state.

Even in states where local governments have achieved a measure of home rule through constitutional, statutory, and charter provisions, it was generally left to state legislatures to determine local nonproperty tax powers. Past restrictions on local nonproperty tax powers took three forms (ACIR, 1962). Outright prohibition of local use of particular nonproperty taxes was the first kind of restriction. Sometimes such prohibitions, rather than being expressed about a particular local nonproperty tax, were used to safeguard the state's right to preempt certain taxes for its exclusive use. A second restriction, Dillon's Rule, which denies the inherent right to local self-government, meant that unless there was explicit authorization, no power to tax existed. A third restriction involved situations where authorization of specific nonproperty taxes carried with it limitations, as in maximum tax rates, restricted geographic or jurisdictional areas, specified purposes for which the revenue could be used, or restrictions regarding the tax base.

Local governments were collecting no revenue from income or consumer taxes at the turn of the century. When localities received nonproperty tax revenue during that period, it came from business licenses, poll taxes, and miscellaneous lesser taxes. At the depth of the depression, nonproperty taxes constituted an insignificant source of local tax revenue, but it was at that time that attempts began to broaden local taxing powers. During World War II, materials and manpower shortages held local spending to a minimum; efforts to obtain new tax sources were few and generally concentrated in large cities. Immediately after the war, the pent-up demand for government services and the large backlog of needed public facilities once again placed local governments in a financial bind. In some states, cities used home rule provisions or general licensing powers to levy broad-based taxes.

According to Aronson and Schwartz (1981), local governments use nonproperty taxes for a number of reasons, in addition to obtaining new revenue, while avoiding property tax increases. Other reasons include achieving a wider distribution of the local tax burden among the recipients of public services; making the tax structure more flexible and more responsive to rising costs and service demands; and, reducing the relatively high taxation rates that arise when the property tax is the major revenue source.

B. Types of Nonproperty Taxation

1. Local General Sales Taxes

As a result of the depression of the 1930s, local revenues had declined to such an extent that jurisdictions sought other sources. In 1934, New York City adopted a sales tax, followed by New Orleans in 1938. The feasibility of the tax for a large number of local governments improved with Mississippi's adoption in 1950 of a system of state-administered local sales taxes. The 1960s and 1970s saw rapid expansion in the use of local sales tax as the number of states authorizing them increased from twelve in 1963 to twenty-six in 1976. In the mid-1970s general sales taxes were authorized for use by local governments in twenty-nine states and the District of Columbia, although in Kentucky, Oregon, and Wisconsin, none of the localities authorized to levy a sales tax had chosen to do so (Aronson and Schwartz, 1981).

Limitations took the form of specific prohibition or simply lack of general authority to enact such taxes. Authorization for the tax may derive from home rule charters, general licensing powers, or specific state statutes; in most localities, it is the latter. Except in states where local jurisdictions administer their own taxes, the base of a local general sales tax levied by localities is almost always mandated to be the same as any existing state sales tax base. Normally, states also mandate certain exclusions or exemptions of goods. In some areas, voter approval of a new sales tax may be mandatory.

2. Local Income Taxes

Philadelphia adopted the first modern income tax in 1938 under authority from the state. Major features of the Philadelphia tax, a flat-rate tax on all earned income, were retained and used as a model for localities in Alabama, Kentucky, Minnesota, Ohio, and Pennsylvania. After 1940, all income taxes adopted by localities followed the Philadelphia type, until Detroit introduced an income tax on all forms of income in 1962. In 1966, New York City produced another major innovation, a personal income tax very similar to the federal income tax. The most recent development occurred in Maryland in 1967 when the state enacted a law that mandated the twenty-three counties and Baltimore City to impose a local income tax on residents at not less than 20% or more than 50% of each individual's state personal income tax liability (Maryland General Assembly, 1982).

Like the general sales tax, the local income tax typically has been adopted in response to constrained fiscal circumstances. Many of the provisions of these taxes are attempts to circumvent statutes or constitutional limits imposed by state governments. According to the ACIR (1983), as of 1982, thirty-nine states did not authorize a local personal income tax. In states where it is authorized, the rate is stipulated, and in some states optional administration is available.

3. Others

Local taxes that are collected on the gross receipts of business function as a general sales tax when applied uniformly to a wide class of businesses. If applied to only one or a limited type of business, they function as a selective sales or excise tax. The bulk of all revenues from selective sales and gross receipts taxes is derived from taxes on public utilities. Very few provisions are found in statutes specifically authorizing local taxation for public utility services, yet in most states public utilities are taxed locally on a sales or gross receipts basis. In general, public utilities are taxed by local governments under their regulatory powers.

Excise taxes are levied by local governments on a wide variety of individual products and services, but the major taxes are those on alcoholic beverages, tobacco products, and motor fuels. Alcoholic beverage taxation is found most frequently in southern cities. The few county and municipal governments that tax distilled spirits, beer, and wine do so either by excise taxes or by occupational license taxes. Some state statutes specifically prohibit the imposition of local alcoholic beverage excise taxes, whereas others supply local governments with explicit but limited statutory authority to impose such taxes. Statutes may also impose rate limits or authorize taxes on one type of alcohol while prohibiting them on others.

No state constitution specifically prohibits local taxes on tobacco products, but some states do prohibit them by statute. Statutory authorization for local cigarette taxes exists to some degree in nine states, but in 1976, localities in only seven states and the District of Columbia taxed tobacco products (ACIR, 1977a). In some states, authorization is restricted to only one or a few local units, usually on the basis of size, whereas other states provide widespread local authority. Legal analysts suggest that municipalities may be able to levy cigarette taxes under home rule charters, but only Colorado cities have cited such powers or authority.

Localities in nine states and the District of Columbia in the late 1970s (ACIR, 1977a) levied taxes on various types of motor fuel. Statutory provisions forbidding local gasoline taxes exist in a number of states, constitutional prohibition in only one. In those states where local gasoline taxes are used, authorization is generally by statute under business or occupational licensing powers, and the rate of taxation is stipulated by all of the enabling states.

Amusement or admissions taxes were used in 1972 by local governments in twenty-five states, although very few states have specific prohibitions against them (ACIR, 1977a). The majority of state laws contain no provisions relating to local admissions taxes, but localities in some states tax admissions under their general sales and gross receipts taxes.

Local governments in ten states and the District of Columbia (ACIR, 1977a) used real estate transfer taxes in the mid-1970s. States authorized such taxes by statutes that usually specified rates.

Most recently, there has been new emphasis among local governments on the imposition of user charges. Precipitated by taxpayer revolts, the trend to move away from property taxes toward other local revenue sources is expected to continue during the 1980s. Charges, as defined by the U.S. Census Bureau, are composed of amounts received from the public for performance of specific services benefiting the persons charged and from sale of commodities and services. Such charges include fees, toll charges, tuition, and other reimbursements for current services. Many localities across the country have been enacting such charges citing general police power; nevertheless, in many states such action can only be taken with express statutory authorization.

IV. DEBT LIMITS

A. Background

States use essentially two major ways to regulate the ability of localities to acquire their own funds. The first, the imposition of specific taxes by localities, has been discussed in this chapter; the second is the regulation of the borrowing of funds by localities. Nowhere is local discretion more limited than in the incurrence of debt. Because of the legal responsibility of the states, they have a legitimate concern over the debt status of their localities. The importance of credit ratings among localities also gives the state a legitimate interest in regulating local government indebtedness.

The origins of the limits are important to their understanding. Tight regulation dates back to the 1860s and 1870s, responding to extensive local government spending and borrowing, coupled with their inability to repay. During that period, localities incurred debts to finance numerous capital projects, including projects designed to lure the railroads. When depressions occurred, cities unable to repay bonds defaulted. As a result, states that had to step in to assist these localities then imposed various regulations to stem what they viewed as excessive borrowing. During the depression of the 1930s, borrowing excesses again occurred among local governments, and the resulting round of defaults led to the enactment of another wave of debt limits. Many of the general limits that exist now in local governments across the country were set during that time.

B. Types of Limitations

Even though the states have an obvious legitimate interest in the health of local government finances, many of the debt restrictions appear to be unduly onerous, complicated, or difficult to administer. Restrictions can be found in state constitutions, in statutes, and even in home rule charters. In designing such restrictions, states may differentiate between types and sizes of localities, apply the limits to only one or a specified number of jurisdictions, or enact special local legislation relating to borrowing practices.

The most common restriction is a limit on the maximum amount of debt that a locality can incur; such limit is usually tied to the assessable base of the local unit. Other restrictions concern: the purposes for which debt can be incurred; the time for bond maturity; the interest rate that a locality may pay; required citizen referenda on issuance of general obligation bonds; procedures for repayment; and, the investment of funds set aside for repayment.

Because of the problem of working with complicated state debt regulations, local government officials have developed numerous ingenious ways to circumvent them. These include: the issuance of revenue bonds, payable from earmarked funds generated by a project and not subject to the usual restrictions applied against general obligation bonds backed by the full faith and credit of the state; the creation of special districts with separate borrowing limits; the use of special funds and assessments that are not part of the state debt limit; the use of leasing rather than buying; and, the use of service contracts or installments.

Data on debt limits are difficult to compare because of variations in state practices. There appears to have been little or no change in the extent of debt limits since 1961 when the ACIR first surveyed them. Of forty-six states responding, forty-five had some debt limit. Responses from all states to an ACIR survey in 1976 (ACIR, 1977a) indicated that forty-five states limited the authority of localities to issue general obligation bonds.

V. CITIZEN TAX REVOLTS OF THE 1970s

Following the dramatic impact of California's overwhelming passage of Proposition 13 in 1978 and the subsequent flood of similar proposals that surfaced in legislatures and on referenda during the following years, local and state governments moved quickly to reevaluate their taxing and spending. Attention focused on the tax burdens of citizens, on the level of governmental expenditures, and the competition for the public's dollars. It is worth noting the various factors that touched off the explosion of fiscal limit measures during the last years of the 1970s (Council of State Governments, 1978a; Danziger and Ring, 1982). Among these were the public's concerns about the growth in government and its spending; the public's frustration with its apparent loss of control over government spending and the inflationary economy; the dramatic increases in the level of property taxation as assessments kept pace with rising market values; the decline in real disposable income for the average family; resentment at rising taxes, especially among those with above-average income; the widespread perception that taxes were too high; and, the deterioration of respect for government and public officials, coupled with the loss of faith that government could solve all or most of society's major problems. Recent citizen-sponsored initiatives across the country have taken various forms as discussed subsequently.

A. Types of Initiatives

1. Limitations on Spending

Expenditure or total revenue limits apply to local or state government or the combined spending of both. Spending limits may be set on types of funds or by the total amount, either in fixed dollars or as a fixed proportion of a specified economic indicator. Rather than try to freeze expenditures, limits may be set on the rate of increase in government spending. For example, in 1978, Tennessee voters approved a constitutional amendment that restricted state spending to the "estimated rate of growth of the state's economy as determined by the growth in personal income." Michigan passed a constitutional amendment that limited the growth of local tax revenue to the growth of the U.S. consumer price index. New Jersey limited spending by counties and municipalities to a fixed percentage of the previous year's expenditures.

2. Limitations or Reduction of Taxes

These initiatives proposed to limit, reduce, and in some cases, eliminate certain state or local taxes. At the state level, the measure generally applied to personal income taxes. Methods for control included indexing the tax rate schedule to overcome the impact of inflation, rollback or reduction of tax rate schedules, or establishment of maximum tax rates. Limitations or reductions of local taxes were the most prevalent of all the initiatives, most of them aimed at limiting or reducing local property taxes. Like Proposition 13, some limited property taxes and future assessment rates. Other initiatives called for tax assessment increases based upon specified economic indicators; a moratorium on future increases; and rollbacks, reductions, or limitations on future increases in property taxes.

3. Full Disclosure Requirements

In some states, citizens proposed initiatives that require governmental entities wishing to change tax or spending ceilings to notify the citizenry first. The procedure used to inform citizens of such proposed changes is called *full disclosure* and has most often been applied to local governments' use of the property tax.

Table 1 Restrictions on State and Local Government Tax and Expenditure Powers (January 1, 1983)

States	Overall[b] property tax rate limit	Specific[b] property tax rate limit	Property tax levy limit	General revenue limit	State-imposed limits on local governments[a] General expenditure limit	Limits on assessment increases	Full disclosure	Limits on state governments
Total	14	29	20	5	8	6	10	20
Alabama	CMS[c]	CMS[d]						
Alaska	CMS[e]		CM[e]					Const.[c]
Arizona	CMS[c]		CM[c]		CMS[c]	CMS[c]		Const.[c]
Arkansas		CMS[d]	CMS[c,f]					
California	CMS[c]				CMS[c]	CMS[c]		Const.[c]
Colorado		CS[d]	CM[d]		S[e]		CMS[c]	Stat.[e]
Connecticut								
Delaware		CS[e]	C[c,f]					Const.[c]
Dist. of Col.								
Florida		CMS[d]	CMS[c]				CMS[e]	
Georgia		S[d]						
Hawaii							C[e]	Const.[c]
Idaho	CMS[c]	CMS[d]	CMS[c]				C[e]	Const.[c]
Illinois		CMS[d]						
Indiana			CMS[c]					
Iowa		CMS[d]	CM[e]			CMS[e]		
Kansas		CM[d]		S[e]	S[e]			
Kentucky	CMS[d]						CMS[c]	
Louisiana		CMS[e]	CMS[c,f]					Stat.[c]
Maine								
Maryland	CMS[c]		CMS[c]			CM[e]	CM[e]	
Massachusetts		M[d]	CMS[c]					
Michigan	CS[d]	CMS[d]		CM[e]				
Minnesota		CMS[d]	CMS[c]				CMS[c]	Const.[e]
Mississippi		CMS[d]	CMS[c]		S[e]			

State							
Missouri			CMS[c]				Const.[c]
Montana	CMS[d]		CMS[c]				Stat.[c]
Nebraska	CMS[d]		CM[e]				Stat.[c]
Nevada	CMS[d]					CMS[e]	
New Hampshire		C[e]					
New Jersey	CMS[d]	CMS[c]		MS[e]			Stat.[e]
New Mexico	CMS[d]				CMS[e]		
New York	CM[e]						
North Carolina		CMS[c]					
North Dakota	CMS[d]	CMS[e]					
Ohio	CMS[d]						
Oklahoma	CMS[d]						
Oregon		CMS[d]			CMS[c]		Stat.[c]
Pennsylvania	CMS[d]						
Rhode Island	[g]						Stat.[e]
South Carolina							Stat.[c]
South Dakota	CMS[d]						
Tennessee	CMS[e]					CMS[c]	Const.[c]
Texas						CMS[c]	Const.[c]
Utah	CMS[d]						Stat.[c]
Vermont							
Virginia			S[e]			CM[e]	
Washington	CMS[e]						Stat.[e]
West Virginia	CMS[d]			S[e]			
Wisconsin	CMS[d]						
Wyoming	CMS[d]						

[a] C, county; M, municipal; S, school district; Const., constitutional; Stat., statutory.

[b] Overall limits refer to limits on the aggregate tax rate of all local governments. Specific rate limits refer to limits on individual types of local governments or limits on narrowly defined services (excluding debt).

[c] 1978 and after.

[d] Enacted before 1970.

[e] 1970–1977.

[f] Limits follow reassessment.

[g] Limit followed transition to a classified property tax.

Source: ACIR staff calculations, *Significant Features of Fiscal Federalism, 1981–82.*

In Maryland, for example, the assessors established a tax rate that provided a levy equal to the previous year's levy when applied to the current tax base. If the locality decided that more revenue was needed, it must comply with a state-mandated disclosure process for the public benefit.

4. Limitations on Fiscal Policy-Making

Such initiatives generally targeted state government and sought to increase the visibility and accountability of the fiscal process by enlarging the number of elected officials who must approve tax increases or new sources of governmental revenue.

B. Results of Limits

Whereas analysts acknowledge that states are compelled to levy taxes in moderation because of the unacceptability to the citizen of a continuously expanding public sector and because high taxes may leave the state at a competitive disadvantage with other states, the fact remains that a number of policy issues are raised by the defects inherent in the whole range of taxing and spending limitations (see Table 1 for a current list of restrictions). Critics point out that many of the recently enacted limits impose unworkable degrees of rigidity and may result in reducing needed services, weakening local self-management, or may lead to more government centralization.

Tough state fiscal limits on localities often necessitate state reimbursement for activities mandated at the local level and, at the same time, may conflict with prior state inducements to encourage greater local fiscal efforts. In addition to making localities more dependent on state aid and state policy decisions, rigorous state limits work against representative government if the only way to alter such laws is by a referendum. According to John Shannon (1977), a state is justified in imposing limits on local tax rates or on local government levies only on a temporary basis to allow such rates to stabilize. He emphasizes the desirability of making state limits or rollback actions temporary. Once a degree of stabilization has occurred, Shannon says that local decision-makers should have full access to local revenue raising, on the assumption that they will be held politically responsible for later increases. Heller and Uhler (1978) say that if a limitation is necessary, that which is least likely to "strangle responsible and flexible democracy" is an expenditure limit that is tied to the growth in personal income, applies to both state and local revenues, allows for emergencies like recessions, and provides for strict truth in taxation.

For states that impose tight limits on local revenue raising, major intergovernmental fiscal consequences are apparent (Shannon, 1977). If all other major factors are held constant, local property tax levels tend to be somewhat lower in such states. At the same time, total state-local expenditures from their own sources are about the same as in the states without such limits. Thus, the general inference is that, rather than cutting overall public expenditures, rigid limits on local revenue raising tend to move expenditures to the state level, which reinforces fiscal centralization.

Centralization, or the perception of a dominant role of the state government in relation to its localities, is evidenced in the state's proportion of revenue collected, its direct provision of services throughout the state, and in its establishment of standards and restrictions to be followed by local governments (Hawkins et al., 1978). Hawkins et al. say that state centralization has increased in recent years, based on the evidence that state direct spending has grown as a proportion of total state and local spending and that state tax collections have outpaced local collections. Other tangible signs of state centralization are found in the fact that state governments have taken over from localities more responsibilities for the operation and financing of such functions as welfare, education, and roads, for example.

VI. OTHER LIMITATIONS

Custom and tradition have left local government heavily dependent on property taxes for major revenue raising. Local governments seeking to incorporate new means of raising funds often encounter not only legislative hostility but citizen opposition and distrust. Thus, local governments, seeking new revenues they can tap, often find that major tax sources have been preempted by other levels of government (i.e., the federal government's use of income taxes and the state government's use of income, sales, and, in some cases, lotteries and gambling revenues).

Intergovernmental fiscal competition is also a limiting factor for localities. If property tax rates differ significantly among counties and cities in metropolitan areas, those with higher rates may observe a significant outflow of population. This problem becomes even more acute when such neighboring jurisdictions sit on opposite sides of state lines. The Washington, D.C. metropolitan area exemplifies the problems in raising revenue when governments must consider the possibility of losing population to other jurisdictions. This type of limitation applies not only to the property tax, but to the sales tax also. On the Delaware-Maryland-Virginia peninsula known as the Eastern Shore, Maryland merchants complain bitterly of their lost trade whenever the state sales tax is increased, because neighboring Delaware has none.

In those cases where a locality possesses or receives state authorization to enact new measures to raise revenue, localities need to consider any negative economic impact that may stem from such measures. On occasion, the local official may find that he or she has the authority to enact new measures for raising revenue that would not necessarily have a negative economic impact or negative intergovernmental implications, but one obstacle remains—public opposition. Considering the tax and expenditure limitations enacted in the various states since 1978, public opposition to increased revenue raising by all levels of government looms as the most potentially imposing limitation of all on local fiscal authority.

VII. RECENT STATE-LOCAL FINANCIAL DEVELOPMENTS

State-local relations have been characterized by major changes over the last several decades (ACIR, 1977b). In addition to the traditional restrictions on taxing and borrowing and the recent imposition of new limits on revenue raising that have been discussed, other developments include the clear emergence of the states as senior partners in state-local spending and the state-mandated growth in local expenditures. At the same time, there has been a rise in state financial aid to localities and increased sharing of expenditures by the two levels in certain functions, such as school finance. A number of states have been the scene of direct state assumption of costs for selected functions, such as court administration. In essence, the period has been one of increasing state control over local fiscal affairs. Besides public demand for tax relief, state governments have made stronger efforts to control both state and local spending because of the perception on the part of some state officials that local officials need or want restrictions imposed by the state as a way of withstanding the intense pressure for additional spending generated at the local level.

In addition to promoting local fiscal solvency through regulation of taxing, spending, and borrowing, states have begun to take a more direct interest in the quality of local financial management. State involvement in augmenting the capacity of locals to manage their own affairs varies from state to state in its emphasis, scope, and means. Generally, however, such involvement relates to accounting, auditing, financial reports, budgeting, debt management, pensions, cash management, property tax assessment, and purchasing (ACIR, 1977b). Accounting, auditing, and financial reporting are basic to sound financial management. In 1978, the ACIR surveyed state constitutional and statutory requirements pertaining to local government auditing and accounting practices (ACIR, 1979). It found that forty-two states required some kind of accounting system in its cities, and six required express conformance with generally accepted principles of governmental accounting. By 1982, six other states had enacted legislation affecting local accounts, auditing, and reporting that imposed more stringent controls over local practices.

Debt management assistance for localities by states ranges from procedures that are very intrusive to those that are less so (ACIR, 1977b). An example of the former is the direct involvement and assistance of the state in local government financial emergencies. Somewhat less intrusive but still highly regulatory is the mandatory requirement for state approval of bond sales, in particular, or as an integral part of close supervision of local budgets and financial decisions. Less intrusive still is the requirement for a state advisory review of the legal and fiscal aspects of bond sales, active involvement in preparation of bond documents, and central bidding of bond issues on a voluntary basis. Finally, in a more cooperative than coercive vein, many states collect information on local finances, maintain central data files, disseminate data, and provide training and technical assistance in debt management and bond sales on an elective basis.

In summary, the states play a crucial role in the well-being of their local governments. They are the key to success in many areas, bearing a significant portion of the cost of local operations, assisting in improvement of management, coordinating and supervising local administration of programs, and, to a major degree, ensuring good local government. The fiscal relationship is at the heart of most of these other activities.

Many streams of reformist thought converge on the relationship of the state to its local governments. A persistent question is the effect of state policies on local services and administration. Differences of opinion abound, but the importance of the state to the localities is expressed best by David and Jeanne Walker (1975:39):

> The acid test of the states' real strength lies in their relationship with their own localities. Here the legal, political, fiscal, functional, and institutional capabilities of the states are the most severely tested. The states, after all, are the chief architects, by conscious or unconscious action or inaction, of the welter of servicing, financial and institutional arrangements that form the substate governance system of this nation.

NOTES

1. For another opinion, see the opinion of Judge Thomas McIntyre Cooley who held the view that localities have an inherent right to local self-government [Cooley, Thomas McIntyre. (1980). *Constitutional Limitations*. Little Brown, Boston]. This view commands only limited judicial recognition and is now defunct [Syed, A. (1966).] *The Political Theory of American Local Government*. Random House, New York.]
2. An example is *Hunter* v. *City of Pittsburgh*, 207 U.S. 161 (1907).
3. *City of Clinton* v. *Cedar Rapids and Missouri Railroad Company*, 24 Iowa 454, 475. See also John F. Dillon (1911). *Commentary on the Law of Municipal Corporations*, 5th ed. Little Brown, Boston.

REFERENCES

ACIR. (1961). *State Constitutional and Statutory Restrictions on Local Government Debt*. U.S. Government Printing Office, Washington, D.C.

ACIR. (1962a). *State Constitutional and Statutory Restrictions upon the Structural, Functional, and Personnel Powers of Local Government*, A-12. U.S. Government Printing Office, Washington, D.C.

ACIR. (1962b). *State Constitutional and Statutory Restrictions on Local Taxing Powers*, A-14. U.S. Government Printing Office, Washington, D.C.

ACIR. (1977a). *Significant Features of Fiscal Federalism 1976-77, M-100*. U.S. Government Printing Office, Washington, D.C.

ACIR. (1977b). *State Limitations on Local Taxes and Expenditures*, A-64. U.S. Government Printing Office, Washington, D.C.

ACIR. (1979). *Information Bulletin No. 79-7*. U.S. Government Printing Office, Washington, D.C.

ACIR. (1982). *State and Local Roles in the Federal System*, A-88. U.S. Government Printing Office, Washington, D.C.

ACIR. (1983). *Significant Features of Fiscal Federalism, 1981-82*, M-135. U.S. Government Printing Office, Washington, D.C.

Aronson, J. Richard and Schwartz, Eli, Ed. (1981). *Management Policies in Local Government Finance*. International City Management Association, Washington, D.C.

Council of State Governments. (1978a). *The Property Tax: A Primer*. Lexington, Ky.

Council of State Governments. (1978b). *Limiting State Taxes and Expenditures*. Lexington, Ky.

Danziger, James N. and Ring, Peter Smith. (1982). Fiscal limitations: A selective review of recent research. *Public Administration Review 1*:45–55.

Elazar, Daniel. (1975). State-local relations: Reviving old theory for new practice. Paper prepared for the 4th Annual Toward '76 Conference, Temple University, Philadelphia, Penn.

Florestano, P. S. (1980). Revenue-raising limitations on local government: A focus on alternative responses. *Public Administration Review 41*:122–131.

Florestano, P. S. and Marando, V. (1981). *The States and the Metropolis*. Marcel Dekker, New York.

Glisson, Patrick C. and Holley, Stephen H. (March, 1982). Developing local government user changes: Technical and policy considerations. *Governmental Finance 11*(1):3–7.

Government Finance Research Center. (1980). Alternative state and local revenue sources. In *Elements of Financial Management*, No. 6. Municipal Finance Officers Association, Washington, D.C.

Hawkins, Brett W. et al. (1978). The effect of state policies on localities: A study of state revenue and expenditure centralization. Paper presented at meeting of American Political Science Association, New York.

Heller, Walter and Uhler, Lewis. (1978). Tax and expenditure limits. Speech delivered before the National Conference of State Legislature's Annual Meeting, Denver, Colo.

Maryland General Assembly. (1982). *Legislator's Guide to State and Local Fiscal Relationships*. Department of Fiscal Services, Annapolis.

National Governors' Association. (1978). *Tax and Expenditures Limitations. 1978.* Research Note 3. Center for Policy Research, Washington, D.C.

Shannon, John. (1977). Questions and answers on property tax reform and relief. Remarks before the Annual Meeting of the National Conference of State Legislators, Detroit, Michigan.

Shannon, John, Bell, Michael, and Fisher, Ronald. (1976). Recent state expense with local tax and expenditure centers. *National Tax Journal 29*(3):276–285.

Stonecash, Jeff. (1979). State policies regarding local government resource acquisition. Paper prepared for American Political Science Association Meeting, Washington, D.C.

Tax Foundation. (1979). *Facts and Figures on Government Finance*, 20th ed. Tax Foundation, Washington, D.C.

Walker, David and Walker, Jeanne. (1975). Rationalizing local government powers, functions and structure. In *States' Responsibilities to Local Governments: An Action Agenda*. Center for Policy Research of the National Governors' Association, Washington, D.C.

Welch, Ronald B. (1980). *The Property Tax Under Pressure: A Policymaker's Guide*. Lincoln Institute of Land Policy, Cambridge, Mass.

Westmeyer, Troy R. and Westmeyer, Wesley. (May, 1981). Fiscal limits not new in United States. *National Civic Review 70*(5):271–276, 282.

U.S. Bureau of the Census. (1979). *Finances of Municipalities and Township Governments, Vol. 4, No. 4*; and *Governmental Finances, Compendium of Governmental Finances, Vol. 4, No. 5.*; and *Finances of County Governments, Vol. 4, No. 5*. U.S. Government Printing Office, Washington, D.C.

7

State and Local Government Productivity and Performance Measurement

Harry P. Hatry State and Local Government Research Program, The Urban Institute, Washington, D.C.

This chapter is divided into six parts: The first introduces and defines productivity and performance measurement; the second discusses the uses for such measurement; the third discusses the measurements state and local governments should collect; the fourth briefly discusses some data collection procedures that will be needed; the fifth discusses the key issue of how a government can tell whether the measured performance is good or bad; and the last section presents suggested steps by which government agencies might develop their own performance measurement process.

I. WHAT IS PRODUCTIVITY AND PERFORMANCE MEASUREMENT?

Productivity and performance measurement is the measurement of both the effectiveness and efficiency of governments in delivering public services. Effectiveness means to what extent is a program, service, activity, or work group accomplishing what it is supposed to—and avoiding doing bad things it is not supposed to do? Efficiency means whatever the program, service, activity, or work group does, to what extent does it do it at minimum cost (i.e., with the least amount of resources)?

Excluded is measurement or tracking of purely "process" accomplishments, that is, the meeting of internal target dates such as for completing reports or for other events that are principally of interest administratively *within* an organization. Also excluded are primarily personnel oriented actions, such as personnel completing a training or educational program.

Thus, for this subject the *results* achieved by groups or individuals are the prime concerns, not the process by which they achieve the results.

II. USES FOR PRODUCTIVITY AND PERFORMANCE MEASUREMENT

Two approaches to measurement should be distinguished: (a) special ad hoc, in-depth examinations of specific programs, services, or work groups, and (b) regular measurement of performance of programs, services, or work groups that is undertaken at least annually and perhaps more frequently.

Special study performance measurement is usually labeled *program evaluation*. Individual program evaluations typically require substantial amounts of resources and one or more staff-years of time. Because of this, only a relatively few evaluations can be done in any given year and thus can cover only selected programs each year. Thus, each individual program or work group will not likely have an evaluation done on it more frequently than perhaps once every few years. Such studies aim at identifying both the extent to which a particular program has been successful, and also the extent to which the program itself has caused the observed results. Program evaluations thus are quite useful in helping governments identify whether a particular program should be continued, dropped, expanded, or contracted. If the evaluation is appropriately designed, it can also provide information on ways to improve the program. These program evaluations are primarily of use to governments for program planning and similar resource allocation purposes. Because they do not provide regular information to governmental agency management, they are not particularly useful in helping guide managers in their ongoing management and control of their operations.

The other form of productivity and performance measurement is called *performance monitoring*. Its focus is on measuring the results of outcomes on a regular basis, at least once a year, and probably for many performance indicators quarterly, monthly, or even weekly.

Performance monitoring thus has two important advantages: (a) it can provide regular feedback to public officials, managers, and supervisors, for managing and controlling operations; and (b) because it is not as costly as special studies, performance measurement can cover a wide range of programs, services, and work groups of an agency. The main limitation of performance monitoring is that, unlike special program evaluation studies, it does not directly address the issue of what has caused the observed results. In effect, it presents a profit-loss statement, a *score card*, but leaves it to more in-depth analysis to determine why the results have occurred.

Surprising as it may be to beginners in the field of public administration (and even to those who have been in it for a long time), little information on results, either effectiveness or efficiency, is currently made available to government managers and other public officials in most government agencies. Only in recent years have attempts been made to develop better data collection procedures that can be used to fill this gap. Productivity and performance measurement, however, is still in its infancy.

For the remainder of this chapter, the focus will be on performance monitoring, rather than in-depth program evaluations. The latter topic and especially its techniques have been well developed and well documented by numerous texts, articles, and reports. On the other hand, performance monitoring, despite its considerable applicability to public management purposes, has been relatively neglected.

Figure 1 lists four major uses for regular performance measurement. Each is discussed below.

A. Resource Allocation/Program Planning/Budgeting

If program performance is continually poor, this indicates the need for correction or cutting back. If performance is good, this suggests the desirability of continuing, or perhaps expanding the program. If an organization undertakes a change in procedures, performance can subsequently be monitored to determine whether or not results improved and whether or not the new procedures should be continued.

B. Contract Monitoring

Regular feedback on performance can be used by government agencies to assess contractor performance on results. Thus, contractors can be held accountable for results and not merely for the quantity of activities performed and the types of resources (such as vehicles, staffing, etc.) applied.

With an ongoing performance measurement system, an agency can introduce *performance* and *incentive* contracting. Performance contracts include performance targets such as timeliness and quality of the services the contractor provides (e.g., that bridge maintenance should be completed by a particular date

---

1. Resource allocation/program planning/budgeting
2. Contractor monitoring
3. Employee motivation
    A. Performance targeting
    B. Performance appraisals
    C. Monetary incentives
    D. Feedback meetings with employees
4. Management control

Fig. 1 Uses for performance measurement information.

or that a certain percentage of clients should give satisfactory ratings to the service). Incentive contracts include bonuses and penalties for meeting, exceeding, or not meeting the specified contractual targets.

Contracting of government activities is becoming more common throughout the United States. This potential use of performance measurement is thus becoming more urgent.

Here are some examples. Milwaukee County for many years has obtained annual feedback from families of clients of social services provided by contractors. This information is used to help select future contractors. Tulsa (Oklahoma) has included penalties for missed collections and not correcting complaints within a specified time in its agreements with solid waste collection contractors. Gainesville and Ft. Lauderdale (Florida), for vehicle repair, and Prince George's County (Maryland), for its data processing facility management, have included bonus and penalty clauses for contractors who exceed or do not meet specific cost targets. Even in human services such as mental health and social services, where new outcome measurement tools are becoming available and where purchase of services is relatively common, it should be possible to include performance elements in purchase-of-service contracts.

C. Employee Motivation

There are four important occasions for performance measurement that are of particular concern to public administrators.

1. *Performance targeting.* Many state and local agencies have in recent years tried some form of performance targeting or management-by-objectives (MBO). Here government managers, with their supervisors, set performance targets for the coming year. Subsequently performance and the extent of target achievement are measured, perhaps quarterly and at the end of the year. Most MBO performance indicators have been process indicators with few being indicators of program efficiency or effectiveness. With regular performance measurement, performance targeting can become considerably more meaningful by including indicators of service quality/effectiveness and efficiency.

2. *Performance appraisals.* A 1977 Urban Institute telephone survey of personnel staff from the fifty state and fifty local governments found that most felt that their current performance appraisal systems were either nominal or counterproductive.[1] A major obstacle was the lack of objective performance measurements. Both those appraising and those appraised are likely to be much more satisfied with performance appraisals if meaningful, objectively obtained measurements are included, thus reducing squabbles and claims of favoritism

[1] John M. Greiner et al. (1981). *Productivity and Motivation: A Review of State and Local Government Initiatives.* The Urban Institute, Washington, D.C.

and unfairness of what otherwise would be primarily subjective, judgmental appraisals.

   3. *Monetary incentives.* Pay-for-performance has in recent years become an attractive concept to many state and local governments as well as to the federal government. There has been a large number of trials of salary and bonus incentive systems for both management and nonmanagement employees. A major problem in implementing such systems is the need for objective, meaningful performance indicators that are acceptable both to potential recipients and to givers of the funds—and that will stand scrutiny from the public and media as being a reasonable basis for providing more money to government personnel. Such cities as Dayton, Phoenix, San Diego, and Montebello (California) have introduced such plans for managers. North Carolina (for workers in its Department of Transportation) and the cities of Flint and Detroit, Michigan (for solid waste collection workers) have experimented with pay-for-performance plans for nonmanagement employees. The existence of sound, regular performance measurement is needed to permit meaningful application of monetary incentives.

   4. *Feedback meetings with employees.* Greater employee participation has been widely promulgated as a way to motivate and tap the knowledge of government employees, especially lower-level employees. If regular performance reports are prepared, supervisors can use such reports as a basis for group "How are we doing?" meetings in which recent performance is examined and compared with previous periods. The group could then identify and discuss problems and obstacles and begin formulation of an action plan to improve future performance. Subsequently, the group could examine further performance reports to see if improved performance resulted after the actions were taken.

   If the performance measurements are client oriented (as will be discussed later), these group meetings can have the additional effect of sensitizing employees to client concerns and needs.

D. Management Control

If performance measurement reports are available frequently, perhaps monthly, managers can use them to help guide work schedules and assignments such as to cover activities or geographical areas where problems appear. For example, New York City assigns waste collection crews based in part on its regular measurements of street cleanliness.

III. TYPES OF PERFORMANCE MEASURES

Figure 2 lists a number of types of performance measures. Each is discussed briefly.

Effectiveness/quality measures
Efficiency measures
  Input ÷ output (work accomplished)
  Output ÷ input
  Actual ÷ "standard" (work standard)
  Effectiveness ÷ input
Productivity indices

Fig. 2 Types of performance measures.

A. Effectiveness/Quality Measures

These measures assess the degree to which a service has achieved its objectives, especially relative to the clients it serves, including the extent to which it avoids unintended, negative effects; for example, the pollution effects connected with transportation systems. Service effectiveness and quality are abstract terms for which precise definitions and general agreement do not exist today. These are best discussed by examples:

- For parks and recreation and library services: indicators of client satisfaction and amount of use of facilities and programs (e.g., attendance and participation rates)
- For road maintenance: indicators of the roughness and ridability of streets
- For fire suppression: estimates of the amount of fire spread after arrival of first firefighting vehicle
- For human service programs such as training and employment, health, mental health, and social service programs: measures of the extent of improvement in clients' employment and earnings, health, and functioning
- For internal support services (e.g., purchasing, data processing, personnel, building and vehicle maintenance): indicators of the correctness and adequacy of the services provided

Characteristics of service "quality," such as its timeliness, accessibility, and courteousness with which the service is performed, should also be included in performance measurement. For example, in most, if not all, services, clients are concerned about the timeliness with which the service is provided to them. Thus, measures of response times should be used to assess most services, such as the amount of time to: make repairs to roads; replace street lights; remove snow; respond to calls for police and fire assistance; fill purchase orders; respond to complaints; process eligibility determinations and provide assistance checks; and provide licenses and other applications processed.

B. Efficiency Measures

1. Input/Output Measures

Efficiency is typically defined as the ratio of the amount of input applied divided by the amount of output produced. If the reciprocal of this ratio is used, output divided by input, the resulting ratio is labeled *productivity*. Both forms give equivalent results.

Input units typically are either the number of employee hours or dollars. The more difficult question is what output units should be used. Generally, governments have used the amount of physical workload accomplished such as the number of repairs made, reports processed, clients served, applications processed, gallons of water treated, and crime or fire calls responded to.

2. Effectiveness/Input Measures

Unfortunately, counts of workload accomplished provide little or no information about the quality or result of the output. Some eligibility determinations are made incorrectly, some clients (whether of health, employment, or social services), though given service, may not be helped to any significant extent, repairs may be defective, and complaints may be responded to only nominally, and so on. Thus, such measures themselves indicate little to public administrators and elected officials as to what has been accomplished and, in the true sense, how efficiently. In fact, if only these indicators are used, the effort may be counterproductive. Output quantity would be encouraged at the expense of service quality.

To reduce this problem, the output measure should to the extent possible: (a) exclude output that is defective and (b), where possible, be a measure that indicates service effectiveness. This can best be illustrated by some examples:

- Since some arrests turn out not to be productive and may be dropped for lack of evidence or improper arrest procedures, instead of merely measuring the number of arrests per police-year, use number of arrests *that survive the first judicial screening* per police-year.
- Provide a quality test for repairs, either through a formal inspection or by deleting from the count of output those repairs where a service callback is required within a certain time interval, such as within a month.
- Instead of using a measure such as cost-per-household that used a recreational facility during the year, use cost per household that used a recreational facility during the year *and* that also expressed overall satisfaction with their experiences. Data for this measure can be obtained through the use of client surveys as discussed later.
- Instead of the measure number of staff hours per social service clients served, use the number of staff hours per social service client *that improved* (to a

certain prespecified degree) within nine months. Data for this measure could be obtained through a variety of approaches as discussed later.

The basic principle here is that persons or groups whose performance is being measured should not be encouraged to emphasize output quantity at the expense of quality, which will occur if efficiency is measured without consideration of service quality and effectiveness.

3. Work Standards

A number of local, state, and federal agencies have used work measurement to develop work standards. This approach was originally developed by industrial engineers for private businesses, especially manufacturers. A particular work activity is closely examined to determine how much time it should take if done correctly by a trained, reasonably proficient worker working at a reasonable rate of effort. This *engineered time standard* approach is primarily applicable to work that is routine, repetitive, and done frequently.

Typical government applications include road repairs, park vehicle, and building maintenance, certain data processing and clerical activities, certain inspection activities, and eligibility determinations. In recent years, various forms of work measurement and standards have begun to be applied to more ill-structured activities, such as social casework and legal activities; it is, however, not clear that these are appropriate.

For activities for which work standards have been developed, an agency can compare actual performance against the standard if appropriate time and input information are collected.

4. Productivity Indices

Productivity indices can be readily calculated for each of the performance measures discussed, but traditionally have been most often applied to measures where output is divided by input.

A productivity index shows the *relative* change in a measure from a base period to another time period. One year, or a set of years, is chosen as the base period. The actual value of the performance measure chosen as the base period (e.g., the number of repairs made per unit of output) is given the value of 100. The index calculated for each succeeding year would be the ratio of the performance measured for that year as compared with the base year. Thus, if a future year's performance is 10% higher than that of the base period, the index for that year would be 110.

The disadvantage of productivity indices is that they say nothing about the absolute level of performance for any time period. They only show relative performance over time. An important advantage of productivity indices is that indices for individual activities can be aggregated to give an overall productivity index that includes a number of quite different activities. This is done by weighting each separate index by the amount of input. For example, if one activity required 25% of the total number of employee years, whereas the second activity required 75% of the employee years, to calculate the overall productivity index, the index for the second activity would be weighted three times that of the first.

5. Pseudo Efficiency Measures

A number of measurements have sometimes been considered to measure efficiency, but do not. Some examples are the following:

- The cost per capita of a particular service
- The cost of a particular service per dollar of assessed value
- Worker-client ratios (including teacher-pupil ratios)
- Number of library books per capita

These measures are expressed as ratios and on the surface resemble efficiency measures. In reality, however, they are indicators of the amount of input applied for a particular activity. They do not say anything about the amount of output or product provided and thus should not be considered as measuring efficiency.

IV. DATA COLLECTION PROCEDURES

Data collection procedures are the key to valid and meaningful performance measurement. It is vital that such procedures measure key aspects of performance with reasonable validity and accuracy, and at reasonably low cost. Performance measurements will be of most use if the measurements can be as objective and quantitative as possible. This does not mean that subjective, qualitative service aspects should not be included where these represent important service objectives. Such performance aspects often can be included in the measurements, but should be obtained in as systematic, objective, and valid a way as possible. Some techniques for using subjective, qualitative judgments will be discussed in the following sections.

There are three primary types of procedures:

- Use of government records
- Trained observer ratings
- Citizen/client surveys

These data sources are applicable to most government agencies. Most of the measurement should be done within individual agencies (an exception is that of some citizen surveys as mentioned later). Though public administrators do not need to know all of the technical details of these approaches, they should have a reasonable grasp of their strengths and weaknesses and a sense of what can be achieved through their use. Each procedure is discussed in the sections following.

A. Use of Government Records

Use of existing recorded data, all other things being equal, is at least on the surface, the most attractive source of data collection for performance measures. Presumably when relevant agency records are available, their use for performance measurement will require little added cost. Agency records are the basic source of such information as cost data and amount of workload completed for use in efficiency measures. Some examples of such workload data are number of repairs, records processed, prison-inmate days, and persons trained.

Agency records often are available for some effectiveness/quality measures including the number of: complaints received by an agency; traffic accidents and injuries; reported crimes; arrests; and incidence of communicable diseases, as well as the response times to requests for services.

Unfortunately, existing records are likely to be somewhat inadequate and may need revision for performance measurement. For example, cost data may not be maintained in such a way as to permit cost or employee-hour breakouts for specific activities associated with specific workload measures (e.g., to distinguish between the cost of commercial and residential collection or between the costs for various types of state promotional activity.) Another example is that, though incoming complaints are processed, many agencies do not actually tabulate these data and aggregate them by the nature of the complaint or by the time that it takes to resolve the complaint.

Two examples of how government records might be made more useful for measuring service quality are the following:

- Calculate response times for responding to service requests, such as maintenance activities, client complaints, eligibility determinations, and so forth, by recording the time of the official request and then the time when the request was satisfied.
- Exclude defective output from output counts, such as by excluding repairs that have to be redone within, say, one month, and identifying the number of arrests that survive the first judicial screening to screen out inappropriate, unproductive arrests. This would also reduce the temptation of police officers to make excessive arrests.

B. Trained Observer Techniques

This is a class of procedures in which an observer (e.g., an inspector) is trained to rate particular performance characteristics of a service. These characteristics are usually physical. Some examples of the use of trained observers are:

- To assess street cleanliness, such as done by New York City and Charlotte, North Carolina
- To evaluate the condition of roads, as done by many state and local transportation agencies
- To assess park maintenance, such as done by Honolulu and New York City
- To assess the condition and extent of improvement in clients in such human service programs as developmental disabilities and mental health, as done by a number of mental health agencies

The accuracy of these procedures depends on a number of factors. If the procedures are too loose or too haphazard, they may be inaccurate. Four ways to make trained observers' ratings more reliable include:

- Provide specific scales for the ratings (i.e., *anchored scales*) so that different observers seeing a condition at different points in time would provide approximately the same rating. Specific descriptions should be used to describe each grade on the rating scale, including quantitative descriptions, such as the height of grass, number of road defects per 100 feet, or the amount of litter. Another type of rating procedure that is gaining popularity is to define the rating categories by preselected photographs representing the different grades, such as grades of road roughness, street cleanliness, or park maintenance quality. Photographs have been used to measure street cleanliness, road conditions, park maintenance, and the condition of traffic signs and signals.
- Use raters who are independent of the work unit rated to avoid the potential for, or appearance of, bias.
- Provide training in rating procedures to all new trained observers.
- Have each observer's ratings checked periodically for possible deterioration in quality. Provide retraining to those for whom problems appear.

Trained observer procedures require time for making the ratings. Thus, they will involve extra costs to an agency unless there are persons available, such as inspectors, with time to do the ratings. A way to reduce the costs of trained observers is to rate only a sample of items (e.g., a sample of streets, park areas, or eligibility determinations). Another way is to use the same observers to rate more than one type of condition, thus reducing the cost for each measurement. For example, inspectors could simultaneously measure both street cleanliness and condition as done in trials by St. Petersburg, Florida, and Nashville, Tennessee.

C. Citizen/Client Surveys

Surveys of a sample of households in the community can be used to obtain performance feedback on a variety of basic services used by most citizens. In addition, surveys can be undertaken of only those persons that have been clients of particular services to obtain information on their experiences with, and their perceptions of the quality of, those services. Surveys can be used to obtain both factual data relating to service effectiveness and ratings by clients of various characteristics of a service.

For example, surveys can be used to obtain such *factual data* as:

- Participation rates, that is, the percent of *different* persons or households that use a service for such services as parks and recreation, museums, libraries, and public transit. Data from fare boxes and from site counts (sometimes obtainable from agency records) tell how many visits and trips were made, but they do not indicate how many different persons made the trips or visits.
- Data on crime victimization of citizens to obtain better information on crime rates than are obtainable from tabulations of crimes reported to the police.
- Information from clients of human service programs (such as employment and training, education programs, mental health, and social services) as to their postservice employment history and earning levels, and the extent of improvement in their functioning to estimate the percentage of clients actually helped.

Surveys can be used to obtain such *client ratings* as:

- Satisfaction with recreational programs and facilities
- The adequacy and quality of transportation services
- The odor, taste, appearance, and pressure of the water received
- The adequacy and promptness of motor vehicle licensing and registration
- Ratings of faculty teaching (by students)
- The timeliness, accessibility (both as to physical location and hours of operation), and the courteousness of government employees in serving clients

Note that client surveys can be used to assess internal support services, such as purchasing, data processing, vehicle repair, payroll, building maintenance, custodial activities, and personnel. The "clients" of internal services who would be surveyed for their ratings are those employees in other government agencies who received the services.

Surveys for performance measurement should be distinguished from the more common opinion surveys that ask citizens' opinion of various policy issues and what the government should do in the future. Many, if not the majority, of the citizen surveys used by governments have emphasized this latter type of question, not performance measurement questions. Survey procedures are then used as a quasi-referendum and are subject to special problems in developing the questionnaires.

The accuracy and cost of the information obtained from citizen/client surveys depend on a number of factors. These include: the size of the sample; the mode of administering the questionnaire; the ease in reaching the persons to be interviewed; and, to a lesser extent, the length of the questionnaire itself. Some suggestions for maintaining accuracy while keeping the costs reasonable are the following:

- Make sure that a representative sample is drawn and that it covers all important parts of the universe that you wish to cover. (For example, the sample should be adequately representative of apartment and trailer-camp dwellers if these are an important part of the population from which feedback is sought).
- Use a random sample to assure that results are representative of the whole population.
- Don't overdo precision requirements. Such confidence as 95 and 99% confidence intervals for most government purposes are excessive; 90% confidence intervals will usually be ample. More precision substantially boosts the size of the sample needed and thus the survey costs.
- Use telephone interviewing, possibly with mail administration. Both cost and accuracy are greatly affected by the mode of interviewing (i.e., whether in-person, telephone, or mail surveys). In-person interviews are by far the most expensive and are probably not practical for most regular, ongoing performance measurement. Mail surveys are the cheapest and can inexpensively be mailed to large populations, but response rates are generally too small to achieve credible results. A 20% response rate for mailing is typical. Multiple mailings can increase this rate somewhat. Mail questionnaires have to be less complex than those that can be used with the other modes. Since over 90% of the population of the United States has access to a telephone, and with the introduction of random digit dialing, permitting telephone surveys to cover persons without listed numbers, telephone interviewing has become popular with professional survey firms. As a general rule, telephone interviews will probably be the appropriate mode for most government surveys. However, combinations such as one or two mailings followed by a telephone followup of nonrespondents may also be appropriate.

What are the costs of these surveys? Cost is probably the major inhibition to greater use by government agencies, along with their unfamiliarity to most government managers. For performance monitoring, annual surveys are needed, perhaps undertaken evenly (e.g., quarterly) over the year to cover different seasons. After the survey procedures and questionnaire have been initially developed, subsequent surveys can be relatively routine. Cities such as Dayton, St. Petersburg, and Nashville have achieved costs of perhaps $10 or even less per respondent once they developed the basic questionnaire. Thus, for a telephone sample of 700 households in the community, the cost for the survey would be approximately $7000.

For *client* surveys, the costs could be significantly less or greater. For example, for surveys of clients of internal support services such as purchasing, data processing, and building and vehicle maintenance, the costs should be quite small, if not negligible. For determining the outcomes of human services such as mental health and social services where clients are interviewed both at intake and after services have been received, perhaps six to nine months later, these costs can become higher, especially if a large proportion of the clients is surveyed.

Can surveys of a very small proportion with populations such as 700 families out of many thousands be sufficiently accurate? If statistical sampling procedures are followed, the accuracy should be quite adequate—plus or minus 3% points with 90% confidence. The Harris and Gallup polls regularly interview about 1600 families across the United States to represent the full U.S. population of over 220 million people.

For sample surveys of the population of a jurisdiction, a considerable savings in cost-per-performance indicator can be achieved by covering several services simultaneously. If several services are covered in a single survey, it probably should be administered out of a central office with each of the several operating agencies contributing sections of the questionnaire. This has been done by several local governments including Dayton (Oh.), Charlotte (N.C.), Dallas (Tex.), Kansas City (Mo.), Randolph Township (N.J.) (a jurisdiction of under 20,000 population), and such states as North Carolina and Wisconsin. The Wisconsin 1976 survey, for example, contained performance measurement questions on road maintenance (road roughness, adequacy of traffic signs, overall transportation adequacy), the convenience and adequacy of vehicle registration and licensing, a variety of health issues such as accessibility to medical care, experiences with mental health and social services, and on employment and family income. Not included, but could have been, are questions regarding use of parks, including reasons for nonuse, and for those respondents found to be users, assessments of various park characteristics.

Two somewhat unusual recent uses in citizen and client surveys have been to obtain feedback: (a) on the adequacy of regulatory agencies (state of Maryland), and (b) from prison inmates as to internal prison security (state of Minnesota).

Figure 3 illustrates the type of information that can be obtained from such surveys. It contains excerpts from a questionnaire surveying recreation facility users. Most of the questions ask about specific service characteristics. If a substantial proportion of respondents rate any of these characteristics as fair or poor, this would suggest to managers that corrective action is needed (the success of which could be assessed in subsequent surveys). The last question in

How would you rate the following?

	Exc.	Good	Fair	Poor
6. Hours of operation				
7. Cleanliness				
8. Condition of equipment				
9. Crowdedness				
10. Safety conditions				
11. Physical attractiveness				
12. Variety of programs				
13. Helpfulness of personnel				
14. Overall				

Fig. 3 Survey of recreation facility users (Nashville and St. Petersburg).

the figure asks the respondent for an overall (global) rating. These surveys can also ask respondents who rate a service "poor" why it was so rated. Such information can provide managers with specific clues as to the problems perceived by their clients.

D. Miscellaneous Data Collection Procedures

This is a catchall category to pick up miscellaneous approaches and leave room for a government's own ingenuity.

A number of measurements currently in use require special equipment to obtain performance data. Measurements of air, water, and noise pollution fit this category. Another example is the use of road roughness measuring equipment, such as ridemeters or "roughometer."

A special problem with such measurements is to make sure that the technical measurements are translated into terms that managers, elected officials, and citizens understand. Technical measurements should be translated into understandable categories, such as whether air quality is excellent, good, fair, or poor. This requires explicit definitions for each such category to avoid subsequent manipulation.

E. A Special Topic: The Need for Measurement Procedures to Consider Differences in the Difficulty of the Incoming Workload

The work coming into any agency or organizational unit will inevitably vary considerably as to its difficulty—whether the work involves different types of mental health or social service clients, different road repair problems, or different crimes needing investigation, and so on. Some clients may be very easy to help;

others may require extensive time and effort and be very difficult to help. Road segments in some parts of a state (depending on soil, weather, and terrain conditions) will take much more effort to keep in good condition than other sections. The ability of investigators to solve crimes depends very heavily on the amount of evidence obtained at the scene of the crime before investigators begin their work.

This aspect of performance measurement has often been overlooked, leading to a focus on aggregate performance that can mislead users of the data. Figure 4 shows an example of what can occur if only aggregate data are looked at. Looking only at aggregate performance indicates that performance has worsened between 1983 and 1984. But when the data are broken down by difficulty category, the opposite is found. The workload mix (e.g., the degree of difficulty) has changed. This mix can vary from one year to the next (as shown in the figure) or can differ among facilities or work groups that are being compared. Therefore, it is quite important for fair and meaningful performance measurement that the difficulty of the incoming workload be considered.

Four key steps are: (a) identify key characteristics of the workload that affect service efficiency or effectiveness; (b) define three to five levels (categories) of difficulty based on these characteristics; (c) classify incoming workload into these categories (for example, clients coming in for mental health treatment might be classified as to the extent of their functioning problems at intake); and, (d) measure separately the cost and service effectiveness for each category.

This is an issue that has only recently been raised as an important problem in performance measurement. It warrants careful consideration.

	1983	1984
Total clients	500	500
Total helped	300	235
%	60	47
Severe cases	100	300
Total helped	0	75
%	0	25
Nonsevere	400	200
Total helped	300	160
%	75	80

Fig. 4 Illustration of need to consider difficulty of incoming workload.

V. HOW CAN WE TELL WHETHER PERFORMANCE IS GOOD OR BAD?

A major issue in performance is how to assess whether the measured level of performance is good or bad. Government managers and other officials need information that will permit them to compare current performance against benchmarks. Figure 5 lists seven types of benchmarks. A government might use some or all of them. Each is discussed briefly next.

A. Existing Standards

If a government has engineered work standards for specific activities, actual performance could be measured against these. These are most applicable for routine, repetitive activities. However, most government activities are not routine and repetitive. Thus, at least today, most governments do not have valid work standards against which to compare actual performance.

B. Previous Performance

Comparing current performance to that in previous periods is the most common form of comparison currently undertaken by governments. It is very appropriate and very useful. Of course, government administrators undertaking these comparisons need to be sensitive to, and consider, special circumstances that are not within the control of the agency and thus explain at least part of the reason for changed performance.

C. Performance of Similar Units

In some instances, there are different facilities, service districts, precincts, or service units that provide essentially the same service within the government. These provide important opportunities for comparisons. The performance of the best facility or unit could be used as the yardstick against which to compare the performance of the others.

---

1. Existing "standards"
2. Previous performance
3. Performance of similar units
4. Outcomes for different client groups
5. Performance of other jurisdictions
6. Private sector performance
7. Preset targets

Fig. 5 Possible benchmarks against which to compare actual performance.

D. Outcomes for Different Client Groups

Sometimes comparisons can be made among different client groups, such as different age, sex, income, or geographical-residence groups, if the groups being compared do not differ widely as to service difficulty. This will indicate whether some groups have a greater need or are being served as well as others. The highest performance level achieved for any one of the groups might be used as the yardstick.

E. Performance in Other Jurisdictions

In some instances, comparable information may be available from other jurisdictions. Such information is most prevalent for indicators that are collected nationally, such as traffic accident rates, air pollution levels, and unemployment rates. Sometimes, however, national data are collected for large geographical areas rather than for individual cities or counties. A problem here is to ascertain that the measurements obtained elsewhere are obtained in a similar way to, and thus are comparable with, that data obtained by one's own government.

F. Performance of the Private Sector

In some instances, data can be obtained on similar activities undertaken by private businesses to provide a comparison. For example, motor vehicle repair activities, printing activities, building maintenance, purchasing (particularly unit prices obtained for common purchased items), and some recreation programs have private sector counterparts. It may not be very difficult to obtain data on private sector costs and service quality. The government agency activity can then be compared with the activity undertaken by the private sector for itself.

G. Preset Targets

Finally, for those agencies that in one way or another establish targets at the beginning of a year for particular performance measures, actual performance can subsequently be measured and compared against those targets. Agencies that have some form of management-by-objectives (MBO) system fall into this category. The targets could themselves be set by using one or more of the previous six types of benchmarks. For example, targets might be set for individual similar facilities by selecting that facility whose performance was best during the previous year, preferably with adjustments to the targets for characteristics of facilities that indicated that their situation was more (or less) difficult.

VI. PROCESS FOR DEVELOPING AND IMPLEMENTING PERFORMANCE MEASUREMENT PROCEDURES

This final section suggests six steps for an agency wishing to develop an improved performance measurement process. The steps are summarized in Fig. 6.

A. Step 1: Establish a Working Group

It is highly desirable to select a group of persons that is knowledgeable about the activity, reflects a variety of perspectives as to the objectives of that activity, and can apply time and effort to guiding the development of the performance measurement process.

The group should contain: (a) program personnel, preferably representing two or three levels within the program organization; (b) representatives of contractors if contractor performance is to be measured as part of performance measurement procedures; (c) analysis personnel, possibly from the central office of management and budget or from outside the government, to assure that the group selects a valid measurement process; and (d) representatives of the services' clients, at least through step 2, to help identify service objectives that should be measured as part of the performance measurement process.

This working group should meet regularly and be responsible for guiding the remaining steps, probably staying formally in existence for a one- to two-year period during formulation and initial testing of the measurement procedures.

B. Step 2: Identify Service Objectives and Relevant Performance Indicators

An early step for a performance measurement process is to identify what objectives and results are to be expected from each service and to identify the specific

---

1. Form a working group
   - Program personnel
   - Contractor representative
   - Analysis personnel
   - Clients
2. Identify objectives and performance indicators
3. Select data collection procedures
4. Identify key workload-difficulty characteristics
5. Develop and implement a utilization plan
6. Test the process

Fig. 6   Steps for developing a performance measurement process.

performance indicators that should be measured to assess progress towards the objectives. Sec. III of this chapter might be helpful as background.

C. Step 3: Identify Appropriate Data Collection Procedures

This step makes operative the performance indicators selected in step 2. The group should consider data validity, the cost of data collection, feasibility of the procedures, and utility of the resulting information. Sec. IV in this chapter could be used as background for this step.

D. Step 4: Identify Key Workload Characteristics Affecting Performance and Develop Procedures for Explicitly Considering Different Mixes of Incoming Workload Difficulty

The importance of this step and needed tasks were discussed in Section IV.E.

E. Step 5: Develop and Implement a Utilization Plan

Early in the activities of the working group, a plan should be developed to identify what specific uses are intended for the data, at least during the first one to two years. Candidate uses were described in Sec. II.

The plan should identify what specific reports should be prepared from the measurement process, what specific comparisons should be shown in the reports (see Sec. V), what the reporting frequency should be, and who should receive the reports. It is vital that reports be carefully planned so as to be fully understandable and clear to users. (The dissemination of overly complex or unintelligible reports has all too often been a major problem in presenting quantitative information.)

F. Step 6: Test the Process

The data collection procedures and reporting methods should be fully tested over a period of a number of months, and preferably over a period of at least one year. Problems that are found should be corrected prior to full-fledged use.

VII. FINAL COMMENTS

There are a variety of measures and data collection procedures available. The technical state of the art seems adequate to provide reasonably decent performance measurements on effectiveness and efficiency for most state and local activities. These measurement procedures are by no means perfect, but they can provide a reasonable perspective on performance of most agencies.

The key hurdle currently for state and local agencies is the interest and motivation of managers and other public officials to undertake and use such measurements. Government managers by and large are not used to such data and have not insisted on it or requested it. Such measurement does take special effort.

Currently, we are in a vicious circle in public administration in which managers are not sure of the utility (the cost-effectiveness) of performance measurement, at least not sufficiently to undertake substantial trials of such procedures to test their utility.

Nevertheless, slow progress seems to be being made. The potential for substantially improved performance measurement is there. Many basic management activities depend heavily on adequate performance measurement, measurement not normally available in most government agencies today. Improved performance measurement seems badly needed. We can only hope that performance measurement continues to be strengthened to permit government managers to manage.

SELECTED BIBLIOGRAPHY

1.   Measuring Productivity in State and Local Government, Donald M. Fisk, U.S. Department of Labor, Bureau of Labor Statistics, Bulletin 2166, December 1983 (U.S. Government Printing Office, Washington, D.C.).

2.   *Using Performance Measurement in Local Government*, Paul D. Epstein, Van Nostrand Reinhold, New York, New York, 1984.

3.   *The Status of Productivity Measurement in State Government: An Initial Examination*, H. P. Hatry, D. M. Fisk, L. H. Blair, A. Schainflatt, and H. Parker, September 1975. (Available from the National Technical Information Service, Stock No. SHR0000422/LLC, $10.75).

4.   *How Effective Are Your Community Services? Procedures for Monitoring the Effectiveness of Municipal Services*, by Harry P. Hatry, Louis H. Blair, 1977. Available from The Urban Institute and the International City Management Association, Washington, D.C. (318 pp.).

5.   Efficiency Measurement for Local Government Services: Some Initial Suggestions, by Harry P. Hatry, Sumner N. Clarren, Therese van Houten, Jane P. Woodward, and Pasqual A. DonVito, 1979. Available from The Urban Institute, Washington, D.C. (204 pp.).

6.   *Effectiveness Measures: Literature and Practice Review*, Public Technology, Inc., 1979. Available from NTIS, 5285 Port Royal Road, Springfield, VA, 22161. Order #HUD-0001225, $8.00 (55 pp.).

7.   *Developing Client Outcome Monitoring Systems: A Guide for State and Local Social Service Agencies*, Rhona Millar, Harry Hatry, *et al.*, 1981. Available from The Urban Institute, Washington, D.C.

8.   *Measuring Urban Services: A Multi-Mode Approach* by Elinor Ostrom and Roger B. Parks. Available from the Workshop in Political Theory and Policy Analysis, Indiana University, Bloomington, Ind. (129 pp.).

9. *Performance Measurement and Cost Accounting for Smaller Local Governments*, 1979. Available from the Rhode Island Department of Community Affairs, Providence, R.I., $7.00 (99 pp.).

10. *Performance Measurement and Improvement of Local Services: Proceedings of National Workshops*, Public Technology, Inc., 1980. Available from NTIS, 5285 Port Royal Road, Springfield, VA, 22161, PB 81-128548, $9.50 (96 pp.).

11. *Productivity Improvement Handbook for State and Local Government*, edited by George J. Washnis, 1980. Available from Wiley-Interscience, Somerset, N.J. (1,500 pp.).

12. *Using Productivity Measurement: A Manager's Guide to More Effective Services*, Management Information Services Special Report, No. 4, May 1979. Available from the International City Management Association, Washington, D.C. (175 pp.).

13. *Improving Productivity Using Work Measurement* (2 volumes: "A Management Report" and "A Technical Guide"), 1977. Available from Public Technology, Inc., Washington, D.C.

14. "Work Measurement in Local Government," Patrick Manion, *Management Information Service Report*, Vol. 6, No. 10, October 1974. Available from the International City Management Association, Washington, D.C.

15. *Obtaining Citizen Feedback: The Application of Citizen Surveys to Local Governments* by Kenneth Webb and Harry P. Hatry, 1973. Available from The Urban Institute, Washington, D.C. (105 pp.).

16. *Total Performance Management: Some Pointers for Action*, National Center for Productivity and Quality of Working Life, 1978. Available from the National Technical Information Service, Springfield, VA (NTIS order #PB-300-249) (49 pp.).

8

Information Systems in State and Local Governments

Edward M. Jackowski Graduate Program for Administrators, Rider College, Lawrenceville, New Jersey

I. INTRODUCTION

Paperwork and the affiliated record-keeping systems that public administrators were required to maintain at the turn of the century were minimal, but as time progressed, the nation witnessed a population explosion and an increase in the number of laws, regulations, policies, and procedures that affected the management of state and local governments. As a result of these expositions and the eminent outcry of the public for government accountability, paperwork multiplied at least tenfold. It was during the 1950s, 1960s, and 1970s that legislative control mechanisms with their corresponding requirements created a horrendous paperwork nightmare and automated information system technologies began to be referenced heavily. Public administrators thought that information systems technologies would provide management a means of coping with the paperwork explosion. They viewed information system specialists as highly organized professionals who, with their resources, would supposedly save not only the public but also private administrators in their plight to digest and understand the wealth of paperwork required by legislative and other enactments. Sadly, as the century moved forward, the paperwork burden continued to enlarge and information systems commitments began to accumulate and lead toward the existence of a period of sour grapes.

The difference that exists between information systems designed for state and local governments and those of the private sector is in the information that resides in their data banks. In keeping with the sour grapes theory, public administrators would strongly agree that information systems grew at suboptimal rates rather than being dynamically designed as decision support systems (DSS).[1] To dispell some of these opinions and enlighten present and future public administrators, this chapter will: (a) provide an overview of state and local information systems and their accompanying methods and architectural designs as foreseen in the 1980s; (b) describe state and local information systems from a data administration and decentralized processing perspective; and (c) review several information system characteristics of state and local governments.

Originally, in their quest to design and operationalize functional information systems, state and local public administrators met with catastrophies in illogically designed systems. This was caused by their use of inadequate tools (i.e., first-, second-, and even third-generation computer hardware and software) and a lack of knowledge pertaining to the administration of information as an organizational resource. To design effective information systems, public administrators of the 1980s and beyond must become technically astute as *information specialists* or, to future-oriented managers, *information engineers.*[2] They must receive an in-depth knowledge of automated information resource management techniques and an explicit and implicit understanding of how data are viewed, manipulated, and constructed. Thus, the public administrator of the future will have a sound repertoire of experiences and an intuitive understanding of a particular situation to make wise decisions.

Compared with several of their counterparts in the private sector (banks, insurance companies, and stock exchanges), state and local governments are paperwork intensive and, as a rule of thumb, should have authorization to appropriate at least 5% of their operating budgets to the development and implementation of information systems (Taggart, 1980:160). This statement is an absolute truth; however, state and local governments that reach this level of spending are a rarity. Even though a 5% funding level is justifiable and financial net present value methods and other capital budgeting techniques can derive positive cost benefits, a 5% level of spending is not reached because this level of funding is a political issue. Qualitatively, however, public administrators and legislatures are cognizant that government organizations have goals and objectives that require them to have information systems for collecting, processing, and reporting on their clients, services, and other operations.

II. INFORMATION SYSTEM OVERVIEW

Federal data collection requests have had a prodigious impact upon the information required in the individual information systems of state and local governments. To alleviate the large number of data collections imposed upon them, the Congress of the United States established the Federal Paperwork Commission in

1975 to study what they considered an unprecedented paperwork burden placed upon state and local governments and other public and nonpublic entities (Horton and Marchand, 1982:28-44). The commission's responsibility was to review the rules, regulations, and other policies and practices of the federal government as they related to the collection, processing, and dissemination of information or data sought. One of the outcomes of the commission was the assistance it provided in the passage of the Paperwork Control Act of 1980. The purpose of the act is (Paperwork Control Act of 1980, 1980: §3501):

(1) to minimize the Federal paperwork burden for individuals, small businesses, States and local governments, and other persons;

(2) to minimize the cost to the Federal Government of collecting, maintaining, using, and disseminating information;

(3) to maximize the usefulness of information collected by the Federal Government;

(4) to coordinate, integrate and, to the extent practicable and appropriate, make uniform Federal information policies and practices;

(5) to ensure that automatic data processing and telecommunications technologies are acquired and used by the Federal Government in a manner which improves service delivery and program management, increases productivity, reduces waste for persons who provide information to the Federal Government; and

(6) to ensure that the collection, maintenance, use and dissemination of information by the Federal Government is consistent with applicable laws relating to confidentiality, including section 552a of title 5, United States Code, known as the Privacy Act.

It is imperative to understand that the federal government's impact was and currently is a driving force in the conceptualization of state and local architectural frameworks for information systems. When the term information system was first used, it had various overtones associated with its meaning. To the uninitiated, an information system was (a) the cure-all to management's problems, and (b) the answer and solution to the decision-maker's complex environment. Today, public administrators are beginning to understand that a properly designed information system can help them resolve problems and provide alternative solutions to a current situation. Information systems cannot, however, make higher-order decisions. Decisions of this type are derived from a combination of structured (algorithmic) and unstructured (heuristic) consequences. During their formative years, the development of information systems was considered a part of the systems and procedures unit of large organizations; whereas, in smaller municipalities, they were part of the responsibility of an administrator that was considered a jack of all trades and master of none. Information systems were believed to be a means of coping with the ever-increasing demand for the plethora of information that top, middle, and operational managers needed to conduct their daily (short- and long-range) operations.

A. Method for the 1980s

Several methods on the design of state and local government information systems exist today. An analogy that best describes two methods available for use by information system specialists in the design of any management system are the *mystery house* and the *mansion* methods. The mystery house method coincides with building a basic one-bedroom ranch that has rooms and/or other structural changes made as the family expands and the household develops. Under this method, future expansions are not normally contemplated or thought out before designing the foundation, thus leaving little room for adequate and efficient expansion. Typical systems using this approach are developed to satisfy only one purpose, never realizing that in the future they may have to be concatenated with a larger integrated system.

Designed with the tools and knowledge of the first generation of information systems architects, the mystery house method was used in the 1950s through the early 1980s. From an organizational standpoint, data were viewed as belonging to a specific department, bureau, program, or project, with fragmentation along organizational responsibility lines a common characteristic of the method (Computerworld, 1983:53-61). Additionally, payroll systems are not seen as logical integrations of larger personnel or finance systems. The sharing of data in the mystery house is looked at with a jaundiced eye because information is power and survival is paramount.

The mansion method, as opposed to the mystery house method, uses a different generation of information systems architecture techniques commonly referred to as data base systems (DBS). Using this method, the public administrator views information as an organizational resource that belongs to the organization as a single entity. The administrator operating within this concept is futuristic, and puts into action the scientific management approach when designing an information system. Over the past several years, numerous state departments and local government units have been employing data base concepts in their information systems: New Jersey, Texas, Minnesota, Florida, Ohio, and Washington are a few. Under this method, systems designed during the immediate future will be limited to nonfragmentation on a departmental basis only. The treasury, police, education, health, and human services, and so on, departments of a state are each viewed as being individually responsible for their own information systems as are their counterparts in local municipalities. Each, in its quest to create nonfragmented systems, is facing many hardships and disappointments; however, they are progressing and, in time, successful information systems are inevitable. Local administrators employing data base concepts are mainly associated with large municipalities such as the Dallas Independent School District which, as early as 1974, installed a widescale financial information system. The Board of Education in Newark, New Jersey, is establishing data base concepts and integrating appropriate data bases throughout the district.

As time progresses, enlightened data base management specialists and information systems engineers will enable the data flowing throughout a state or local government to be viewed holistically. This can occur because the computer hardware and software necessary for a state or local information system to be installed from a totally nonfragmented approach are now available. However, to accomplish this the scientific method and use of the theories and practices of several disciplines are necessary. These include:

1. Organizational development and theories pertaining to changing the status quo
2. Organizational behavior and the team approach to managing an organization's resources
3. Operations research with its qualitative and quantitative methods to project future status
4. Data base management principles that are associated with scientific management theories of structuring, coding, and encoding data

Information systems as they are currently conceived by state and local public administrators are a hodgepodge of computer applications that the organization uses to make intelligent decisions. As few as five years ago, if ten to twenty administrators were interviewed within the same organization, inferences from the study would reveal that each interviewee had his or her own description of an information system. These administrators did not regard information systems as a structured integration of information at various levels of operation within a particular organization. Today, isolated instances of integration are occurring across the country. In the future, state and local administrators that use data base management (information center architecture) methods will be able to concatenate data throughout an entire organization.

B.   Information Center (IC) Architecture

The architecture of information centers in an organization is shown in Fig. 1 (information center structural model) as the building block for state and local government administrative information systems.[3] Five levels are shown in the structural model (column 3). This model is generic in nature and not absolute, thereby enabling adaptations to be easily made to suit individual needs. When working with the model, the main criterion that should be held constant

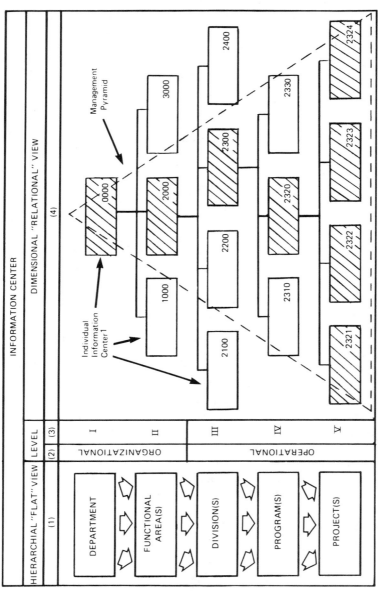

1The information contained in each individual center is: financial, facility, client, service, and other types of internal and external data that depict their goals and objectives. They also contain appropriate performance data about centers responsibilities. Columns one and four depict the same organization, except column one is a flat view and column four a relational view of the information center(s).

Fig. 1 Information center structural model.

is: No matter how large or multifaceted an organization is, it should only have one comprehensive structure. In Fig. 1 (column 2), levels I and II are referred to as organizational levels. The operational levels where the everyday functions of government occur begin at level III. Each of these levels (excluding level I) have multiple information centers associated with them. This is clearly depicted in the dimensional or relational view of the information centers (column 4). The code in the rectangles (IC) represents the key elements for processing and identifying where a particular item or information/data originated. For example, program level (IV) contains three rectangles, which signifies that three programs operate under division (level III) 2300. The shaded rectangles provide a complete example of how the code follows a step-down process. Level IV rectangles can represent a program within a municipal police, fire, or street division, or even a program within a school district, state department, or other functional entity. Each individual information center (column 4) is a total management information system (MIS) in itself, because an information center requires information to be generated, processed, and disseminated to its own top, middle, and operational management staff.

The management pyramid superimposed over the organization chart in Fig. 1 (column 4) indicates that the overall MIS requires information attributes ranging from detailed, hard, exact, past, often, and current data and their base (level V), to summary, soft, approximate, future, occasional, and delayed data at its top (level I) (Taggart, 1980:48–56). Specifically, the concept of the information center model should be used in all organizations with terms such as responsibility center, investment center, cost center, and so forth, currently found within the literature (Garrison, 1982:432–436). The rationale behind this statement stems from the fact that state and local governments (including the private sector) require a broad base of operations information. Governments need and want information relevant to their financial situation, the clients served, the services or products produced, the facilities occupied, and the personnel employed. Additionally, the information center concept allows managers responsible for the overall organization (levels I and II) to evaluate the context, inputs, processes, and products of all organization aspects. A unified information system capable of delineating, obtaining, and providing information is needed to accomplish this (Stufflebeam et al., 1972).

This section provided an overview of information systems by reviewing the Federal government's necessity for information and state and local enactments that cause the public administrator to obtain and report information in an orderly fashion, thus giving rise to the information center concept. Furthering this notion, Sec. III identifies the resources available to public administrators responsible for collecting, processing, and disseminating information to all organization levels, the public, and institutions to which they are accountable.

III. INFORMATION SYSTEM RESOURCES

Dictated by the needs and wants of outside groups and internal administrators, numerous types of information are maintained within the data banks of state and local governments. It can be assumed that needs assessment techniques can be applied against existing government data banks to help assess future directions and current requirements. By fully maximizing information systems resources available to them in advanced technology and scientific management techniques, public administrators will be able to use their information systems as a decision support system (DSS).

Until recently (the last ten years), automated on-line interactive processing of data was expensive and not considered cost justifiable; thus, this capability was not readily available to lower operating levels in state and local governments. The use of scientific management methods to design the basic architectural structures for viewing and coordinating data collection in an orderly and timely fashion was also not understood. The latter condition is the largest drawback for accessing information in state or local government data bases. Public administrators have had three options to choose from when designing information systems. Systems could be (a) manual, (b) automated, or (c) a combination of these processing modes. As a result of the proliferation of microprocessors, the majority of the information systems designed in the 1980s and beyond will be a combination of manual and automated systems. The resources necessary to design these information systems are farsighted administrators and advanced computer hardware and software.

Information systems developed for state and local governments in the 1960s and 1970s were not integrated. The system designers were first-generation information systems specialists whose understandings of systems were myoptic and followed the traditional "black box" or mystery house method. They used computer hardware that had limited capability, and communication interfacing was not fully developed. Software emphasized single-application design and followed a traditional file management system (FMS) approach where the location of the physical file of data was contained and accessed through an application program. It was during this period that users complained vehemently about data processing department/data center results. Additionally, there was a lack of understanding that the information resource belonged to the entire organization—a resource that must be managed at each individual information center level within a state or local government. The transition toward this view began in the late 1970s and will continue through the 1980s with data base system design (DBS) techniques encouraged. DBS emphasizes the integration of files and access of data through query languages and report writers. The physical residence of data contained in its files is transparent to whomever accesses the data.

A. Data Administration

Today's second-generation information systems engineers in state and local governments are employing new concepts in the design of information systems with emphasis on knowing the uses and attributes of information from a total organizational standpoint. The information center concept aids in this achievement by becoming the focal point for information system designs. Administrators responsible for coordinating an organization's comprehensive data structure must be aware of each information center's needs, wants, political constraints, and interactions with other information centers. To accomplish this, the organization of the future needs the services of a data administrator who can be an individual, group, or committee responsible for knowing the logical view of data as they relate to an overall state or local government. Logical views are referenced in DBS and signify the user's view of data versus how data are maintained and stored in the computer (the physical view of data). State and local governments with futuristic sights are performing data administration as an overview function not necessarily associated with the specific responsibilities of a data center. The magnitude of this essential function is such that it warrants a separately staffed organization reporting directly to senior administrators with its main purpose something other than the physical layouts of data.

Data administration relies heavily on scientific management principles and the viewing of data from a relational standpoint. Information must be known up and down, backwards and forwards, sideways, and related to every other piece of data (data element) within the organization. Data administration specialists should be generalists that understand deductive and inductive reasoning with a special emphasis on classifying and codifying each and every data element. A tool that can aid the data administrator in this massive effort is the data element dictionary/directory.[4]

Data element dictionaries are new undertakings within an organization, and depending upon an administrator's function, they can be seen from two different perspectives: a data processor's (DP) and a data administrator's (DA). As more sophisticated computer software is designed, both perspectives will become unified.

1. Data Element Dictionary (DP Perspective)

Data processing staffs across the country are familiar with data element dictionaries/directories as they relate to data base management system (DBMS) software packages (Kroenke, 1978). The data dictionaries in this sense are linked to intricate data description languages (DDL) that together enable the user to describe their needs from a logical view without having to know where the data physically reside in the computer. Several DBMS software packages exist, with each containing their own logical (hierarchical, network, and relational) schema of how data should be referenced and cross-referenced (Veazie, 1981). Dictionaries designed with this perspective are predominately driven by the data elements resident within the computer; they do not pertain to the full gamut of data elements resident within the macroorganization.

2.   Data Element Dictionary (DA Perspective)

The data administrator's view of a data element dictionary/directory is from the perspective of the entire organization, not the development of an isolated DBMS. The purpose of its construction is the ability to physically locate data in the computer and also several other attributes about each data element. Examples of the benefits that can be derived by state and local governments are (Jackowski, 1979:24):

1.   Increased data sharing within the organization by identifying what data are collected, when they are collected, by whom, and in what format.
2.   More timely availability of data to users by indicating where data are located and how data are stored and accessed.
3.   Reduction of respondent burden by identifying multiple collectors and users of the same data, as well as by identifying data which are collected without sufficient justification.
4.   Increased confidence in the data being collected by building the validity and reliability of data through agency-wide use of common terms, definitions and reporting procedures.
5.   Greater capacity to manage, control and/or coordinate the data collection process by developing knowledge of the data collection activities of an agency.

Data element dictionaries are a necessity to understand the flow of data within an organization; however, their development must follow scientific management principles. The reason for stressing this fact is that, if data administration is to occur in an orderly fashion, data elements must be viewed uniformly across the organization. Each data element must be categorized according to an overall schema that has divisions or subschemata to represent where a particular data element can be placed or found. The National Center for Educational Statistics (NCES) developed for state and local education agencies a series of handbooks that lend themselves to this. Based upon these and other categorization principles, structural frameworks for generic data element dictionaries can be designed for data administrator/data processing in various types of organizational settings in tomorrow's state and local governments (Jackowski, 1977).

In 1978, the Federal Education Data Acquisition Council (FEDAC) made a major attempt to understand the data elements contained in state and local educational agencies. FEDAC was initially housed within NCES and later transferred to the Office of Management and Budget (OMB). The council aimed to identify who was collecting educational data elements and then develop a plan to reduce, as much as possible, those data elements that were redundant and did not pertain to federal regulations. Extensive data review committees were initiatied with federal, state, and local participation.

B. Decentralized Processing

First-generation information systems relied heavily on the skills of information system specialists who perceived their clients as unwary participants. Administrators held this perception because clients responsible for the management of a particular state or local program were not trained to interpret and manipulate data, especially the processing of data through automated means. Today, computers are becoming as familiar as the radio or television, and information systems clients are accepting the computer as another piece of machinery. Not only are they understanding that the computer can benefit them, they are also beginning to perceive data from a multipurpose dimension. Administrators realize that data can be arrayed to suit their personal needs as well as other administrators' and that data can be extracted from data banks without a burdensome task having to be performed. This familiarity, coupled with the development of client-friendly computer software, is enhancing the notion of decentralized processing of data (Martin, 1982). When decentralized processing is contemplated or existent, state or local government administrators must insist that standards and procedures for the shared processing and use of these data be immediately developed.

Hardware compatibility needed for decentralized processing in widely dispersed geographical areas exists, and is formally entitled distributive data processing (DDP).[5] It is paramount that control and documentation of the data elements and report formats processed in this mode be centralized for decentralized concepts to function effectively and efficiently. One way of accomplishing this objective is through the data element dictionary and an organization's readiness to develop:

1. A thorough knowledge of the concepts of centralized information management within a decentralized context
2. A top-level commitment to centralized, yet dispersed, data banks
3. A disciplined information/data accountability and control system

The information resources required to design second-generation information systems are available in advanced communications hardware, client-friendly software, and control processes necessary to coordinate the information throughout the organization. The cognizant public administrator should realize that he or she is on the threshold of second-generation information systems concepts and that many person-years of logical thought processes and effort must be put forth before achieving a totally integrated system. Section IV of this chapter provides the public administrator with a review of several characteristics relevant to automated information systems.

IV. INFORMATION SYSTEM CHARACTERISTICS

State and local information systems have broad ranges of characteristics associated with the tasks they are responsible to perform. They range from general organizational characteristics to ones concerning specific development efforts. The purpose of this section is to review: (a) the general characteristics associated with system applications and the resources required to manage information systems, and (b) the characteristics of information system data centers.

A. General Characteristics

Information systems are big business and governments realized, in 1970, that application development expenditure efficiencies occur through the initiation of system and application transfer programs. A transfer program is responsible for creating an atmosphere of sharing automated information systems designed and implemented in different governments. For example, in 1972 California transferred a Highway Maintenance Management System to Minnesota and Pennsylvania; in 1981, Ohio transferred to California the Hospital Automation Systems (NASIS, 1982:33-39). Local governments, in 1976, transferred sixty-nine application programs to other state or local governments and planned no increase in the volume of transfers over the next couple of years. A majority of the local-application programs dealt with accounting, budgeting, law enforcement, and fire protection transfers (Kraemer, 1977:377-378). These illustrations represent substantial system design and programming cost savings; yet, governments tend to share among themselves on a limited basis (Kraemer, 1982).

In 1977-1978, twenty-six states transferred systems or programs into their state from either another state or the federal government; twenty-five states transferred systems or programs out for a total of fifty-one transfers. These figures can be compared with forty-four (transferred in) and nineteen (transferred out) for a total of sixty-three transfers in 1981-1982 (NASIS, 1982:33-39). The federal government, to encourage transfer programs, has provided states with funds that enable them to visit other states with systems similar to the one they are proposing to design. Federal assistance in the development of state information systems has been mainly in health and welfare, labor, and environmental protection. Additionally, the federal government has had limited amounts of funds available to states capable of designing generic information systems with turnkey caveats.

As a general rule, information systems require "as much as ten percent to 25 percent of" (Taggart, 1980:329) their design time devoted to system documentation. The need for documentation is critical to program preparation, and numerous studies have been conducted on strengthening the reasoning as to why it is an absolute requisite. A ranking of external and internal problems related to state information systems reveals that out of twelve possible problem categories (NASIS, 1982:21, 22):

1. The highest-ranking external problems were the recruitment of qualified personnel and gaining management's understanding.
2. The lowest-ranking external problems were need for a common data base and need for documentation.
3. The highest-ranking internal problems were missed programming schedules and costs too high.
4. The lowest-ranking internal problems were inaccurate output and poor operating documentation.

Governments need to develop formalized, organizationwide plans for information systems; to date, only thirty-two states have formal plans, twenty-one of which were developed since 1980. Maryland and Ohio were the first states with formal plans in 1974; and by 1976, five additional states' plans were developed (NASIS, 1982:23, 24).

B. Data Center Characteristics

Large computer mainframes account for about 26% of the total population of computers used for state information systems. Equipment used in and among the states ranges from the predominant IBM, Digital, Burroughs, and Hewlett-Packard, to Control Data and Prime computers (NASIS, 1982:Appendix B). Over the past five years, the tendency has been for large computer purchases to remain constant as a percent of total computers employed; however, a shift is occurring toward more minicomputers (Whicker, 1983:494–496), with a corresponding decrease in medium and small computers. In 1981, the method of computer procurement favored (leased or purchased) was about equal for large, medium, and small computers with minis having a preference for leased agreements (NASIS, 1982:13, 14). Under current economic conditions, state data centers are using lease-purchase agreements to spread expenditures for large hardware configurations over several fiscal years. At the same time they acquire ownership at the end of the contractual period.

Statistically, in 1981, computer inventory trends showed Texas, California, and Washington each having between sixty and seventy-nine computers as compared with Mississippi, South Dakota, Hawaii, and Tennessee with two to four. The types of computing power available to states range from machines with 16 million bytes (IBM 3033MP, Washington) to those with less than 16 thousand bytes of core storage (NASIS, 1982:Appendix B). The average mixture of personnel needed to operate a state data center in 1981 were: (a) management, 17%; (b) systems and programming, 38%; (c) operations, 28%; and (d) data entry, 17% (NASIS, 1982:17). On the average, a percentage breakdown of the expenditures associated with state data centers is: hardware, 29, software, 2, communications, 3, consultants, 6, personnel, 46, and other, 14% (NASIS, 1982:31). These expenditures are normally billed to clients through software packages designed specifically to monitor the resources a particular client uses. For example, the New Jersey Department of Human Services uses the Value Computing software package. Resource usage can be in hours of systems or programming time, seconds of CPU/KWS, seconds of disk or tape channel time, number of lines printed, and so on.

Regarding the instructional method used to train personnel in a state data center, approximately 50% is formal internal training with the majority of external training supplied by a vendor or consultant. Systems analysis and application programmers receive the predominant amount of training, accounting for about 48% with a client's staff accounting for at least 27% (NASIS, 1982:20). As data base software use continues to increase, future training endeavors will be heavier in systems programming and client awareness (Martin, 1983).

V. CONCLUSION

The impact that federal paperwork, the population explosion, and high technology have had on the design of state and local government information systems is astonishing. The Congress of the United States, cognizant of this issue, passed the Paperwork Control Act of 1980 to minimize duplicate and unwarranted information generated by legislative enactments. An overview of information systems concepts reveals that a causal relationship exists between the federal government's requirements, technological advancements, and the development of state and local information systems. The federal government, because of the need for various and sundry types of information, is the driving force in the conceptualization of the architectural frameworks that are crucial to the concatenation and extraction of information. Aided by the population explosion of the 1960s, the pure volume of information required by the public administrator is catastrophic. These reasons coupled with high technology (advancements in computers and telecommunications) brought about present-day information system theories and concepts.

Numerous problems existed in the past that kept the public administrator from using information system technologies to their fullest potential:

the newness of the computer, nontransferability of computer application software, and systems software incompatibility. Computer hardware and telecommunications have expanded their horizons with the use of very large-scale circuitry and are no longer a limiting factor. Likewise, software transferability and utility capabilities have advanced through the use of data base management techniques. And in the future they will offer the same potential that current-day hardware is now capable of performing. An awareness of information systems architecture and accompanying data administration concepts, with their underlying principles of integrated nonfragmented data structure techniques, is of paramount importance. Synoptically, public administrators of the 1950s, 1960s, and 1970s were placed in a state of "future shock" as they witnessed (a) the growth in paperwork and (b) the uneasiness of being unfamiliar with high technology terminology. Technological advances have occurred at the rate of 30% per year.

This chapter suggests several implications or recommendations for future public administrators contemplating the design of a state or local government information system. The following propositional inventory of future trends is offered:

1. Public administrators of the 1980s and beyond must become technically astute as information systems engineers.
2. State and local administrators that use data administration and data base management methods will be able to concatenate data throughout an entire organization.
3. Enlightened data base management specialists and information systems engineers will require the data flowing throughout a state or local government to be recorded in data element dictionaries.
4. Information resident within state and local government data banks can be assessed to determine possible future directions and information requirements.
5. Second-generation information systems engineers in state and local governments will emphasize knowing the uses and attributes of information from a total organizational standpoint.
6. The organization of the future necessitates the services of a data administrator responsible for knowing the logical view of data as it relates to a particular state or local government.
7. State and local governments with futuristic sights are performing data administration as an overview function not necessarily associated with the specific responsibilities of a data center.
8. Public administrators should realize they are on the threshold of second-generation information systems concepts and that many person-years of

logical thought processes and effort must be put forth before a totally integrated system can be spawned.

9. The utilization of data base software requires future training endeavors to be heavier in the area of systems programming and clients' awareness.

NOTES

1. Systems designed in the DSS mode use various technological forecasting techniques to project future states about the conditions of an organization. They provide management with the means to choose a course of action that is based upon a review of several variables about a condition. The DSS module of an information system is used when questions are asked about data resident in the system.

2. Information engineering concepts came into existence as a need to understand the structure, classification, and codification of data. They are ". . . an integrated set of analysis and design methodologies that can significantly reduce today's application development and maintenance bottleneck" (see Finklestein and Martin, 1981:1–43).

3. Within the context of this chapter, the term information center refers to an operating/administrative unit within an organization. See *Accountant's Handbook*, 1970:4.4. Martin uses the term information center in his textbook, *Application Development Without Programmers* (1982), to mean an organizational unit within a data center whose overriding objective is "to greatly speed up the creation of applications which end users require."

4. Data element dictionaries/directories contain information about the uses and attributes of each data element resident in the data banks of an organization. Dictionaries define each data element; whereas, directories contain less descriptive information.

5. Distributive data processing is the ability of two or more computers located in separate geographical areas to communicate among and between themselves; this enables state and local governments to utilize computers as the main form of communication within an organization.

REFERENCES

Danziger, J. N., Dutton, W. H., Kling, B., and Kramer, K. L. (1982). *Computers and Politics: High Technology in American Local Governments*. Columbia University Press, New York.

Finklestein, C. and Martin J. (1981). *Computerworld* reprint of issues dated May 11, 1981, May 25, 1981, June 1, 1981, June 8, 1981, and June 15, 1981, on principles of information engineering. Computerworld, Framingham, Mass.

Freedman, A. (1981). *The Computer Glossary: It's Not Just a Glossary*! The Computer Language Company, New York.

Garrison, Ray H. (1982). *Managerial Accounting*, 3rd ed. Business Publications Inc., Plano, Texas.

Goodbody, T. (1983). Information systems engineering. *Computerworld 17*(9): Depth/11–18.

Horton, F. W. and Marchand, D. A., eds. (1982). *Information Management in Public Administration*. Information Resources Press, Arlington, Va.

Jackowski, E. M. (1977). An educational data element dictionary. *Journal of Systems Management 28*(8):38–43.

Jackowski, E. M. (1979). Uses and attributes of an educational data element dictionary. *Association of Education Data Systems 17*(7–9):24–27.

Kraemer, K. L. (1977). Local government, information systems, and technology transfers: Evaluating some common assertations about computer application transfers. *Public Administration Review 4*:368–382.

Kroenke, D. (1978). *Database: A Professional's Primer*. Science Research Associates, Chicago.

Martin, J. (1975). *Computer Data-Base Organization*. Prentice-Hall, Englewood Cliffs, N.J.

Martin, J. (1982). *Application Development Without Programmers*. Prentice-Hall, Englewood Cliffs, N.J.

National Association for State Information Systems and the States (1980). *Information Systems Technology in State Government*. The National Association for State Information Systems, Lexington, Ky.

National Association for State Information Systems and the States (1982). *Information Systems Technology in State Government*. The National Association for State Information Systems, Lexington, Ky.

New Jersey State League of Municipalities, New Jersey County and Municipal Government Study Commission, and New Jersey Department of Community Affairs (1982). *Computer Use: A Guide for Local Officials in New Jersey*. New Jersey League of Municipalities, Trenton.

Northrop, A., Dutton, W. H., and Kraemer, K. L. (1982). The management of computer applications in local government. *Public Administration Review 3*:234–243.

Stufflebeam, D. I. et al. (1971). *Educational Evaluation and Decision Making*. F. E. Peacock, Itasca, Ill.

Taggart, William M., Jr. (1980). *Information Systems: An Introduction to Computers in Organizations*. Allyn and Bacon, Boston.

Whicker, M. L. (1983). Budgets and computers in government. In Rabin, J. and Lynch, T. D., eds., *Handbook on Public Budgeting and Financial Management*. Marcel Dekker, New York.

Wixon, R., Kell, W. G., and Bedford, N. M., eds. (1970). *Accountants' Handbook*, 5th ed. The Ronald Press, New York.

Veazie, S. M. (1981). Data handling takes sophisticated effort. *Hospitals 55*(20): 115–121.

9

Fiscal Stress in the American States

David P. Rebovich Department of Political Science, Rider College, Lawrenceville, New Jersey

I. INTRODUCTION

In the early 1970s Ira Sharkansky, an eminent political scientist and student of state government, claimed:

> too many people malign the states unjustly. State governments are not the weak sisters of the federal system. They provide an increasing portion of the money for domestic services. (1972:53)

Professor Sharkansky endeavored to understand and publicize the increasing importance of state government in the lives of Americans. Although intelligently and judiciously critical of the states in a number of areas, Sharkansky believed that state government did and should play an integral role in the American political system.

These views were not shared by many other political scientists or citizens in the 1970s. The states were seen as havens of ". . . corrupt, evil or simply ineffective politicians and bureaucrats" (Sharkansky, 1972:1) who were incapable of, or unwilling to, address economic, educational, racial, and urban problems. Few scholars emphasized the responsibilities and accomplishments of state governments in providing a broad range of goods and services or the states' potential to make further contributions to the public good.

By the end of the decade the states did begin to receive notice. This attention was not due to the states' impressive accomplishments. Rather, the states entered the political limelight because of tax and expenditure cuts that they enacted. Students of government, somewhat ironically, became concerned with what a decreased state role in revenue raising and spending would mean for American society, the economy, and politics (Rose, 1982; Stedman, 1982). In recent years state governments have been subjected to careful study in an effort to understand state policy-making and perhaps reform it.

A necessary and perhaps the paramount prerequisite of purposeful state government is fiscal solvency—the ability to obtain revenues to fund the costs of government operations and policies. In a democratic political system, governments can achieve fiscal solvency only if the citizenry is willing and able to pay the costs of government. Throughout the 1970s, state government costs grew considerably. As spenders of public monies, the states have become more important and powerful in the American political system. However, within a relatively few years, the ability and willingness of citizens and particular state governments to support policies and expenditures have varied considerably.

Following nearly twenty years of extended growth in revenue, twenty-one states in 1978 and thirty-three states in 1979 enacted tax reductions (Wright, 1982:252). These reductions were possible because many states had accumulated large budget surpluses. During the 1970s, the states were aggressive revenue raisers; increases in state taxes and high inflation rates produced large revenue gains for state treasuries. In many states, citizens questioned the need for huge budget surpluses and, indeed, the increasing levels of state and local taxes and expenditures. The conservative mood that would carry Ronald Reagan to the White House manifested itself first at the state and local levels in the form of the so-called taxpayers revolt (Rose, 1982:3).

Citizens across the country, spurred by California's Proposition 13, called for decreases in taxes and expenditures at all levels of government. In twenty-eight states legislative resolutions calling for a balanced federal budget were approved. Governors echoed the concerns of voters. At their national conferences in 1978 and 1980, the governors criticized the growth of federal spending and federal programs to aid the states and cities. They complained that large federal deficits perpetuated high inflation rates and the conditions attached to federal grants compromised the ability of the states to govern effectively. The chairman of the National Governors' Association stated: "to me, there is no doubt that the federal umbilical cord is beginning to strangle us. If something can't be done, then I fear that my successors . . . ultimately will be relegated to mere clerks of the federal establishment (Broder, 1980:C7).

Soon after Ronald Reagan was elected, some governors began to modify their views. President Reagan's "New Federalism" plan, which the President hoped would be implemented throughout the 1980s, proposed

> a phased swap of some $47 billion in programs beginning in 1984
> . . . (and) . . . a dramatic shift of some 40 social, transportation and

community development programs—and revenues to help pay for
these in the early phases—to states . . . (and) . . . a "swap" of the
three principle welfare programs for the poor. The federal government would assume the full costs of the Medicaid health programs
while the States took over food stamps and Aid to Families with
Dependent Children (AFDC). (*Congressional Quarterly Weekly
Report*. Jan. 30, 1982:147,148)

Many governors reacted favorably to the creation of bloc grants in place of
several categorical grants that detailed the purposes for which federal monies
could be spent by the states. However, during 1982 and in early 1983, governors
of both parties campaigned vigorously against President Reagan's proposed swap
of programs with the states. The argument most frequently made was that
income maintenance programs were so important to American society that they
should remain a federal responsibility. In March 1983, the National Governors'
Association (NGA) adopted a resolution that called for the federal government
to reduce its deficits by slowing military spending and certain domestic expenditures. The NGA recommended a continuation of federal funding at current
levels for most social programs for the poor (*The New York Times*, March
2, 1983:1).

Why had the governors' perspectives changed so dramatically in a few
short years? One explanation involves political factors; Democrats sat in more
state houses throughout the country than in 1980. And, according to opinion
polls, President Reagan's popularity had declined among the electorate. But
behind these political factors was the reality of state fiscal conditions. Halfway
through President Reagan's term, the states had already endured large cuts in
federal aid; high interest rates meant high borrowing costs for the states; and, the
recession had eroded state tax collections while increasing pressures for more
state expenditures. In late 1982 and early 1983, numerous states had either
approved or were considering tax increases to cover large projected deficits
(Gold and Benker, 1983:i).

These changes in state perspectives and policies between 1978 and 1983
are more dramatic than one expects to encounter in the American political
system. These seemingly contradictory developments in such a short time span
also suggest that it is difficult to generalize about the interests and capabilities of
the American states. However, these recent events do reveal a variety of factors
about the states that will continue to influence their performance:

1. The states' role in the American political system has grown considerably;
   state revenues and expenditures have increased to the point that in the late
   1970s citizens called for tax and spending cuts.
2. The states have been successful in raising their own-source revenues but still
   depend on federal aid in order to provide citizens with high levels of goods
   and services.

3. The states, as one would hope and expect in a democracy, are subject to citizen pressures to increase and/or decrease expenditures and taxation.
4. The states can be the beneficiaries or the victims of national economic trends over which they have negligible control.

In order to understand the conditions of state governments, one scholar recommends that we view the states as "middlemen" in an intergovernmental game. According to Deil S. Wright, ". . . state governments are the focal points for enormous political, fiscal and other pressures exerted by national officials on the one hand and local officials on the other" (1982:262). Whereas the states have demonstrably improved their ability to raise revenues and deliver goods and services to the public, these pressures challenge state officials to formulate and adopt purposeful policies and maintain fiscal solvency.

II. STATE FISCAL STRESS

As the states entered 1983, a variety of pressures contributed to making the states' fiscal conditions "exceedingly grim," according to a survey conducted by the National Conference of State Legislatures (NCSL). The NCSL staff reported that:

> at the end of the current fiscal year (FY 83), 19 states project deficits in their general funds and another 12 states anticipate having a year end balance of 1 percent or less of their annual general fund spending. At the other extreme, only six states expect a balance of more than 5 percent, which has traditionally been regarded as the minimum prudent balance. . . . Thirty-five states have reduced their spending for the current fiscal year below the level in their original budgets for Fiscal Year 1983. . . . The reason for these cutbacks is a plague of revenue shortfalls that has afflicted nearly every state. As the recession has persisted much longer than expected, all but three states have seen their tax revenue flow in more slowly than antici-pated in their budgets. (Benker and Gold, 1983:i)

At the same time that states were experiencing revenue shortfalls, unemploy-ment rates were at a post-World War II high. The already heavy demands made on state governments for goods and services also increased because of the reces-sion. Most states in 1983 were faced with the prospects of cutting back pro-grams, deferring capital expenditures, laying-off employees, and increasing state taxes.

This crisis confronted by the states is called *fiscal stress*. Specifically, fiscal stress refers to the ". . . gap between the needs and expectations of citizens and government employees for government services and benefits, and the inability of the economy to generate enough economic growth to expand (or even sustain, in some places) tax-supported programs without putting unacceptable demands on tax-payers' take-home pay" (Levine, 1980:1). Fiscal stress is both an *objective* and *subjective* condition. It is objective in the sense that the fiscal conditions of the states depend on economic trends, constitutional authority, and limits of state governments and the statutory requirements of state governments to provide certain goods and services to the public. It is subjective in the sense that the fiscal conditions of the states depend on public demands and preferences for state expenditures and the public's willingness to make sacrifices in the forms of increased taxation or program cuts.

Charles Levine (1980:8) offers a list of factors that can impinge on the fiscal conditions of government. His list captures the objective and many of the subjective aspects of fiscal stress. Levine presents ten factors related to fiscal stress and divides them into two categories, situational factors and management factors. These factors can be readily adapted to the analysis of state government fiscal conditions.

Situation factors that can contribute to fiscal stress are:

1. The economic base of the states
2. The states' taxing capacity
3. The organization of taxing and spending authority within the states and between state and local governments
4. The scope of state government service responsibility
5. Citizen service demands and expectations
6. Interest-group and public employee demands

These situational factors are not, Levine suggests, in the short-run readily amenable to change by state government officials and are the proximate causes of fiscal stress. As discussed previously, these factors can and do change and recently have done so in a way that has made achieving fiscal solvency at the state level more challenging.

Managerial factors are:

1. State government decision-making methods, particularly those regarding budgeting
2. State resource mixes; the means by which states generate revenue
3. Productivity improvements in state agencies and programs
4. Cutbacks and terminations of state programs and personnel

These managerial factors contain policies and procedures that are amenable to change to address fiscal stress (Levine, 1980:8). However, the effort to effect changes in these areas usually results in political conflict, given the high demand and resource scarcity that marks periods of fiscal stress.

Progress has been made in identifying various factors that may contribute to fiscal stress. However, it is still difficult for students of government and public officials to predict the occurrence of fiscal stress or measure levels of stress (Bahl, 1980:20). This makes averting fiscal stress, or preparing for it, more difficult, and ultimately complicates efforts at managing fiscal stress if it does occur.

Although fiscal stress is a possible threat to all fifty states, situational factors can and often do vary from state to state. Although state officials have limited influence over these situational factors, it is important to attempt to identify which factors are primarily responsible for the fiscal problems experienced by particular states. This determination is useful for several reasons. It would assist state officials in their efforts to: project the demands made on state governments; and, consider appropriate and financially realistic policies in response to these demands. It would enable students of state government to evaluate the reasons for, and the feasibility of, the policies pursued by particular states in response to their specific situations.

Along the same lines, it cannot be assumed that each state government possesses the same ability to change the managerial factors listed previously. Some state constitutions and political processes make bold policy changes more difficult to effect. In others, political forces—historically strong groups within and outside of government and groups mobilized by fiscal decline—can act as barriers to even the strongest governors and legislatures. The likelihood of managerial reforms often depends on certain "structural" situational factors. In some states, local governments have significant spending authority. Under these circumstances, changes in state decision-making methods may have a limited impact on actual expenditure policies within a state.

Two other qualifications about managerial factors must be mentioned. During fiscal stress, state governments are likely to attempt to increase efficiency in program operations and encourage savings in nonessential programs. However desirable efficiency and savings are, the student of fiscal stress should be cognizant of the amount of savings produced by such managerial reforms when measured against demands for goods and services. Productivity improvements themselves are unlikely to balance budgets (Bahl, 1980:105). Second, particular attention should be devoted to the substance of government spending and revenue-raising during fiscal stress. The relevant questions are: To what extent do state policies have an immediate impact on the expenditure-revenue gap?; and, What is the relationship of policies to the factors that are causing fiscal stress? Managerial or policy changes (e.g., cutbacks in goods, services, and personnel; terminations of programs; or, revenue-raising reforms) may indeed balance state budgets. But, new state policies may make no contribution to overcoming the circumstances that give rise to fiscal stress. Indeed, one should query if a state's policies will, in the long-run, intensify fiscal stress.

III. STUDYING FISCAL STRESS: THE BUDGETARY APPROACH AND THE EXPENDITURE DETERMINANTS APPROACH

Two approaches have been used for attempting to predict and measure fiscal stress. Budgetary studies have concentrated on examining the relationship and balance between service level needs and the revenues available to the states (Bahl, 1980:32). Expenditure determinants studies focus on identifying factors and trends that are likely to lead to substantial demands on state governments for goods and services (Bahl, 1980:92-94). Both approaches provide information useful for understanding state fiscal conditions.

State budgets provide tangible evidence of demands made on that governments—"citizen service demands and expectations"—, objects of state expenditure, and the statutory responsibilities of state governments—"the scope of state government service responsibility." The study of state budgets over time reveals levels and the scope of expenditure that, given state budget processes and politics, are difficult to change. Budgets also provide information on state revenue raising—how states raise revenue and the extent to which states rely on particular revenue sources.

Expenditure determinants studies provide information on demographic and economic base factors—population growth, urbanization, per capita income, economic growth rates—that are often related to the substance and levels of citizen demands and government tax capacity. Some ambitious studies have attempted to establish statistical relationships between state government expenditure and revenue raising and state economic and demographic characteristics. The factors most frequently identified as increasing state government expenditure are increases in school-age children, welfare recipients, and urbanization (Bahl, 1980:94). No definite relationships have been established.

As mentioned previously, the significance of these factors for determining citizen demand for state government expenditure should be considered within the context of a state's budgeting history and political circumstances (Maxwell and Aronson, 1977:36). A state may be experiencing increasingly higher scores on an expenditure determinants scale but not increase its expenditures significantly. This lack of response could be due to the lack of policy development in a particular area because of marginal support among active voters for certain expenditures. In this sense, expenditure determinants studies by themselves do not capture the complex political dimension of state fiscal policies.

A similar criticism can be made of budgetary studies. Almost all the states are constitutionally or statutorily required to end the fiscal year with balanced budgets. The fact that states do balance their budgets and end the fiscal year with surpluses by no means implies that states have overcome fiscal stress. Balanced budgets may hide the fact that certain expenditures have been temporarily deferred or that express and latent demands of citizens have not been satisfied.

With these important qualifications and considerations in mind, it is more comfortable to discuss state expenditure and revenue-raising trends and their fiscal conditions as states entered the 1980s. The focus will be on: the growth of state service responsibility; expenditures and revenues; situational factors influencing state fiscal policies; changes in state managerial factors, particularly state resource mixes; political considerations relevant to state expenditure and tax policies; and, some differences among the states. This chapter will conclude with a brief discussion of state responses to fiscal stress in 1982 and 1983.

IV. STATE GOVERNMENT EXPENDITURES

Analyses of state expenditures and revenues are frequently based on combined state and local figures. Since some state governments may perform functions that are in other states local responsibilities, comparing state government expenditures is a difficult task (Maxwell and Aronson, 1977:3). Isolating state expenditures for particular goods and services and comparing funding levels across the states do not solve this problem given the differences in state responsibilities. A more meaningful method to compare state expenditures is to calculate the per capita amount spent by both state and local government in each state for particular functions. It is important to distinguish state responsibilities from local ones. But, local governments have limited revenue-raising capabilities, and state governments are paying a larger portion of the costs of local programs. This trend suggests that increases in citizen demands, at the local level, for expenditures will ultimately reach state governments. In the absence of increased state revenues, these local demands will contribute to fiscal stress.

State and local expenditures have dramatically increased since World War II and, since 1960, have significantly increased as a percentage of the gross national product. State and local governments have also come to spend a larger proportion of the public funds expended in the United States. In 1948, the federal government was responsible for 67.5% of public expenditures; state and local governments for 32.5%. By 1980 the state and local figures had increased to over 40% of total government spending (Maddox and Fuquay, 1981:190).

The various functions for which the states have appropriated large amounts of money in 1980 are detailed in Table 1. As has been the case for many decades, education dominates state expenditures, although in recent years welfare and health care have become larger items in state budgets. The variation of expenditures among the states, per capita and for specific functions, is particularly interesting. Table 2 reveals that most northern industrialized states spend more per capita than southern rural states. This suggests that public service levels are lower in southern states than in the North. Given the shift in economic activity to the Sunbelt states in the 1970s, one can project that some southeastern and southwestern states will be required to increase government expenditures in the future (Bahl, 1980:78). While there is already evidence that substantiates this prediction, it should be noted that the lower level of state expenditures and taxation in the Sunbelt is considered an important factor for its economic growth.

Most southern states allocate larger percentages of their expenditures to education and health care than do northern states. The latter devote a significantly larger portion of their budgets to welfare payments and programs. Indeed, one scholar claims that ". . . if southern states were to make the same per capita welfare expenditures as northern states, the north–south gap in per capita expenditures would be cut from 17 to 9 percent" (Bahl, 1980:78). A relevant statistic that might cause some surprise is that public employment levels per capita are higher in the southern states than in northern ones. One reason for this difference may have to do with labor economies of scale; in the more densely populated northern states, fewer employees are needed to deliver services.

Nearly all the states (Vermont is the exception) require balanced budgets, and many have adopted specific spending limitations (The Council of State Governments, 1982:368). Nonetheless, state governments do borrow money, primarily to finance capital expenditures. Once again, there is variation in state borrowing practices. States in the northeast have, by comparison, more long-term outstanding debts than other states. Interest payments on debts and repayment make claims on state revenues, and these are considered state government expenditures.

State and local expenditures have grown since 1950. It should be noted, however, that federal aid to state and local governments has increased as a percentage of state and local revenues and thus expenditure. This suggests that the expenditure levels of state and local government reflect and are dependent on federal funding. To generalize about state expenditure growth and levels, one must understand the relationship of federal aid to state expenditures. To the extent that state expenditure growth is related to federal aid, the spending patterns and fiscal performance of state and local governments are uncertain measures of state fiscal performance and capabilities. This consideration is particularly important given the cuts in federal aid to the states enacted in the Reagan administration.

Federal aid impacts on state expenditures in another way. The federal government has added large sums of money to state and local coffers via revenue sharing, categorical grants, and bloc grants. In certain cases, states are required to provide matching funds to receive federal aid. One study estimated that in the period from 1958 to 1972, state funds to match federal aid subsumed approximately one-third of the increase in state own-source resources (Wright, 1982: 251–252). What this means is that the states have gained large amounts of money from the federal government but have had to spend large amounts of

Table 1 Direct General Expenditure of State and Local Governments, for Selected Items, by State: 1979–80 (in millions of dollars)[a]

State or other jurisdiction	Total	Other than capital outlay	Education		Public welfare	Health and hospitals	Highways		Interest on general debt
			Total	Local schools only			Total	Other than capital outlay	
United States	$367,339.9	$314,389.6	$133,210.8	$92,930.0	$45,552.2	$32,173.5	$33,173.5	$14,177.8	$14,746.8
Alabama	5,159.8	4,428.9	1,992.9	1,175.1	549.8	697.4	518.1	251.7	168.9
Alaska	2,502.7	2,001.4	725.0	539.0	115.2	60.1	223.6	88.2	216.4
Arizona	4,204.7	3,351.7	1,828.6	1,176.7	185.3	299.3	427.0	135.4	121.8
Arkansas	2,742.3	2,264.5	1,084.5	748.3	322.3	266.1	406.4	173.4	65.0
California	43,412.7	39,177.7	15,062.8	9,967.9	6,761.5	3,641.2	2,311.9	1,264.9	902.0
Colorado	4,558.4	3,877.5	1,924.3	1,295.7	402.1	383.5	474.2	222.2	124.2
Connecticut	4,918.8	4,362.6	1,715.5	1,311.4	658.9	306.2	356.7	189.2	289.1
Delaware	1,076.5	932.3	435.3	249.6	98.3	49.2	99.3	47.6	63.2
Florida	12,753.7	10,545.9	4,486.0	3,309.1	760.8	1,512.0	1,201.6	369.6	436.6
Georgia	7,462.6	6,067.4	2,602.2	1,887.3	707.1	1,179.5	820.5	256.1	206.9
Hawaii	1,876.8	1,524.4	559.7	337.6	231.9	136.7	130.3	38.8	112.2
Idaho	1,289.1	1,074.2	483.6	317.8	116.4	117.6	170.6	63.3	28.8
Illinois	18,122.1	15,394.0	6,407.0	4,630.2	2,543.1	1,152.2	1,838.9	720.5	738.7
Indiana	6,826.7	5,784.6	2,920.0	1,955.8	662.6	732.9	692.7	281.5	203.4
Iowa	4,910.6	4,192.6	2,032.6	1,355.3	550.3	506.1	697.8	338.1	81.8
Kansas	3,748.2	2,955.6	1,376.8	920.0	373.6	303.1	570.0	230.9	114.8
Kentucky	5,406.3	4,191.7	1,853.5	1,149.8	648.3	334.1	981.7	240.0	358.4
Louisiana	6,558.2	5,495.4	2,242.9	1,550.9	645.6	749.1	793.6	324.6	306.2
Maine	1,581.0	1,399.5	544.0	396.9	264.4	71.9	211.0	116.7	63.8
Maryland	7,626.1	6,251.0	2,691.0	1,854.5	756.0	607.7	679.4	234.8	323.3
Massachusetts	10,301.3	9,419.5	3,230.4	2,653.6	1,800.6	848.1	616.8	347.3	493.0
Michigan	17,401.8	15,234.9	6,442.8	4,404.4	2,705.5	1,620.1	1,263.4	536.8	569.7

Minnesota	7,723.6	6,384.1	2,658.8	1,877.0	1,035.6	640.5	892.3	385.0	318.3
Mississippi	3,412.2	2,866.1	1,264.7	776.9	393.0	433.8	492.8	192.1	99.9
Missouri	6,294.6	5,275.9	2,324.9	1,689.5	659.3	669.8	701.4	280.3	164.9
Montana	1,392.0	1,121.9	544.2	422.0	107.8	75.8	244.5	100.0	43.9
Nebraska	2,424.6	1,965.1	972.9	651.6	191.0	224.6	359.7	127.2	52.1
Nevada	1,491.9	1,153.3	459.5	332.8	77.0	142.0	188.3	64.9	57.3
New Hampshire	1,233.9	1,0582.	432.7	298.6	167.9	59.4	176.7	93.6	70.6
New Jersey	12,427.1	11,058.2	4,452.4	3,403.6	1,532.1	796.0	780.3	430.3	591.9
New Mexico	2,156.0	1,758.4	924.2	631.7	166.4	177.2	252.7	92.4	83.6
New York	38,689.9	35,009.1	11,774.0	8,748.8	6,286.7	3,459.1	2,159.9	1,097.3	2,692.7
North Carolina	7,639.3	6,561.1	3,186.4	2,060.6	769.3	727.7	702.4	289.2	185.4
North Dakota	1,201.2	952.7	426.5	259.5	91.6	52.7	197.8	72.0	35.9
Ohio	15,447.0	13,022.3	5,929.2	4,334.4	1,827.7	1,624.5	1,180.6	535.4	509.0
Oklahoma	4,254.6	3,505.2	1,683.2	1,087.6	548.2	353.7	454.4	210.8	120.7
Oregon	5,000.9	4,170.9	1,955.4	1,318.9	476.3	286.7	473.2	188.2	314.2
Pennsylvania	17,429.8	15,328.4	6,123.3	4,761.5	2,803.4	1,112.6	1,128.8	740.7	1,067.9
Rhode Island	1,661.0	1,509.2	549.2	349.0	298.7	139.9	83.9	44.8	109.0
South Carolina	3,958.4	3,405.5	1,698.5	1,061.1	363.1	564.7	286.6	141.6	95.7
South Dakota	1,094.6	906.6	399.3	270.4	104.7	49.7	205.7	108.3	39.2
Tennessee	5,928.6	4,022.0	2,113.4	1,380.9	596.0	762.1	688.5	278.4	229.2
Texas	19,376.0	15,204.6	8,238.6	5,643.9	1,500.9	1,779.8	2,285.3	613.8	696.2
Utah	2,359.0	1,827.4	1,073.6	699.3	188.0	148.4	279.3	83.9	61.6
Vermont	817.5	719.8	321.1	190.8	95.5	44.4	100.3	60.9	41.3
Virginia	7,700.0	6,420.7	2,909.9	1,960.1	768.2	682.5	935.0	371.0	282.7
Washington	7,358.9	5,992.8	3,009.1	2,031.1	788.0	459.5	802.0	297.0	230.3
West Virginia	2,966.1	2,372.1	1,068.1	753.9	253.7	210.5	601.5	210.4	151.3
Wisconsin	8,464.2	7,423.9	3,292.8	2,145.1	1,227.5	656.6	917.4	494.0	261.1
Wyoming	1,100.0	804.9	430.3	297.0	42.8	96.2	179.6	49.7	57.0
Dist. of Col.	1,896.6	1,761.9	383.4	305.6	332.3	178.1	75.2	53.2	95.8

aNote: Because of rounding, detail may not add to totals.

Source: U.S. Bureau of the Census. (1979–1980). Governmental Finances in 1979–80.

Table 2 Per Capita Direct General Expenditure of State and Local Governments, for Selected Items, by State: 1979–1980 (in dollars)

State or other jurisdiction	Total	Other than capital outlay	Education		Public welfare	Health and hospitals	Highways		
			Total	Local schools only			Total	Other than capital outlay	Interest on general debt
United States	$1,621.77	$1,388.00	$ 588.11	$ 410.28	$201.11	$142.04	$147.04	$ 84.47	$ 65.11
Alabama	1,326.42	1,138.52	512.32	302.08	141.33	179.28	133.19	68.48	43.41
Alaska	6,256.70	5,003.53	1,812.41	1,347.39	288.06	150.16	558.94	338.60	541.02
Arizona	1,547.00	1,233.17	672.77	432.92	68.16	110.12	157.10	107.28	44.83
Arkansas	1,200.13	991.04	474.62	327.50	141.06	116.46	177.84	101.98	28.43
California	1,834.16	1,655.23	636.39	421.14	285.67	153.84	97.67	44.23	38.11
Colorado	1,577.85	1,342.16	666.09	448.50	139.18	132.73	164.12	87.24	42.99
Connecticut	1,582.63	1,403.67	551.96	421.93	211.99	98.51	114.78	53.90	93.02
Delaware	1,809.18	1,566.82	731.58	419.42	165.16	82.76	166.85	86.91	106.29
Florida	1,309.42	1,082.74	460.58	339.74	78.11	155.24	123.36	85.42	44.82
Georgia	1,365.77	1,110.43	476.24	345.41	129.41	215.87	150.17	103.20	37.86
Hawaii	1,944.88	1,579.69	580.05	349.81	240.29	141.70	135.01	94.81	116.31
Idaho	1,365.57	1,137.97	512.25	336.69	123.29	124.54	180.73	113.67	30.55
Illinois	1,587.15	1,348.23	561.13	405.52	222.72	100.91	161.05	97.95	64.70
Indiana	1,243.47	1,053.65	531.88	356.25	120.70	133.49	126.17	74.91	37.06
Iowa	1,685.76	1,439.29	697.78	465.25	188.91	173.75	239.54	123.49	28.09
Kansas	1,586.20	1,250.76	582.65	389.34	158.10	128.26	241.23	143.49	48.58
Kentucky	1,476.72	1,144.96	506.27	314.06	177.09	91.26	268.14	202.59	97.91
Louisiana	1,560.00	1,307.18	533.52	368.92	153.57	178.19	188.77	111.55	72.84
Maine	1,405.33	1,244.04	483.52	352.82	234.99	63.87	187.57	83.82	56.70
Maryland	1,808.85	1,482.70	638.87	439.87	179.32	144.15	161.15	105.45	76.69
Massachusetts	1,795.59	1,641.88	563.08	462.55	313.85	147.83	107.52	46.97	85.93
Michigan	1,879.65	1,645.60	695.92	475.74	292.24	174.99	136.46	78.48	61.53

Minnesota	1,894.42	1,565.87	652.16	460.40	254.00	157.09	218.87	124.43	78.07
Mississippi	1,353.51	1,136.89	501.66	308.16	155.91	172.09	195.48	119.29	39.61
Missouri	1,280.18	1,072.99	472.83	343.60	134.09	136.22	142.65	85.64	33.54
Montana	1,768.80	1,425.57	691.48	536.24	136.94	96.27	310.62	183.64	55.77
Nebraska	1,544.35	1,251.71	619.70	415.02	121.67	143.05	229.12	148.11	33.18
Nevada	1,867.19	1,443.35	575.07	416.48	96.31	177.78	235.68	154.46	71.72
New Hampshire	1,339.74	1,148.92	469.79	324.24	182.31	64.45	191.89	90.27	76.70
New Jersey	1,687.55	1,501.66	604.61	462.19	208.06	108.09	105.96	47.54	80.37
New Mexico	1,658.44	1,352.59	710.94	485.92	128.03	136.31	194.36	123.29	64.29
New York	2,203.67	1,944.02	670.62	498.31	358.07	197.02	123.02	60.52	153.37
North Carolina	1,300.53	1,116.98	542.45	350.80	130.97	123.89	119.57	70.34	31.56
North Dakota	1,839.55	1,458.96	653.09	397.37	140.33	80.69	302.88	192.61	54.94
Ohio	1,430.67	1,206.10	549.15	401.44	169.28	150.46	109.35	59.75	47.14
Oklahoma	1,406.47	1,158.73	556.44	359.53	181.22	116.94	150.20	80.52	39.91
Oregon	1,899.31	1,584.09	731.26	500.91	180.90	108.87	179.72	108.24	119.33
Pennsylvania	1,468.76	1,291.68	515.99	401.24	236.24	93.76	95.12	32.70	89.99
Rhode Island	1,753.96	1,593.62	579.96	368.57	315.39	147.73	88.61	41.25	115.13
South Carolina	1,269.13	1,091.87	544.55	340.20	116.42	181.05	91.89	46.50	30.67
South Dakota	1,586.37	1,313.89	578.72	391.92	151.74	71.96	298.08	141.22	56.86
Tennessee	1,291.35	1,072.08	460.33	300.79	129.82	165.99	149.98	89.33	49.92
Texas	1,361.82	1,068.64	579.04	396.68	105.49	125.09	160.62	117.48	48.93
Utah	1,614.64	1,250.80	734.81	478.64	128.66	101.59	191.15	133.71	42.16
Vermont	1,599.83	1,408.64	628.32	373.35	186.97	86.81	196.18	77.04	80.73
Virginia	1,440.33	1,201.03	544.03	366.65	143.69	127.67	174.89	105.50	52.88
Washington	1,781.81	1,451.04	728.60	491.80	190.79	109.08	194.19	122.28	55.77
West Virginia	1,521.09	1,216.47	547.72	386.61	130.11	107.92	308.48	200.54	77.58
Wisconsin	1,798.99	1,577.89	699.84	455.92	260.90	139.55	194.99	89.99	55.50
Wyoming	2,335.46	1,708.91	913.63	630.58	90.85	204.25	381.42	275.73	120.96
Dist. of Col.	2,972.71	2,761.66	600.92	479.02	520.90	279.19	117.82	34.50	150.21

Source: U.S. Bureau of the Census. (1979–1980). *Governmental Finances in 1979–80.*

their own money to do so. And, given federal aid requirements, states have gained revenues but not necessarily the ability to determine the precise purposes for which these revenues can be used.

A similar point can be made about state aid to local governments. This state expenditure item has increased in recent years, particularly in northern states. State aid to local governments reveals the importance of the states as spenders but also suggests that certain states have less control over their expenditures than others. In states where local governments have more spending authority, increased expenditures can be understood as ". . . responding to the pressures and claims of local government for more state aid" (Wright, 1982: 263). Once again, the growth in state spending does not necessarily indicate the ability of state governments to effect purposeful policy aimed at upgrading services, satisfying citizen demands, or encouraging economic growth—all factors relevant to fiscal stress. There is no real evidence to suggest that *centralized* states—states in which the state government dominates direct spending and revenue raising—spend more efficiently, effectively, and responsibly (Walker, 1969). However, it would seem that centralized states possess greater potential for planning their expenditures and adapting to changing circumstances. The southern states, with their history of weak local governments, seem to be at an advantage in this regard. In the South, the possibility of urban annexation—cities subsuming surrounding communities—also exists to a greater degree than in the North. Annexation can take revenue-raising expenditures off decaying urban centers and decreases the need for state expenditures in the form of aid.

One final point about state expenditures. As stated previously, state expenditures have grown dramatically since 1950. But dollar increases in expenditures do not necessarily mean proportional increases in state service levels. In the 1960s, more than one-half of state expenditure increases can be accounted for by inflation (Wright, 1982:251). In the mid-1970s, it is estimated that inflation constituted nearly all the increases in state expenditures (Bahl, 1980:59).

V. STATE GOVERNMENT REVENUE-RAISING

State revenues have also significantly increased since 1950 in order to fund the higher expenditure demands made on state governments. In the last three decades, state tax revenues have experienced almost a 10% annual increase. In the same period, local taxes increased 8.4% annually and federal taxes 6.7% annually (Advisory Commission on Intergovernmental Relations, 1980:58). Although this state revenue increase is consistent with the growth of state service responsibilities, two important developments stand out: there have been large changes in the relative amounts of income for state and local governments—the states are collecting more revenues; there have been significant changes in the resource mix of the states—their revenue sources (Maddox and Fuquay, 1982: 202–203). State revenues have increased, but the percentage of state revenues obtained through state taxes has declined given the large amount of federal aid the states receive. The contribution of local tax revenues to state–local resources has also declined, given the unpopularity of property tax increases. Throughout the 1970s, states were aggressive revenue raisers and adopted and increased a variety of taxes. This fact reflects the revenue-raising potential of state governments themselves. But, as stated previously, state and local governments received sizable contributions from the federal government in the form of revenue sharing and grants. And, local governments became more dependent on state governments for revenue.

The states have relied on a variety of sources to obtain revenues (see Table 3). In the early part of the century, property taxes played a large role in state revenue systems. Since the depression, other state-imposed taxes and federal aid have far outdistanced the property tax as a source of revenue for state governments. By 1980, sales taxes—both general retail sales taxes and excise taxes on such items as cigarettes, liquor, and automobile fuel—provided the states with approximately one-half of their total tax revenues. Nearly all the states utilize the sales tax, and twenty-nine states obtain more than 50% of their revenues from this form of taxation. Personal income taxes have also become an important source of state revenue, and in 1980 provided the states with more than one-quarter of their own-source revenues. Since 1950, income taxes have been the fastest growing state own-source revenue-raising tool.

Most states tax corporate income; by 1980 corporate income taxes accounted for about 10% of state tax revenues. Only a few states rely heavily on corporate income taxes for revenue. Thirty-one states impose severance taxes on natural resources, and energy-rich states obtain a sizable portion of their tax revenues from these taxes. Other state revenue sources include taxes on insurance, utilities, estates, gifts, corporate licenses, stock transfers, and drivers' licenses. States also obtain revenues through user fees, such as highway and bridge tolls and state college tuition (Hansen, 1983:421–425).

The states as a whole have a broad and diverse resource mix. However, the revenue-raising capabilities of the states depend on the productivity of taxes—the ability of particular taxes to generate revenue. Different taxes respond differently, in terms of their ability to provide revenue, to economic fluctuations. State taxes ". . . differ by how much or at what rate they respond to a specified change in an important economic indicator, such as personal income, gross national product (GNP), or rising property values" (Wright, 1982:257). Personal income taxes, particularly progressive income taxes, have a high elasticity. As income increases due to economic growth, inflation, or favorable wage settlements, states utilizing income taxes obtain more revenue. On the other hand, states that rely heavily on income taxes are vulnerable to economic

Table 3 State General Revenue, by Source and by State: 1980 (in thousands of dollars)

State	Total[a] general revenue	Taxes Total	Sales and gross receipts Total	General	Motor fuels
All states	$233,592,124	$137,075,178	$67,854,790	$43,167,534	$9,721,569
Alabama	3,633,716	1,856,789	1,146,256	577,089	172,922
Alaska	3,011,436	1,437,601	54,422	0	26,175
Arizona	2,566,150	1,684,399	1,056,991	814,588	118,158
Arkansas	2,102,719	1,160,767	625,315	371,825	136,166
California	29,603,059	19,366,696	8,599,792	6,695,242	854,185
Colorado	2,791,974	1,490,898	757,961	537,379	113,442
Connecticut	3,110,767	1,839,678	1,326,202	802,950	153,155
Delaware	892,558	515,715	74,169	0	29,319
Florida	7,303,596	4,804,298	3,544,031	2,252,113	417,133
Georgia	4,583,376	2,728,961	1,506,923	931,976	330,485
Hawaii	1,636,835	998,383	614,237	498,293	34,778
Idaho	917,331	490,346	223,490	137,114	52,793
Illinois	11,045,235	7,073,077	3,681,186	2,379,123	388,097
Indiana	4,322,869	2,695,759	1,761,331	1,331,594	256,149
Iowa	2,957,634	1,746,828	778,242	502,055	167,463
Kansas	2,161,779	1,269,671	634,819	418,389	118,937
Kentucky	3,743,692	2,144,941	1,007,078	607,604	187,446
Louisiana	4,792,318	2,397,215	1,190,267	739,347	188,281
Maine	1,178,755	619,160	347,675	214,113	51,652
Maryland	4,833,162	2,760,818	1,247,724	712,815	186,658
Massachusetts	6,748,678	3,927,303	1,349,502	745,996	212,035
Michigan	10,277,168	5,947,650	2,556,716	1,706,728	473,593
Minnesota	5,253,033	3,202,581	1,216,226	650,138	204,955
Mississippi	2,482,408	1,257,932	899,777	671,086	127,647
Missouri	3,670,190	2,094,540	1,146,337	792,290	203,177
Montana	945,678	435,751	95,191	0	51,089
Nebraska	1,419,516	816,767	446,856	277,014	104,331
Nevada	829,112	476,604	391,327	182,925	34,625
New Hampshire	672,172	267,495	133,372	0	48,046
New Jersey	7,147,524	4,265,830	2,091,599	1,180,267	288,264
New Mexico	1,984,036	926,048	537,085	402,909	69,999
New York	22,051,223	12,716,772	4,607,665	2,844,869	474,798
North Carolina	5,369,967	3,215,348	1,413,025	693,564	295,143
North Dakota	907,133	371,861	191,814	124,012	33,488
Ohio	8,230,517	4,766,665	2,658,567	1,445,788	397,133
Oklahoma	3,135,059	1,776,044	678,807	317,578	129,545
Oregon	3,079,327	1,455,352	172,186	0	92,880
Pennsylvania	11,277,432	7,240,808	3,518,743	1,995,829	575,891
Rhode Island	1,186,593	550,787	297,993	169,061	39,260
South Carolina	2,905,665	1,678,049	939,284	576,489	173,412
South Dakota	703,253	270,518	232,851	147,171	41,809
Tennessee	3,571,842	1,886,992	1,415,967	982,251	226,785
Texas	11,926,955	6,758,706	4,368,968	2,536,805	480,946
Utah	1,557,722	785,755	433,964	324,744	74,074
Vermont	630,156	266,317	128,010	40,836	21,745
Virginia	5,034,342	2,743,325	1,212,363	595,060	275,141
Washington	4,830,772	2,917,445	2,176,618	1,625,006	254,637
West Virginia	2,177,916	1,219,492	845,791	598,512	101,467
Wisconsin	5,596,130	3,366,310	1,305,000	853,863	194,684
Wyoming	801,644	388,125	215,075	163,134	37,576

[a]Total general revenue equals total taxes plus intergovernmental revenue plus charges and miscellaneous revenue. Columns do not add to totals due to rounding.
Source: U.S. Bureau of Census. *State Government Finances in 1980.*

Taxes				Intergovern-mental revenue	Charges and miscellaneous general revenue
Licenses		Individual income	Corporation net income		
Total	Motor vehicle				
$8,690,435	$4,935,633	$37,089,481	$13,321,331	$64,326,479	$32,190,467
116,586	38,344	396,570	109,570	1,252,576	524,351
39,136	10,960	100,481	565,329	380,637	1,193,192
88,039	58,180	287,498	117,764	557,616	324,135
105,565	72,964	316,644	83,714	723,598	218,354
629,387	414,881	6,463,736	2,507,183	7,257,017	2,979,346
93,434	49,153	461,325	110,607	781,549	519,527
111,142	69,951	100,953	246,139	815,919	455,170
144,468	23,007	235,763	40,553	206,657	170,186
379,845	244,009	0	371,405	1,790,579	708,719
85,896	46,797	872,073	239,713	1,427,845	426,570
15,892	8,398	311,404	50,259	373,608	264,844
58,510	35,163	159,138	42,604	284,566	142,419
459,805	349,804	1,900,676	797,927	2,869,941	1,102,217
127,788	98,411	556,709	179,191	898,400	728,710
176,985	132,742	602,385	138,564	781,538	429,268
103,096	70,063	336,061	149,517	587,664	304,444
94,969	51,133	505,832	158,846	1,100,282	498,469
162,152	41,560	247,438	249,338	1,304,273	1,090,830
56,179	33,782	142,689	45,086	411,739	147,850
112,453	81,390	1,097,009	165,857	1,164,803	907,541
93,375	55,556	1,860,033	532,383	2,097,467	723,908
340,358	248,587	1,916,626	910,732	2,816,792	1,512,726
194,485	134,506	1,262,697	381,217	1,274,458	775,994
80,247	26,612	150,296	64,369	929,212	295,264
178,442	108,107	603,319	135,103	1,156,044	419,606
38,026	21,188	135,012	45,623	370,572	139,355
67,038	42,489	235,821	57,579	389,420	213,329
64,193	23,467	0	0	241,219	111,289
40,768	21,917	10,474	62,786	255,892	148,785
469,863	256,307	1,004,781	497,205	1,856,391	1,025,303
55,534	34,423	46,846	46,272	438,166	619,822
496,160	312,044	5,780,045	1,235,340	7,373,613	1,960,838
240,715	128,089	1,180,507	291,752	1,561,501	593,118
41,424	25,631	53,346	36,348	246,633	288,639
367,242	209,315	1,039,728	517,344	2,235,588	1,228,264
173,470	118,998	361,895	89,869	797,599	561,416
159,261	102,189	867,976	177,425	952,828	671,147
748,786	278,116	1,671,842	861,682	2,854,579	1,182,045
23,270	18,466	153,912	53,620	358,799	277,007
65,557	31,905	494,789	153,475	849,619	377,997
24,690	15,770	0	3,292	269,558	163,177
181,522	93,089	30,800	198,222	1,241,306	443,544
741,680	302,348	0	0	2,917,195	2,251,054
33,661	18,364	265,327	40,377	505,902	266,065
27,467	20,174	83,182	22,425	245,133	118,706
149,138	99,121	1,103,006	193,847	1,391,394	899,623
153,134	78,162	0	0	1,236,987	676,340
71,480	49,987	252,362	32,889	712,959	245,465
161,745	99,035	1,430,475	311,321	1,533,017	696,803
41,377	30,979	0	0	245,829	167,690

Table 4

State	Per capita state[a] and local revenue from own sources (in dollars)	Effort[b] relative	Expenditure[c] relative	Tax[d] capacity
U.S. average	$1,321.35	100	100	100
Alabama	985.56	94	82	89
Alaska	7,840.68	445	386	215
Arizona	1,309.39	110	95	116
Arkansas	902.28	87	74	78
California	1,545.34	103	113	115
Colorado	1,407.23	103	98	111
Connecticut	1,309.07	83	98	106
Delaware	1,493.14	105	111	111
Florida	1,077.44	89	81	104
Georgia	1,116.57	101	85	83
Hawaii	1,629.35	121	120	105
Idaho	1,075.92	95	85	91
Illinois	1,341.08	90	98	112
Indiana	1,031.29	79	77	97
Iowa	1,315.18	97	104	106
Kansas	1,269.79	88	98	107
Kentucky	1,005.84	91	91	86
Louisiana	1,275.47	114	96	108
Maine	1,061.53	100	87	80
Maryland	1,484.03	105	118	98
Massachusetts	1,478.22	106	111	91
Michigan	1,467.51	101	116	102
Minnesota	1,582.20	115	117	102
Mississippi	947.83	103	83	71
Missouri	1,003.16	79	79	95
Montana	1,355.65	114	109	111
Nebraska	1,372.43	102	95	96
Nevada	1,435.68	100	115	164
New Hampshire	987.24	79	86	97
New Jersey	1,413.30	97	103	101
New Mexico	1,507.75	134	102	105
New York	1,842.59	130	136	87
North Carolina	982.90	90	80	82
North Dakota	1,485.42	115	114	106
Ohio	1,100.13	82	88	99
Oklahoma	1,175.02	93	86	113
Oregon	1,460.45	110	117	105
Pennsylvania	1,231.61	94	90	92

Table 4 (Continued)

State	Per capita[a] state and local revenue from own sources	Effort[b] relative	Expenditure[c] relative	Tax[d] capacity
Rhode Island	1,335.90	103	108	84
South Carolina	978.55	95	78	77
South Dakota	1,146.23	99	98	92
Tennessee	937.03	86	80	81
Texas	1,160.58	90	84	122
Utah	1,165.97	112	99	88
Vermont	1,192.99	110	99	86
Virginia	1,137.68	88	86	93
Washington	1,429.48	101	110	103
West Virginia	1,074.61	97	94	95
Wisconsin	1,429.87	108	111	96
Wyoming	2,126.85	145	144	179

[a]From U.S. Bureau of the Census. (1979–1980). *Governmental Finances in 1979–80.*
[b]Calculated by the author, based on data from the U.S. Bureau of the Census. (1979–1980). *Governmental Finances in 1979–80.*
[c]Calculated by the author, based on data from the U.S. Bureau of the Census. (1979–1980). *Governmental Finances in 1979–80.*
[d]As reported in *Congressional Quarterly Weekly Report.* (1982). January 30:153.

downturns during which personal income declines. The same is true, although to a lesser degree, about sales taxes. Most state tax structures are moderately elastic; state revenues increase or decrease at essentially the same rate that personal income increases or decreases.

Since the states have little influence on economic base factors within their borders, their revenue-raising capabilities are strongly determined by forces beyond their control. This explains to some extent why states have adopted certain resource mixes. Reliance on both inelastic and elastic taxes enables the states to assure themselves of revenues during downturns and capture more revenue during growth periods. State revenue mixes can be understood in terms of this calculation. However, states have pursued a variety of revenue-raising devices because the states' primary revenue sources—income taxes, sales and excise taxes, and user fees—are also utilized by the federal government and in some cases local governments. Since the depression the states have proven to be adaptable and by and large successful revenue raisers. Nonetheless, it is important to realize that ". . . the states do not have, in the aggregate, a single preponderant revenue source as do the national and local governments" (Wright, 1982:

255). Since the states have no unassailable claim to any one tax, they make tax decisions within the context of federal and local government tax policies.

As can be seen in Table 3, state reliance on taxes varies. In general, the industrial, urban states of the north rely more on income taxes; southern states favor sales taxes. States also differ in terms of the revenue effort they make. Table 4 shows the per capita general revenue of state and local governments derived from their own sources. It can be seen that northern states obtain more revenue from their residents than southern states. However, it is somewhat misleading to compare the states as revenue raisers in terms of per capita own-source revenue. Given their different economic bases, states vary in their ability to obtain revenues. A more meaningful method to compare the states is to ascertain the *revenue effort* each makes.

State revenue effort is measured by determining the amount of own-source revenues raised per $1000 of personal income. To compare the states, one determines the national average, assigns the figure of 100 to this average, and computes a score for each state that relates its revenue effort compared with the national average. The resultant figure is called state "efforts relative" (Maxwell and Aronson, 1977:38–39). States efforts relative for 1980 and expenditures relative, a similar comparison of state expenditures, are listed in Table 4.

States with higher per capita income have to exert less revenue effort in order to maintain relatively high levels of expenditure. The revenue systems of poor states are challenged to provide funds for expenditures approaching the national average. Table 4 indicates that many southern states have revenue efforts significantly higher than their expenditure efforts. These states would have to dramatically increase their revenue efforts, well-above the national average, in order to increase their expenditure efforts.

The staff of the Advisory Commission on Intergovernmental Relations (ACIR) developed another measure to determine the fiscal health of the states. The ACIR staff attempted to ascertain the taxing capacity of the states and established an index based not only on state per capita income but other factors such as real estate values and energy resources (*Congressional Quarterly Weekly Report*, January 30, 1982:53). The results of the ACIR staff's study are listed in Table 4. It is interesting to compare the various measures of state fiscal conditions and performance listed in Table 4. In terms of per capita income and efforts and expenditures relative, the northeastern states appear to be fiscally healthier than states in the southwest and Rocky Mountain regions. According to the ACIR staff's index, states in the southeast are less healthy on all measures.

What explains these differences in tax utilization and revenue effort? As is the case with expenditures, economic, historic, and political factors all influence state revenue-raising policies and resource mix. Industrialized states with high per capita income rely on individual and corporate income taxes. States with lower per capita income and lower-quality housing have favored sales taxes. The energy-rich states make heavy use of severance taxes. An important study on state revenue raising (Bingham, 1978) suggests that the states that have utilized particular taxes for many years are better able to make state tax policy increases than states that have recently adopted certain taxes.

State political circumstances are also relevant. In many states there are constitutional and statutory limitations on revenue and expenditure increases. Such measures decrease the ability of state legislatures and governors to pass new revenue measures or increase existing measures. Some states require referendums on tax measures or large majority support in their legislative bodies to increase taxes.

In many states, a portion of state revenue is earmarked for certain expenditures, such as education, highways, and aid to the elderly. Earmarking is aimed at assuring funds for programs deemed particularly important. However, this practice limits the budgeting flexibility of state officials since earmarked monies cannot usually be transferred to fund other highly demanded or desirable programs (Maxwell and Aronson, 1977:220–228).

Political ideology and political culture also have a bearing on state tax policies. The more conservative southern states tend to have fewer taxes and more regressive tax systems; liberal states are more likely to have higher and more progressive taxes (Hansen, 1983:428). The importance of political ideology generally, and public opinion specifically, cannot be overstated. As our earlier discussion of the taxpayers revolt indicated, state government officials are extremely sensitive to the public's views on tax matters. While it is true that states with a strong governor and legislative majority of the same party have been daring and innovative in revenue raising (Bingham et al., 1978:203), it has generally been the case that citizens regard state expenditures as less important and effective than federal and local expenditures (Advisory Commission on Intergovernmental Relations, 1980:2).

Although states have increased their own-source revenue, post-1950s state and local governments have increasingly relied on federal aid. The federal government has provided state and local government with aid for welfare, education, and highways. Federal aid amounts for the states are in part based on state tax effort. States that exert a greater tax effort, have poor revenue-raising capacities, and have larger numbers of poor people receive more federal aid. In recent years southern states have received less per capita aid than northern states. However, federal aid constitutes a slightly larger percentage of the total general revenue received by southern states than northern ones. In aggregate, the states have come to depend on the federal government for approximately 20% of their general revenues. One scholar suggests that ". . . federal aid to the states has a far greater impact on state spending than have efforts by the states to increase revenues from their own sources, even in states that have made considerable changes in their tax structures since 1960" (Hansen, 1983:440).

VI. THE FISCAL FUTURE OF THE AMERICAN STATES

The roles of the states as spenders and revenue raisers and the complex environments in which state fiscal policy is pursued affect both the demands made on state governments and their ability to meet these demands. Predicting the occurrence of fiscal stress is extremely complicated. Nonetheless, there have been some developments that suggest that almost all of the American states will experience fiscal challenges in the 1980s.

The older, industrialized states in the North seem to be particularly susceptible to fiscal stress, primarily because their economic bases are declining. Urbanization has been correlated with higher citizen demand for government services, and decaying northern cities pose serious challenges to government officials. Although population growth in the North has declined, it will not necessarily result in decreased demand for government goods and services. This is more relevant if the percentage of poor residents of a state increases, which is the trend in the North. This may explain why state per capita expenditure increased faster in northern states than per capita income.

In one sense it seems reasonable to expect that states that have a declining economic base will experience some decrease in demand for goods and services. When population growth slows and levels of industrial and commercial activity decline, there is less public demand for such goods and services as highways, sewage facilities, and schools. However, states in economic decline face the challenge of replacing a decaying infrastructure in order to perpetuate current levels of economic activity and become attractive to investors. Such demands can make large claims on state revenues at a time when most older industrial states already have high debts.

Some states may be victims of their own past successes in raising revenues and providing goods and services. Citizens have come to expect high levels of goods and services from the states, and powerful interest groups, government bureaucrats, and state employee unions play important roles in perpetuating state programs. In states where local governments possess significant spending authority, local interests can undermine the efforts of state officials to contain or redirect certain expenditures. On the revenue side, states with diversified resource mixes may be assured a certain level of revenue. But, the historically higher tax rates in the North seem to limit the possibility of raising state tax rates significantly. In states where greater party competition exists, public officials may be less willing to gamble their political futures on tax increases.

Other states, particularly those in the southwest and Rocky Mountain regions, seem to be in a more favorable fiscal position given recent shifts in economic activity. These states may be in the position to increase revenues and possess the potential to diversify their resource mixes if fiscal conditions and program goals warrant. The primary constraint on this would seem to be political, given the historically lower and fewer taxes in these states.

The economically growing states are also experiencing population growth, which will likely result in higher demand for education, health, and perhaps welfare expenditures. Economic growth will also bring demand for infrastructure expenditures. The question remains to what extent economic growth will support population growth and increased demands for goods and services. In the southern states public employee wages are lower than in the North. Increases in the professionalization of state workforces, unionization, and higher private sector wages, are likely to create wage pressures on state governments.

Overall the American states can expect to experience a variety of pressures that will make achieving fiscal solvency and purposeful government more difficult. As the states entered 1983, these pressures had combined to subject the states to their worst conditions in forty years (Gold and Benker, 1983:1). Although states from all parts of the country were suffering from fiscal stress, those in the New England, Great Lakes, and Far West regions faced the most challenging fiscal problems. These problems were not altogether unexpected, although the severity and extent of budget crises were surprising. In 1982 the states also had fiscal difficulties; they responded by holding the line on spending and making minor adjustments in taxes. Only nine states felt compelled to raise taxes in 1982, since many state officials believed that the national economy would recover. When the economy did not rebound as quickly as anticipated, the states faced even more serious budgeting problems.

The national economic recession was the most important factor contributing to fiscal stress in the states in the early 1980s. The high unemployment rates throughout the country resulted in increased demands for public expenditures and cut into the projected revenues of state governments. Even the oil-rich states were affected; economic decline, conservation, and world oil glut suppressed demand and prices, and state severance taxes yielded less revenue than anticipated. The decline in the inflation rate, however welcomed, also hurt state revenue raising; state sales and income taxes were negatively affected by lower inflation rates and smaller private sector wage hikes. From 1982 to 1983 state revenues increased by 5.5% and expenditures by 6.4%. "These increases are lower than the inflation rate for goods and services purchased by the states" (Gold and Benker, 1983:i).

Two other political factors also contributed to the states' fiscal stress. The decreases in federal aid recommended by the Reagan administration cost the states almost $13 billion in revenues (U.S. News & World Report, March 8, 1982: 49). All states were affected by these cuts, but northern states were hardest hit. The states were also victims of their own tax policies. Between 1978 and 1982 state taxes decreased from about 7% to 6.5% of personal income (Gold and Benker, 1983:i). Given the long duration of the recession, the wisdom of state tax cuts in the late 1970s was questioned in 1983.

But the states did not attempt to manage fiscal stress by immediately raising taxes. Rather, they focused on certain incremental and short-run changes to overcome their revenue shortfalls. Some states postponed payrolls, accelerated tax payments, transferred money between various funds, entered the short-term debt market, enacted hiring freezes, postponed employee raises, and reduced or deferred spending. Where states did try to raise revenues, they favored increases in sales and excise taxes (Gold and Benker, 1983:8–12). The success and appropriateness of the latter measure will depend on how much the federal government uses excise taxes to increase its own revenue.

The states will no doubt consider it necessary to increase taxes during the 1980s to meet their service responsibilities and to satisfy citizen demands. One can expect a broader and further utilization of personal income taxes by the states. There is already evidence to suggest that citizens will tolerate revenue-raising increases to fund needed and desirable expenditures. During 1982 most state and local bond issues were approved by voters, and Democratic candidates in gubernatorial elections had great success (U.S. News & World Report, Nov. 15, 1982:92,93). And, citizens and public officials at all levels of government expressed serious reservations about President Reagan's "New Federalism" proposals.

The states, nonetheless, must be prepared to deal with lower levels of federal aid in the coming years. Even if the major components of the "New Federalism" are not approved, the trend is for the states to assume more service and thus more revenue-raising responsibilities. The American states will thus continue to be in the "middle," dependent on federal aid and pressured by citizens and local governments for more and better goods and services. Under such conditions the states will be frequently maligned. But, in facing the challenges of fiscal stress, citizens may also develop a greater appreciation of state governments and the importance of state policies and effective state government administration for their lives.

REFERENCES

Advisory Commission on Intergovernmental Relations (1981). *Significant Features of Fiscal Federalism, 1978-79, 1980-81*. U.S. Government Printing Office, Washington, D.C.

Advisory Commission on Intergovernmental Relations (1980). *Changing Public Attitudes Towards Taxes*. U.S. Government Printing Office, Washington, D.C.

Bahl, R. (1980). State and local government finance in the changing national economy. In *State and Local Finance: Adjustments in a Changing Economy*. Joint Economic Committee, Congress of the United States, Washington, D.C.

Bingham, R., Hawkins, B. and Hebert, F. (1978). *The Politics of Raising State and Local Revenues*. Praeger, New York.

Broder, D. (August 24, 1980). The governors, feeling burned. *The Washington Post*:C7.

Congressional Quarterly Weekly Report (January 30, 1982). Congressional Quarterly, Inc., Washington, D.C.

Council of State Governments (1982). *Book of the States 1982–83*. Council of State Governments, Lexington, Ky.

Gold, S. and Benker, K. (1983). *State Fiscal Conditions Entering 1983*. National Conference of State Legislatures, Denver, Col.

Hansen, S. (1983). Extraction: the politics of state taxation. In *Politics in the American States*, 4th ed., Gray, V., Jacobs, H., and Vines, K. (eds.). Little Brown, Boston.

Levine, C., ed. (1980). *Managing Fiscal Stress*. Chatham House, Chatham, N.J.

Maddox, R. and Fuquay, R. (1981). *State and Local Government*, 4th ed. Van Nostrand Company, New York.

Maxwell, J. and Aronson, J. (1977). *Financing State and Local Government*, 3rd ed. The Brookings Institute, Washington, D.C.

The New York Times. March 2, 1983.

Petersen, J. and Spain, C. (1980). *Essays in Public Finance and Financial Management*. Chatham House, Chatham, N.J.

Phares, D. (1980). *Who Pays State and Local Taxes?* Oelgeschlager, Gunn and Hain, Cambridge, Mass.

Rose, J., ed. (1982). *Tax and Expenditure Limitations*. Center for Urban Policy Research, New Brunswick, N.J.

Sharkansky, I. (1972). *The Maligned States*. McGraw-Hill, New York.

Stedman, M. (1982). *State and Local Governments*, 3rd ed. Little, Brown, Boston.

U.S. Bureau of the Census (1981). *Government Finances in 1979–80*. U.S Government Printing Office, Washington, D.C.

U.S. News & World Report. March 8, 1982; November 15, 1982.

Walker, J. (1969). The diffusion of innovation among the American states. *American Political Science Review 63*:880–889.

Wright, D. (1982). *Understanding Intergovernmental Relations*, 2nd ed. Brooks/Cole, Monterey, Calif.

10

Fiscal Dependency and Governmental Capacity in American Cities

John J. Gargan   Department of Political Science, Kent State University, Kent, Ohio

I. INTRODUCTION

The viability of American cities as governing units has been a recurring theme in popular and scholarly commentary and analysis. Current pessimism regarding the effectiveness of urban administrative structures, quality of urban life, and opportunities open to the urban poor is not new. Although the reasons for pessimism have varied over the past century, the degree of pessimism about urban conditions has remained relatively constant.

Much of the concern about the governing capacity of cities in the 1980s has related to the state of city finances. Issues of social unrest have been crowded off political and governmental agendas by fiscal issues. Mayoral rhetoric has changed from questions like "Can we afford not to do it?" to the question of "What can we afford to do?" Knowledge of the techniques of budget reduction and productivity enhancement has replaced community organizing as the test of administrative competency.

To a greater extent than in the past, the ability to govern cities has come to be perceived as the ability to finance. The reasons for the perception are well known and real. Inflation rates of the 1970s increased the costs of providing labor-intensive services and of borrowing money. Voter-approved limitations on taxing and spending, most spectacularly evidenced in California's Proposition 13 and Massachusetts' Proposition 2½, legally constrained fiscal decisions by public officials where adopted and undoubtedly politically constrained such decisions even where not adopted. A recessionary economy in the mid-1970s and early

1980s increased the need for social services and eroded the tax base that funded those services. Finally, the reductions in domestic spending achieved by the Reagan administration in 1981 and the New Federalism initiatives proposed by the administration in 1982 altered fiscal and programmatic relations between the national government and cities.

Whereas all the changes are important, those in the patterns of fiscal federalism are especially so. For some observers adjustments represent a major departure from governing patterns of the past fifty years and especially of the past fifteen years. Commenting on this pattern, Richard Nathan (1981:530) has noted:

> Cities, . . . , are now major recipients of federal grants. Federal grants to local governments account for approximately half of all non-welfare federal grants to states and localities. The growth in direct federal-local grants over the past fifteen years is one of the most fundamental changes in our intergovernmental finances in the recent period. The heightened flow of federal grants directly into city coffers . . . is of such consequence as to challenge the basic characterization of the American governmental system as federal.

The implication of Nathan's observation for the governing of cities is clear. If the national government has become an important source of municipal revenue, then any reduction in the amount and scope of that aid would have obvious adverse effects on the capacity of city governments to function. Similar adverse effects on city governing capacity have been predicted by Coleman and Ross (1983:34) with regard to Reagan's New Federalism proposals: "The proposed changes in the federal grant-in-aid system are drastic. Fully implemented, these changes would require a major restructuring of state and local governments' public service financing and delivery systems."

That the fate of cities is intimately tied to decisions made in the Executive Office of the President, congressional subcommittee deliberations, and federal district courtrooms is a well-established fact in the current wisdom of American government and politics [Advisory Commission on Intergovernmental Relations (ACIR) 1980a]. The penetration of the federal government by way of programs, grants, and regulations into problem areas traditionally the sole purview of local governments has brought about a redefinition of the key participants and power holders in local politics. The expanded federal presence has also resulted in considerable fiscal dependency of cities on federal aid. Indeed, the argument goes, whatever earlier constitutional authorities might have held about the legal relationships between the national, state, and local governments, a new order exists. All general-purpose local governments are directly linked to Washington, and the larger the government, particularly in the case of cities, the stronger the link.

This analysis is concerned with the relationship between fiscal dependency and the governing capacity of cities. Little attention is given to the specific actions taken by cities to cope with revenue shortages; a growing body of sophisticated literature documents these actions.[1] A principal thesis is that the complexity of city fiscal dependency has been understated and the public administration community's dominant paradigm of governing capacity is inadequate for dealing with that complexity. The problems of fiscal dependency are primarily political; their resolution will be determined by the political patterns that define the governing capacity of individual cities.

II. GROWTH IN THE PUBLIC SECTOR

The fact of increased direct federal-city relations is indisputable. The importance of those relations is problematic. The extent of city fiscal dependency resulting from those relations is questionable. All three matters—direct relations, importance of the relations, and dependency resulting from the relations—are by-products of dramatic alterations not simply in the outlines of federalism or intergovernmental relations but in the role of the public sector in American society.

The most elemental of these dramatic alterations is the sheer expansion of the public sector (combined federal, state, and local) over the last fifty years. In 1929, total public sector spending accounted for 9.8% of gross national product (GNP); in 1959, 26.9%; in 1975 nearly 35% (34.4%); and since the mid-1970s approximately one-third. In constant dollar terms (1972 dollars) total per capita spending was $258 in 1929, $1090 in 1959, and over $2000 from 1977 to the present (ACIR, 1983:12-15).

Measured as a percent of GNP or in constant dollars, public sector growth has involved an increase in the scope of services provided by all levels of government as shown in Table 1.

The two major trends of overall expansion in the public sector and the growing importance of intergovernmental transfers are revealed by the figures. The first trend is most evident in the "From Own Funds" line for the federal government in Table 1; federal expenditures grew from 2.5% of GNP in 1929 to 23.4% in 1981. The import of the second trend is indicated by the pair of lines reported for local government. Including transfers from other governments, local expenditures increased from 5.9% of GNP to 8.9% in 1975 and declined since then; own-fund expenditures by local governments amounted to a smaller percentage of GNP in 1981 than in 1929.

Table 1 also documents the maturation of the welfare state and the legitimation of governmental involvement in more activities. Despite attention to projected spending increases for national defense, growth in domestic programs has dominated public sector expansion in recent decades. (In 1959, federal

Table 1 Government Expenditures as Percent of GNP from Own Funds and After Intergovernmental Transfers: By Level of Government for Selected Years

	Year (%)				
	1929	1959	1975	1979	1981
Level of government					
Federal					
From own funds	2.5	18.7	23.0	21.1	23.4
After transfers	2.4	17.2	19.6	17.8	20.5
State					
From own funds	2.0	3.8	6.2	5.6	5.6
After transfers	1.6	3.6	6.0	5.3	5.3
Local					
From own funds	5.3	4.4	5.2	4.6	4.5
After transfers	5.9	6.0	8.9	8.1	7.7

Source: Advisory Commission on Intergovernmental Relations. (April 1, 1983). *Significant Features of Fiscal Federalism, 1981-82 Edition*. Advisory Commission on Intergovernmental Relations, Washington, D.C., pp. 12-15.

expenditures accounted for 18.6% of GNP, of which 10.9% was for defense and 7.7% for domestic expenditures; in 1981 comparable figures were 23.4% of GNP of which 7.5% was allocated to defense and 15.9% to domestic.) The maturing and legitimation has been systemwide. That local government from own funds expenditures, in the aggregate, represented a smaller percentage of GNP in 1981 than in 1929 does not mean an absence of increased direct spending by local officials; between 1929 and 1981 per capita own-funds expenditures by local governments grew from $137 to $295 in constant 1972 dollars.

For cities and other local governments, increases in spending are an important manifestation of dramatic changes in legal, social, and political definitions of entitlement and equity. Whether medical care, food, and shelter are basic human rights is, in the end, an issue of normative political theory. Whether those basics—or such additional matters as tertiary treatment of sewage, subways, equal education opportunities for the handicapped, access to legal counsel, and day care for the children of unwed mothers—are treated as rights will be determined, in the present, by dominant attitudes and decisions of those exercising political control. Over the past decades, these attitudes and decisions have been generally supportive of expanding definitions of rights and entitlements.

As Table 1 suggests, the expanded definitions have involved substantial fiscal costs. To a considerable degree, since the rights and entitlements have been viewed as associated with national citizenship, their implementation has required some redistribution of financial resources by the national government to meet minimal levels of adequacy in all states and communities. The extent to which these communities have come to depend on these resources is an important empirical question with implications for the operations of a federal system (Elazar, 1979; Landau, 1969). In federal systems, national programs of intergovernmental aid have an economic rationale since they address the problems of spillover effects of program benefits, fiscal disparities between jurisdictions, and income distribution in the population (Break, 1980:76). If the national programs are less the product of national problems than the access of hyperactive interest groups to Congress (Beer, 1978; Anton, 1980), then a local citizenry is forced to bear costs it may not want. Undue dependence of cities on federal or state aid means that effective control of city affairs is exercised by nonlocal (and typically nonelected) public officials. Should significant reductions in that aid limit the ability of city political leaders to meet voters' expectations or bring about a redefinition of entitlements, the political leaders may be faced with a situation of governing capacity failure.

III. THE ISSUE OF FISCAL DEPENDENCY

In considering the governing capacity of cities in the 1980s, it is necessary to distinguish between urban fiscal dependency and urban fiscal stress. Dependency connotes some reliance on external sources of revenues to finance functions and activities for which the city government is legally responsible. The extent of a city's fiscal dependency can be demonstrated by such measures as the percentage of revenues contributed by noncity government sources.

Fiscal distress implies an extremely adverse condition under which a city lacks the financial resources to achieve some desired level of performance. Used in recent years to describe city problems, fiscal stress (or distress) is a vague concept, the meaning of which is influenced by the analyst's measurement instrument. As Roy Bahl (1982:8) notes:

> Fiscal health or distress is a qualitative term, so it is not surprising that it means different things to different people.
>   In fact, there is no best measure of the fiscal health of cities and states. In one sense, all are in trouble because the level of public services is never adequate and taxes are always too high.

By way of illustration, Bahl cites seven comparative studies based upon differing statistical measures. Of twenty-nine cities meeting some criterion of fiscal stress in at least one of the studies, only seven cities received a stress ranking in four or more studies. Included are well-known and highly publicized sites of financial problems during the 1970s—Newark, St. Louis, Boston, Cleveland, Baltimore, New York, and Philadelphia.

Fiscal dependency may be one consequence of fiscal stress. However, fiscal dependency does not necessarily equate with distress so long as there is no extended disruption in the transfer of funds from external sources to city treasuries.[2] Although all cities have become dependent on federal and state aid, most cities are not smaller (or larger) versions of Newark, St. Louis, or New York.

Distinguishing between city fiscal stress and fiscal dependency is important; it separates out a distinct minority of cities with special problems from the larger number of cities with more limited problems. Yet, the separation does not eliminate ambiguity in analysis. If judgments of fiscal stress are shaped by the variables included in measurement, judgments of fiscal dependency are shaped by the vantage point of observation and the level of data aggregation.

The prevailing view of fiscal dependency is simply stated. For city finances, state and federal aid (direct and passed through the states) is increasingly important. Though both types of aid decreased in constant dollar terms during the last years of the 1970s, in 1980 federal and state aid combined amounted to nearly 60% (56.2) of municipal own-source general revenue (ACIR, 1981:59). And this slowdown came after a period of very rapid growth. Between 1972 and 1977, municipal general revenue grew at an annual average rate of 11.6%; during the same years, federal and state aid increased at an annual average rate of 28.4 and 10.8% (ACIR, 1980b:7). In 1980, federal and state aid accounted for 25.8% of current revenue of all respondent cities combined and 33.6% of current revenues of the forty-four largest cities.

The general outline of municipal fiscal dependency is suggested by the national overview and by aggregated data. However, the general outline masks considerable variation across cities in the degree of dependency. Some sense of this variation can be gained from a brief examination of published data. In the 1981–1982 edition of *Significant Features of Fiscal Federalism*, the Advisory Commission on Intergovernmental Relations reports individual state fiscal profiles. Included in each profile are data on the percentage distribution, by source, of 1980–1981 general revenues of the state government, local governments combined, and of counties, municipalities, and independent school districts. Percentage distribution of general revenue is included for seven sources: federal aid, state aid, property tax, general sales tax, income tax, other tax, and charges and miscellaneous.

These data permit interstate comparisons of the relative importance of each revenue source to each type of local government. Listed in Table 2 for each municipal revenue source are the five highest- and five lowest-ranking states and the fifty state average percentage. Even a cursory examination of the groupings of states demonstrates the diversity of municipal revenue sources. Thus, the property tax, the historic mainstay of local government finance, constitutes over one-half general revenues of *all municipalities combined* in Rhode Island,

Connecticut, New Hampshire, and Massachusetts; the tax contributes less than 10% of municipal revenues in eight states and less than 7% for Arkansas, Oklahoma, and Wyoming. Municipalities in Ohio rely heavily on the municipal income tax (29.4%), Oklahoma municipalities on general sales tax (30.3%), and municipalities in North Dakota (51.4%) and Nevada (47.4%) on charges and miscellaneous sources.

Interstate differences are also evident for municipal reliance on federal aid, state aid, and federal-state aid combined. Clearly, the extent of municipal dependence on either type of aid, or both combined, is not uniform. In 1980–1981, federal aid accounted for over one-quarter of municipal revenue in four states but less than 10% in six (the five listed plus Wisconsin). Similarly for state aid, the range of dependence is considerable, from a high of nearly 45% for New Jersey cities to a low of under 2% for those in Texas. With both sources combined, the importance of aid is obvious, accounting for one-sixth and one-fifth of municipal general revenues in even the five lowest-ranking states and approaching or exceeding 50% in the five high-ranking states.

For students of municipal finance these comments are familiar. It has long been recognized, for example, that fiscal comparisons of cities can be made only in light of the assignment of municipal functional responsibilities (for what specific activities is the city responsible for under state law and/or the city charter) and the division of functional and financing responsibilities between municipal (or other local) governments and the state government. Any understanding of the effects of fiscal dependency on city governing requires a sensitivity to the complexity of municipal finances.

Efforts have been made to decipher the complexities of comparative local government finance.[3] One approach is to shift focus from jurisdictional to functional comparisons so that the question is not how much does city A spend on fire, police, and education in comparison with city B, but rather what is the level of state-local combined spending for fire, police, and education in state Y versus state Z. Such comparisons highlight interstate policy differences; they do not tell much about city government and politics. A second approach has involved the formulation of public finance typologies. One such typology has been developed by state-local finance authorities at Syracuse University. As reported by the Advisory Commission on Intergovernmental Relations (1982:36), the Syracuse University typology groups states according to three variables: "state financing share of state-local direct expenditure, state expenditure share of state-local direct expenditure, and state-local per capita expenditure." Each variable is scored high, medium, and low. Of the twenty-seven possible combinations, ACIR finds the states grouping into eighteen.

Given the groupings produced by the Syracuse typology, the most appropriate response to the question of how fiscally dependent cities are in the 1980s and what effects that dependency has on their governing capacity is, "It depends."

Table 2 Municipal General Revenue Sources, 1980–1981: Percentage Distribution, by Source, U.S. Total, Five Highest- and Five Lowest-Ranking States, Mean ($\overline{X}$) Percentage All States

Federal aid		State aid	
U.S. Total	13.6	U.S. Total	20.4
Delaware	32.5	New Jersey	44.8
Vermont	29.6	Wisconsin	42.2
Kentucky	27.3	Maryland	41.8
South Carolina	26.2	Wyoming	40.0
Indiana	24.0	Alaska	37.2
—		—	
Connecticut	7.6	Hawaii	5.0
New York	7.4	Vermont	3.2
Alaska	7.1	Oklahoma	3.1
Nevada	5.5	West Virginia	2.5
New Jersey	3.5	Texas	1.5
$\overline{X}$	16.1	$\overline{X}$	17.0
Federal aid plus state aid		**Property tax**	
U.S. Total	34.0	U.S. Total	22.0
Maryland	58.6	Rhode Island	56.6
Wyoming	52.1	Connecticut	54.2
Wisconsin	50.5	New Hampshire	53.5
New Jersey	48.3	Massachusetts	50.0
Mississippi	45.1	Maine	47.5
—		—	
Utah	20.3	West Virginia	8.3
Alabama	20.0	Arkansas	6.9
Oklahoma	20.0	Alabama	6.4
Texas	17.7	Oklahoma	5.4
Nevada	16.5	Wyoming	3.8
$\overline{X}$	33.1	$\overline{X}$	23.0
Other taxes		**Charges and miscellaneous**	
U.S. Total	6.8	U.S. Total	25.1
West Virginia	20.7	North Dakota	25.1
Georgia	17.1	Nevada	47.4
Florida	16.7	Kansas	46.1
Nevada	15.7	Minnesota	45.9
Missouri	15.6	West Virginia	45.6
—		—	
Indiana	0.7	Maryland	13.8
Connecticut	0.7	New Jersey	13.3
Rhode Island	0.5	Connecticut	11.7
Maine	0.5	Massachusetts	11.7
Massachusetts	0.4	Rhode Island	5.4
$\overline{X}$	6.5	$\overline{X}$	30.1

Table 2 (Continued)

General sales tax[a]		Income tax[b]	
U.S. Total	6.8	U.S. Total	5.4
Oklahoma	30.3	Ohio	29.4
Colorado	27.1	Pennsylvania	26.5
Utah	20.2	Kentucky	18.7
Arizona	18.6	Delaware	11.5
Louisiana	18.3	New York	11.1
$\overline{X}$ (N = 22)	11.3	$\overline{X}$ (N = 9)	13.3
$\overline{X}$ (N = 50)	5.0	$\overline{X}$ (N = 50)	2.4

[a]General sales tax was a reported revenue source for municipalities in twenty-two states.
[b]Income tax was a reported revenue source for municipalities in nine states.
Source: Advisory Commission on Intergovernmental Relations. (April 1, 1983).
Significant Features of Fiscal Federalism, 1981-82 Edition. Advisory Commission
on Intergovernmental Relations, Washington, D.C., pp. 85–136.

For any particular city, the factors affecting the degree and nature of fiscal
dependency are essentially three:

- The state in which the city is located.
- The scope and level of public services, mandated and discretionary, provided
  by the formal city government.
- The mix of revenue sources chosen and used by the city government from
  the range of sources available.

Individually and in combination the three factors indicate the central role
of state government in defining the conditions of city fiscal dependency; in
point of legal, fiscal, and political fact, local governments, including cities,
continue to be creatures of the state. The location of a city determines, in effect,
the allocation of functional responsibility and the division of state-local burdens
for funding and direct expenditures on the function. State law, as filtered
through city charters and decisions by local officials, defines what services must
be and may be delivered by city government. State law also defines what options
are available locally for financing those services.

The point being emphasized is that cities vary in the extent of their
reliance on external revenue sources. This variation is especially great with regard
to direct federal funding. That federal grant programs have been enacted does
not mean that all cities receive, or even apply for, those grants. Reporting on a
National League of Cities (NLC) survey of member attitudes toward general
revenue sharing, Frank Viscount (1982) writes: "For cities under 10,000

63 percent indicated it was the only grant they received. For cities under 50,000, 41 percent indicated it was the only grant received."

The finding is, in part, a function of city size; no city of over 250,000 population reported general revenue sharing as its only source of federal funds. And the finding does not dispute the importance of federal funds. Respondents to the NLC survey indicated that elimination of revenue sharing would result in significant spending reductions, tax increases, and capital expenditure delays. Nevertheless, for a very large number of cities under 50,000 the direct fiscal lifeline to the federal government is a thin one. Overall, revenue sharing represents, on the average, 6.3% of own-source revenues and 10% or more in smaller cities. Whether 6 or 10% is considerable is a question of perspective, but to the extent that the cited NLC conclusions can be generalized to the universe of American cities, most cities are not unduly dependent on direct federal help.[4]

Discussion of the data reported in Table 2 and the choice of selected findings from an NLC survey can be faulted for understating the real extent of city fiscal dependency on nonlocal sources. Aggregating municipal revenue sources by state allows for more accurate description; it also masks intrastate differences by combining cities regardless of size. *Ceteris paribus*, size is a surrogate for a number of other variables—social heterogeneity, organizational complexity, scale of public programs, and so on—and any consideration of fiscal dependency needs to consider its effects. Typically, the urban fiscal crisis has been portrayed as a crisis afflicting the largest cities.

Table 3 provides an overview of dependence on outside revenues for the twenty largest U.S. cities, except for Washington, D.C. Reported for each city is the percentage of total general revenue (1980–1981) obtained from state government, federal government, and state-federal combined. Also reported is each city's general revenue sharing allocation, expressed as a percentage of total general revenue.

Big-city budgets are dependent upon external revenue sources; the mean value of federal and state revenue as a percentage of total general revenue is 36% for the twenty largest cities. However, there is considerable variation about that mean. Again, the difficulty of generalizing on the extent of city fiscal dependency is evident. Although they all rank among the largest cities, the dependency on federal and state aid of Baltimore and Detroit is qualitatively different from that of Houston and Dallas. The differences in the federal and state contributions make Baltimore decidedly more interested in decisions in Annapolis than in Washington, and Detroit somewhat more concerned with developments in Washington than in Lansing.

Table 3 also allows comparison of individual large cities and thereby provides a more accurate indication of dependency than do the state-aggregated

Table 3 Big City Fiscal Dependence: Percent of Total General Revenue (1980-1981) from State Government, from Federal Government, Total State and Federal, and General Revenue Sharing as Percent of Total General Revenue, for Twenty Largest Cities[a]

City	Percent of total general revenue		Total state and federal	General revenue sharing as percent of total general revenue
	From state	From federal		
New York[a]	34.8	6.9	41.7	1.7
Chicago	13.3	26.8	40.1	4.0
Los Angeles	8.6	15.8	24.4	3.0
Philadelphia[a]	18.4	11.1	29.5	3.1
Houston	1.7	14.1	15.8	2.8
Detroit	19.1	35.2	54.3	3.0
Dallas	1.8	13.2	15.0	3.6
San Diego	13.1	15.8	28.9	2.6
Phoenix	19.1	19.6	38.7	2.6
Baltimore[a]	45.8	16.6	62.4	1.9
San Antonio	2.5	31.9	34.4	3.6
Indianapolis	25.1	27.4	52.5	2.8
San Francisco	27.3	14.3	41.6	1.7
Memphis	26.4	12.0	38.4	2.3
Milwaukee	41.4	10.7	52.1	3.8
San Jose	11.9	7.7	19.6	3.1
Cleveland[a]	9.5	18.1	27.6	3.8
Columbus	9.0	20.2	29.2	3.3
Boston[a]	27.5	9.2	36.7	2.2
New Orleans	11.1	26.7	37.8	3.9

[a]Cities meeting the fiscal stress criteria of at least four of seven studies.
Source: U.S. Bureau of the Census. (1981). *City Government Finances in 1980-81*, Series GF81, No. 4. U.S. Government Printing Office, Washington, D.C.

totals in Table 2. City size may be a determinant of dependency, but it is not an overriding determinant. Presumably as important as size is the geographic location of the cities. It is not coincidental that the four cities most dependent on state and federal aid are located in economically declining Mideast and Great Lakes regions, and that the four cities least dependent are in the economically growing Southwest and Far West regions. To compare Dallas and Houston with Baltimore and Detroit is not to compare large cities but economic-revenue base apples and oranges.

A relationship between city fiscal dependency and geographic location exists, but it is not perfect. Of the eleven cities in Table 3 ranking above the mean value (36%) of state and federal contributions to city general revenue, seven are located in states of the Great Lakes, Mideast, or New England, but the remaining four are in states of the Southeast, Southwest, or Far West. Of the nine cities ranking below the mean value, six are in states of the Southwest or Far West, but three are in states of the Mideast or Great Lakes. At least for the twenty largest cities, to the extent that geographic location is an indicator of general economic conditions and, therefore, of revenue need, the figures in Table 3 do not provide clear evidence that all cities in economically declining regions are disproportionately dependent on intergovernmental help.

Nor is the evidence clear that even those cities acknowledged to be most fiscally distressed are equally dependent on state and federal revenues. Seven cities were cited earlier as meeting the fiscal stress criteria of at least four of seven studies. Five of the cities (New York, Philadelphia, Baltimore, Cleveland, and Boston) are marked with an [a] in Table 3. For the other two cities, total state-federal revenues as a percent of total general revenues were 69.4% for Newark (64% from the state and 5.4% from the federal government) and 39.3% for St. Louis (14.7% state and 24.6% federal). As to the dependency on nonlocal revenues of these seven distressed cities, the results are mixed. In terms of the percent of total general revenues derived from the state and federal governments, two of the seven (Cleveland and Philadelphia) more resemble Dallas than Detroit, and another two (Boston and St. Louis) are just above the mean state and federal percentage figure for the twenty cities. Only the remaining two distressed cities, Baltimore and Newark, evidence a reliance on state and federal funds that sets them clearly apart from the nondistressed (or less distressed) large cities.

A. Summarizing City Fiscal Dependency

This section has attempted to clarify the issue of city fiscal dependency as a precondition of considering its effects on governing capacity. Clarity is not easily achieved because city fiscal dependency is multidimensional, and its extent and meaning are conditioned by the dimension examined. Extent and meaning are also conditioned by the level of data aggregation. In recent years, a number of studies have summarized revenue and expenditure data for all U.S. cities or for classes of different size cities (Bowman, 1981; Merget, 1980). Such summaries are not inherently flawed and may be viewed as useful by national-level urban policy-makers. Yet, the big picture created by averaging and combining does not and cannot reveal the critical details of fiscal differences between cities.

A segment of the critical detail was reported in Table 2 showing interstate differences in major municipal revenue sources. Although these figures reveal state-by-state differences, they are subject to the same criticism as national aggregates. Within any given state, cities operating under the same state law will utilize, depending upon specific local conditions, different revenue combinations to provide different combinations or levels of public services. Only when individual cities are analyzed individually is it possible to make judgments about the magnitude of city fiscal dependency. Across the twenty largest cities dependence on state and federal revenues is evident, although the level of dependence varies significantly and is not totally related to regional location or distressed conditions.

To this point, discussion and comparison of cities have been based upon a relatively limited definition of city government fiscal dependency. At least implicitly, fiscal dependency has been equated with reliance on state and/or federal aid. Given the attention to changes in the distribution of that aid, the equating is justified. However, regardless of the number of dollars forthcoming from the national or state capitals, all cities are fiscally dependent in the obvious sense that they must have resources. The capacity of any city to function and survive is constrained by the degree of its dependence on particular revenues and the stability of those revenues. At the logical extreme is the city totally dependent upon a single revenue source, the yield of which is determined by nonlocal factors. Adequate governing capacity can never be fully developed in the city since local officials lack meaningful control over the nonlocal factors.

The logical extreme is not the same as the logically absurd. Although probably no city is totally dependent upon a single revenue source, most cities do depend upon several sources, each of which is susceptible to, albeit to varying degrees, nonlocal factors. By way of illustration, the revenue yield to many Ohio cities that use the municipal income tax (Table 2) is susceptible to employment trends in steel, automobile, and rubber industries.[5] In recent years, employment levels in those industries, and therefore city revenues, have been affected by the actions of Japanese manufacturers, German steel companies, and OPEC oil producers. Less dramatic cases could be made for each of the other municipal revenue sources in Table 2. Where property tax levels are subject to voter approval in referenda, returns from sales taxes and user charges are determined by discretionary spending of consumers, and amounts of state and federal aid are dependent upon shifting legislative coalitions, local revenue stability is not assured. To the extent that economic health is the crucial exogenous variable for local fiscal health, local officials, however sophisticated, operate primarily from a reactive stance. The best they can do is think in terms of contingent situations, of the range of options available to them to take action, given a set of developments. Whether actions taken by individuals or communities will have any appreciable effect is debatable. As to the realities of the modern-day international economy, Rose (1980:223) notes: "Both electors and elected today often find themselves powerless. Whereas elections are about what people want, economics is about what people can have with scarce and uncertain resources."

IV. RELATING TO CITY GOVERNING CAPACITY

Throughout this analysis, city fiscal dependency is assumed to be measured as some percentage of a city's total general revenue. So defined, fiscal dependency is properly stated for the formal city government but is understated for the city as community or as site of public service delivery. Where a city government is formally responsible for education, hospital, or welfare functions, city budgets (and the *City Government Finances* series of the Bureau of the Census) will reflect the responsibility. Where the functions are not the formal responsibility of the city government but of some other unit (an independent school board, a hospital authority, a county welfare department), their relevance to city residents will not be evident in the city's total general revenue or in the amount of intergovernmental revenue recorded in the city budget. If the total amount of intergovernmental aid transferred to a city is calculated (adding, for example, state aid to an independent school district within the city to federal and state aid to the city government), the city, as community or service site, will be more fiscally dependent than when the formal city government is considered alone.[6]

The decision to consider all public revenues in a city or only those of the general-purpose city government involves more than an exercise in sophistry. Revenue bases and flows of intergovernmental aid are related to functional assignment; functional assignment, in turn, fundamentally shapes governmental and political patterns of a city. With schools and hospitals as city government services, the mayor or city manager and city council are legally and politically accountable for their administration. Developments that complicate those services—a strike by hospital employees, a decline in the number of school-aged children, changes in state school aid formulas—directly influence the decisions of elected city officials. Alternatively, when education and health care are not provided by city government, elected officials have greater flexibility in deciding on the extent of involvement in service problems. This suggests that two basic questions underlie any assessment of the impact of fiscal dependency on governing capacity. The first is, "Whose capacity?" And the second is, "Governing capacity to do what?"

Governing capacity is the ability of locally elected officials (mayors, members of city council, and so on) and their appointed surrogates (city managers, finance directors, police chiefs, and so on) to govern—*to do what they are required to do by law, and what they wish to do in light of local political culture, dominant community attitudes, and available resources.* This view is both more conservative and more expansive than prevailing ones of capacity. The centrality of elected officials assumes that, by the fact of election, they, and by extension their appointees, are the only ones legitimately empowered to govern on behalf of the city. It is recognized that other community elements (neighborhood associations; religious, business, and labor groups; organized crime) sponsor and conduct activities that shape the quality of city life. These elements advise, influence, and in some places even control elected officials. The groups and individual citizens can be praised for their contributions to the city or imprisoned for anticity actions, but unless they are elected they cannot be held liable for the city's governance.

Viewed in this way, governing capacity is contextually defined. The ability of elected officials to govern is determined much less by prevailing standards of model city government or the state of the art in municipal management practices than by the context within which the standards are imposed and the practices implemented. Responses to fiscal dependency and to fiscal stress are determined in the long and short term by the quality of leadership produced from the local political recruitment pool.

A.   The Dominant Paradigm of Local Governing Capacity

A contextual approach differs from a body of work done on local government capacity. Out of that work have come substantive findings, recommendations, and how-to action plans for moving city governments to more highly developed stages. For a portion of this important work the study premises and policy recommendations are updated versions of an old reform approach to structural change; governing capacity is to be enhanced by altering the formal organization and structure of city and metropolitan governments.[7]

For another portion of the work, governing capacity is management based, and a city's capacity level is determined by the adequacy of its performance of management activities. Philip Burgess (1975) sees capacity building as directed to three management functions: policy, resource, and program. These functions, according to Burgess (1975:708), "together constitute the core elements of public management and administration." It is to inadequacies in these core elements that capacity-building programs are formulated and directed. From a somewhat different approach, although with the same orientation, Beth Walter Honadle (1981:577) posits that capacity involves the ability to:

- Anticipate and influence change.
- Make informed, intelligent decisions about policy.
- Develop programs to implement policy.
- Attract and absorb resources.
- Manage resources.
- Evaluate current activities to guide future action.

Given acceptance of certain assumptions, the logic, reasoning, and conclusions of Burgess, Honadle, and others cannot be faulted. Two assumptions are overriding. First, is that governing capacity is determined primarily by management functions and a derived set of activities necessary to the accomplishment of those functions. Second, is the existence of valid, universal, and accepted performance standards for the functions and activities. Once the assumptions are made, it is relatively easy to assess the governing capacity of cities as a class or individually. The task can be performed by the capacity diagnostician who compares a city's performance to the universal standards. Any gap constitutes the target of capacity-building treatment.

Governing capacity as organizational structure, management activities, and universal standards constitutes a dominant paradigm. The paradigm, in one form or another, is of longstanding and essentially nonpolitical or apolitical. It is also widely accepted. That cities are labeled ungovernable, not because of a prolonged breakdown of civil order but because of accumulated "fragmentation" in their decision-making structures, presumes some achievable model city against which the ungovernable city can be measured.[8]

The paradigm's model city and the practices followed by its officials have been made concrete. Much of the stimulus for local management capacity building has been from the national level. Federal agencies have promulgated obligatory standards, by way of regulations as conditions of grants-in-aid, and provided management capacity-building assistance and lessons for local officials.[9] National professional groups put forth standards of exemplary behavior for their members. Local finance directors can learn of, and be urged to follow, generally accepted accounting principles. City managers can build a library of specialized handbooks on various aspects of their job. And elected officials can obtain coherent and well-written self-improvement workbooks on topics such as integrated financial management. All the materials are available from national organizations and are designed for use in cities in all regions.

The dominant capacity paradigm holds that many, if not most, local governing problems result from an ignorance of effective management practices. Ignorance can be overcome, management improved, and governing capacity expanded by way of new legislation, skill acquisition, and technical assistance. During periods of real stress, cities are challenged, and their governing capacities are tested. Thus, for example, the prominence of city fiscal problems has heightened interest in, and the salience of, financial management as a component of governing capacity. Approaches to revenue and fiscal-dependency problems are management approaches. Well-developed modified accrual accounting schemes, as part of a management information system, provide officials current and accurate information on conditions in the city. Future revenues can be estimated by regression or econometric-based forecasting models. Minimal disruptions in essential services are achieved by way of a rationally formulated priority structure of spending reductions. Any harm resulting from the cuts are checked by ongoing policy evaluation and compensated for by way of productivity improvements. Finally, a goal-setting process, as a preliminary to a strategic plan, allows a city and its officials to control their futures and minimize dependency.

Available studies suggest that local governments with good management practices in place deal more effectively with fiscal problems, including revenue shortfalls and reductions in aid, than those without (Levine et al., 1981). Lacking a rank ordering of cities by capacity scores, it is not known whether the highest-capacity cities are those with exemplary practices. More likely than not, the relationship does exist. Cities and their elected officials are not dumb. On recognition of the inadequacies of existing administrative arrangements, changes may be made. Since the late 1960s, there has been considerable transfer of functions between local governments and the state and between municipalities, counties, and special districts (ACIR, 1982:9-17). Without significant alteration in structural form, county governments have become increasingly important service providers in metropolitan and nonmetropolitan areas. Regarding adoption by cities of the city manager form between 1970 and 1980, Richard Stillman (1982:184) comments that:

> The pattern of change from mayor to manager government follows an established historical trend. Manager plan adoptions occur as small cities grow and encounter governmental and management problems that cannot be handled by part-time elected officials. The change in government is often accelerated by rapid population change, which can simply overwhelm small cities.

Although most cities and their elected officials are not dumb, they are not necessarily similar in other respects. The faith in a causal relationship between the adoption of new management forms or practices and increased governing capacity is essentially an optimistic one. If true, the solution to fiscal crises arising from capacity weakness would be management strength. The solution implies a sophisticated state of the art in management techniques and performance evaluation standards of universal applicability. But given the limited success of such techniques as zero-base budgeting at the local level, the management arts may still be evolving. And the diversity of state laws and fiscal systems complicate the adoption of universal standards (Gargan, 1983).

A management approach to governing capacity also implies that cities and their elected officials are able to learn and to respond quickly to environmental challenges. Most local governing in the United States is by governments of limited scope,[10] small management staffs, and elected officials more concerned with feasible than with optimal approaches to local problems. It is not that local officials fail to recognize the potential payoffs of management improvement; they do (McGowan and Stevens, 1983:132). Nonetheless, the press of daily business and the resistance to innovation from city councils and bureaucracies are such that limited attention can be given to capacity-building initiatives, whatever the recommendations of external observers.

B. Contextually Determined Governing Capacity

If city governing capacity is defined as the ability of local elected officials to do what they are required and wish to do, capacity is determined by local context rather than level of management sophistication. This ability of officials is always influenced by the interplay of a city's resources, expectations, and problems (Gargan, 1981). Governing capacity does not exist outside of a specific and real context. In all cities, the expectations held by segments of the community and key individuals as to how city government should perform, and to what they are entitled from city government, liberates and/or constrains elected officials. In cities where local affairs are dominated by an upper middle-class cosmopolitan citizenry, officials may well be able (and required) to perform by the canons of effective management. In such places, Larry Schroeder's (1982:124) judgment about the political risks of revenue forecasting is probably true:

> Dissemination of forecast results, even those that include the "warts," can produce political capital for public officials, especially if they fully understand what the forecast is telling and how it was produced. To an enlightened electorate (and surely an electorate that becomes accustomed to regular forecasts that do not shy from impending difficulties will grow increasingly enlightened), the fact that their public officials are attempting to anticipate trouble spots and make preparation for them should be seen as evidence of good management.

In cities of cosmopolitans, effective management might well handle the strains imposed on governing capacity by fiscal dependency. Reductions in external aid are absorbed or their effects are mitigated by creative approaches to service delivery.

For cities not dominated by enlightened citizens, the challenge to elected officials is more difficult. The exponential rate of growth in federal and state programs, aid, and regulations from the mid-1960s to the late 1970s was based in a heightening of expectations and a redefining of entitlements. One major factor contributing to the fiscal dependency of cities has been their role in implementing policies to satisfy heightened expectations and to comply with externally imposed mandates (Lovell, 1981; Muller and Fix, 1980). As local resources become increasingly scarce and problems become increasingly complex, elected officials can maintain existing governing capacity by lowering the expectations of the electorate as to what are appropriately the responsibilities of government.

Regardless of urban fiscal conditions, proposals for a lowering of expectations and acceptance of more limited entitlements are more easily stated than achieved. For many cities, governing capacity and fiscal dependency have been complicated by the politics of race, expectations, and entitlement. During the early months of 1983, mayoral primary elections in Chicago and Philadelphia involved debates over the quality of city administration and the accuracy of revenue forecasts; they also involved the racial characteristics of the candidates and neighborhood perceptions of likely service costs and benefits. Similarly, the appointment of a new chief administrator for the New York City public school system received much attention because of the need for management skill, at a time of fiscal shortages, but also because the leading contenders for the office were from different ethnic and racial groups. Also in early 1983, questions of city governing capacity in Boston related to the incumbent mayor's decisions on curtailing of basic services and to his political organization, fund-raising techniques, and work practices of city employees.

How events in Chicago, Philadelphia, New York, and Boston are viewed is fundamental to an understanding of the differences between the dominant management-oriented paradigm of city governing capacity and one that sees capacity as contextually determined. Highly visible and conflictual episodes in a city's life history may have little to do with either governing capacity or service delivery. Although widely publicized, the charges and countercharges of candidates might well be a diverting sideshow to the real conduct of government by career administrators. Whatever the division in city council or between the mayor and city unions, streets are repaired, buildings are inspected, and fires extinguished. This represents the local equivalent of the classic politics-administrative dichotomy, a kind of "boys will be boys" view of local politics.

The assumption of a separation of city politics and city administration, *even for purposes of analyzing management-improvement initiatives in the abstract*, is an optimistic one. Where the political and administrative domains are congruent rather than separate, management and service decisions are made not in isolation from political conflict but as manifestations and instruments of the conflict. Exercised in its highest form, this approach to city government makes extensive use of current symbols of administrative capacity building and reform rhetoric. Advocacy of change in organizational structure—replacement of an elected mayor with a city manager or a multimember county commission with an elected county executive—can be motivated by a desire to improve governmental performance; it can also be motivated by the desire of an out-of-power faction (which if in power would resist structural change) of the dominant party to replace its intraparty rivals. Cutback management processes designed to maximize rationality and group participation in budgetary reduction decisions (Coke and Moore, 1981) can be adopted and subsequently used to punish enemies and reward friends, irrespective of the economy or equity implications.

Where the condition of overlapping domains exists but participants are less sophisticated in the use of the symbols and rhetoric of administrative capacity building or reform, political dominance of governing can be more overt and heavy-handed. In small- to medium-sized cities the approach can employ the petty or bothersome—withholding public documents from political foes, delaying delivery of services to certain areas, or allocating funds to incumbent office holders solely on the basis of their party affiliation. The approach can also employ more serious practices such as the selective indictment of opponents for technical, but minor, violations of state statutes.

The implications should be clear. The degree of overlap of the administrative and political domains defines the context for administrative or management capacity-building initiatives. That political and administrative domains are congruent and political criteria dominate and guide even technical specialists does not necessarily imply low-quality or poorly administered public services. Indeed, the reverse is often the case. The elected local official, ambitious for reelection or higher office, may be considerably more sensitive to constituent demands for high-quality management and service delivery than the appointed functional professional. It was a practicing political philosopher, Richard M. Daley, that allegedly claimed, "Good government is good politics."

Highly politicized cities can be cities of quality public sector operations, and the political pressures on the administrative and management cadre to perform in an exemplary manner can be intense. But in such cities (and in their highly politicized counterparts where the quality of services is low and political pressures are exerted on administrators to violate professional norms), the political context reflects the distribution of community power. Understandably, power holders do not view favorably threats to the existing distribution. To the extent management capacity-building initiatives threaten, or even make less certain, this existing power distribution, they will not be welcome.

The intensity and style of city politics do change. In Cleveland, for example, Mayor George Voinovich has been elected and reelected as a Republican in a predominantly Democratic city. Prior to his election the city had suffered through a period of acrimonious political conflict, charges and counter-charges of mismanagement, and fiscal distress resulting in default on short-term notes. In office, the mayor has been required to install new financial management practices by a state-mandated fiscal oversight commission. He has also been able to attract competent financial managers to office and to begin actions designed to relieve Cleveland's fiscal stress (City of Cleveland, 1980). Mayor Voinovich's strategies have been well received in the area's businesses and good government circles and, in light of his reelection, presumably by most of Cleveland's voters. The strategies have had, if not tacit approval, at least not active opposition from other political power holders. Although important and commendable, Mayor Voinovich's financial management initiatives reflect only movement toward enhanced governing capacity. Whether fiscal reforms will outlast the mayor is an open, and the crucial, question. Given the history of municipal reform in many cities, and the strife of Cleveland politics in the recent past, there is no guarantee.

V. CONCLUSION

This analysis has followed a circuitous path to reach a simple point. It is local political context that produces a set of elected officials. Any governing capacity that exists in a city is reflected in the ability of that set of officials to govern— to do what they are required to do by law and what their communities wish them to do, given local expectations, resources, and problems. Governing capacity in a city (or any political system) is ultimately determined by, and must be evaluated in terms of, its political context.

Obviously, both political context and governing capacity are affected by the availability of revenues. In the 1980s, the relationship between fiscal dependency and governmental performance is seen as a paramount issue. However, despite the attention to the issue, the relationship is neither simple nor direct. That is, adequate financing is a necessary, but not sufficient, condition of local governmental capacity. What constitutes adequate, sufficient, and necessary is subject to ongoing reinterpretation. As the data on municipal finances suggest, the nature and extent of fiscal dependency vary considerably across states and across individual cities within the same state.

Reductions in federal and state aid will shift the dependency to other sources. Cities have used a number of options, including new user charges, privatization of services, and deferring action on problems. Actions to shift dependency sources have strained, and will continue to strain, the ability of local officials to govern. As fewer public dollars are available for public sector employees and public sector-dependent clients, local politics will undoubtedly become more intense and uncompromising. Particularly in the most fiscally distressed cities, officials will be much less concerned with matters of entitlement, equity, and social need, and more concerned with the conventional style of urban politics, allocating scarce resources on the basis of the power bases of requestors.

The outlook for many cities is bleak. Although governing capacity and policy outcomes in a city are determined by local political patterns, the city exists within a broader framework of interdependent governmental and economic systems. Developments in this broader framework are, for the most part, beyond the control of local politicians. When these developments are of an incremental sort, minor shifts from the normal, local adjustments can be thought out and implemented. But when, as in recent years, the developments take the form of system shocks, major and unanticipated departures from the normal, meaningful local responses may not be available.

The facts of interdependency and locally uncontrollable economic factors are more than givens, they condition the potential utility of specific practical management techniques advocated by the dominant governing-capacity paradigm. As a simple example, any revenue forecasts based upon a regression model must assume, by definition, a best-fit line. Where there is substantial variation about the line as a result of short-term changes in the revenue yield to a particular community over time, the significance of the model is minimized. The dilemma is familiar. It is during periods of uncertainty that the need and incentive for local officials to use management techniques with predictive capability is greatest, whatever their usual decision rules. Yet, during such periods the required capability is not always evident.

When the next three to five years are assumed to be much like the past three to five years, projections can be made as to the future costs of current decisions. The validity of the assumptions about the future is the key determinant of projections, a fact recognized by those involved in basic research on forecasting techniques. During periods of rapid economic and social change, assumption-making may be more art form than science, more in the vein of astrology than astronomy.

The point is more than a banal comment on the difficulty of coping with future uncertainty. It is meant to illustrate a fundamental issue of local governing capacity and capacity building. Management practices, procedures, and techniques are not intrinsically good, nor is their value self-evident to public officials. Adoption of innovative practices requires receptivity in target communities. If changes are externally imposed, by state law or federal regulations, there is no assurance that they will be viewed locally as legitimate. Naomi Caiden's (1981: 12) observation regarding budget reform is equally applicable to management capacity-building efforts in general:

> Budget reformers seem to believe that behavior follows form since they concentrate so much on the formal processes of budgeting and rarely deal with budgeting behavior. The trouble with this view is that new procedures may simply be subverted by old ways instead of mandating real changes in decision-making behavior. Reforms are formally instituted but the old ways continue in practice.

For negative local political factors and resistant governing coalitions to be overridden by proponents of modern management practices, there must be potential payoffs to local officials. When the capacity builders cannot deliver the payoffs, such as valid projections during periods of economic and social instability, success is unlikely. Where the future appears to be a simple continuation of the past, the impetus for disrupting established routines is not strong. Progressive leaders in progressive communities may be amenable to innovative techniques or fads simply because they are already capable. Those leaders and communities most in need of improved capacity may resist change simply because they are less capable.

NOTES

1. On the management and politics of revenue reduction the work of Charles Levine and his colleagues has been especially important. The details of coping with fiscal stress in four local governments (Oakland, Cincinnati, Prince George County, and Baltimore) are analyzed in Levine, Rubin et al. (1981). Important too is the work of Terry Nichols Clark, especially Clark and Ferguson (1983). Discussion of a number of the issues related to fiscal dependency and stress, as well as a very comprehensive bibliography, can be found in the edited volume by Burchell and Listokin (1981) of the Center for Urban Policy Research of Rutgers University.

2. Fiscal and political problems develop in local governments when there are disruptions in the flow of funds from federal and state sources. So in mid-1983, many local officials were apprehensive over the local fiscal consequences of a failure of Congress to renew general revenue sharing. In Ohio, local schools have been confronted with midfiscal year announcements of reductions in state aid. The issue is, of course, not fiscal source but fiscal stability. For a cross-cultural discussion of local government reliance on external revenue sources, see Ashford (1980).

3. Among the most important centers of deciphering has been the Metropolitan Program at the Maxwell School of Syracuse University. During the 1960s, the research and teaching of Seymour Sacks and Alan K. Campbell influenced a generation of students. Given the quality of work that continues to be produced in the program, their successors maintain an important tradition.

4. Obviously, the statement is debatable. Although a loss of 10% of own-source revenue would cause a lowering of service levels, it would not necessarily render cities incapable of governing. In an era of slow economic growth, it is unrealistic not to expect a decline in the level and quality of municipal services, despite calls for increased productivity and better local management (see Thurow, 1983).

5. During periods of high employment, those Ohio cities that are manufacturing centers have enjoyed high municipal income tax returns relative to cities more dependent on the property tax. Of course, the reverse is also true. High unemployment has had an especially negative impact on cities most dependent on the income tax.

6. The distinction is important. Governing capacity as viewed here is determined primarily by political factors rather than aggregate level of services provided. Inclusion of all intergovernmental aid in calculations complicates political analysis since the receipient units may function as autonomous entities, not necessarily requiring any interaction or coordination. For one example of the consequences of combining different forms of aid to define fiscal dependency, see the analysis and testimony of George Sternlieb et al. (1982) presented to the Joint Economic Committee during its hearings on the Reagan National Urban Policy Report.

7. At least some of the studies of the Advisory Commission on Intergovern-
    mental Relations relate to a longstanding faith in structural rearrange-
    ments. See, for example, the units of analysis and recommendations in the
    1982 study, *State and Local Roles in the Federal System.* It is not that
    structure is unimportant; the seminal works of Robert Bish and Elinor and
    Vincent Ostrom have demonstrated the crucial relevance of structural
    arrangements for service and policy consequences (Bish and Ostrom, 1973;
    Ostrom and Ostrom, 1980). Neither the metropolitan structure nor the
    public choice schools have given much attention to the relationship
    between structural factors and political leadership factors. On this point
    see Dahl's study of New Haven (1961) and the important article by
    Pressman (1972) on mayoral leadership.
8. A persuasive case is made by Douglas Yates (1978) that it is structural
    arrangements that make cities "ungovernable." But note the still relevant,
    if not more relevant, argument of Edward Banfield (1974) that urban
    problems are at base a function of the presence of significant numbers of
    lower-class, present-oriented individuals in cities.
9. An important source of capacity-building assistance has been the U.S.
    Department of Housing and Urban Development. For an assessment of the
    department's activities, see Warren and Aronson (1981).
10. By 1980, more than half (55.5%) of the total U.S. population and the pre-
    ponderance of local government units were accounted for by places of
    under 25,000 population. Only slightly more than one-quarter (25.4%) of
    the total 1980 population was in a small number of places over 100,000
    population.

REFERENCES

Advisory Commission on Intergovernmental Relations. (1980a). *The Federal
    Role in the Federal System: The Dynamics of Growth, a Crisis of Confi-
    dence and Competence.* ACIR, Washington, D.C.
Advisory Commission on Intergovernmental Relations. (1980b). *Recent Trends
    in Federal and State Aid to Local Governments.* ACIR, Washington, D.C.
Advisory Commission on Intergovernmental Relations. (1981). *Significant
    Features of Fiscal Federalism, 1980–81 Edition.* ACIR, Washington, D.C.
Advisory Commission on Intergovernmental Relations. (1982). *State and Local
    Roles in the Federal System.* ACIR, Washington, D.C.
Advisory Commission on Intergovernmental Relations. (1983). *Significant
    Features of Fiscal Federalism, 1981–82 Edition.* ACIR, Washington, D.C.
Anton, T. J. (1980). Federal assistance programs: The politics of system trans-
    formation. In Ashford, D. E., ed., *National Resources and Urban Policy.*
    Methuen, New York, pp. 15–31.
Ashford, D. E., ed. (1980). *National Resources and Urban Policy.* Methuen,
    New York.
Bahl, R. (1982). The fiscal health of state and local governments: 1982 and
    beyond. *Public Budgeting and Finance 2*:5–21.

Banfield, E. C. (1974). *The Unheavenly City Revisited*. Little Brown, Boston.

Beer, S. H. (1978). Federalism, nationalism, and democracy in America. *The American Political Science Review 70*:9–21.

Bish, R. and Ostrom, V. (1973). *Understanding Urban Government*. American Enterprise Institute, Washington, D.C.

Bowman, J. H. (1981). Urban revenue structures: An overview of patterns, trends, and issues. *Public Administration Review 41*:131–143.

Break, G. F. (1980). *Financing Government in a Federal System*. The Brookings Institute, Washington, D.C.

Burchell, R. W. and Listokin, D., eds. (1981). *Cities Under Stress: The Fiscal Crisis of Urban America*. The Center for Urban Policy Research, Piscataway, N.J.

Burgess, P. M. (1975). Capacity building and the elements of public management. *Public Administration Review 35*:705–716.

Caiden, N. (1981). Public budgeting amidst uncertainty and instability. *Public Budgeting and Finance 1*:6–19.

City of Cleveland. (July, 1980). *City of Cleveland Operations Improvement Task Force Final Report*.

Clark, T. N. and Ferguson, L. C. (1983). *City Money*. Columbia University Press, New York.

Coke, J. G. and Moore, C. (1981). *Toward A Balanced Budget: Making the Tough Decisions*. National Association of Counties, Washington, D.C.

Coleman, H. A. and Ross, J. P. (1983). The new federalism strategy and state and local government finances. *Journal of Urban Affairs 5*:29–40.

Dahl, R. (1961). *Who Governs?* Yale University Press, New Haven.

Elazar, D. J. (1979). Statement before the U.S. House of Representatives Subcommittee on the city on "Revenue Sharing with the States." In *Revenue Sharing with the States*. Subcommittee on the City of the Committee on Banking, Finance and Urban Affairs, House of Representatives. U.S. Government Printing Office, Washington, D.C.

Gargan, J. (1981). Consideration of local government capacity. *Public Administration Review 41*:649–658.

Gargan, J. (1983). Financial management capacity: A political perspective. Unpublished manuscript.

Honadle, B. (1981). A capacity-building framework: A search for concept and purpose. *Public Administration Review 41*:575–580.

Joint Economic Committee, Congress of the United States. (1982). *Trends in the Fiscal Condition of Cities: 1980–1982*. U.S. Government Printing Office, Washington, D.C.

Landau, M. (1969). Redundancy, rationality, and the problem of duplication and overlap. *Public Administration Review 29*:346–358.

Levine, C. H., Rubin, I. S., and Wolohojian, G. G. (1981). *The Politics of Retrenchment: How Local Governments Manage Fiscal Stress*. Sage Publications, Beverly Hills.

Lovell, C. H. (1981). Evolving local government dependency. *Public Administration Review 41*:189–202.

McGowan, R. P. and Stevens, J. M. (1983). Local governments' initiatives in a climate of uncertainty. *Public Administration Review 43*:127–136.

Merget, A. E. (1980). The era of fiscal restraint. In *The Municipal Yearbook, 1980*. International City Management Association, Washington, D.C.

Muller, T. and Fix, M. (1980). Federal solicitude, local costs: The impact of federal regulation on municipal finances. *Regulation 4*:29–36.

Nathan, R. P. (1981). Federal grants—How are they working? In Burchell, R. W., and Listokin, D., eds., *Cities Under Stress: The Fiscal Crises of Urban America*. The Center for Urban Policy Research, Piscataway, N.J.

Ostrom, E. and Ostrom, V. (1980). Public economy organization and service delivery. In Mathewson, K., and Neenan, W. B., eds., *Financing the Metropolis*. Praeger, New York.

Pressman, J. (1972). Preconditions of mayoral leadership. *American Political Science Review 66*:511–524.

Rose, R. (1980). Misperceiving public expenditure: Feelings about "cuts." In Levine, C. H., and Rubin, I., eds., *Fiscal Stress and Public Policy*. Sage Publications, Beverly Hills.

Schroeder, L. (1982). Local government multi-year budgetary forecasting: Some administrative and political issues. *Public Administration Review 42*: 121–127.

Sternlieb, G., Burchell, R. W., Carr, J. H., Florida, R. L., and Nemeth, J. (1982). Growth and characteristics of the transfer-dependent, intergovernmental city. In *The Administration's 1982 National Urban Policy Report*. Joint Economic Committee, Congress of the United States. U.S. Government Printing Office, Washington, D.C.

Stillman, R. J., II. (1982). Local public management in transition: A report on the current state of the profession. In *The Municipal Yearbook, 1982*. International City Management Association, Washington, D.C.

Thurow, L. C. (January, 1983). Economic outlook. *Public Management*.

U.S. Bureau of the Census. *City Government Finances in 1980–81*. U.S. Government Printing Office, Washington, D.C.

Viscount, F. (November 22, 1982). Cities' response to NLC survey shows dramatic need for revenue sharing. *Nation's Cities Weekly*.

Warren, C. R. and Aronson, L. R. (1981). Sharing management capacity: Is there a federal responsibility? *Public Administration Review 41*:381–387.

Yates, D. (1978). *The Ungovernable City*. The MIT Press, Cambridge, Mass.

Unit Three

POLICY-MAKING IN STATE AND LOCAL GOVERNMENTS

11

Chief Executive Support and Innovation

James L. Perry Graduate School of Management, University of California, Irvine, California

I. INTRODUCTION

Technological and managerial innovations are viewed as primary means to improve the productivity and effectiveness of state and local governments (Perry and Kraemer, 1979). Large investments have been made in the development and diffusion of various physical and management technologies such as minipumpers, modular housing, team policing, and computerized assessment. These and other innovations have become a way for state and local governments to confront the dilemma posed by conflicting demands from the public for more and higher-quality services and lower taxes.

State and local government chief executives (e.g., governors, mayors, city managers) are perhaps the most influential participants in their organizations (Abney and Lauth, 1982); recent studies of technological innovation in local governments suggest that their influence in the adoption and implementation of innovations is no exception to this generalization. Chief executives interject themselves into the technological decision-making processes of line agencies (e.g., fire, police, and public works departments), stimulate line agencies to perceive performance gaps that might be closed by technological innovations, and provide moral and financial support for innovation adoption. Thus, although technological leadership is primarily a characteristic of specific line agencies within a government organization, Robert Yin and his colleagues from the Rand Corporation contend:

> Although it is generally useful to analyze the activities of a police department or a public health agency as an autonomous organization,

such an agency is highly dependent on the general jurisdiction and its "overhead" agencies and executives, e.g., the local legislative body, the chief executive of the jurisdiction, and such related staff offices as the budget bureau. (Yin et al., 1976:74).

At the outset of the chapter, it will be helpful to provide some definitions so that the reader has a frame of reference for understanding the chief executive's role. First, when we refer to innovation we mean "the successful utilization of processes, programs or products which are new to an organization and which are introduced as a result of decisions made within that organization" (Rowe and Boise, 1974:285). This definition is quite broad, but it conveys the central idea that an innovation is something "new" that has been successfully and voluntarily introduced to an organization. Using this broad definition, government innovations may take many forms. As Donald Stone (1981:508) suggests: "They [innovations] apply to objectives and policies, character of product or services, hardware and software technology, procedure and process. They also involve structure, management style and systems, external and internal relationships."

Second, it is important to be aware that innovation occurs over time and can be divided into four stages (Eveland et al., 1977; Syracuse Research Corporation, 1977): *preadoption, adoption, implementation, and incorporation.* It is in the preadoption stage that a state or local government becomes aware of a problem or performance gap that requires attention. At the adoption stage, a decision is made to choose among various solutions and whether to adopt a particular solution. If a particular innovation is selected to conclude the adoption stage, then it must be implemented in the next stage. Over time a successful innovation will be used and accepted and thereby fully incorporated into government operations.

This chapter focuses primarily on how the chief executive can promote innovation by the design of important relationships inside and outside a state or local government. It emphasizes the mechanisms by which state and local chief executives direct and encourage subordinates to pursue their independent goals and thereby facilitate the innovation process. For the sake of brevity and simplicity, the chapter takes essentially a positive approach to innovation by assuming that the chief executive is competent, well informed, motivated by the broad interests of the organization and the constituents served and, is interested in facilitating change. The situation in any government jurisdiction will vary from this ideal. In some instances, a chief executive's intervention will lead to dysfunctions in the innovation process (Perry and Kraemer, 1977, 1980). For example, the chief executive may support adoption of an innovation because of anticipated power shifts, regardless of the organizational benefits generated by the innovation (Dutton and Kraemer, 1977; Kraemer and Dutton, 1979; Kraemer and King, 1976). Thus, the reader should be aware that how a chief executive actually behaves may deviate considerably from the ideal type discussed.

II. CHIEF EXECUTIVE CONTROL OF THE INNOVATION PROCESS

There are three general ways in which a chief executive can influence innovation in an organization. One has the chief executive develop expectations among staff, clients, and constituents that support the innovation process. Another structures the organization's climate to support and sustain innovative activity. A third provides the resources—political, technical, and economic—for the successful implementation and incorporation of innovations. Each of these avenues by which the chief executive can influence innovation is integral to success and can be characterized by unique tactics.

A. Staff, Client, and Constituency Expectations

For most employees and clients of state and local governments, the chief executive, together with the governing body and line department heads, is the most visible reference point. The chief executive's actions can be powerful messages to employees that either generate bursts of creativity or as easily retard the development of new technologies or processes. The image the chief executive portrays to staff about innovation and change is, therefore, of continuous and genuine importance. As two local government participants, one a city manager and the other a technology coordinator, described the process:

> The truth of the matter about innovation is that we do it all the time
> as we adjust to new demands and shifts in policies. And, probably
> the greatest innovators are our employees who adapt so well that
> they have figured out how to survive almost any social threat, city
> council, or administration. (Donaldson and Singleton, 1975:8)

And just as state and local government employees must continuously adjust internal processes to meet new demands and policies, clients and constituents must also adapt.

Whereas the chief executive's importance as a communicator with these groups is evident, the tactics the chief executive employs in facilitating innovation are less well defined. As an "agenda setter" and "gatekeeper" in the innovation process, the chief executive can influence both demand, by manipulating perceived performance gaps, and supply, by bringing new ideas to the staff's attention. Among the tactics through which the chief executive alters the supply/demand perceptions of others are: leading the informal information system (Quinn, 1982), signaling support of innovation proposals (Bingham et al., 1981), and legitimizing new viewpoints among staff, clients, and constituents.

Effective chief executives develop informal networks with an array of organizational and extraorganizational individuals and groups to sense possible needs for change (Quinn, 1982). These networks are used by the chief executive to overcome the filtering of information. Thus, state and local chief executives build relationships with other executives, interest groups, career civil servants, and business and university representatives.

State and local government chief executives have come to rely on professional associations, such as the International City Management Association (ICMA) and the Council of State Governments, as important network elements. Jack Walker (1969), a political scientist, argues that such associations serve as information sources and policy cues and as "occupational contact networks" that expedite the transfer of personnel between jurisdictions. Bingham et al. (1981:15), citing earlier research by Dwight Waldo who characterized them as "hinge" institutions, make the case for the centrality of professional associations in the public sector innovation process: "Professional-specialist organizations . . . are part of whatever societal transformations are underway. Solutions to problems cannot be accomplished without their input. Public service professional associations are at the center of 'what's happening,' and must be so viewed." The chief executive's professional association contacts help to: identify innovations for potential adoption; define performance gaps by comparisons with salient reference points; and, recognize possible future threats to the status quo. As a linking pin between the professional association and the organization, the chief executive integrates this information into the messages sent to employees, clients, and constituents, and the formal agenda set for the organization.

Of course, the chief executive is neither the only organizational member with professional association linkages nor the only initiator of change. When the chief executive is not the initiator, he or she must be aware of the need to facilitate the activities of others. Donaldson and Singleton (1975) suggest the chief executive must permit the staff to view him or her as their supporter when they take the initiative to innovate. Research also indicates (Bingham et al., 1981) that an elected or appointed chief executive's opinion about the importance of innovation is the primary determinant of a movement toward adoption, suggesting that the chief executive's support of change performs a significant gatekeeping function.

A logical extension of the chief executive's role in responding supportively to the ideas of others is that the chief executive also must actively work to make new ideas legitimate. For new ideas that entail significant uncertainties or concern, chief executives may seek to "create forums and allow slack time for their organizations to talk through threatening issues, work out the implications of new solutions, or gain an improved information bank that will permit new options to be evaluated objectively in comparison with more familiar alternatives" (Quinn, 1982:192). This type of activity by the chief executive may receive little notice, but it is a significant way of facilitating the generation, development, and acceptance of new ideas.

B. Creating an Innovative Environment

The stimulation of expectations and ideas for change requires systematic organizational support so that innovations are not prematurely rejected. The goal in creating an innovative environment is to institutionalize the innovation process and make it productive. Incentives must be created for organization members with new ideas to help them overcome resistance from opponents. Donaldson and Singleton describe this process as follows:

> In any organization one will find a few people willing to attempt change, with others attempting to block such activity. For those who try to innovate there is often so little room to maneuver that their attempts are rebuffed and they fail. Thus, the manager is faced with making changes in the organization itself and the staff relationships if efforts to innovate are to succeed. (Donaldson and Singleton, 1975:9)

Three aspects of the organization's climate that affect innovation appear particularly responsive to the chief executive's influence. They are professionalism, technical competence of staff, and concern for results. Professionalism refers to a climate designed to sustain rational behavior, (i.e., largely structured, systematic, and coordinated) (Rowe and Boise, 1974). Professionalism embodies several attributes. It implies that organizational members are integrated with external professional communities and have relatively extensive channels for interpersonal communication. It also presumes a division of labor within the governmental unit with appropriate coordination among specialists and their roles. Finally, professionalism assumes orderly internal communications so that innovative ideas and proposals can be adequately conveyed. Although these attributes are not equally important at all stages, they would appear to be particularly important for the latter stages of adoption and implementation.

Each of these attributes of professionalism is largely under the chief executive's control and therefore can be influenced in a variety of ways. Resources for and approval of staff participation in professional organizations is one means. A cursory review of a local government's line-item budget will very quickly indicate whether the chief executive actively supports such linkages. The development of orderly communication may also include efforts by the chief executive to inform and update legislators, making them aware of the organization's goals and preventing inadvertent sabotage of the innovation process.

Within the organization, the chief executive may encounter defensive responses to innovative proposals. Insight about the reasons for departmental defensiveness and parochialism is provided in a study by Pettigrew (1973) of the organizational politics surrounding a large-scale computer innovation. He argued that innovations invoke political behavior because they involve individuals or organizational subunits making claims against the current distribution of organizational resources such as salaries, new equipment, information, or control over a new activity. An innovation may generate a demand for new resource allocations to an individual or subunit that has not previously been a claimant. And, consequently, other claimants might resist the innovation introduction because they see their interests threatened by a potential change in the current resource distribution.

The chief executive can minimize defensive behavior and encourage professionalism by balancing departmental and organizational perspectives. One means for achieving this balance is to develop incentive systems that reward and recognize the organizational perspective. Another means is through interdepartmental committees. Donaldson and Singleton offer an example of how committees operated in Tacoma, Washington:

> Balance in the operating structure was accomplished by revising decision-making procedures. Extensive use of interdepartmental teams has drawn staff into interdepartmental decision-making and has encouraged reviewing of procedures. Innovative staff have the opportunity to legitimately introduce their ideas, and there is less chance of being rebuffed without reason. (Donaldson and Singleton, 1975:10)

In addition to promoting a professional climate, the chief executive must take the lead in assuring that the organization has an adequate reservoir of talented staff. The staff's skill and experience is an important component of innovation (Perry and Danziger, 1980). Because the chief executive selects so many of the organization's top personnel, he is directly responsible for the quality of key personnel and, indirectly, by his example and the decisions of subordinates, for many other appointments. Stone (1981:511) suggests that many executives fail in this activity because of "one of the deep-rooted human vanities . . . the assumption that the competencies of prospects for a managerial post can be determined in a brief interview."

A state or local government climate characterized by professionalism and a technically skilled staff is incomplete unless it includes concern for results. Performance norms within the organization are critical for innovation because they affect so many phases of the process. For example, performance expectations are necessary for triggering a performance gap at the preadoption stage and also for evaluating an innovation at the adoption phase. The chief executive's leadership is central for creating a pervasive and constructive concern for results. In particular, the chief executive's example of and support for meaningful performance evaluations of subordinates and subunits are important indicators of this concern.

As to the assessment of specific technologies, the chief executive's concern for results also is critical. Because the chief executive needs to approve the initiatives of others, he or she must reserve judgment about the value of a particular innovation until it can be shown to improve services or reduce costs (Kraemer and Dutton, 1979). Kraemer and Dutton describe as "faith" a chief executive's support for an innovation that is offered independent of specific and identifiable benefits. They suggest that faith reflects deep sentiments about the value of a particular technology that are not easily depleted through disappointments with the technology. The chief executive's failure to judge innovations objectively based on identifiable benefits and, more importantly, the failure to demand the same from subordinates, risk the adoption of unsuccessful and costly changes.

C. Resource Provider

Whereas the chief executive may be successful in setting an agenda for innovation and creating a supportive climate, most efforts to innovate will fail without a third ingredient—resources. These resources are not only financial, but technical and political as well. The chief executive's primary role is to bring together the various coalitions needed to assure an adequate supply of resources. This is perhaps the most challenging of the chief executive's roles. As Donaldson and Singleton (1975:10) note: "Our experience is that the extent of the need for not only resources, but for several types of resources, easily is underestimated."

Coalition building is the central requirement of resource acquisition. Lambright and Flynn (1977) offer some useful insights about coalitions in local governments. They studied the adoption of fourteen technologies in the Syracuse/Rochester, New York area. They found that adoption of most of these innovations cost more than existing budgets could support, and the lead agencies therefore had to build coalitions to provide additional financial support from community, state, and federal sources.

Lambright and Flynn also found the ideal technological innovation coalition has two axes. One axis is intergovernmental and is based on state and federal officials as fund sources. Therefore, as outside promoters of innovation, they are generators of change within the local system. The second axis is community based and consists of citizen groups, interest groups, the media, suppliers, clients, and strategic employee groups.

The intergovernmental coalition is essential at the outset of the adoption phase of innovation. It is an important asset for bureaucratic entrepreneurs, such as department heads and bureau chiefs, in identifying performance gaps and innovative ways to deal with them. Once an innovation is adopted, however, the community-based coalition is a means for sustaining the innovation process through implementation and routinization. Bureaucratic entrepreneurs must forge alliances with suppliers, clients, and strategic employee groups to make sure that what is adopted will be implemented and used (Lambright and Flynn, 1977:116).

How does the chief executive influence these coalition-building processes? For particularly important or significant issues, the chief executive may lead the coalition. In Lambright and Flynn's Syracuse/Rochester study, for example, the Onondaga County executive led in championing adoption of a $50-million resource recovery plant by securing major grants from the state and federal governments.

According to Lambright and Flynn (1977), successful demonstration projects are among the most effective strategies administrative leaders can use to build coalitions. A demonstration project is a small-scale test of a proposed innovation. It is a way of establishing commitments of financial and other support from intergovernmental actors and of making a visible show of results for community members. Demonstrations are therefore helpful for building coalitions at relatively low cost and risk. They are useful for testing the technical feasibility of a new technology or process prior to a commitment to full-scale adoption. Demonstrations also reduce political risks because they are reversible if the results prove the demonstration to be a social or political liability.

Another way in which the chief executive may facilitate the development of coalition support for innovation proposals is to assist bureaucratic entrepreneurs within the organization (i.e., usually the heads of line agencies) in putting coalitions together. This may entail shifting slack resources to help overcome impediments to the creation or operation of intergovernmental or community-based coalitions. This commitment of support to an innovation coalition may extend throughout the innovation process, from the preadoption phase to incorporation. For example, from their experience in Tacoma, Donaldson and Singleton suggest that:

> Once agreement has been reached on a program, it is important for the manager to create a position on his staff dedicated to the implementation of the agreed program. . . . It becomes the job of the person in this position to utilize the staff, organization, and resource facilitation that the [city] manager has done to make the program work. (Donaldson and Singleton, 1975:10)

By creating a new staff position as part of the adoption of an innovation, the chief executive's support continues into the implementation phase of the innovation process.

III. CONCLUSION

Although there is little empirical research in the area, anecdotal and case study evidence suggest that the chief executive plays a pivotal role in a state or local government's innovation process. The chief executive appears to influence the innovation process in three ways: by developing appropriate expectations among staff and constituents; by creating a supportive organizational climate; and by providing adequate political, technical, and economic resources.

Even when the chief executive is successful in providing all these conditions, there are still many other constraints that might sidetrack the process (Feller and Menzel, 1977). The lack of appropriate technologies and legal uncertainties are but two reasons why the process may fail even with the chief executive's support. However, despite the fact that the results are seldom certain, active support from the chief executive can increase considerably the probability that the innovation process will run its course.

REFERENCES

Abney, G. and Lauth, T. P. (1982). Influence of the chief executive on city line agencies. *Public Administration Review 42*(2):135–143.

Bingham, R. D., Hawkins, B. W., Frendreis, J. P., and LeBlanc, M. P. (1981). *Professional Associations and Municipal Innovation*. University of Wisconsin Press, Madison.

Donaldson, W. V. and Singleton, H. R. (1975). The manager as catalyst. *Public Management 57*(4):8–10.

Dutton, W. H. and Kraemer, K. L. (1977). Technology and urban management, the power payoffs of computing. *Administration and Society 9*(3):305–340.

Eveland, J. D., Rogers, E. M., and Klepper, C. (1977). *The Innovation Process in Public Organizations*. University of Michigan, Department of Journalism, Ann Arbor.

Feller, I. and Menzel, D. C. (1977). Diffusion milieux as a focus of research on innovation in the public sector. *Policy Sciences 8*(1):49–68.

Kraemer, K. L. and King, J. L. (1976). Computers, power, and urban management: What every local executive should know. *Sage Professional Papers in Administrative and Policy Studies 3*(03-031). Sage Publications, Beverly Hills.

Kraemer, K. L. and Dutton, W. H. (1979). Urban technology, executive support, and computing. *Urban Interest 1*(2):35–42.

Lambright, W. H. and Flynn, P. J. (1977). Bureaucratic politics and technological change in local government. *Urban Analysis 4*:93–118.

Perry, J. L. and Danziger, J. N. (1980). The adoptability of innovations, an empirical assessment of computer applications in local governments. *Administration and Society 11*(4):461–492.

Perry, J. L. and Kraemer, K. L. (1977). The chief executive in local government information systems: Catalyst or barrier to innovation? *Urban Systems 2*: 121–131.

Perry, J. L. and Kraemer, K. L. (1979). *Technological Innovation in American Local Governments*. Pergamon Press, New York.

Perry, J. L. and Kraemer, K. L. (1980). Chief executive support and innovation adoption. *Administration and Society 12*(2):158–177.

Pettigrew, A. M. (1973). *The Politics of Organizational Decision Making*. Tavistock, London.

Quinn, J. B. (1982). Managing strategic change. In Tushman, M. L. and Moore, W. L., eds., *Readings in the Management of Innovation*. Pitman Publishing, Marshfield, Mass., pp. 188–206. Reprinted from *Sloan Management Review* 2(4):3–20.

Rowe, L. A. and Boise, W. B. (1974). Organizational innovation: Current research and evolving concepts. *Public Administration Review* 34(3): 284–293.

Stone, D. C. (1981). Innovative organizations require innovative managers. *Public Administration Review* 41(5):507–513.

Syracuse Research Corporation. (1977). *Adoption and Utilization of Urban Technology: A Decision-Making Study*. Report to the National Science Foundation, Washington, D.C.

Walker, J. L. (1969). The diffusion of innovations among the American states. *American Political Science Review* 63(3):880–899.

Yin, R., Heald, K., Vogel, M., Fleischauer, P., and Vladek, B. (1976). *A Review of Case Studies of Technological Innovations in State and Local Services*. The Rand Corporation, Washington, D.C.

12

The Governor as Administrator

Alan J. Wyner   Department of Political Science, University of California, Santa Barbara, California

The contemporary governor performs several overlapping roles. An appreciation of any one role requires some awareness of the full picture. Although this chapter focuses on governors as administrators, this activity is only a segment of gubernatorial responsibilities. How a governor performs as an administrator, the amount of time and energy devoted to administrative chores, and the extent of success as an administrator are all conditioned by the competing demands of other roles. To provide a context for the primary topic of this chapter, it seems appropriate at the start to survey briefly the territory today's governors must cover.

I. GUBERNATORIAL ROLES

At the top of any list of gubernatorial roles is the most ubiquitous one—politician. No man or woman can be elected governor without adopting this mantle, campaign rhetoric notwithstanding. The campaigning does not stop on election day because all successful gubernatorial candidates carry the hopes and aspirations of their winning electoral coalition for certain tangible and symbolic policy actions and outcomes. Keeping the coalition viable during the term of office is a central concern of governors, and thus they play the political role.

Partly as a consequence of the political role, and partly because of widespread expectations by the public, the media, and other governmental actors, governors become policy formulators. They are expected to have policy preferences that they articulate in the form of concrete proposals for governmental action. Of course, the policy formulator role dovetails with the requirement to act as a politician; the two roles are mutually reinforcing. Formulating policy proposals, however, requires more attention to substantive detail and practicality than is necessary when making speeches on the campaign trail.

All governors have certain legally mandated responsibilities, although the list of such tasks is not uniform in each state. These responsibilities include functions such as deciding upon the appropriateness of bills sent to the governor by the legislature (except in North Carolina where the governor has no authority to veto legislation), making appointments to certain positions in the executive and sometimes the judicial branch, presenting a proposed state budget to the legislature, and handling requests for the extradition of suspected criminals. Every governor chooses a personal style for meeting these legally imposed aspects of the job, but it is virtually impossible to avoid them.

A gubernatorial role that does permit wide latitude in definition, and sometimes even the possibility of ignoring it, is the ceremonial aspect of being governor. Welcoming visiting dignitaries, cutting ribbons to open new buildings, putting in an appearance at a charity fund-raising event, and other similar activities are somewhat discretionary because governors may select only those ceremonies that benefit them or a cherished cause. No governor, however, can completely escape ceremonial responsibilities because too many groups and important individuals expect gubernatorial support for their activity. But at least governors can work most of these chores into the schedule according to their own priorities.

Through a combination of constitutional mandate, political necessity, and public expectations, governors must also perform an administrative role. Executive decisions must be made about how public policy will be interpreted and implemented. Personnel must be selected to administer state programs. Within certain limits, organizational responsibilities must be delegated and articulated and lines of authority established. Resources must be allocated and priorities for executive branch actions established. All this is conditioned by, but not necessarily dominated by, the guidelines and provisions of legislative actions. Governors are commonly referred to as the *chief executive*, with the connotation that they are in complete charge of the executive branch in its performance of administrative tasks. Because of numerous constitutional and legal obstacles, as well as extenuating political circumstances, governors are rarely supreme commanders in administrative matters. By picking and choosing times and issues carefully, a governor can become a forceful and successful administrator, but success in the administrative role is not guaranteed. Explaining how and why this is the case becomes the underlying purpose of this chapter.

Governors, then, can be thought of as politicians, policy formulators, bearers of certain legally mandated responsibilities, performers of ceremonial tasks, and administrators. These roles overlap in both complementary and conflicting fashion. In the performance of one role a governor may be simultaneously helping to perform another role. Presiding at a public ceremony may also be generating good will with persons from whom the governor needs support for political or policy goals. On the other hand, directing a state agency to implement a program in a certain fashion based on an efficiency criterion may alienate individuals whose support the governor needs in an upcoming political fight. Another point to keep in mind in this discussion of gubernatorial roles is that each governor will choose a style and a set of role priorities that are comfortable and advantageous. There is no automatically right or wrong set of priorities among roles. Unless a governor goes to the extreme of absolutely ignoring state law or the constitution, judgment about the correctness of a governor's choices of how the roles are fulfilled becomes a highly subjective matter.

This chapter is about governors' performance of administrative responsibilities. The preceding discussion of the various gubernatorial roles is meant not only as setting an introductory context, but also as a reminder that severing one role, administrator, from the full picture is a somewhat arbitrary exercise. It is defensible, however, because administrative activities have an identifiable character to them and because we will try not to lose sight of the larger context. From a governor's perspective, being an administrator involves three major activities.

1.   Appointing persons to executive branch leadership positions
2.   Directing the implementation of public policy
3.   Preparing and implementing state government budgets

Each of these activities requires almost constant decision-making. Decisions must be made about the administrative process (e.g., who will make policy and what organizational arrangements are appropriate) and about the actual substance of policy (e.g., what will be done and in what priority). Some of the flavor of the administrative function is captured by Thompson and Tuden when they observe that "an important role for administrators is to manage the decision process" (Thompson and Tuden, 1969:326).

II. CHAPTER ORGANIZATION

After providing a very brief review of important historical trends in the development of contemporary gubernatorial roles, the chapter turns to a consideration of three major topics: personal staff, appointments to executive branch leadership positions, and executive branch management activities. The section on executive branch management will consider the governor's involvement in budgetary matters, the use of cabinets, and the management styles that can affect administrative actions. A picture of the governor as administrator should emerge by examining these major topics.

As a final introductory comment, a caveat about data should be entered. A systematic, state-by-state examination of the gubernatorial administrative role is beyond the scope of the chapter. Specific examples and selected comparisons will be offered, but most of the subsequent narrative will speak of general patterns or trends. Original data have not been collected; the chapter relies upon the existing—and incidentally, growing—literature. That literature will be sifted, interpreted, and categorized.

III. HISTORICAL TRENDS

The functions, responsibilities, and expectations of governors have changed dramatically over time. Whereas the very early state governors in the post-Revolutionary War period were usually men of some prominence, both they and the governments of their states were weak and small in any comparison with contemporary governors and state government. The trend has not been without interruption or reversal, but it has resulted in governors with considerable constitutional prerogatives and opportunities for political influence.

Some observers claim that contemporary governors still fall short of the power they need to be effective. Thomas Dye argues that, "Despite a generation of recommendations by political scientists and public administrators that governors' control over their administration should be strengthened, governors still do not have control over their administration that is commensurate with their responsibility for it" (Dye, 1981:161). Dye and others who share his views may be right, and this is a theme considered subsequently, but it does not undercut the historically based proposition that the office of governor has evolved into a more important and powerful position.

Coming out of the Revolutionary War, the early state constitutions reflected an anti-executive bias that was a heritage of the fight against the English crown and the king's governors in the American colonies. The first American state governors were restricted in many ways. (At the national level, the bias resulted in the lack of any executive authority in the Articles of Confederation.) Most early governors held office for only one year, without prospect of another term, and they were usually elected by the legislature. They could not perform executive duties, such as they were, without the advise and usually the consent of a council of state appointed by the legislature. Only New York and Massachusetts permitted the governor to veto a legislative act. As Leslie Lipson concludes, these early state constitutions were "meager in their grant of executive power" and "in general, legislative supremacy is the keynote" (Lipson, 1968:14).

Coincidental with Andrew Jackson's presidency (1828–1836), many of the formal restrictions on governors were eased, and like the presidency, the governorship in most states became more robust. Terms of office were lengthened, reelection made possible, the gubernatorial veto was initiated, and some independent administrative powers granted. Displeasure with legislative omnipotence also led to gubernatorial selection by voters. This period, however, was a mixed blessing for future governors because along with the gubernatorial enhancement came the beginning of a constitutionally mandated plural state executive. One of Jacksonian democracy's messages extolled the virtues of popular election of as many public officials as possible. Therefore, as the need for a more active executive became accepted, state constitutions required that the new executive functions be performed by officials elected separately from the governor; governors were not given any formal authority over these newly created executive positions.

By the end of the nineteenth century, governors had achieved a place of prominence in American politics that could not have been predicted by looking at their predecessors a century earlier. This turnabout occurred because of the previously mentioned expansion of constitutional prerogatives and the growing acceptance of executive power. Partly as a consequence, the governorship became an attractive political position, and many ambitious politicians saw it as an important goal in its own right and as a possible springboard to national office. The biggest cloud on the gubernatorial horizon at the turn of the century was the continuing proliferation of independent executive agencies, with the resulting decentralization of authority. Referring to New York, Sabato points out that "there were only 10 state agencies in 1800. By 1900 the number had mushroomed to 81, and by 1925 the state bureaucracy claimed 170 constituent parts" (Sabato, 1983:6). The irony is that as the plural and decentralized executive grew in the early twentieth century it was partly as a result of a wave of Populist reform led by some governors such as Hiram Johnson in California, Robert LaFollette in Wisconsin, and Theodore Roosevelt in New York.

The depression of the 1930s pointed out state government's inability to stem the tide of human and economic desolation. Governors appeared as impotent political leaders, although one of them, Franklin D. Roosevelt of New York, was elected president in 1932. The New Deal and Roosevelt's style marked the beginning of a tremendous surge in the power and financial resources of the national government, and the consequent establishment of states and governors as the junior partners in the federal system. World War II accentuated this trend. But as we have seen before, nothing in American politics moves in an unambiguous fashion. In the face of the nationalization of politics and the economy in the postwar era, there were still efforts to preserve state responsibilities. Along with that preservation were many successful efforts to rationalize state executive branch organization so as to centralize more authority in the governor's office. Since 1965, twenty-one states "undertook comprehensive executive branch reorganization and almost all states have carried out some form of functional reorganization" (Beyle, 1983:199). These reorganizations have increased the governor's formal authority over executive functions.

Just as some observers in the 1950s and 1960s were predicting the demise of state government, growing popular suspicion and even mistrust of the federal establishment sparked a new effort to revitalize state government. The U.S. Supreme Court's "one-person-one vote" decisions on state legislative reapportionment (*Baker v. Carr* and *Reynolds v. Sims*) made state government more visible and important to urban and suburban political activists. State financial resources increased and that made state government decision-making more important to more people from different interests. Governors became central figures in the new resurgence of the 1960s and 1970s. Once again governors were nationally prominent figures, and they were working with an executive branch organizational structure that was not as decentralized as in earlier decades.

This short historical survey only conveys the flavor of the development of the American governorship. The long-term trend has been toward an expansion of gubernatorial power and prominence.[1] With this as background, we now turn to an examination of the contemporary governor's performance of the administrative role.

IV. PERSONAL STAFF

One of the first things any newly elected governor does is to assemble a personal staff. This staff must be personally and politically compatible with the governor; their physical proximity and access to the governor, as well as their responsibilities, demand compatibility. Governors rely heavily upon staff in carrying out their administrative responsibilities. In many cases, governors delegate certain aspects of administrative responsibilities to staff members, and the governor retains little or no personal involvement. Weinberg calls the personal staff the governor's most important "enabling resource" (Weinberg, 1977:63). Thus, an understanding of governors as administrators should begin with a discussion of the composition and functions of the governor's personal staff.

A. Size

Gubernatorial staffs have dramatically grown in number during the last three decades. The average staff size in 1956 was eleven, with the range being three to forty-three. By 1979 the average size had increased threefold to 34, whereas the range advanced to 6-262 (Council of State Governments, 1982:142). Not surprisingly, the size of staff is related to a state's population. Although the governor's staff size varies with population, the smaller states actually have a higher ratio of staff to population than the larger states. Some basic functions must be performed regardless of state population, and this demands a certain minimum staff size independent of population size. Nevertheless, the complexity and quantity of activities demanded of gubernatorial staff does bear a strong relationship to population size.

These data on staff size beg the obvious question of why the increases have occurred. The answer is tied to the governor's resurgence as the state's preeminent political figure with more constitutionally mandated authority than before and to the widespread increases in state government activity and financial resources. As a governor is told to be in charge of more executive branch functions, and as the scope and intensity of those functions increase, more gubernatorial staff assistance becomes necessary.

B. Recruitment and Background[2]

Serving in a gubernatorial staff position is a prestigious and much-sought after opportunity. Competition for positions can be fierce. The governor's personal involvement in most staff recruitment further charges the recruitment process. A rough composite picture of the staff emerges from some generalizations about staff background characteristics.

Virtually all staff members have had political, public administrative, or political party experience prior to their appointment. Novices are a very rare breed on the governor's staff. Most staff members acknowledge developing an interest in politics as teenagers, and they have pursued a career pattern that has placed them in the political arena. Very few staff members, however, have ever held elective office.

Staff members tend to be relatively young. Sprengel (1972) says that 54% of the staff he studied were under forty. The staff's previous political or governmental experience is apparently gained at a young age. A large percentage of staff are lawyers by training, although they rarely hold positions in the office that require someone with a legal education. By training and inclination most staff members are generalists, including the lawyers, who have personal experience and skills that are transferable in a helpful way to the governor's office. These skills include analytic and strategic thinking, attention to detail, and an understanding of the state and the capitol politics. A noticeable minority of staff also have some expertise in a specialty such as budgeting, law enforcement, or public relations.

A majority of staff members had some association with the governor prior to their appointment. The most common form of association was in the governor's election campaign. Casual acquaintances of the governor may gain a staff position, but "key staff positions are not entrusted to individuals who have not had a long acquaintance with the governor" (Sprengel, 1972:114). Trust and confidence are not built too quickly and governors need the unquestionable loyalty of competent persons in the most important staff positions.

Both Democratic and Republican governors pay close attention to their staff appointments, but there appears to be a slight difference in the way Democrats and Republicans assemble their entourage. "Democratic governors have been acquainted with a larger proportion of their staffs for a longer period of time than their Republican counterparts. This tendency supports the notion that Democrats recruit personal coalitions for staff while Republicans recruit an electoral coalition" (Sprengel, 1972:114). The difference between a personal coalition and an electoral coalition refers to the length of time staff members have been associated with the governor. A personal coalition consists of persons who have been associated with the governor for several years prior to the gubernatorial election campaign whereas an electoral coalition contains individuals assembled immediately prior to the campaign kickoff.

By at least one indicator—length of staff service—the governors' recruitment efforts have usually been successful. There is a low rate of turnover among gubernatorial staff. It is not uncommon for a large percentage of the original staff to still be in the office on the day the governor leaves the position. Governors can usually enjoy the benefits of an experienced staff for most of their tenure.

C. Organization

As the size of the staff has grown, so too has the need for delineating an organizational structure. If an office only has three or four staff persons, it is not necessary to develop an elaborate statement of authority relationships and task responsibilities. But if confusion is to be held at a minimum, and efficiency valued, those authority relationships and task responsibilities must be articulated as staff size grows. No group of thirty-four people (the average staff size) can accomplish much with an ad hoc, ever-changing division of responsibilities and no established authority structure.

The organization chart in most governors' offices is relatively flat. Three or four layers of hierarchy are quite common except in the very largest office where five or six layers may exist.

Typically a governor designates someone as the chief of staff or executive assistant. This is the person who makes the office function on a daily basis: handing out staff assignments, arranging necessary coordination among staff, keeping communication flowing, dealing with personnel issues in the office, and making sure the governor is benefiting from staff work on policy and political issues. Because the executive assistant is usually a close confidant of the governor, most of them become very authoritative figures within the office. Some governors encourage the executive assistant to develop a strong external position with agency personnel, media, and legislators. Other governors want a less visible role for this staffer so that there are no allegations that the governor had delegated "excessive" responsibility. The governor's own style will dictate the extent of the executive assistant's extra-office responsibilities and visibility. But regardless of the governor's idiosyncracies, the executive assistant is at the top of the staff hierarchy and almost inevitably makes certain decisions in the governor's name.

The governor's personal secretary is directly responsible to the governor. This person manages the flow of paperwork for the governor and frequently controls access to the governor. Both of these functions can lead to conflict with other staff members, all of whom think that they "must" see the governor and that the governor should read their latest memo immediately. Developing a workable modus operandi between the executive assistant and the governor's personal secretary is crucial to office efficiency.

Most of the other major staff positions are at an equal level in the hierarchy. These positions indicate not just the number of staff, but also the importance a governor attaches to certain functions. The most common staff designations are:

Press secretary: liaison with media
Legal advisor: liaison with state attorney general and advises on extradition and clemency
Appointments secretary: organizes the selection of gubernatorial appointees

Additional staff work is performed by persons responsible for mail and casework, intergovernmental relations, and policy recommendations to the governor. The latter category varies by governor, but it often includes a staff person in charge of education, health and welfare, environmental protection, economic development, or long-range planning. Governors vary in their policy priorities, and their priorities often change during a term, so assignment of a staff member to one of these policy areas is an indication of current gubernatorial priorities.

Designation of a staff person to coordinate intergovernmental relations, primarily with the federal government, is relatively recent in most governor's offices. As Deil Wright concludes, "No governor or governor's office can function effectively today without devoting time and staff to state/national relationships" (Wright, 1982:294). The application for and utilization of federal funds, as well as the impact of numerous federal regulations, require the governor's attention because of the heavy impact these funds and regulations can have on state government. And what is of importance to a governor always becomes the subject of staff attention.

In the smaller offices, a single staff member may work on, for example, media relations or appointments. The larger offices do not necessarily perform more tasks, but more people are needed to carry out the same jobs. So in a large office there may be four of five persons who deal with the media or help organize the appointments to various state and local positions. The hierarchy, in other words, gets deeper in larger offices.

Two important caveats must be made about gubernatorial office organization. The use of the term *hierarchy* in the foregoing discussion should not convey the image of a military chain of command with clearly defined channels of communication and lines of authority. Governor's offices are not that rigid. They need too much flexibility and spontaneity to adhere to a fixed set of organizational rules. Another qualification about office organization also refers to formal organizational structure: as in any organization, the formal structure in a governor's office only explains part of the staff's behavior. Informal norms and relations sometimes guide behavior. Because the executive assistant, for instance, is supposed to coordinate all staff work for the governor does not necessarily prevent a staff member from bypassing the executive assistant to approach the governor directly about a particular matter.

D. Role Perception

Another way to examine the functioning of the personal staff is to consider what the staff perceives as their roles. This leads away from the substantive tasks staff perform and to the way staff members define their job vis-à-vis the governor. Wyner (1970) indicates the most frequently mentioned responses when gubernatorial staff were asked, "What do you think should be the role of a governor's staff?" In order of frequency, staff replied:

1. Organize information for the governor.
2. Create a favorable image of the governor.
3. Handle details.
4. Take blame for mistakes.
5. Coordinate executive branch activities.
6. Serve as a complaint bureau for the public.

These responses serve as a reminder of how extensively staff define their roles in relation to the governor's needs. Press and VerBurg summarize gubernatorial staff requirements in this way: "The key requirements are a willingness to work long hours, put the needs of the governor above one's own, work with little or no personal credit outside the governor's office, take the blame and absorb the shock for mistakes, and accept a policy decision once it's made" (Press and VerBurg, 1983:313).

E. Conclusion

What emerges from this section on gubernatorial personal staffs is a picture of a handpicked group of individuals who are organized to perform the substantive tasks that reflect the governor's priorities and political needs. The relatively low turnover in staff suggests both care in the initial staff selections and the apparently high level of job satisfaction felt by staff members.

V. APPOINTMENTS TO EXECUTIVE BRANCH POSITIONS

In a handbook prepared for newly elected governors, the National Governors' Association emphasizes the importance of gubernatorial appointments to executive branch positions: "Perhaps the most challenging task facing the new Governor is the appointment of individuals to hundreds of state government positions in the administration. . . . Few other early decisions will have such a long-term effect on the success of the administration" (National Governors' Association, 1978:70).

Most governors can make hundreds of executive branch appointments; this includes top-level administrators as well as members of boards and commissions. Wyner (1968) found that the average number of statutory appointments was approximately 400. In the larger states the number of appointments rises to substantially more than the average. The California governor, for example, appoints about 170 top-level agency personnel and about 2200 members of various boards and commissions (Bell and Price, 1980:218-219).

Executive branch appointments are usually considered very important for governors because of the underlying assumption that governors will be able to influence (some say control) the persons appointed. Through these appointees, the reasoning goes, governors stand their best chance of shaping the direction of policy development and policy implementation in the various agencies. Some authors have also pointed out the relationship between appointments and relations with the legislature. Coleman Ransone says that "the governor's appointment power when used as patronage can be a useful tool in building support in the legislature and thus help the governor in achieving a legislative bloc necessary for passage of his administration bills" (Ransone, 1982:34). These advantages and opportunities that supposedly flow from the appointment process are widely cited (Morehouse, 1980; Fox, 1974; Beyle and Dalton, 1981). An important exception will be noted subsequently.

As was discussed previously in the section on historical trends, the governors' liberation from colonial era restrictions was accompanied by the creation of numerous executive agencies headed by independently elected officials. The resulting executive branch structure in most states was characterized as a plural executive. The post-World War II reorganizations have almost always reduced the number of separately elected executive officials and increased the number of agency heads appointed by the governor. At the extreme, the governor is the only statewide-elected executive official in Maine and New Jersey. Speaking generally, the plural executive still exists, but it is less prevalent now than at any time in the last century.

This does not mean, however, that most of the top executive officials are gubernatorial appointees. Ransone (1982) has analyzed the percentage of executive agency heads appointed by the governor in each state.[3] He finds a wide range: 89% in New York and 86% in Virginia, but 24% in Texas and 21% in South Carolina. The median is 48.5%. Putting the data differently, Ransone observes that "in only 22 states does the governor appoint 50% or more of the state's administrative officials" (Ransone, 1982:36).

Beyle and Dalton (1981) suggest that the movement to increase the governor's appointments may be spent. They find only very small changes between 1965 and 1980 in the number of independently elected agency officials. However, when the authors constructed a scale to measure gubernatorial appointive powers, they found a few interesting changes during that time period. First, more governors are now able to appoint, with the legislature's consent, the heads of human services and development agencies as contrasted to previous appointive power being lodged in an independent board or commission. Second, more states now require legislative consent for gubernatorial appointments to head state police and safety organizations and regulatory agencies. This is actually a slight decline in gubernatorial appointive powers in the affected states.

Appointments below the top agency positions are often available to governors. Second- and third-echelon positions in many executive agencies are not part of the civil service and, therefore, persons in those positions serve at the governor's pleasure. Governors must make a careful choice about their strategy for filling these subordinate positions. On the one hand, a governor wants persons in all the agency management positions who are loyal to the governor and judged as competent; this tempts governors to appoint not just the top person, but also the key subordinates. Yet, a strong argument can be made for allowing an agency head the freedom to select his or her own subordinates without the governor's involvement. After all, if the agency head will be held responsible for the agency's performance then he or she ought to be able to pick their own management team. Some governors adopt one or the other of these appointment strategies. But most governors utilize a mixture of approaches, depending upon the agency involved and the particular person selected to head it.

Diane Blair (1982) tries to explain an apparent irony about the gubernatorial appointment process. The trend has been toward increasing the governors' number of appointments, and it might appear that governors and their personal staff would appreciate this trend. When asked, however, governors and their aides talk about the time-consuming nature of appointment making, the internal arguments it generates within the governor's electoral coalition, and the political risks from the possibility of a "bad" appointment (Blair, 1982: 88,89). The answer to this irony, Blair finds, requires separating high-level administrative appointments from the more numerous appointments to the boards, commissions, and advisory committees every state has. Speaking about the latter type of appointments, Blair says that "the decision-making process is elaborate and exhausting, the policy consequences may be negligible, and political consequences are frequently a net minus" (Blair, 1982:91). Thus the power to appoint is not an unmitigated blessing.

What qualities do governors look for in their appointees? When Beyle and Dalton posed this question to fifteen former governors, the responses fell into three major categories:

(1) "management and administrative skills"
(2) "experience, expertise, and competence"
(3) "basic commitment to the administration and its policy direction" (Beyle and Dalton, 1981:9).

Partisanship also is an operative criterion, but the authors felt that partisanship was subsumed under the "loyalty" criteria and from the natural tendency for governors to simply know more potential appointees of the same party. Partisanship works to ensure that virtually all gubernatorial appointments are from the governor's party, although all the different party factions are not always accommodated.

VI. EXECUTIVE BRANCH MANAGEMENT ACTIVITIES

Apparently many governors do not find executive branch management a difficult task. When fifteen former governors were asked to indicate the most difficult aspects of being a governor, management of state government ranked last of the eleven topics that received mention (Beyle, 1979:105). There are a few different ways to interpret those responses. The former governors may have been excellent administrators who were so adept at executive branch management that it was an easy and almost incidental part of their daily responsibilities. Or perhaps those governors decided to make executive branch management a very low priority in their offices and therefore it did not appear to be a difficult task. Or in a variation on the last explanation, perhaps the governors faced so much initial frustration in exercising leadership over the agencies that they essentially gave up trying and by the time they left office the task did not seem so onerous. The predominant tone of the literature on gubernatorial management favors the last two explanations. Starting with some illustrations of the type of management style governors can choose, this section considers executive branch management activities, some reasons for gubernatorial frustration, and some ways governors attempt to deal with it.

In the handbook for newly elected governors, the National Governors' Association (1978:86) suggests that governors usually choose one of three approaches (or styles) to management:

(1) "active managers of government ... concerned with all issues that affect state residents." These governors adopt a "broad set of policy pronouncements."

(2) a narrow "focus on the management of state government." These governors "set specific policy goals for agency directors and actively participate with them to attain results."

(3) the setting of "broad policy goals" and allowing department heads "to develop their own objectives." These governors "focus only on issues of major interest to the administration."

The difference between the first and third management approaches turns on the range of issues in which the governor becomes involved. The second style reflects a governor who wants a very active involvement in executive branch management. There is no evidence about the frequency with which governors choose these different styles; nor is there much systematic evidence about the consequences of choosing one or the other of these styles.

However, Weinberg's (1977) case study of the management activities of former Massachusetts Governor Francis Sargent suggests the difficulty and impracticality of successful gubernatorial management across the full range of policy matters handled by the executive branch. She argues forcefully that a governor must choose "strategies, devoting energy and resources to some tasks and not to others . . ." (Weinberg, 1977:20). A governor must be selective in executive branch management because neither the personal staff nor the governor have the time, even if they had the inclination, necessary for comprehensive management efforts; too many nonadministrative roles require attention. Furthermore, not all agencies are susceptible to gubernatorial management. Weinberg (1977:67-70) creates a typology of agencies derived from the circumstances of the governor's involvement with them:

(1) Agencies requiring constant scrutiny—those that spend large sums of money or have large numbers of employees and those in which a crisis or malfunction would be intolerable.

(2) Agencies receiving constant scrutiny because of the governor's personal preferences.

(3) Agencies that receive attention only because a specific crisis emerges.

(4) Agencies that receive little or no attention from the governor or staff.

Lynn Muchmore (1981) has offered another way of thinking about governors' managerial style. Muchmore says that a "governor fulfills his executive role through a mixture of four relationships" (Muchmore, 1981:72). They are:

(1) Ensure minimum standards of decency and ethical behavior in the executive branch.

(2) Establish a capacity to respond to natural or man-made crises.
(3) Ensure performance of routine administrative functions by agencies.
(4) Manage agencies in the full sense of setting goals and overseeing their accomplishment.

The first and second functions call for very minimal gubernatorial involvement or staff activity. Muchmore claims that the third function predominates and that most relationships between governors' offices and executive agencies focus on the routine or "custodial" performance of previously assigned agency tasks. Rarely do governors "manage" as in the fourth function.

Further evidence and refinement of this view of gubernatorial executive branch management comes from a survey of approximately 1100 state department heads. Abney and Lauth (1983) asked department heads about their relationship with the governor's office and the extent to which the governor, the legislature, interest groups, and local and federal officials influenced their agency programs and objectives. Their major conclusion is that "governors do not dominate administrative branches of government despite the attempts of reorganization efforts in recent years to strengthen their positions as chief administrators" (Abney and Lauth, 1983:41). By a margin of 43-38% their respondents cited the legislature over the governor, respectively, as the political actor most influential with them. Governors do fare better with department heads appointed by them. Not surprisingly, then, "governors tend to limit the exercise of their administrative roles to those departments which come within the purview of their appointment power" (Abney and Lauth, 1983:44). The most common reasons cited for gubernatorial involvement with departments were efficiency and coordination concerns. Governors want to promote efficiency, and they realize that their office can be a major center of interagency coordination.

Most governors recognize the importance of their administrative role, and they are willing to devote their office's attention to it, but roadblocks and opportunities for frustration abound. A quick summary of the major factors impeding gubernatorial management will illustrate why the contemporary governor still is not fully in charge of the executive branch, despite the reforms and reorganizations that have increased the governor's executive prerogatives.

The plural executive still lives, although in diminished form. Independently elected executive officials have a separate popular mandate and constitutional status, so they are not required to accede to the governor's efforts to influence them.

Increasing professionalism among agency personnel makes them less willing to follow the governor's political direction (Hebert and Wright, 1982; Abney and Lauth, 1983). An extensive civil service, with its protections for agency personnel, reinforces their independence.

Governors and their staff simply do not have the time to give continuing attention to the full range of agencies under the governors' formal control. A selective approach is almost a practical necessity. The political importance of an agency to the governor, or a crisis in an agency or in its policy arena, often become the catalysts that lead to gubernatorial efforts at agency management. This in turn establishes priorities among agencies.

Because governors and their staff cannot possibly have extensive expertise on all major issues, they must depend upon agency personnel for information and advice on many important items of policy or policy implementation. Such dependence can undercut authority.

Upper-level agency personnel have contacts and influence with legislators, interest groups, and relevant federal officials. This gives them access to other political actors and can reduce their reliance upon the governor.

In a slightly different vein, it must also be acknowledged that some governors simply are not interested in administrative chores. Given this predilection, administrative responsibilities fall almost exclusively to staff. Staff success without apparent, direct gubernatorial involvement is problematic.

With determination, governors can exert some leadership over executive agencies. They must rely upon their political skills, those of their staff, and the inclinations of bureaucrats to follow their lead in policy development and implementation. Two important aspects of this effort are the state budget and the use of a cabinet.

A. Budgets

States spend large sums of money. In fiscal year 1980, the range of expenditures was from a low of $600 million in Vermont to a high of $32.8 billion in California (Lorch, 1983:334, 335). Seven states spent over $10 billion. State expenditures have increased dramatically since World War II. Total state government expenditures per capita (in constant dollars) have gone from $139.11 in 1950 to $398.43 in 1975 (Sharkansky, 1978:55). Formulating a budget requires the development of a plan to spend the money and, implicitly, a plan to raise the necessary revenues.

This expenditure plan (and sometimes the revenue plan) becomes the primary vehicle for governors to articulate their policy preferences and, thus, extend their influence over the executive agencies. It is never a simple matter, however. Passage of a budget inevitably creates a power struggle involving virtually all of the important political actors in the state. Yet governors in almost every state enjoy certain advantages that usually give them a prime, but not exclusive, role in the budgetary process. The governor's advantage stems from the constitutional mandate in forty-four states that the governor prepares a budget for submission to the legislature and from the governor's right to veto (usually an item veto) budgetary provisions passed by the legislature.[4] Governors cannot control all aspects of the budget, but they are extremely influential.

One of the major reforms earlier in this century that increased gubernatorial stature was the adoption of constitutional provisions requiring an executive budget; that is, a budget prepared by the governor and submitted to the legislature for consideration. Giving the governor the task of organizing the budget document has several important consequences. In the context of executive branch management, the executive budget gives the governor a very important tool in the effort to exert leadership. Agencies must annually negotiate with the governor's staff over the total agency budget request and the specific ingredients of the request. This process puts agencies in the position of seeking the governor's approval, with the obvious opportunities for the governor. Of course, agencies still get their day with the legislature, but the executive budget process allows governors to influence agency policy and gives governors a chance to circumvent partially the impediments discussed previously.

Two important features of state finances limit the extent to which governors can use budgets as opportunities for agency management. A large percentage, often reaching 50%, of most state budgets are earmarked for specific purposes and are not subject to gubernatorial change. For instance, in most states all taxes on gasoline must be used only for highway or transportation-related purposes. Furthermore, it is unrealistic to imagine that a state's budget is created from scratch every year. Rather, the primary basis for this year's budget is last year's budget. In a word, budgets develop incrementally. By custom and because of time pressures or insufficient interest, no governor can have the staff reconsider the desirability of every aspect of the budget every year. Therefore, incremental budgeting is a de facto limitation on the potential gubernatorial use of budgets as an agency management technique.

B. Cabinets

Another technique most governors use to help with administrative responsibilities is the cabinet meeting. The cabinet is composed of agency heads, with the exact membership being defined by either the constitution, statute, governor's order, or simply custom. With the exception of a few states, cabinets are only advisory to the governor; they have no formal decision-making power. Bodman and Garry (1982:93) report that "in 16 of the 40 states with cabinets, the authorization for existence is either constitutional or statutory; 13 are created by governor's directive or executive order; and the remainder have their roots in tradition or a combination of the above sources."

Regardless of its origin, a cabinet is what the governor wants it to be. Most governors convene regular cabinet meetings, but it is the governor's choice as to the agenda: meaty, substantive issues or trivial, housekeeping matters. (Cabinet meetings are open to the press and public in some states, and this may inhibit the discussion somewhat.) If a governor chooses to use cabinet meetings as an occasion for seeking advice about important current policy issues, a message is conveyed to agency personnel that can enhance both the governor's and the agency head's position with subordinates. The message is that the governor cares about administrative policy matters and the agency head is giving advice directly to the governor.

Some governors choose not to utilize cabinet meetings for anything of importance and instead make them almost a social occasion where top-level administrators can see each other and share "war stories." The primary drawback to the cabinet as an advice-giving body is the disparate nature of the membership. After all, what advice can the head of the Department of Forestry give about implementing a new welfare regulation? Nevertheless, many governors find cabinet meetings beneficial because they force the governor and the staff to concentrate regularly on administrative responsibilities.

VII. SUMMARY AND CONCLUSIONS

The administrative role is only one of the many roles governors must play. The competition for time and the political rewards from the nonadministrative roles can sometimes overwhelm administrative responsibiltiies. Yet, it is virtually impossible to absolutely ignore executive branch activities.

Despite the predictable ups and downs, the historical trend shows governors moving from weak and unassuming positions to their contemporary prominence in state government. An effective and compatible personal staff is essential for a governor. In assisting a governor conduct administrative tasks, staff members can help coordinate the work of executive agencies, organize personnel matters, provide trusted advice about agency activities, and serve as the governor's surrogate with agencies if the governor's style dictates this approach. Appointing carefully selected men and women to top-level positions in executive agencies is probably the most beneficial way for a governor to extend gubernatorial influence in the executive branch. Persons who have a basic loyalty to the governor and who are in fundamental agreement about how to approach policy matters are more likely to follow the governor's lead as they direct their agencies. There are numerous forces working against gubernatorial influence over agency activities, and having "good" appointees at the top helps counteract the tendency for bureaucracies to ignore political leadership.

The plural executive, professionalism in agencies, competing time pressures on the governor and the personal staff, and opportunities for agencies to seek alliances with political actors other than the governor are all factors that mitigate attempts at gubernatorial influence over agencies. The budget, however, is a tool available to governors in their management efforts. Some governors also use regular cabinet meetings to reinforce their own interest in administrative matters and reassert some leadership.

A mixed picture emerges after this examination of governors as administrators. Governors are probably more prominent and possess more formal authority than at any previous time in this century, and, arguably, at any time since colonial days. As Sabato (1983) has concluded, the governorship has been "transformed." The contemporary governor is clearly in a better position to exercise leadership over executive agencies. Many governors do just that.

There are also several forces at work to undercut gubernatorial executive branch management attempts. It would be quite an exaggeration to conclude that governors are in total command of the executive branch. But those governors who have the desire now have the potential to exercise significantly more leadership over the executive branch than their predecessors.

NOTES

1. There are some observers who are skeptical about the permanence of the apparent increase in gubernatorial power. For example, see Dometrius, Nelson C. (1980). State government administration and the electoral process. *State Government 53*:129–134.
2. Most of the information in this section is a summary of two articles: Sprengel, Donald R. (1972). Governors' staffs—Background and recruitment patterns. In Beyle, Thad and Williams, J. Oliver, eds., *The American Governor in Behavioral Perspective*. Harper & Row, New York, pp. 106–118; and Wyner, Alan J. (January/February, 1970). Staffing the governor's office. *Public Administration Review 30*:17–24.
3. As Ransone acknowledges, his technique of calculating the percentage of executive agency heads appointed by the governor does not take into account the relative importance of the various executive positions.
4. The six states in which the governor must share responsibility for budget preparation are: Kansas, Louisiana, Mississippi, North Carolina, South Carolina, and Texas. North Carolina's governor has no veto authority, and the governors of Indiana, Maine, Nevada, New Hampshire, Rhode Island, and Vermont can veto legislation but not with an item veto. All other governors have an item veto.

REFERENCES

Abney, G. and Lauth, T. P. (1983). The governor as chief administrator. *Public Administration Review 43*:40–49.

Baker v. Carr (1962). 369 U.S. 186.

Bell, C. G. and Price, C. M. (1980). *California Government Today*. The Dorsey Press, Homewood, IL.

Beyle, T. L. (1979). Governors' views on being governor. *State Government 52*: 103–109.

Beyle, T. L. (1983). Governors. In Gray, V., Jacob, H., and Vines, K. N., eds. *Politics in the American States*. Little, Brown, Boston, 180–221.

Beyle, T. L. and Dalton, R. (1981). Appointment power: Does it belong to the governor? *State Government 54*:2–12.

Blair, D. K. (1982). The gubernatorial appointment power: Too much of a good thing? *State Government 55*:88–92.

Bodman, L. and Garry, D. B. (1982). Innovations in state cabinet systems. *State Government 55*:93–98.

Council of State Governments. (1982). *Book of the States, 1982-83*. Lexington, Ky.

Dometrius, N. C. (1980). State government administration and the electoral process. *State Government 53*:129–134.

Dye, T. R. (1981). *Politics in States and Communities*. Prentice Hall, Englewood Cliffs, N.J.

Fox, D. (1974). *The Politics of City and State Bureaucracy*. Goodyear, Pacific Palisades, Calif.

Hebert, F. T. and Wright, D. S. (1982). State administrators: How representative? How professional? *State Government 55*:22–28.

Lipson, L. (1968). *The American Governor From Figurehead to Leader*. Greenwood Press, New York.

Lorch, R. S. (1983). *State and Local Politics*. Prentice Hall, Englewood Cliffs, N.J.

Morehouse, S. M. (1980). *State Politics, Parties and Policy*. Holt, Rinehart and Winston, New York.

Muchmore, L. (1981). The governor as manager. *State Government 54*:71–75.

National Governors' Association. (1978). *Governing the American States: A Handbook for New Governors*. Washington, D.C.

Press, C. and VerBurg, K. (1983). *State and Community Governments in the Federal System*. Wiley, New York.

Ransone, C. B. (1982). *The American Governorship*. Greenwood Press, Westport, Conn.

Reynolds v. Sims (1964). 377 U.S. 533.

Sabato, L. (1983). *Goodbye to Good-Time Charlie*. CQ Press, Washington, D.C.

Sharkansky, I. (1978). *The Maligned States*. McGraw-Hill, New York.

Sprengel, D. (1972). Governor's staffs—background and recruitment patterns. In Beyle, T. and Williams, J. O., eds. *The American Governor in Behavioral Perspective*. Harper & Row, New York, 106–118.

Thompson, J. D. and Tuden, A. (1969). Strategies in decision-making. In Lyden, F. J., Shipman, G. A., and Kroll, M., eds. *Policies, Decisions and Organization*. Appleton-Century-Crofts, New York, 310–330.

Weinberg, M. W. (1977). *Managing the State*. The MIT Press, Cambridge, Mass.

Wright, D. S. (1982). *Understanding Intergovernmental Relations*. Brooks/Cole, Monterey, Calif.

Wyner, A. J. (1968). Gubernatorial relations with legislators and administrators. *State Government 41*:199–203.

Wyner, A. J. (1970). Staffing the governor's office. *Public Administration Review 30*:17–24.

13

State and Local Officials and Their Personal Liability

W. Bartley Hildreth   Graduate School of Management, Kent State
University, Kent, Ohio

Gerald J. Miller   Institute of Public Administration, Rutgers, The State
University of New Jersey, Newark, New Jersey

State and local governments, as well as their officers and employees, are vulnerable to tort liability suits. This legal accountability rests on both state and federal laws. Whereas governmental entities face a threat from state law or common law, the most significant personal liability exposures for officials and employees come from recent interpretations of a century-old federal law. Legal developments in both areas impact on public management.

This discussion is to provide a basic introduction to relevant legal rules and their consequences. Legal rules that structure the liability challenge are first reviewed. Special attention is given to the law that effectively provides a national liability policy—the Civil Rights Act of 1871. The chapter closes on a discussion of management and policy issues.

I. LEGAL RULES STRUCTURING THE LIABILITY CHALLENGE[1]

Legal rules are used by our society to define acceptable behavior, and are contained in federal and state constitutions, statutes, regulations, and court decisions. For example, legal rules prohibit the violation of a person's constitutionally protected right of due process. The violator of the legal rule assumes a liability.

A liability is the responsibility to others for a possible or actual loss, expense, or burden implying the obligation to make something good or to discharge a duty. Thus, liability is the obligation in law to do, pay, or make good something.

There are three basic types of liability—criminal, contractual, and tort (Prosser, 1941:8). The focus here is on tort liability, or the interference with the interests of others that is unreasonable. Using again our example, a violation of a person's due process rights permits the wronged, or injured, person to seek recovery from the wrongdoer.

This chapter explores legal rules and consequences when the alleged or actual wrongdoer is a public agency (a state government, a municipality, or even a county department, for example) or its agents (i.e., elected or appointed officials or public employees).

A. Tort Liability Matrix[2]

These are several sources for tort liability that have both personal and official implications. Briefly, *personal liability* refers to the penalty or responsibility, usually but not always financial, a court may place on public officials or employees themselves. Personal liability carries with it the risk of loss of personal assets.

To complicate matters, these same public agents face *official* liability. That is, an injured citizen can sue a public official or employee as the occupant of a formal position (as governor, mayor, manager, supervisor, and so on) on the assumption that the position occupant can right a wrong.

The governmental entity (e.g., a city, county, state agency, school district, and so forth) also faces tort liability. For example, a city might face a suit to restore lost earnings due a developer who was unfairly denied a zoning variance. In such cases, the government itself, not an individual officer or employee, is held directly responsible for an injury or loss. This situation is referred to as governmental liability.

Legal rules on personal and official liability emanate from both the state and federal levels.[3] These authoritative rules prescribe actions that stop action (through injunctions), nullify action (through declaratory relief), and/or compensate injured citizens at the public official's or governmental entity's expense for actions done by the public official or the entity (damages).

The variety of tort liability rules leads to confusion. A matrix is presented in Fig. 1 to help reduce the confusion. Basically, public policy-makers and managers must contend with each of the four quadrants in the tort liability immunity matrix:

1. State law on personal liability
2. State law on official liability

Application of Legal Rules

	Personal	Official
State as Source	Absolute or Qualified Immunity: —Position —Duties **1**	Governmental or Sovereign Immunity **2**
Federal Law As Source	**3** Civil Rights Act of 1871	**4** Civil Rights Act of 1871

Law (vertical label on left)

Fig. 1.   Tort liability immunity rule matrix.

3. Federal law on personal liability
4. Federal law on official liability

The following sections review each quadrant in summary fashion. A later section focuses in more detail on the controlling federal law.

B. State Law Liability

State law and state court rulings provide that state and local officials and employees face *personal* responsibility for some acts under some conditions and *official* responsibility for other acts under specific conditions. To clarify these concepts, personal liability and then official liability under state law will be examined.

1. Quadrant One

Public agents (officials and employees) face tort liability depending upon their functions performed and the scope of their duties. By performing particular functions, certain public agents enjoy broad tort liability immunity. For instance, judges typically have received immunity for judicial acts even though the judge might have acted maliciously or corruptly. The same situation dominates for legislators and high government executive officials. When acting within the scope of legitimate authority and jurisdiction, these officials generally receive absolute immunity from tort reprisals. The rationale is to insulate these officials from the intimidation that might come from tort liability threats (*Gregoire v. Biddle*, 1949:579).

Lower officials and employees do not enjoy the absolute immunity and have only qualified immunity, depending upon that person's scope of duty. The scope of duty question is resolved by examining the amount of job discretion. Government executives exercising independent judgment in making policy and in performing duties are viewed as having *discretionary* duties. Officials involved in tax assessment, job hiring and firing, prosecuterial bargaining, and so on, all use a wide degree of discretion in their work. These officials have been generally granted latitude in making decisions and absolute immunity from suit, especially if their actions are performed in good faith.

On the other hand, *ministerial* duties are where public agents have specified tasks to perform and no choice or discretion on how to do them. The negligent performance of the duties or nonperformance makes such officials and employees potentially liable for the consequences. Blanket immunity is not granted because performance can be measured by conformity with legal duties (negligence) or nonperformance of duties (failure to act). Examples of ministerial acts include the signing of licenses once they are authorized, the filing of papers, and the collection of taxes.

Despite the complex legal rules, the *potential* for liability has traditionally fallen short of the *actual* results. The reason is that ministerial and discretionary duties differ more clearly in legal theory than in actual practice. Because most managerial jobs require discretion, public officials have enjoyed an effective shield to suits brought to contest public decisions. In recent years, a change toward more liability has occurred, however.

2. Quadrant Two

Until recently, state and local governments enjoyed absolute or sovereign immunity from suit.[4] Sovereign, or governmental, immunity denies a citizen the right to sue the governmental unit. The doctrine evolved from the principle that it was a contradiction of the sovereignty of the king to force him to submit to suit in his own courts. States either allowed the doctrine to stand as part of common law (judge-made law), or the concept was incorporated into state statutory law.

In the last two decades, sovereign immunity has fallen due to the lack of an overwhelming reason to support the position that an injured party should not find recompense against an injury-causing government or its agents (Floyd and Associates, 1978; Spector et al., 1983). Just because the government or its agent caused the injury, so goes the argument, the injury remains, nevertheless.

As a result, either through legislative or judicial actions, sovereign immunity has been substantially restricted. Table 1 reveals that most states have limited

Table 1 Tort Liability Immunity of States and Their Local Governments

	Total waiver	Partial waiver	Immunity retained
States with immunity of local governments	7[a]	38	5[b]
States with state government immunity	4[c]	41	5[d]

[a]Alaska, Louisiana, Massachusetts, Nevada, New York, Rhode Island, and Washington.
[b]Arkansas, Georgia, Maryland, Mississippi, and West Virginia.
[c]Alaska, Louisiana, Nevada, and New York.
[d]Alabama, Arkansas, Georgia, North Dakota, and West Virginia.
Source: Susan A. Spector et al. (January 10, 1983). Governmental tort liability: A national survey. Law Department, City of New York, mimeograph, New York. pp. 41, 42 and 53, 54.

the immunity of their governmental entities and agents (Floyd and Associates, 1978; Spector et al., 1983). States that have totally waived immunity of their local governments are Alaska, Louisiana, Massachusetts, Nevada, New York, Rhode Island, and Washington. In other states, citizens wronged by the action of government agents can sue the government only within limits provided by state courts or state legislatures or both.

A later section on indemnification options provides a fuller discussion of alternative designs of state laws defining limitations on liability.

3. Quadrant Three

The primary area of personal liability for public officials under federal laws is covered by the Civil Rights Act of 1871, or Title 42, Section 1983 of the *U.S. Code Annotated*. The statute covers an official's acts that violate the constitutional or federally protected rights of citizens. Many different actions are protected under this law, including such items as failure to provide hearings, inadequate due process considerations when condemning or destroying property, discrimination in providing government services, and many others. Suits under this law have provoked widespread judicial scrutiny and, therefore, an extensive body of law. To understand this law requires a review of separate parts of the act in more detail, as is provided later in this chapter.

4. Quadrant Four

Official tort liability also arises from the Civil Rights Act of 1871. According to the U.S. Supreme Court in 1978 (*Monell v. Department of Social Services of the City of New York*, 1978), city governments are liable for actions *implementing* an unconstitutional statute, policy, or custom having the status of a policy.

The "policy or custom" provision raises many more questions than it answers. Surely, standard operating procedures (SOPs) or formally adopted procedural rules constitute policy. In the case at issue, the New York City department of social services required women employees to take unpaid sick leave in the latter months of pregnancy. This was clear policy, although later held to be unconstitutional.

Less clear is what constitutes a "custom." By definition, a custom is something not likely to be written in an SOP manual. A custom is defined as a practice that has not received formal approval through an organization's decision-making channel. Furthermore, a custom can be established by almost anyone in an organization, not just duly recognized policy-makers. The Houston Police Department, for instance, was found (*Webster v. City of Houston*, 1982: 1220) to have a custom of police use of "throw-down" pistols to justify a shooting. There were no official policies condoning the practice, nor did officials know of the direct situation when a pistol was thrown down after a shooting to make it look as if the victim had had a gun. Officials did not condone or try to stop the custom. The court ruled that the city had a custom that would make the city liable for the injuries caused by three officers operating under the custom.

II. A NATIONAL LIABILITY POLICY

The federal law that creates substantial liability for state and local governments, as well as individual officers and employees, is the Civil Rights Act of 1871. The statute constituted legal reaction to Ku Klux Klan (KKK) terrorism in the South after the Civil War. The KKK terrorism was directed against politically active blacks and their sympathizers. State and local officials were said to tolerate this lawlessness.

Congress reacted by enacting the Ku Klux Klan Act. The formal title is the Civil Rights Act of 1871, and it has been codified as Title 42, Section 1983 of the *U.S. Code Annotated*. The act states:

> Every *person* who, *under color of* any statute, ordinance, regulation, custom, or usage, or any State or Territory *subjects, or causes to be subjected*, any citizen of the United States or other person within the jurisdiction thereof to the *deprivation of any rights, privileges, or immunities secured by the Constitution and laws*, shall be liable to the party injured in an action at law, suit in equity, or other proper proceeding for redress. (author's italics)

Due to the national significance of Section 1983, as it is commonly known, each of the italicized words or phrases is examined in some detail. This review is not intended as a definitive or timely legal brief due to the constant litigation over

Section 1983 provisions. Instead, the discussion is intended to convey the broad significance of the law by a review of major court interpretations.

A. Person Acting Under Color of Law

Since the word "person" is not explicitly defined in the law, congressional records have been used to try to clarify the meaning. In confronting the issue for the first time in 1961 (*Monroe v. Pape*, 1961), the U.S. Supreme Court interpreted the debates to hold that the word "person" was not meant to include a municipal corporation. The implication was that all other individuals, groups, and corporations were persons within the act's meaning.

A second review in 1978 (*Monell v. Department of Social Services of the City of New York*, 1978) led the U.S. Supreme Court to reverse its earlier position. In its new interpretation, the Court declared municipal corporations to fall under the law's definition of person. Municipalities thus joined a long list of persons, including counties, states, school districts, private firms, and private individuals.

The color of law clause further defined the word person. In the 1961 Court interpretation, the color of law provision was found to apply to officials, employees, or individuals responsible for the enforcement of state (and local) laws. Interestingly enough, this effectively excluded sanctions against the Ku Klux Klan; only those who represented a state in some capacity and who were *unwilling* to enforce a state law fell within the definition of person accountable under Section 1983. According to this interpretation, public persons as well as private persons representing the state in some capacity (e.g., contractors) faced liability for implementing an unconstitutional law or abusing public authority.

Added complexity results from the court allowing under color of law to encompass two unconstitutional actions: one when authorized by the state, and the other taken without state authority. Both are reviewed in the following sections.

1. Unconstitutional Acts Authorized by State Law

The U.S. Supreme Court suggested in its 1961 interpretation that public officials implementing unconstitutional actions face *personal* liability, even if those actions were authorized under state law. Merely executing an existing state law does not provide individual public officials and employees with immunity from suit.

In the 1978 Supreme Court case (*Monell v. Department of Social Services of the City of New York*, 1978:167) that first subjected municipal corporations to liability under Section 1983, the issue centered upon unconstitutional actions authorized by state law. Specifically, New York City's social services department required women employees to take unpaid sick leave in the latter months of pregnancy. Some of the women employees sued to stop the sick leave policy and to force the department to pay for wages lost during the forced leaves. Before the New York case reached the U.S. Supreme Court, the Court overturned similar sick leave policies in another case. When confronted with the New York City case, the Court held that women employees could sue the city—the government—to gain wages lost because of an unconstitutional policy.

2. Unconstitutional Acts Not Authorized by Law

The second application—action taken without state authority—applies primarily to public officials personally. For instance, in the 1961 case cited earlier, a Chicago resident sued police officers personally for breaking into his home, searching it without a warrant, and arresting and detaining him without a warrant or arraignment. He argued that the police officers should be liable for depriving him of his rights, privileges, and immunities secured by the Constitution. The Court agreed, holding that the officers violated both the U.S. Constitution *and* the laws of Illinois. Unlike the New York case where city policy or law commanded an unconstitutional act, the Chicago police violated both state and federal law. As a result, the Court ruled that the officers were personally liable for damages due to their actions that were contrary to existing law that protects citizen rights.

In summary, the Court has interpreted the under color of law provision to protect individuals from misconduct by a variety of persons abusing public responsibilities.

B. Subjects or Causes to Be Subjected

Public officials who deprive an individual of a federally protected right face Section 1983 liability. A public official may fall under the act's purview when serving in any of three capacities: policy-maker (i.e., official acts), individual (i.e., personal acts), and, supervisor of a subordinate who violates a citizen's rights. Each job setting is briefly reviewed here.

1. Official Acts

A person subject to Section 1983 faces legal liability for actions taken (or not taken) in his or her official responsibility. This occurs when, for example, governors, mayors, councilpersons, or managers have primary responsibility for adopting or changing an unconstitutional policy, ordinance, regulation, decision, or custom. According to the U.S. Supreme Court, government officials are liable "when execution of a government's policy or custom, whether made by its lawmakers or by those whose edicts are acts may fairly be said to represent official policy, inflicts the injury that the government as an entity is responsible" (*Monell v. Department of Social Services of the City of New York*, 1978:167).

The New York City mandatory sick leave policy for pregnant employees provides an illustration of this point. The Court allowed the employee's suit against New York City's social services department administrators because the sick leave policy was unconstitutional. Whereas the administrators were not personally responsible for paying the damages awarded, the administrators were in a position to officially correct the situation by changing policy and processing the city's payment of back wages to the wronged parties.

2. Personal Acts

Public officials may be held *personally* liable for violating another individual's rights. Until recently, for the wronged party to prevail, the wrongdoing public official had to act in *bad faith* and *unreasonably*, a so-called two-prong test. Whereas each of the two tests are defined here, recent Court cases[5] suggest movement towards a single operating rule: the known or should have known test.

The Reasonable Official Test. The more subjective of the two prongs—the reasonable official test—centered on the wrongdoer's "good faith" belief. The test served to differentiate between what an official did, and what a reasonable person would have done or should have done under the circumstances. In one noteworthy case, a suit was brought against Ohio's governor, Kent State University's president, and high-ranking officers in the Ohio National Guard. These officials were charged with unnecessarily deploying the National Guard to quell a 1970 riot at the university and instructing soldiers to use force if necessary. Four students died in the ensuing activities. The U.S. Supreme Court required that the reasonable officials' rule be used to determine whether the governor could be held liable for the deaths (Kattan, 1977:986; *Scheuer v. Rhodes*, 1974:232). As is evident, a level of subjectivity is involved in applying this decision rule.

The Known or Should Have Known Test. A more objective prong has now become controlling law. In this test, knowledge of the law is dominant. The question depends on whether the official knew or should have known that an act was illegal (*Wood v. Strickland*, 1975:308) To apply this decision rule, a court first examines whether an action (or inaction) was illegal at the time of the alleged wrongdoing. Then, the court determines whether the official should have known the act was illegal. Although more clear than the reasonable official test, this test leaves much room for ambiguity too. For example, when was an action ruled illegal? And, should the official have been cognizant of the correct legal status of the action at the time of his or her decision? Must the official be his or her own constant legal advisor? In attempting to clarify and establish the boundaries of the known or should have known rule, the U.S. Supreme Court (*Harlow v. Fitzgerald*, 1982:2727) declared that "the decisive factor in granting or withholding of immunity is the state of law at the time of the" alleged wrongful action.

3. Supervisory Actions

Serving as a supervisor can lead to liability exposure. In fact, suits are often filed against supervisors instead of, or in addition to, the injury-causing subordinate. Several reasons explain such a tactic by the injured party. For one, supervisors can better afford the cost of any judgments because they usually receive more pay than their subordinates. Also, injured citizens may not be able to identify the lower-level employee who actually caused the injury. Third, supervisors have more chances to change or end illegal subordinate actions since supervisors have the power to discharge subordinates and correct procedures (Kattan, 1977: 1206, 1207).

Lacking a definitive U.S. Supreme Court ruling, circuit courts follow different decision rules in dealing with supervisory liability. Two common rules are reviewed below.

Personal Involvement.   A person suing a supervisor must prove that the supervisor had personal involvement in the illegal actions of his or her subordinates. This requires that a supervisor must participate, encourage or direct the illegal subordinate conduct (Kattan, 1977:1206, 1207). This may rest on facts showing the supervisor was actually present when an illegal act was committed and in a position to end or prevent the subordinates' illegal conduct (Days, 1978:61).

Personal Knowledge and Failure to Act.   The premise of this broader rule is that supervisory inaction is just as dangerous to citizens as supervisory action. Supervisors may be liable for a subordinates's illegal action when the supervisor failed to take reasonable steps to halt the subordinate's actions or prevent its recurrence (Days, 1978:61). Supervisors can thus face liability for failing to discipline, retrain, or otherwise deal with subordinates prone to violating an individual's federally protected rights.

C. Definition of Deprivation of Rights

To initiate a suit under Section 1983, an individual's *rights, privileges, or immunities secured by the Constitution and laws* must be violated. The ultimate legal definition of just what is a right, privilege, or immunity is, of course, subject to court determination. Basically, Section 1983 coverage is expanded as Congress and the courts clarify individual rights, privileges, and immunities.

Despite the act's title, the Civil Rights Act of 1871 does not only protect civil rights. In 1980, the U.S. Supreme Court addressed the phrase "and laws," and ruled that the coverage of Section 1983 includes any federally protected right (either based on constitutional or statutory grounds) (*State of Maine v. Thiboutot*, 1980:4859). By this redefinition, the Court incorporated numerous federal entitlement programs (such as Aid to Families of

Dependent Children) into the protective grasp of Section 1983. Thus, as substantive rights increase, public officials face a wider window of liability vulnerability.

D. Section 1983 Summary

Section 1983 is a century-old, one paragraph legal guide for holding public officials accountable for their actions. Interpretations of the law's provisions have changed over the years. Extensive litigation has taken place and is forecasted to continue as long as Congress hesitates to replace the law. The next part of the chapter focuses upon management and policy responses to the law.

III. POLICY AND MANAGEMENT RESPONSES

Why are public organizations and their agents facing the liability challenge, and what options are available for dealing with this issue? The answer is not simple. To help answer the question, this section opens with a discussion of megapolicy issues. With this broad view as a guide, the discussion then turns to organizational options in managing risks, first through risk management and then through the use of indemnification laws. A review of the range of financial risks facing the organization and its agents leads into a discussion of why transferring the financial risk to an insurer is employed more now than in the past.

A. Megapolicy

What have courts and legislatures intended by defining the tort liability of governments, officials, and employees? One intention is to compensate individuals injured by governments or public agents. A second is to deter official misconduct. This is achieved by holding officials accountable in courts for violations of citizen rights.

These goals, however honorable and desirable, compete with the needs of government administration. Discretion is a necessary part of most public officials' jobs, and, no doubt, the responsibilities of most offices require it. Damage suits can easily limit the motivation of public servants to use discretion. Thus, courts and legislatures have recognized the need for swift and effective administration of government policies through the use of immunities for officials having discretion.

As a policy issue, the primary question about liability turns on how courts and legislatures reconcile compensation or deterrence with the reality of government administration. The answer is that efforts are made to balance the competing concerns. As such, policies must balance four needs: (1) to promote effective administration of government policies; (2) to deter misconduct of public officials; (3) to protect individual rights; and, (4) to compensate individuals for injuries received through the actions of public officials.

B. Risk Management

What can a public organization do to deal with the liability threat to itself and its officers and employees? A systematic effort for dealing with personal and official liability requires an effort now known as risk management. The management of risks (such as tort liability) depends upon a process of identifying risk exposures, evaluating the risks with the threats they pose, and deciding upon planned strategies to prevent or reduce the risks. Few governments, however, actually follow this route. A national survey conducted in 1981 reported that only one-fourth of the responding cities and counties adopted formal risk management policies (Roos, 1982). State-level surveys provide similar results (Texas Advisory Commission on Intergovernmental Relations, 1978a).

A problem faced by governmental units that neglect the significant liability threat is that its response, if any, may well be disjointed and reactive. When a single organizational member has the responsibility to oversee organizational responses to liability issues, a coordinated response may be more likely to result. To what degree have governmental units assigned risk management duties to an organizational member? The earlier cited 1981 survey indicated that less than 25% of surveyed cities and counties employed full-time risk management (Roos, 1982). State-level data reveal even less formal risk management efforts (Texas Advisory Commission on Intergovernmental Relations, 1978a). In contrast, the private sector has significantly embraced risk management (Green and Serbein, 1978). In government, however, the practice of risk management is:

> still the function of a government employee who wears several hats and spends only a portion of his or her time attending to these concerns. For example, in a number of municipalities, assistant city managers are performing this function (Roos, 1982).

Why do public agencies exhibit such little reliance upon risk management programs? A key reason is a basic misunderstanding of the risk management concept and process. For example, a 1977 survey of Oklahoma cities reported that risk management was rated as only slightly important in dealing with liability problems, yet respondents wanted improved information about insurance premiums and law suits as well as improved loss control (Oklahoma Municipal League, 1978:11-24). Thus, though professing little interest in risk management per se, respondent governments welcomed elements of the risk management process.

A random sample survey in 1979 of New York local governments found similar results. Only 15% of the reporting jurisdictions used formal risk management programs, but approximately 57% wanted outputs normally associated with such programs (N.Y. State Legislature, 1980:132-141). Despite management interest in the work of risk managers, the innovation has not yet achieved significant diffusion throughout public management.

A reason for the low adoption of risk management activities may rest on public officials having a preference that higher-level policy-makers (legislators at the federal or state level) eliminate or reduce the liability threat. Fundamentally, this is exhibited in the call for laws restoring absolute (or near) immunity on governments and its officials and employees. Some state legislatures have responded by enacting various indemnification laws.

C. Indemnification Laws to Reduce Liability

Public organizations, officials, and employees seek to shift liability exposure by indemnification laws. State laws providing indemnification are effective ways to restore most, if nearly not all, protections provided under sovereign immunity (Floyd and Associates, 1978; Spector et al., 1983). This method is *not* an effective means for limiting Section 1983 liability because state law cannot limit federal law; Congress alone has the responsibility to make statutory changes in Section 1983.

Two state-level indemnification approaches have evolved. One indemnification design attempts to replace the loss of sovereign immunity with specific legal protection. It is referred to here as official liability. The second form of indemnification design is labeled personal liability to convey that Section 1983 liability is not limited by state law, but rather just redirects the payor of any civil damages from the individual public officer or employee to the public budget.

1. Official Liability

In the absence of sovereign immunity, states have to enact laws that restore all or part of the immunity. The effect of such laws is to direct citizen suits away from the wrongdoing individual officer or employee and to the governmental entity that has certain immunities from suit. This constitutes *official liability* since it serves to immunize officials directly. The resulting state laws follow one of two basic designs: open-ended, and closed-ended (U.S. Advisory Commission on Intergovernmental Relations, 1978:22).

Open-Ended Approach. Open-ended indemnification provides broad governmental responsibility for civil wrongs. As such, the governmental unit becomes liable for activities of its officers and employees, unless otherwise specified. The areas that generally receive absolute immunity from civil suits include legislative, judicial, and executive (discretionary) functions as well as decisions related to taxing, inspecting, and licensing. All other areas of governmental activity are susceptible to civil suits.

Under such laws, the liability of employees and the entity itself are merged. That is, the government entity defends any wrongdoing employee and pays judgments rendered if the employee was found acting within the scope of his or her powers. However, open-ended statutes often place a dollar limit (or cap) on the amount of liability that the public jurisdiction may have to pay. In Oklahoma, (Spector et al., 1983:36; 11 *Okla. Stat.* 23-103:102) for example, the limit was set by law at $1 million per occurrence and $100,000 per person as of July 1, 1983. The Oklahoma law also established procedures for bringing claims against a government; citizens must observe filing deadlines or else the claim is not acceptable for review. Oklahoma political jurisdictions can also purchase insurance as protection against the financial risks associated with the liability threat.

Closed-Ended Approach to Indemnification. Closed-ended liability narrowly defines liability. This approach provides for the exclusion of suits against governments except in certain instances (U.S. Advisory Commission on Intergovernmental Relations, 1978:22). Missouri law, for example, provides that governments are generally immune except for damages caused by a public vehicle or a dangerous condition on public property—two areas dealt with in a 1977 state supreme court decision (*Mo. Rev. Statute*, § 537.606; Spector et al., 1983:33). Even within this narrow liability, states often place caps on the financial risks facing public organizations. Missouri law, for instance, limits public entities to a cap of $100,000 per person, $800,00 per occurrence.

2. Personal Liability[6]

State laws enacted to deal with liability created by Section 1983 and other federal laws cannot remove the federally imposed liability. Rather, states can only specify who will ultimately bear the liability. That is, the governmental entity may defend and pay all costs, including settlements or court awards, if any, resulting from a Section 1983 citizen suit.

State indemnification laws covering Section 1983 claims generally do not provide absolute protection to the wrongdoing public official or employee. Three general tests have evolved for determining a government's assumption of the financial consequences of Section 1983 liability.

The first test rests on an objective determination of whether or not the wrong occurred as a result of an official or employee performing official duties or operating within a defined scope of employment. If the wrong occurred outside the scope of official duties, the wrongdoer is left personally exposed to Section 1983 remedies, including the requirement to *personally* pay litigation costs and any court-imposed monetary damages.

The second test rests on the nature of the wrongdoing. The governmental entity may deny indemnification when an officer or employee operates in a grossly negligent, willful, or malicious manner. In a related manner, indemnification can be limited to those acts or omissions conducted in good faith.

A third test depends on after-the-fact behavior by the wrongdoing official or employee. To receive governmental indemnification, an alleged wrongdoer has to cooperate in good faith in the case defense. Employees thus have an incentive to reasonably challenge the complaint. Without such cooperation, the employing jurisdiction would be unable to mount an effective defense. Absent the cooperation of the alleged wrongdoing public official or employee, state laws permit the removal of any otherwise provided indemnification effort.

D. Monetary Implications of Liability

Tort liability suits have a monetary implication for governments and their agents (i.e., public officials and public employees). The public organization faces various costs in managing its liability risks, including the cost of training, supervision, and insurance premiums. In addition, the organization faces the expenses and awards associated with liability claims. This section outlines some of the most important monetary implications of tort liability claims (or suits) and some indemnification provisions that seek to reduce the financial uncertainty facing governments and their agents.

1. Litigation Expenses

Litigation is not inexpensive. Just to get a frivolous suit thrown out by a judge requires legal time and expenses. As a result, most indemnification statutes authorize governmental entities to pay legal defense costs. According to a late 1982 California survey, more than $2.5 million was paid in legal fees by 84 cities from 1980 to late 1982 with many of the suits lacking any substance (*Western City*, 1983:17-19,30).

Another approach for handling legal fees and costs is to have the jurisdiction direct its legal counsel to defend the employee. State laws clarify the circumstances under which this might be permitted. The Oklahoma statute (11 *Okla. Stat*, 102), for instance, provides that the affected official or employee must request the political jurisdiction's legal assistance within 14 days after notification of a suit. The jurisdiction then must conduct an inquiry into case facts. If the act or omission was performed during employment and in good faith, the employee will be indemnified. Upon such a finding, the jurisdiction's legal officer has a responsibility to appear and defend the employee.

It is not always advisable for a public official or employee to rely upon the jurisdiction's legal counsel. The reason is that the defense strategy is decided upon by the jurisdiction's legal officer, not the alleged wrongdoer. As a result, the jurisdiction's interest in a case may differ from the sued officer/employee. Whereas the jurisdiction's legal counsel would appear to have two clients—the jurisdiction and the officer/employee—the legal counsel is paid by and beholding to the jurisdiction, not the alleged wrongdoing public official or employee. To avoid this potential conflict of interest, the official or employee has to engage the services of a personal legal representative and directly pay all legal expenses.

In many cases, the jurisdiction's insurance company decides which legal counsel will be used and the defense strategy. An insurance company has an interest in making sure any settlement or judgment is low. If settlement offers a more effective financial result than litigation, an insurance company has an incentive to settle rather than risk expensive litigation. Police officers dislike this practice since it makes them appear to have been wrong when they feel (and the evidence may well show) that they did nothing wrong.

2. Damage Awards

If the alleged Section 1983 complaint is taken through the court process, the government and/or its agents may face monetary liability through compensatory, punitive, or nominal damages. The monetary implications of each is reviewed here.

Nominal damages are merely designed to provide symbolic relief. For example, two students were suspended from school without the school following procedural due process. These actions violated the students' constitutional rights, yet the court found no actual harm done. The court placed a symbolic value of $1 on the loss (*Carey v. Piphus*, 1978:1042).

Compensatory damages, also known as actual damages, serve to make the injured person whole again. This can take the form of back pay for improper personnel procedures (e.g., requiring pregnant employees to take unpaid sick leave) or loss of business earnings due to unfair zoning procedures, for example. These awards range from inconsequential sums to relatively high awards.

If the wrong was adjudged to have been done with "malice," or intent to harm, *punitive damages* may be awarded the injured party. Punitive damages are designed to punish the wrongdoer. As such, punitive damages present a special problem for indemnification efforts. In fact, punitive damages have been expressly excluded in most state laws. The reason is that punitive damages are based upon intent or malice to harm and, furthermore, are designed to punish the wrongdoer. State lawmakers find it difficult to justify using taxes to indemnify in such situations. As a result, the wrongdoing officer or employee is generally left directly responsible for punitive damage award payments. In some cases, the government may pay the awarded punitive damages, but will later recover it from the offending officer or employee.

Governments and their agents are treated differently in punitive damages. The U.S. Supreme Court has interpreted Section 1983 to give municipal governments immunity from punitive damages (*City of Newport v. Fact Concert, Inc.*, 1981:247), but the same immunity does not extend to government officials and employees. A U.S. Supreme Court decision in 1983 further clarified the punitive liability of public officials and employees (*Smith v. Wade*, 1983:3021). In this case, a prison guard's "reckless or callous indifference" to an inmate's rights resulted in an inmate's rape. The facts were that the inmate was placed in a cell with another inmate who had a history of violence. The guard did not attempt to determine if another cell was available with less risk. Following his rape, the inmate sued under Section 1983, and the court awarded $5000 in punitive damages (combined with $25,000 in compensatory damages) against the state prison guard.

3. Attorney's Fees

Even when no monetary damage awards result from the litigation, Section 1983 suits may still end up causing a direct outlay of money to pay the attorney's fees and court costs for the person injured. The reason is that Section 1983 is linked to the Civil Rights Attorney's Fees Award Act of 1976, codified as 42 U.S. Code, Section 1988 (Texas Advisory Commission on Intergovernmental Relations, 1978b:138–142). Section 1988 allows the court, at its discretion, to award a reasonable attorney's fees to the prevailing party. One effort to put a stop to frivolous suits against governments and their agents is the movement toward allowing the defendant—the sued government, official, or employee—to recover attorney's fees from the person bringing the suit (the plaintiff). Recently proposed changes in the Attorney's Fees Act seek to codify this option (*The National Law Journal*, 1983:3,36).

E. Transfer the Financial Risk: Insurance

The financial risk resulting from the liability threat has increased the interest in transferring the risk to an insurance company. For a set premium, the insurance company agrees to assume all litigation, settlement, and award costs that conform to the actual provisions of the insurance contract.

Due to the relatively recent growth of Section 1983 as a relief against alleged wrongs, the insurance industry has a limited data base of claims and judgments upon which to base sound insurance policies. The frequency and severity of Section 1983 claims are only now starting to provide the basis for expectations about future losses. One recent study revealed that insurance rate-making for insurance products designed to deal with Section 1983 and other liability exposures were fraught with myths without empirical justification (Hildreth, 1983).

Although early surveys indicated that governments faced some difficulty in acquiring and retaining insurance protection for personal liability risks (Texas Advisory Commission on Intergovernmental Relations, 1978a), more recent accounts show that insurance options are more available (*Journal of American Insurance*, 1980:16–20). Yet general liability insurance policies often exclude civil rights coverages. As a result, a specialized insurance product called public officials liability has evolved. The acquisition of special insurance policies can lead to potential overlaps or basic incompatibility of an insured's total insurance package. Simply stated: Who covers what, when, where and under what conditions? Litigation can be required to sort out all the insurance contracts.

Even when some form of insurance is found, all employees and officials may not be covered. For instance, separate police professional liability policies are required to cover police departments. Public health staff and physicians are usually excluded from standard policies; special coverages are required.

To make matters even more complex, some state laws make the mere purchase of insurance a waiver of any otherwise provided immunity. State indemnification laws often have to address this point.

Public jurisdictions have come to rely upon insurance protection despite its costs. A 1981 survey of public official liability experiences in six states— California, Illinois, Maryland, Michigan, Texas, and Virginia—found that 70% of the surveyed cities and townships and 62% of surveyed counties purchased liability insurance (The Wyatt Co., 1982). Respondents cited the reasons for not purchasing public official liability insurance as: insurance was unnecessary; insurance costs were too high; or, insurance purchase conflicted with legal advice.

Besides finding and entering into an insurance contract, governments must contend with escalating premium costs. Some governments report escalating premiums despite the lack of any claims submitted under the policy (U.S. Advisory Commission on Intergovernmental Relations, 1978:22). This could indicate, however, that the insurance company considers the jurisdiction prone to claims or lackadaisical about the prevention of liability claims.

IV. CONCLUSIONS

The liability of public jurisdictions and their agents, including elected, appointed, and career employees, reflects the trend toward more accountability of public entities and agents to citizens. Some state tort environments have changed due to the loss of sovereign immunity. State tort reform laws serve to restore some, if not all, of the previously enjoyed state-provided immunity from citizen suits. In contrast, the Civil Rights Act of 1871, better known as Section 1983, serves as a national policy to force public organizations and their agents to be more cognizant of citizen rights. Developments in this federal law have a significant impact on public budgets and the personal assets of public officials and employees. We do not now know the degree to which the law influences decision-making by officials and employees. This area of state and local government demands more research.

NOTES

1. This section builds off earlier research reported in Rabin, Jack, Hildreth, W. Bartley, and Miller, Gerald J. (1979). *Public Officials Liability*, International City Management Association, Washington, D.C.
2. The major source on this subject is Rhyne, Charles S., Rhyne, W. S., and Elmerdorf, S. P. (1976). *Tort Liability and Immunity of Municipal Officials*, National Institute of Municipal Law Officers, Washington, D.C., p. 349.
3. To be precise, state law in this categorization refers to state courts' interpretations of the common law. Federal law refers to courts' interpretations of the Civil Rights Act of 1871. The reader must realize that state courts can interpret the Civil Rights Act of 1871 and, that until the early 1970s, federal courts interpreted the common law similarly to state courts.
4. For example, under statutes such as tort claims acts; under private laws passed to compensate specific persons; under common law for proprietary or nongovernmental functions such as water works in some states; through insurance and indemnification that will be discussed later; and under constitutional provisions limiting sovereign immunity, such as eminent domain.
5. A recent court case is *Harlow v. Fitzgerald* (1982), 102 S.Ct. 2727. For background on the two-prong test, see Developments in the law: Section 1983 and federalism. 90 *Harvard Law Review* 1213.
6. This section uses as examples the civil rights indemnification laws of Oklahoma (see Spector et al., 1983:151; 11 *Okla. Stat.* 23–103,102); Massachusetts (*Mass. Gen. Laws*, Chapter 41, 100–1001) and New Hampshire (*N.H. Rev. Stat. 31*:106).

REFERENCES

Carey v. Piphus (1978). 98 S.Ct. 1042, 435 U.S. 247.

Days, D. S., III. (February 8, 9 and May 3, 1978). Statement before Subcommittee on the Constitution, Committee on the Judiciary. U.S. Senate, *Civil Rights Improvements Act of 1871, Hearings*. 95th Congress, 2d Session, p. 61.

Developments in the Law: Section 1983 and Federalism. *Harvard Law Review* 90:1133–1361.

Floyd, Kennedy and Associates, Inc. (1978). *The New World of Municipal Liability*. The National League of Cities, Washington, D.C.

Green, M. and Serbein, O. N. (1978). *Risk Management*. Reston Publishing, Reston, Va., and issues of the weekly publication *Business Insurance*.

Gregoire v. Biddle (1949). 177 F. 2d 579.

Harlow v. Fitzgerald (1982). 102 S.Ct. 2727.

Hildreth, W. B. (1983). The municipal liability market and rate-making revisions. Loman Foundation Research Fellowship Award.

Kattan, J. Knocking on wood: Some thoughts on the immunities of state officials to civil rights damage actions. *Vanderbilt Law Review 30*:941–1003.

League surveys "deep pocket" costs. (June, 1983). *Western City 30*:17–19.

State of Maine v. Thiboutot (1980). 48 LW 4859.

Monell v. Department of Social Services of the City of New York (1978). 436 U.S. 658.

Monroe v. Pape (1961). 365 U.S. 167.

New York State Legislature, Ways and Means Committee (1980). *Municipal Insurance Pools*. State Legislature, Albany, N.Y., pp. 132–141.

City of Newport v. Fact Concerts, Inc. (1981). 453 U.S. 247.

Oklahoma Municipal League (1978). *Oklahoma Municipal Liability and Insurance*. Oklahoma Municipal League, Oklahoma City, Okla., pp.11–24.

11 *Okla. Stat.* 23–102, 103.

5 *Okla. Stat.* 151, *et seq.*

Prosser, W. L. (1941). *Handbook of the Law of Torts*. West Publishing Co., St. Paul, Minn., p. 8.

Rabin, J., Hildreth, W. B., and Miller, G. J. (1979). *Public Officials Liability*. International City Management Association, Washington, D.C.

Rhyne, C. S., Rhyne, W. S., and Elmerdorf, S. P. (1976). *Tort Liability and Immunity of Municipal Officials*. National Institute of Municipal Law Officers, Washington, D.C., p. 349.

Roos, N. R. Risk management: Selected characteristics for individual cities and counties. In *Urban Data Service Reports*, Vol. 14, No. 2. International City Management Association, Washington, D.C.

Scheuer v. Rhodes (1974). 416 U.S. 232.

Sims v. Adams (1976). 537 F. 2d 829.

Smith v. Wade (April, 1983). 33 Cr.L. 3021.

Spector, S. A., Fischetti, A. M., Lubow, F., Notterman, A., and Roessel, K. (January 10, 1983). Governmental tort liability: A national survey. The City of New York Law Department.

Sweetened attorney-fee proposal set. (October 17, 1983). *The National Law Journal*, pp. 3, 36.

Texas Advisory Commission on Intergovernmental Relations (August, 1978a). Tort liability experience of public employees and officials of Texas political subdivisions. *Intergovernmental Report*, Austin, Texas.

Texas Advisory Commission on Intergovernmental Relations (August, 1978b). *Personal Tort Liability of Texas Public Employees and Officials: A Legal Guide*. Austin, Tex., pp. 138–142.

U.S. Advisory Commission on Intergovernmental Relations (1978). *Intergovernmental Relations 5*:22.

Webster v. City of Houston (1982). 689 F.2d 1220 (5th Cir.).

Why municipal liability insurance is alive and well. (Summer 1980). *Journal of American Insurance 56*:16–20.

Wood v. Strickland (1975). 420 U.S. 308.

The Wyatt Company (1982). *National Report on Public Officials Liability*. Chicago, Ill.

14

State Budgeting and Appropriations Processes

James E. Skok   Department of Public Administration, Pennsylvania State University, Middletown, Pennsylvania

I. STATE BUDGETING AND FISCAL STRESS

Since the early 1960s, governmental budgeting has been one of the most dynamic subfields within public administration. Based on the rich and rapid development of decision-making theory, this awakening of interest has induced a generation of M.P.A. students to choose budgeting careers with executive and legislative staffs. As the surpluses of the 1960s give way to the shortages of the 1980s, budget analysts are moving ever closer to center stage in the ritualized budget dramas of the fifty states.

The 30 years of unprecedented economic growth that followed World War II afforded economic theorists an opportunity that comes to social scientists once in a generation, at most—the chance to apply social science theory to the task of improving the equity and rationality of the governing system. "Increasing governmental revenues must be allocated rationally among the many competing demands for public services," was the message of economists and systems analysts whose academic disciplines excelled among all the social sciences in the theories of choice and rational allocation. Receptivity to that message was truly impressive during the 1960s and 1970s as wave after wave of decision-making reforms swept through federal, state, and city governments. However, the effectiveness of the many attempted reforms has still to be evaluated and placed into historical perspective by academicians and practitioners of public administration.

Neither government surpluses nor application of social science theory can remain immune to political and economic events. Thus, a recent Associated Press survey (*New York Times*, February 22, 1983) found state governmental surpluses replaced by massive deficits ($5.7 billion in twenty-two states) and nearly all states moving to cut budgets and increase taxes. The period of experimentation in state budgeting seems to have ended with the inception of the new era of retrenchment, and the states today find their budget systems and procedures resting firmly in the hands of cutback managers. The budget, seen by some as primarily a financial control mechanism, is clearly a planning process as well. If the reformers of the 1960s and 1970s tended to emphasize the planning function, today's managers in state government are being forced to emphasize control of expenditures and the limiting of governmental growth. Budgeting in the 1980s has become the central process through which a new generation of managers is planning and implementing a slowdown in the growth of state government.

In order to balance their 1983 and 1984 fiscal years' budgets, approximately half of the fifty states have been forced to raise taxes—a policy choice distasteful under any circumstances, but absolutely life-threatening to a state governor and members of his political party during recovery from a recession. The volatile political environment facing state leaders today results from a combination of economic and political circumstances. First, state revenues from their own tax sources fell short of estimates due to the faltering national economy in the period from 1981 through 1983. Second, many state income taxes are tied to the taxpayer's federal tax liability; thus, federal income tax cuts have had the effect of lowering tax yields even further. Third, federal grants to state governments are being consolidated into block grants and funded at reduced levels. Consequently, state governments have been forced to reassess their program priorities, raise taxes, and cut public services. The long-term effects of these massive economic and political changes should not be underestimated; instead, one should expect substantial political and administrative realignments to follow. The budget process in state government is likely to become more highly politicized as interest groups mobilize to limit their losses and legislative bodies struggle to maintain some degree of control over state appropriations. Legislatures will be forced to fight tendencies toward a centralizing of state decision-making processes that threaten to enhance the power of executive branch agencies at the state level. Finally, state-local relations may very well enter a period of increased turmoil as state agencies replace federal agencies in the allocation of grant funds.

Two primary themes are developed in this chapter: (a) budgeting practices have evolved through a series of reform movements resulting in a slowly improving management capability in state government; and (b) budgeting is an analytic process requiring professional decision-making skills, but in a broader sense it is ultimately political in nature and thus inextricably bound to the current of political events in the state. Recent efforts to reform the budget preparation process (planning-programming-budgeting systems and zero-base budgeting) are discussed to explain the evolution of analytic methods in budgeting, and the role of the state legislatures in appropriating funds is explained to relate budgeting to the broader political process.

II. BUDGET REFORM AND MANAGEMENT IMPROVEMENT

Modern state budget systems trace their parentage to progressive governmental reform movements that spread across the country during the first two decades of the twentieth century. The keystone of these early reforms is the principle of the executive budget, a legal arrangement that centralizes the responsibility for preparing a balanced budget in the governor's office. In most states, a four-phased budget cycle developed and a standard set of procedures grew to enhance the governor's control over the process. Thus, budget requests generally are prepared in the executive branch during summer and fall (phase 1: preparation), submitted to the legislature for enactment of appropriations during the winter and spring (phase 2: appropriation), administered by the executive branch throughout the fiscal year (phase 3: execution), and audited by an agency independent of the governor after completion of the fiscal year (phase 4: postaudit). Sets of highly ritualized procedures developed in each of the phases with institutional participants playing and replaying their designated roles year after year. Stereotypically, the literature on budgeting portrays administrative agencies as aggressive seekers of new programs and bigger budgets, the governor's central budget office as responsible fiscal strategists, the legislative appropriations committees as fiscally conservative budget cutters, and legislators in general as pork-barrel bargainers negotiating to advance their particular interests (LeLoup, 1977:74–174; Wildavsky, 1974:18–62).

During the budget preparation phase bureau-level administrators throughout the executive agencies respond to budget instructions issued by the central budget office.[1] Standardized forms are provided and, in some states, analytic methods and standardized formulas are specified. Methods of analysis vary from state to state and agency to agency, but generally they may be described as a collage of object-of-expenditure, programmatic, and zero-base projection techniques.

In budget analysis, form clearly affects substance. Thus, reformers and zealots have spent much energy on attempts to induce change from object-of-expenditure approaches to newer programmatic and zero-base forms of budgeting. With most reform efforts being designed and directed by central budget office staffs, one should not be surprised to find a strong centralizing tendency in recent budget reforms such as the planning-programming-budgeting

systems (PPBS) of the 1960s and 1970s and the zero-base budgeting (ZBB) of
the 1970s and 1980s (Schick, 1973:152; Wildavsky, 1974:188). In fact, these
recent reforms have sought enhancement of centralized executive power, deploying governor against bureaucracy and maintaining the momentum begun during
the early reform period. A look at PPBS and zero-base budgeting, particularly
the analytic methods advocated in these reforms, will serve the dual purpose of
explaining budget preparation and confirming the trend toward executive
centralization.

A. PPBS Versus Creeping Incrementalism

The task of deciding which governmental functions to fund, and at what levels,
lies at the heart of public policy. This observation is particulary true for the
United States because, lacking a broad public planning process such as that
found in other economies, individual funding decisions determine public
priorities in a de facto sense. Policy choices in state governments have tended to
emerge incrementally from the budget and appropriations process.

  Among the many reformers to appear in the 1960s, that most unsettled of
recent decades, was a group of economists and systems analysts whose vision of
a rational-comprehensive, decision-making system for government captivated
both academics and practitioners of public administration. Many compelling
arguments supported the reforms. Thus, one was told that modern social science
and decision-making theory would support rational choice among alternative
government programs, the competitive position of the United States in the world
would be enhanced through a more wise use of scarce resources, and state
governments could become instruments for advancing social equity. The
reformers' objectives were no less than the supplanting of deeply ingrained
processes of incrementalism.

  According to the PPBS reformers, budgeting should be linked to programs
(i.e., interrelated sets of activities with identifiable objectives and target groups),
not to bureaus or other organizational units whose objectives were unstated, at
best, and unknown, at worst. The government's performance in achieving its
objectives could be evaluated through empirical data secured by measuring
output (quantity of work or activities produced) and impact (effects of the
activities upon specified target populations.) Empirical studies would become
the means of evaluating alternative governmental programs, and poor performers
would be replaced by more effective alternatives. Instead of focusing budget
analysis on objects-of-expenditure (i.e., things being purchased), such as salaries,
supplies, consultant services, and equipment, analysts could concentrate upon
identifying the better program through cost-benefit analysis. Five-year projections of costs and benefits, quantified through impact data, would enhance
rational choice.

State governments were told that the "old" style of budget analysis encouraged decision-makers to look at prior-year expenditures for each governmental department in the various object-of-expenditure categories and to estimate coming-year needs by adding amounts for new or expanded services (such as costs for new positions, salary increments, fringe benefit increases, and so on). This process, labeled *successive-limited-comparison*, tended to legitimatize existing activities (known as the *base*), most of which escaped evaluation of any sort (Lindblom, 1959). Furthermore, argued the reformers, it encouraged the worst in the political process by allowing real issues and choices to remain buried in semilatency. Politicians could avoid alienating their constituents by avoiding the explicit identification of objectives and the hard choices that would ensue. The political bargaining process was seen as reinforcing this tendency toward unplanned incrementalism as organized interest groups fought in state legislatures to protect their base (i.e., existing programs and appropriations favorable to them) and to secure their share of the increment (i.e., new funds available).

Although many states implemented some form of PPBS during the 1960s and 1970s, few, if any, experienced the many advantages suggested by the reformers. Dropped by the federal government in 1971, PPBS in the states met a similar fate throughout the 1970s with most states deemphasizing and simplifying the complex planning and analysis routines set up in the early stages of the PPBS reforms.

One recent study (Ramsey and Hackbart, 1979) reports that by 1977, eleven states still claimed to be using PPBS; however, scholars disagree over the authenticity of these systems: that is, are those states actually conforming to the essential theories and procedures as spelled out by the PPBS reformers? Pennsylvania's system, probably the most successful of all the state systems, has been studied in some detail; and even there the conclusions are cautiously optimistic, at best, with one study reporting some use of PPBS-generated data in the central budget office and very selective use by a legislative appropriations committee during one legislative session (Skok, 1977). It should be noted, however, that some of the PPBS routines, most notably the practice of empirical program evaluation, have left their impact upon state decision-making. As pointed out in a 1975 survey by the National Association of State Budget Officers, thirty-two states now perform program-evaluation analyses in the central budget office (Lee and Staffeldt, 1977).

Somewhat less successful have been the PPBS procedures designed to enhance central budget office control over agency budgets. The case of Pennsylvania is illustrative. "Program Policy Guidelines" issued each spring by the governor's budget office specify gubernatorial policy priorities for the coming year's budget. The "Guidelines" provide policy cues for the agencies in preparing their budget requests, and the agencies are to respond by submitting appropriate

"Program Revision Requests," outlining and analyzing alternatives for implementing the gubernatorial policies. These "Requests" are to take the form of data-based, empirical analysis using measurement concepts such as need-and-demand indicators, program output and impact measures, and cost-benefit ratios. The one preferred program alternative is to be selected and defended. Through these procedures, hard data, essential to rational decision-making, were to be injected into the budget analysis process, and gubernatorial policy was to become the prime force in setting the policy agenda, thus substantially enhancing the governor's role and limiting the more uncontrolled style of selecting policy priorities inherent in the traditional incremental-political budget-making process. Although these procedures are still followed in Pennsylvania, research reports indicate the "Program Revision Requests" generally are not agency responses to the gubernatorial policy guidelines and that agencies do not take seriously the mandate for data-based analysis of programmatic alternatives (Silverman and Gatti, 1975; Skok, 1977). The many reasons cited by Schick (1973) for failure of the federal government's PPBS experience are also relevant to Pennsylvania and the other states (e.g., the high cost and other burdens associated with empirical analysis; limitations on data, empirical theory, and analytical capabilities; fear held by agency administrators that they would lose control over budgetary decision-making to central office analysts and politicians who might misunderstand and misuse the analyses; and, finally, the widespread perception that the data analyses lacked real substance and thus were ignored and unused by decision-makers).

B. ZBB: Controlling Growth by Cutting the Base

Zero-base budgeting attained national prominence during the 1976 presidential election when candidate Jimmy Carter extolled the virtues of the system he had introduced while governor of Georgia. Touted by management consultants such as Peter Pyhrr (1973), the main goal of ZBB is to force agencies to analyze their current program activities (the base) rather than to focus their analysis only on new programs they are seeking to justify. This is accomplished by forcing agency administrators (beginning with those at the lower organizational levels) to define agency functions and to build "decision packages" for each of the functions. Decision packages are to include: (a) a description of goals and activities; (b) consequences of not performing the particular activity; (c) performance measures, costs, and benefits at various levels of activity; (d) alternatives for accomplishing the stated goal; and, (e) the preferred (cost-effective) alternative. Priority rankings for all decision packages are developed at lower levels throughout each agency and are grouped into larger decision packages at higher administrative levels, although theoretically the priorities assigned at lower levels are to remain visible as options in the higher-level packages. Through the ranking process those administrators close to the service-delivery level propose a prioritized list of agency functions specifying the desired funding level for each. The prioritizing allowed higher-level supervisors to excise rather easily the less critical functions from the bottom of the list and thus to remove them from the agency's budget. Administrators throughout the agency would be forced to become more familiar with the agency's operations and to develop a sense of what functions were most critical. Theoretically, a minimum funding level would be identified for each function below which its effectiveness would be reduced to the point that its elimination would be recommended. Top-level agency management thus would be shown the lower priority functions and could see the consequences of their elimination. As the decision packages are passed up the management ranks, they are aggregated through combination of many small packages into fewer large ones, and new priority rankings are established until the chief agency administrator (and ultimately the governor's budget office) would complete the desired combination of packages. The unique features here are the prioritizing and the minimum funding levels, two operations designed to force program administrators at least to delve into the base of their ongoing operations and to make hard choices.

Adopted in some form by eighteen states (Dimock et al., 1983:384) as well as the federal government, ZBB seems to have had little impact upon state decision-making (Lauth, 1978). Sold as a system that would decentralize budgetary decision-making by involving lower-level program administrators in budget preparation, in fact ZBB systems generated overwhelming amounts of paperwork and a complex process of ranking and reranking decision packages (Schick, 1978). Dropped by the federal government in 1981, states that adopted ZBB reverted to more simplified versions with a minimum of decision packaging and ranking processes. With the coming of economic hard times, Schick and Keith (1976:1) perceptively suggested that ZBB might become another tool of central-office budget staffs to force agencies to cut back their programs. Today it is used primarily as a tool for decremental budgeting under which agencies are forced to produce decision packages outlining agency priorities under 5, 10, or 15% cuts below current-year budget levels (Dimock et al., 1983:384). Thus a system designed to decentralize the budget process has become a means for the further enhancement of centralized control over agency budgets.

III.   BUDGETING AND THE LEGISLATIVE PROCESS

A reason often given for the failure of PPBS in the federal government is the lack of interest shown by Congress in promoting the system or using its data (Schick, 1973:154). It is true that meaningful reform of the budget process can occur only if the traditional routines of the legislative process become receptive to new forms of data and information. One should not assume from this, however, that reform is hopeless. Recent experience in the states suggests that legislatures can become receptive to new forms of data and decision-making as long as their essential political character is given deference. This section discusses two recent reform thrusts in state legislatures—the massive increases in legislative staffing and the development of new procedures for legislative control over public policy—for the dual purpose of explaining the legislative process and assessing the possibility of improving budgetary decision-making.

The legislative function in budgeting is essentially a bifurcated process (Bozeman and Straussman, 1982). On one hand, it is a top-down process directed by the political party leaders in the legislature and chairpersons of the major standing committees whose aim it is to forge a document that will implement partisan ideology and programs. On the other hand, it is a bottom-up process, the nondirected building of coalitions of support from among competing interests. The first process is somewhat more synoptic and centralized with party leaders developing strategies for drawing together a voting majority behind the party banner. The second process is basically spontaneous and nondirected with special-interest legislators competing and forming alliances of convenience necessary to logroll in support of their group's budget position. Reformers expecting to change the legislative appropriation processes in state government must recognize this dual reality.

On one level, the fifty state legislatures present a wide array of differing institutions and procedures (Rosenthal, 1981:286–308). The executive budget system is the standard practice in virtually all states. In only four states (North Carolina, South Carolina, Texas, and Arkansas) does the legislative branch share responsibility for budget preparation; and, in these four, joint legislative-executive budget commissions share responsibility. Although there are some significant state-to-state variations in the formal processes of appropriating funds, the similarities are more significant than the differences. In general, state legislatures, like the U.S. Congress, tend to be decentralized institutions reflecting the individual legislator's orientation toward the needs of his or her district. Forces for institutional centralization are found in the legislative leadership, the appropriations committees, and the finance (tax-writing) committees. Generalizing about legislative process runs the risk of error by oversimplification. However, it can be argued that states with two-party competitive political systems generally tend to be somewhat more highly organized with more force lodged in the top-down legislative process, whereas the one-party states generally are somewhat more fragmented in their legislative processes, emphasizing the bottom-up features of budget coalition building.[2] As Rosenthal (1981:167) points out, the leadership of the majority party in the legislature can exercise considerable control over the law-making process, including appropriations, through their control of the legislative agenda and their domination of the standing committees. Although one should be careful not to overestimate the power of the legislative leadership in today's milieu of generally weakened political parties, the two-party competitive state in which one party controls the governorship and both houses of the legislature generally will tend to be more centralized in its decision-making capability and top-down budgeting will be more pronounced.

The driving environmental factor in state budgeting today is, undoubtedly, the condition of financial shortages and looming budget deficits. Bozeman and Straussman (1982) argue that these hard realities are pushing the federal government toward top-down budgeting in which a supine Congress is more than willing to allow a forceful president to suffer the political slings and arrows associated with massive budget cutting. A similar phenomenon may be occurring in the hard-pressed states. As one state official (State Budget Officer, 1981) suggested recently,

> The state legislature has not fought the governor over implementation of (the new) Federal Block Grants because they are scared to death they will have to consider new taxes.

In fact, what has been happening in the states over the past several years is a complex pattern of institutional change in which the legislatures have been seeking selectively to reassert their powers over the purse strings to arrest the flight of policy control to the executive branch.

A. Legislative Staffing and Budget Reform

A massive increase in professional staffing of our state legislatures has been in process for the past decade; this phenomenon accounts for a substantial transformation in the legislative process. Rosenthal (1981:206) cites a 130% growth in professional staff from 1968 to 1974, with states such as New York, California, Florida, Michigan, Texas, and Pennsylvania each boasting complements of over 400 professionals. Although many of the smaller states remain woefully understaffed with legislative professionals, there appears to be a continuing commitment to this professional buildup across the nation, and an understanding of this trend is to be found in legislative attempts to hold their own against the ever-increasing development of executive branch power.

Since the 1950s, state legislatures have perceived an erosion of their policy-making power. Assisted by grants of unrestrained authority from their unwary legislatures, state administrative agencies eagerly expanded their control over burgeoning state programs. Simultaneously, the federal grant-in-aid system contributed to an erosion of the state legislature's traditional control of the purse strings. With 25% of the average state budget being composed of federal funds, budget officers and program administrators in the states' administrative agencies and governors' offices rapidly became the primary decision-makers in programs involving billions of dollars nationwide. Understaffed and nonprofessionalized, state legislatures had neither the time nor expertise for budget analysis. Prior to 1970, many state legislatures did not extend their appropriation processes to include federal funds, and state funds required for matching purposes often were given little or no meaningful analysis. Since the early 1970s, state legislatures have been extending appropriation control to include federal funds and have been increasing professional staff and data processing capabilities for their appropriations committees. In short, they have begun the monumental task of stemming the flow of policy control to the executive branch.

It would be tempting to assume from these developments that state legislatures today are competently and effectively analyzing budgets and controlling policy development; but, alas, such would be a false assumption. One has only to look at several recent case studies from the state of Pennsylvania (Skok, 1977; 1980a, b) to discover that professionalizing legislative staffs may be easy, but incorporating their data and analyses into legislative decision-making to a meaningful extent is a tortuous process under even the most favorable conditions.

In 1975, reports circulated around the Governor's Budget Office in Pennsylvania that the House Appropriations Committee, for the first time ever, actually used data and information supplied in the governor's PPBS budget as the basis for questioning departmental officials at the appropriations hearings. Analyses of the committee's behavior confirmed that most of the departments were being challenged by some programmatic-type questioning from committee members and staff analysts who were attempting to pursue program evaluation, compare programmatic alternatives, or identify program goals. The committee used some of these data to make cuts in the governor's requests for a number of state programs and the House Appropriations Committee chairman successfully defended the cuts in the Democratic party's caucus and on the floor of the House of Representatives. To this extent, there is clear evidence that professional staff work and the availability of data-based analyses paid off in the sense that determined participants in the legislative process influenced decision-making through rational analyses provided by the PPBS processes. In fact, the top-down (leadership-directed) budget process in the House was receptive (at least to a small degree) to the rational budget reforms that had begun in the state in 1970. These successes are illustrative, further, of the workings of the top-down process. This receptiveness was possible only because it served the broader needs of the political process. The Democratic party leadership of the House had barely survived a bitter attack upon its handling of the budget; and, to secure its own position and restore confidence in its stewardship of the budget process, the leadership recruited professional staff members for the Appropriations Committee who developed a strategy of using the PPBS data for a rational approach to appropriating funds. In short, the legislative leadership chose to use the PPBS approach because it fit their broader political needs at the time.

As the 1975–1976 budget headed for final passage, however, the top-down, leadership-dominated process became supplanted by a more traditional process of political bargaining among competing interests. Thus, a reversion to bottom-up budgeting occurred as House-Senate bargaining over final appropriations became necessary to develop a majority coalition of support behind the governor's budget. This final-stage bargaining was political in character, featuring across-the-board percentage cuts in all programs and line-item cuts designed to preclude a special investigation into alleged corruption in the City of Philadelphia. Much of the painstaking analysis done at earlier stages of the budget process, therefore, was negated by the last-minute political bargaining endemic to the bottom-up budgeting process. Thus, on the positive side one has seen that rational reform of the appropriations process is possible if decision-makers are willing to settle for limited results and to recognize that the needs of the political process inevitably must take precedence in a democratic system. Illustrative of the main point is the fact that none of these successes, limited though they were, would have been possible without the professional staffing of the Appropriations Committee.

B. The Legislative-Executive Struggle for Dominance

If the use of rational analysis in the legislature is so limited in its prospects, why, then, have legislatures embarked on a course of professionalizing? The answer seems to lie in the nature of executive-legislative conflict. Always present in the U.S. system of government, the conflict increases when control of the two branches is divided between the two political parties or among factions of the same party. In the Pennsylvania case recounted previously, the Democratic governor was thwarted in his effort to fund a special investigation of alleged corruption in the City of Philadelphia by a coalition of hostile members of his own party. For the following two years, the budget process was poisoned by this same intraparty feud. In 1977, factions of both parties in the state legislature formed an alliance to limit policy discretion of the Democratic governor. The outcome was a successful move to extend the power of the state legislature to appropriate federal funds coming into the state. Pennsylvania's action was part of a nationwide move by state legislatures to counter executive power. By 1980, approximately twenty states had requirements for the appropriation of federal funds by the state legislature, and a national movement to expand and strengthen this function became a primary objective of the National Conference of State Legislatures. Advocates of this movement had come to realize that adding staff to legislative committees might enrich the general knowledge base and analytical capability of the legislatures, but in and of itself, could not make fundamental changes in the legislatures' control over policy. To accomplish this, the legislatures would have to force themselves into a decision-making stream now dominated by the state executive branch agencies and their counterpart federal bureaucracies. Increased staffing was a necessary, but not sufficient, step toward legislative resurgence; perceptive reformers seeking this goal have now launched a new phase in the continuing saga of executive-legislative struggle for control over public policy.

Undoubtedly, legislative modernization as reflected by increased staffing and reassertion of policy control will continue throughout the decade. Whether or not state legislatures will be successful in these moves to wrest policy control from their governors and state executive agencies remains to be seen.

NOTES

1. Although there is considerable state-to-state variation in organizational structure, all states have an executive budget staff responsible for overall preparation and administration of the governor's budget. In some cases this staff is located in an executive office of the governor, whereas in others it resides in a separate executive department of budget, finance, administration, planning, or some combination of these functions. In thirty states the power to appoint the chief budget officer resides with the governor (*Book of the States*, Council of State Governments, Chicago, 1982; *State Administrative Officials*, Council of State Governments, Lexington, Ky., 1982).

2. Although one-party dominance is declining throughout the states, it is still a factor in many state legislatures. One recent survey found that there are seven one-party Democratic-dominant states; twelve one-party Democratic-majority states; six one-party Republican-majority states; and twenty-five two-party competitive states (Jewell and Olson, 1978:34–35).

REFERENCES

Bozeman, B. and Straussman, J. D. (1982). Shrinking budgets and the shrinkage of budget theory. *Public Administration Review 42*:509–515.

Dimock, M. E., Dimock, G. O., and Fox, D. M. (1983). *Public Administration*, 5th ed. Holt, Rinehart and Winston, New York.

Jewell, M. E. and Olson, D. M. (1978). *American State Political Parties and Elections*. Dorsey Press, Homewood, Ill.

Lauth, T. P. (1978). Zero-base budgeting in Georgia state government: Myth and reality. *Public Administration Review 38*:420–430.

Lee, R. D. Jr. and Staffeldt, R. J. (1977). Executive and legislative use of policy analysis in state budgetary process: Survey results. *Policy Analysis 3*:395–405.

LeLoup, L. T. (1977). *Budgetary Politics*. King's Court Communications, Brunswick, Oh.

Lindblom, C. E. (1959). The science of muddling through. *Public Administration Review 19*:79–88.

New York Times, 22 February 1983, p. A1.

Pyhrr, P. A. (1973). *Zero-Base Budgeting.* Wiley, New York.

Ramsey, J. and Hackbart, M. M. (Spring, 1979). Budgeting: Inducements and impediments to innovations. *State Government 52*:65–69.

Rosenthal, A. (1981). *Legislative Life: People, Process, and Performance in the States.* Harper & Row, New York.

Schick, A. (1973). A death in the bureaucracy: The demise of federal PPB. *Public Administration Review 33*:146–156.

Schick, A. (1978). The road from ZBB. *Public Administration Review 38*: 177–180.

Schick, A. and Keith, R. (1976). *Zero-Base Budgeting in the States.* Council of State Governments, Lexington, Ky.

Silverman, E. and Gatti, F., Jr. (July 1975). PPB on the state level: The case of Pennsylvania. *The Bureaucrat 4*:117–146.

Skok, J. E. (Fall, 1977). Sustaining PPBS in state government: Pennsylvania's second generation adaptations. *The Bureaucrat 6*:50–63.

Skok, J. E. (1980a). Budgetary politics and decision making: Development of an alternative hypothesis for state government. *Administration & Society 11*: 445–460.

Skok, J. E. (1980b). Federal funds and state legislatures: Executive-legislative conflict in state government. *Public Administration Review 40*:561–567; *41*:296–297.

State Budget Officer. (December 8, 1981). Department of Budget and Fiscal Planning, *Personal Interview*, Annapolis, Md.

Wildavsky, A. (1974). *The Politics of the Budgetary Process*, 2nd ed. Little, Brown, Boston.

15
The Legislative Staff *

Alan P. Balutis[†]   Office of Systems and Special Projects,
U.S. Department of Commerce, Washington, D.C.

I. INTRODUCTION

The young aide is twenty-nine, but his long hair and gold-rimmed glasses make him look ten years younger. As a member of the Florida senator's staff, he usually works at a small, paper-strewn desk adjacent to his boss' office. This morning, though, he is sitting near the rear of a hearing room while the Health Committee, which the senator chairs, is holding a session on a bill affecting nursing education. The committee has been in session for almost an hour and is close to a vote on the proposal, yet some legislators are only now arriving. One of them, a moderately conservative Republican like the senator, hurries into the room. Spotting the young aide, the senator comes over to where he sits taking notes about the issue under discussion. "How are we voting on this?" he asks. The aide looks up and says, "We're voting yes." The senator walks to the front of the hearing room, takes his seat, and votes yes.

At 4:00 P.M., a tall, young woman who is a recent graduate of New York University is at her desk in the Legislative Office Building, outside the office suite of her boss, a third-term legislator from Manhattan. The assemblyman is scheduled to speak next week in his home district to the Association for Retarded Children (ARC). The staffer flips through some research material, then

*The views expressed in this chapter are solely the author's, and should not be attributed to the Office of Systems and Special Projects or the U.S. Department of Commerce.

†Present affiliation: Office of Management Analysis and Control, U.S. Department of Commerce, Washington, D.C.

rolls a sheet of paper into her typewriter. She begins to type: "Alexis de Tocqueville noted in the early 1800s that a great strength of this country lay in its citizens' participation in voluntary organizations." After a few more sentences, she's into a discussion of the ARC in New York State and its value as a voluntary organization. The assemblyman will give the speech almost exactly as the aide has written it.

The recent law school graduate is standing in the rear of the chamber as members of the Wisconsin Senate debate an amendment his boss has just introduced. As the issue is debated, the aide takes notes, circling passages on several typed sheets. As one of the speakers is concluding his remarks, the aide passes several sheets to the senator. The senator studies them briefly and, when he rises again to defend his amendment, he reads directly from the data the staffer has given him.[1]

If one were to visit any of a number of capitol buildings in the United States and ask someone there what has been the most important change in the legislature during the last few decades, the likely response would be a single word—staff. Walking about the building, an observer would get a visual confirmation from the plethora of staff offices. Staff members today are inexorably involved in all aspects of the legislative process.

Yet, staffing as a factor in the legislative process has been, until fairly recently, almost completely ignored by political scientists. Moreover, to the extent that professional staff has been a subject of study, the utility of this research for students of legislatures has been limited by a major perceptual bias. That is, that legislative scholars have seemed to believe that Congress, and Congress alone, is worthy of study. Alan Rosenthal (1973:55) touched upon what might be termed "the Washington bias" in existing studies: "State legislatures are neglected institutions of American government. Compared to Congress, for example, they are ignored by the public and are given little attention by political scientists."

The purpose of this chapter is threefold. First, to survey briefly current trends in the movement for modernization and improvement of our state legislatures. Second, to examine from a number of perspectives the backgrounds, norms, activities, functions, and effects of professional staff members in state legislatures. Finally, to analyze the direction of current reform efforts in the states and to speculate about the most appropriate research strategies for the future.

II. LEGISLATIVE REFORM IN THE STATES

A wide variety of aides currently services our legislatures, and the use of the generic term *staff* conceals their diversity. Jewell and Patterson (1973:250) have noted two broad types of legislative staffs for American legislatures: the housekeeping staff and the specialist or professional staff. The housekeeping staff performs various clerical, secretarial, and service tasks and includes the clerk of the House, the sergeant-at-arms, the parliamentarian, and a wide variety of other aides. The professional staff performs policy-related tasks and may be characterized in several subtypes: research, bill-drafting, investigating, subject-matter expert, and political. Moreover, staffs may serve individual legislators, committees, committee chairpersons, the leadership, an entire chamber, or the whole legislature, and may be either partisan or nonpartisan.

In the face of such a wide array of staff aides, it becomes necessary to conceptualize some classificatory scheme to begin to cope with their diversity. Norman Meller (1967) once suggested that legislative service agencies could be arranged along two axes, the horizontal one oriented to "clientele" and "graduated from facilitating the whole legislature at one extreme to individual legislator service at the other." The vertical axis was to measure personal identification, and was similarly graduated from "personal involvement" at one pole to "anonymous objectivity" at the other. Four quarters of the matrix were delineated by crossing the clientele and identification axes at their midpoints.

The staffing reforms advocated as offering a means of solving the legislatures' ills seem, in the main, to be of a nature as to be classified above the midpoint along the vertical identification axis in their tendency to anonymous objectivity and oriented more toward service to the legislature rather than to individual legislators.[2] Of the roughly 100 or so permanent state legislative service agencies created during the period 1973-1982, 74% appear to be oriented more toward the legislature as an institution than to individual members. In addition, 65% of the total were nonpartisan (which would seem to indicate a tendency to anonymous objectivity), whereas 29% were partisan appointments (indicating some personal involvement with the fate of their employer, be it the party or an individual member). Six percent were not classified or classifiable.

Yet, several observers have noted that legislative staffs of all types have grown fairly steadily in recent years. A survey conducted by the Citizens Conference on State Legislatures (1972) revealed that more respondents noted changes in staffing and services—mainly improvements—than in any other category. More recently, Malcolm Jewell (1981) found that since the 1960s all state legislatures have expanded their staffs, but that the most dramatic staff development had taken place in the urban, industrialized states with highly professionalized legislatures. In California, for example, the legislature was investing nearly $32 million in legislative employees by 1981. The staff of the New York legislature has mushroomed to more than 1500 employees.

Given this marked increase in the size and variety of legislative service agencies, there seems to be a very real danger that legislators and legislative reformers may have come to regard staffing as a panacea. If a little staffing is good, it does not necessarily follow that a lot is much better. As Norman Meller

(1967:388) has pointed out, indiscriminate staffing "could well lead to the institutionalizing of the legislator, and eventually to each legislator becoming the captive of his own staff. . . . For this reason, flat recommendations for larger staff fall short of the mark."

Perhaps the best way to resolve such matters is to see how professional staffs are functioning in our state legislatures at the present time.[3]

III. CHARACTERISTICS OF THE LEGISLATIVE STAFF

As noted earlier, little is known about the role of professional staff in the legislative power structure. As Ralph K. Huitt (1969:226–227) has noted:

> His [the staff man's] influence has been underrated and overrated. Surely he is more than a facilitator, more than extra hands to relieve the legislator of errand-running, more than a trained research mind to end legislative dependence on bureaucrat and lobbyist. Surely he is less than the real power behind the throne, as the frustrated lobbyist, and even the staff man himself, sometimes thinks he is.

Huitt goes on to raise an interesting question: "What is he like, this bright and ambitious man who submerges his own career aspirations in those of another? What does he want, what does he think he can get? How does he perceive his role, its satisfactions and limitations?" It is to a consideration of these questions that we now turn.

IV. BACKGROUND[4]

A survey of the educational backgrounds of the professional staff of several state legislatures indicates that their educational qualifications are rather impressive. Of the sixty-five professional staff aides interviewed, all had B.A.s or B.S.s; thirty-three, M.A.s or M.S.s; twelve, L.L.B.s, and three, Ph.D.s.

As Kenneth Kofmehl (1962:85,86) noted in his landmark study of congressional staffs, a legal education is viewed as exceeding valuable. It helps in mastering such tasks as bill drafting, preparing briefs, and analyzing legislative proposals. It is the staffer's view that being of the same profession and knowing the legal vocabulary are assets in dealing with the many lawyer-legislators. In fact, several expressed a feeling of inadequacy because of a lack of legal training.

In terms of previous political or governmental experience, twenty-eight of the professional staff members surveyed had been employed in the executive branch of the state government, nineteen in the same general field as their legislative work. Fifteen had prior legislative staff experience. Four had experience as federal or local government employees. Two had been newspapermen.

Nine had been (or still were) practicing lawyers. Three had held responsible positions in private business concerns. One had taught in college, and one in high school.

Previous legislative staff experience and prior employment in the executive branch were viewed by senior staffers in charge of recruiting and staffing as being very valuable to a legislative aide. Again, as Kofmehl (1962:86–88) noted, previous legislative staff experience familiarized an individual with the unique environment of the legislature and helped him to gain an appreciation of the political factors that members of the legislature have to take into account in performing their work. Prior employment in the executive branch often had been a primary source of the aide's substantive knowledge of his specialty on the legislative staff, and usually provided a network of personal acquaintances that made securing assistance easier.

The legislative recruitment process in the United States tends to select the middle-aged—men in their forties and fifties—for careers as legislators. Staffers seem to be quite a bit younger than the legislators they serve—normally in their twenties and thirties. The hoary adage has been that politics is a man's game. Male domination continues to be the rule in the legislature. But women are making inroads in many of the legislative staffs, and using the positions as steppingstones to run for office themselves. Professional staff members as a group are well paid, with salaries ranging from $12,000 for a beginning research assistant to over $40,000 for staff directors.

Because many of the professional staff are new, it is difficult to determine whether a career pattern exists. However, there seems to be developing an increasing desire to make work with the legislature a career. Of the fifty-seven aides who responded to a question concerning their future plans, thirty-four stated that they would like to stay on in legislative staff work.

V. NORMS AND CONSTRAINTS

Donald Matthews (1960), in his description of the folkways of the United States Senate, stated that every group of human beings has its unwritten rules of the game, its norm of conduct, and its approved manner of behavior. Legislative staffers clearly do have such unwritten rules and, not surprisingly, their norms were legislative norms.

Staffers tend to adopt the norms and orientations of the members of the committees (or the leaders) for whom they work. The general legislative norms that staff members identified were courtesy and reciprocity; limited advocacy; loyalty; deference; anonymity; specialization; partisanship; institutional patriotism; and, legislative work. The frequency with which each rule was mentioned is indicated in Table 1.

Table 1 Rules of the Game Perceived by Staff and Legislators: Percentage of Respondents Naming Rule[a]

Rules of the game	Staff (n = 65) (%)	Legislators (n = 46) (%)
1. Legislative norms	100	52
2. Limited advocacy	80	30
3. Loyalty	83	91
4. Deference	73	26
5. Anonymity	47	19
6. Specialization	100	11
7. Partisanship	53	13
8. Apprenticeship	50	9
9. Institutional patriotism	33	7
10. Legislative work	60	39

[a]Percentages total more than 100 since most respondents named more than one rule.

These norms have been briefly defined (Patterson, 1970) as follows:

- *Courtesy and Reciprocity* — Political disagreements shouldn't influence personal feelings. Legislators trade votes; staffers swap information and insights;

- *Limited Advocacy* — Staffers shouldn't press their own views or preferences too far. The staffer presents options; the legislator draws conclusions;

- *Deference* — The staff "should be on tap, not on top;"

- *Anonymity* — The staffer should remain behind the scenes; public recognition and credit should go to the legislator;

- *Specialization* — Staff people are expected to specialize and develop a subject-matter expertise;

- *Partisanship* — A staffer is expected, at the very least, to be of a similar political philosophy as his/her employers. In certain cases, an identical political affiliation is required;

- *Institutional Patriotism* — Staffers are expected to defend the legislature and members against outsiders and to not behave in a manner that might reflect on the legislature as a body;

- *Legislative Work* — Staff members are expected to devote a share of their time and energy to what are sometimes characterized as highly detailed, dull, and unrewarding tasks.

VI. THE FUNCTIONS OF THE STAFF[5]

A. Intelligence

One of the visible staff capabilities involves the intelligence function of the legislature. The whole legislative process is built around acquiring information and intelligence and applying it to the fashioning of laws. Information provides the premises for decision or action. By one definition, decision-making is simply "the process of converting information into action." Information—intelligence, news, facts, and data—is essential to all phases of the process. It is a common assumption that bad or wrong decisions in politics as in business stem from insufficient or improperly processed information, and increased legislative staffs are often justified on the basis of providing more complete and accurate information.

Research on Congress has found that the legislative staff is a major information source, and recent research on the legislature resulted in similar findings. Staffers are "facts-and-figures" men and women, and they spend a great deal of their working time engaged in processing information and supplying it to legislators.

Staffs investigate, research, schedule, edit, compile, and distribute much of the information on which legislative decisions are based. The staff network, in fact, is the only organization with sole responsibility for directing and filtering information to the legislature.

B. Integration[6]

Legislative staffs contribute to the integration of committees; they contribute to intercameral integration, and they contribute to legislative-executive integration. Staff members interact with other participants in the political subsystem— members of the governor's staff, executive agency staffers, budget personnel, interest group representatives, other staffers in the same chamber and in the other house, rank-and-file legislators, and the legislative leadership. These relationships provide much of the cement that holds the legislature together and binds the legislative and executive branches together.

This network of staff interactions helps to establish lines of communication to and from the legislature through which staff members can obtain information and oversee administrative action. Personal friendships, previous work relationships, and membership in the same professional organizations are crucial elements in this network.

C. Innovation

Legislative staff members see themselves as having innovative capabilities. One of the reasons members of the legislative staff like their work is that they have the opportunity to innovate, to initiate public policy, or to see it initiated.

Innovation and initiation are somewhat slippery concepts to be sure, but a number of staff people and legislators described projects that the staff was undertaking at their own initiative and many staffers described legislation that they themselves were working on. Staff members, especially those with long tenure in key staff positions, are about as likely to initiate legislation as are legislators themselves.

D. Influence

Staff members see themselves as being important participants in the legislative process and are seen as being influential by legislators, lobbyists, and members of the executive branch. Staffers emphasized expertise, specialization, and the staff's role as an information filter to the legislature in explaining staff influence. They noted the increasingly heavy load on legislators as a factor in staff influence. A staff member serving an assembly leader stated:

> Legislators would be hopelessly bogged down in detail and trivia without staff to relieve them of the routine tasks given them by constituents, other legislators, the governor, etc.
>
> The assemblyman can only deal with bills with major implications statewide or those that directly impact his district. We're his extra hands, arms, legs, etc. to deal with the other 10,000 or so bills that are introduced each year.

Interest group representatives in New York go where power is, or where they think power is, and the leadership staff is not shortchanged when it comes to contacts with lobbyists. As a lobbyist pointed out:

> A lot of lobbyists would rather talk to the staff than try to get in to see the leaders themselves. Staff members are more accessible than the leaders. They're going to be gathering the information anyway, so why not talk to them at the beginning. They're more expert in the subject matter, therefore they're more likely to understand your argument. And besides, the leaders and their staff people are so intertwined that talking to a staffer is just like talking to the legislator.

The staff influence can be seen in many ways: changes in the amount of information available to legislators; changes for the better in the technical characteristics of legislation; a decline in the trend toward the sweeping delegation of increasing amounts of authority to the executive branch; an increase in the ability of the legislature to legislate in detailed instead of broad terms; an increase in the ability of the legislature to oversee executive agency activities; the legislature's resumption of an initiatory stand in several policy areas; and, a reinforcement of the legislature's customary fiscal economizing role. Staff members see themselves as having influence in the legislative process and are seen as influential by legislators, executive officials, and lobbyists. The difference increased professional staffing has made was described best by Eugene Farnum, director of the Senate Fiscal Agency in Michigan:

> In Michigan, the advent of a strong legislative staff only has proven to make a strong legislature stronger. Through the use of staff, the legislators and committees have been able to increase the depth and scope of their committee hearings; perform more intensive and extensive reviews of new and existing programs; maintain an effective overview of state government concerning legislative intent; propose as well as dispose of proposals for new programs; and, perhaps, feel more confident that they have the best information available when they are required to make a decision.

There is, of course, the problem that large and efficient staffs may be a mixed blessing. Critics of large legislative staffs fear that they may develop into independent power centers in the legislative process. They may develop cozy relationships with legislators, agency personnel, and interest group representatives that are difficult for both the executive and the legislature to control. As a Republican assemblyman said, there is an "inevitable tendency of all busy persons to get rid of routine tasks which they think staff assistants will be competent to perform. Sometimes it turns out that the tasks are not routine at all but are in fact policy determining." It is this fact that alarmed an assistant budget director:

> Certain staff members have become too influential. Last year, when we were discussing the tax program, we were dealing with [a Ways and Means staffer] and [an aide to the Senate Majority Leader]. They were acting as if they had a personal stake in the thing. They represent themselves as just staff of their bosses, the legislative leaders. But they were dealing on their own; their own views were very much evident. I think the legislators are assuming a certain neutrality as the legislative leaders should have the facts presented to them. The legislators are being manipulated by the staff. Some of the staff members are acting like they're legislators.

VII.   CONCLUSIONS

Our state legislatures have been almost universally denounced of late as the "sick men" of American government, and the consensus appears to be that legislative institutions everywhere have suffered a notable decline during the twentieth century. The task of salvaging the institution has been perceived as necessitating an extensive reorganization, and the weapon for this reorganization has been increased professional staffing.

Although most proposals for increased professional staff do not discuss the type of man or woman necessary for this position, there is the implication of a model of legislative staffing very close to the classic organization theorist's prescription for the executive. The Brownlow report (1937:5), for example, called for a president's staff that would "remain in the background, issue no orders, make no decisions, emit no public statements . . . possessed of high competence, great physical vigor, and a passion for anonymity." And Leonard White (1945:3) once pleaded that what Congress "needs is a Committee on Congressional Management to do for it what the President's Commission on Administrative Management did for him."

A wide array of staff aides now serve Congress and our state legislatures. This chapter has:

- Examined the norms and constraints of staff aides serving several state legislatures
- Examined these norms as indicators of the way in which the legislative environment molds, shapes, and limits the behavior and influence of the professional staff
- Discussed the functions staff members perform for the legislature and individual members
- Raised questions about the power of the staff and the political role they play

Proposals for strengthening the legislature have often been made in a void. Those advocating increased professional staffing for legislatures, for example, have continued to advocate scientific detachment from values and denied that the staff takes any part in the actual shaping of policy. It has been argued (Heaphey, 1975), however, that this traditional concept of staff is an anachronism. The traditional staff concept is, as Golembiewski (1961) has pointed out, a derivative from a general theory of organization whose purportedly empirical propositions inadequately reflect reality.

As Bernard Crick (1964:ix) argued, "to have ideas on reform is no substitute for knowing how things work and relate to each other." In one area of legislative reform, that of professional staffing, a great deal of careful work needs to be done. We have a number of prescriptive, polemical studies; we lack descriptive and analytical studies. This author feels strongly that recommendations and normative statements regarding the proper role of professional staffs of legislatures need to be grounded on empirical evidence, if we are to know what will happen when specific changes are introduced.

The contribution of political science and public administration to this endeavor can take several forms. First, the most obvious type of involvement is empirical. As noted earlier, the role of professional staffers in the legislative process is far from clear, perhaps because so few attempts have been made to determine precisely what the role is. Research is needed on the backgrounds, career aspirations, norms, functions, roles, and so on of the members of the legislature's bureaucracy. Under what conditions do staff members exercise influence on legislative deliberations? How do they interact with legislators, lobbyists, and the members of the executive branch? How do various staff subgroups interact with each other? Such studies could contribute significantly to our understanding of the legislative process.

Legislatures ought to be a part of the *study* of public administration; but they should also be part of the *practice* of public administration. The constantly increasing pressure and complexity of affairs have, in recent years, induced legislative institutions to provide themselves with a variety of staff agencies, technical services, and administrative facilities. These services and facilities, however, have grown up in a haphazard manner and operate quite independently of each other. They are scattered, duplicated, and uncoordinated. Recent progress in methods of administrative management has been made in the executive branch, but has for the most part passed our legislatures by. It may be argued that the ability of the legislative branch to realize its potential in the years ahead depends considerably on the development of effective mechanisms for administering itself. Thus, there are questions such as how should staffers be recruited, trained, and so on. How should staffs be organized? Who should staffers serve—individual legislators, committees, the leadership, the party caucus, the legislature as a whole? And how can the legislature be made more efficient and effective; how can it be properly administered, without sacrificing its unique aspects as a political entity?

Public administration (PA) is a logical and relevant field within which to deal with the subject of legislatures and legislative improvement.[7] But the application of the principles and concepts of PA to legislative institutions must be subject to a clear understanding of the differences between the legislative and executive functions of government and the differences between the legislatures and a business corporation. For example, as to how the houses of the legislature conduct their business, any number of inefficient practices are apparent. However, closer examination of these practices, and careful consideration of possible improvements would (this author believes) lead us to conclude that many of the apparent inefficiencies actually have their positive value in the legislative process. To take an example from the federal level, Senate Rule XVII (the filibuster rule) apparently contributes to Senate inefficiency; but an attempt to deal with it *solely* with respect to legislative effectiveness and efficiency would be to risk subverting a constraint that the Senate has adhered to under the most severe attack and that is valuable in the protection of minority rights. A similar situation may exist in the case of the apparent duplication of fiscal services, personnel, procurement, and so on between the houses of the legislature and even within each chamber.

Although much public attention and the nation's administrative talents have gone toward making the executive branch an institution equal to the demands of the twentieth century, nothing of the kind has been true of the legislature. Now public administration is turning its attention to the legislature. The challenge awaits us as scholars and practitioners.

NOTES

1. These examples of staff activities paraphrase cases cited by Marlene Cimons in "Girls of Capitol Hill," *Cosmopolitan*, 1972.
2. This is based on an analysis of information presented in *The Book of the States Series* in their review of legislative modernization efforts. Volumes from 1973 through 1982 were reviewed to determine what agencies were created, who they were intended to serve, how staff members were chosen, were they to be partisan or nonpartisan, and so on. Although admittedly a crude index, the direction of current reforms in state legislatures seems clear.
3. This study is based on interviews conducted over the last two years at meetings of the National Conference of State Legislatures and on previous work on state legislative staffing. See Balutis, Alan P. and Butler, Daron K., (1975). *The Political Pursestrings: The Role of the Legislature in the Budgetary Process.* Sage Publications, Beverly Hills.
4. This section relies heavily on the work done and the framework suggested by Kenneth Kofmehl (see references).
5. This section draws heavily on the work done and the staff capabilities suggested by Samuel C. Patterson (see references).
6. Integration is here defined as the degree to which there is a working together or meshing together or mutual support among legislative and executive subgroups.
7. See Heaphey, J. (1975:478–508).

REFERENCES

Brownlow, L. (1937). *Report on the Committee on Administrative Management.* U.S. Government Printing Office, Washington, D.C.

Citizens Conference on State Legislatures (1972). Legislatures move to improve their effectiveness. The Conference, Kansas City.

Crick, B. (1964). *The Reform of Parliament.* Weidenfield and Nicholson, London.

Golembiewski, R. (1961). Toward the new organization theory: Some notes on "staff." *Midwest Journal of Political Science* 5:237–259.

Heaphey, J. (1975). Symposium on public administration and legislatures. *Public Administration Review* 35:478–508.

Huitt, R. K. (1969). Congress: The durable partner. In Huitt, R. K. and Peabody, R. L., eds. *Congress: Two Decades of Analysis.* Harper and Row, New York.

Jewell, M. E. (1981). The state of U.S. state legislative research. *Legislative Studies Quarterly 6*:1–25.

Jewell, M. E. and Patterson, S. C. (1973). *The Legislative Process in the United States*. Random House, New York.

Kofmehl, K. (1962). *Professional Staffs of Congress*. Purdue University Press, West Lafayette, Ind.

Matthews, D. R. (1960). *U.S. Senators and Their World*. Vintage Books, New York.

Meller, N. (1967). Legislative staff services: Toxin, specific, or placebo for the legislature's ills. *Western Political Quarterly 20*:381–389.

Patterson, S. C. (1970). The professional staffs of congressional committees. *Administrative Science Quarterly 15*:22–38.

Rosenthal, A. (1973). Contemporary research on state legislatures: From individual cases to comparative analysis. In *Political Science and State and Local Government*. American Political Science Association, The Association, Washington, D.C.

White, L. D. (1945). *New Horizons in Public Administration*. University of Alabama Press, University, Al.

16

Municipal Service Delivery Alternatives

David R. Morgan   Bureau of Government Research, Department of Political Science, University of Oklahoma, Norman, Oklahoma

As cities are asked to do more with shrinking resources, local officials must search for ways of improving performance and lowering costs. Confronted with recalcitrant taxpayers, a decline in federal support, inflation, and a troubled national economy, municipalities may respond with various approaches— reorganization, new technology, or efforts to motivate workers to increase output. As part of this quest for cost savings, various service delivery alternatives may also be considered. Perhaps contracting with the private sector or with another government might save money or provide better services for the same outlay. Or perhaps voluntary or self-help efforts by local citizens can be encour- aged as a way of alleviating fiscal pressures. In fact, evidence (Berenyi, 1981; Kirlin et al., 1977:112) shows that the greatest impetus to the use of alternative delivery mechanisms is a fiscal crisis. Since it now appears that cities may be in a financial squeeze for the indefinite future, local officials are likely to be increasingly interested in the pros and cons of using alternatives to the tradi- tional city department in delivering urban services.

This chapter considers the rationale for alternative structures and the issues involved in using such arrangements. Special attention is devoted to contracting out, intergovernmental agreements, and the use of citizen volunteers. Several examples will be discussed as well as the frequency with which these arrangements are being employed. Finally, some of the broader equity issues associated with the movement to shrink government programs will be addressed briefly.

I. ALTERNATIVE SERVICE MECHANISMS

What alternatives exist to the traditional municipal service monopoly? Although E. S. Savas (1982:57-58) identifies some eight arrangements, a recent survey (Shulman, 1982) for the International City Management Association (ICMA) reveals that only four are used much at all—contracting (both to profit and nonprofit agencies), intergovernmental agreements, franchising, and voluntary service. A surprisingly large number of services are being handled by one or more of these four alternative means, with contracting and intergovernmental agreements by far the most widely used.

Before examining these options in more detail one might consider the extent of their use. Consider first franchises, an arrangement under which a municipality grants one or more private firms the right to provide a local service. The price of the service is ordinarily regulated, and the service consumer pays the private provider directly. Of the 1500 or so cities and counties responding to the ICMA survey, in only 4 cases were franchises used more than 10% of the time—for commercial solid waste collection (17%), residential waste collection (15%), street lighting (14%), and utility meter reading (10%).

Voluntary service arrangements, although somewhat more common than franchises, nonetheless were largely limited to cultural, arts, recreation, or social service programs. To illustrate, 31% of the cities and counties reported using volunteers for the operation of cultural and arts programs, 20% for the operation of museums, 19% for recreation services, and 18% for programs to serve the elderly.

Contracting out and intergovernmental agreements were quite commonly used for a host of services. Several studies (Fisk et al., 1978; Florestano and Gordon, 1981) show that two types of urban services are most frequently contracted to private firms: (a) repetitive services using unskilled labor such as solid waste collection or janitorial services; and, (b) highly specialized technical and support services such as architectural, engineering, or legal services. When contracting to nonprofit agencies is included, several health and human services also appear on the list. The ICMA survey, for example, reveals the following percentage of cities and counties relying on private contracting, to both profit and nonprofit agencies:

	Profit (%)	Nonprofit (%)
Vehicle towing and storage	78	0
Day care facility	33	40
Cultural/arts programs	7	45
Hospital operation	25	25
Legal services	48	2

Another survey (Florestano and Gordon, 1981) among a more limited group of strictly municipalities finds the most extensive contracting for architectural services (79%), followed by street construction (74%), and engineering services (66%). Surprisingly, none of these three services are shown among the fifty-nine services listed in the ICMA study. Solid waste collection, about which most is written, ranked fairly high on both lists—about 34–38%, all which was performed by profit-seeking firms. Florestano and Gordon (1981) note that among their group of 170 cities the average number of contracted services is 7.8.

Among the ICMA's group of cities and counties, at least 1% used intergovernmental agreements for each of the fifty-nine services listed. Operation of public/elderly housing was first (41%), followed by bus system operation/maintenance (38%), sanitary inspection (33%), and operation of mental health programs/facilities (32%). These figures suggest that intergovernmental agreements are somewhat less commonly used than private contractors.

II. CONTRACTING

Contracting to the private sector is not only widespread among cities of all sizes but appears to be expanding. Why? It was suggested at the outset that a principal reason has to do with hoped-for cost savings. But more is involved. Under what conditions then does contracting make sense?

A. When Contracting Appears Promising

Perhaps the most compelling reasons why a city might consider contracting are to save money and/or improve service quality. In particular, proponents of contracting contend that private provision will be more cost-effective because of increased competition and economies of scale (see Bennett and Johnson, 1980). As opposed to a private business, a public monopoly presumably has little incentive to hold down production costs. Additionally, municipal workers are often seen as a relatively strong political force that use their power to keep wages and benefits abnormally high. Economies of scale may be possible because the municipality's boundaries may not be coterminous with the optimal service area. This is especially likely in public utilities and in some social and health services.

Several other arguments are also advanced in behalf of contracting out (Savas, 1982:89,90):

- It permits the municipality to take advantage of specialized skills lacking in its own workforce.
- It avoids large capital outlays or start-up costs for a new service.
- It allows flexibility in adjusting the size of the local workforce to changing service demands.

- It permits a quick response to new service needs and facilitates program experimentation.

Such benefits appear impressive indeed. But as with everything else, certain disadvantages may exist as well. For example, some of the following are offered in rebuttal (Fisk et al., 1978:7-9):

- Poorer service may result since private firms could skimp on service to maximize their profit.
- Corruption is increased since pressures arise for contractors to engage in various questionable or illegal practices such as payoffs, kickbacks, or bribery.
- Contracts are very difficult to draw up to assure that the municipality gets what it wants and agrees to pay for.
- Contracts require close monitoring, which is an added cost and may enlarge the chance for corruption.

Pros and cons aside, from a practical point of view several other considerations may enter into the decision to contract. First, are legal issues. State law or city charter may restrict or prohibit contracting some services. Legal questions are more likely to arise with intergovernmental agreements than with private contracts, but this issue should be resolved before any further steps are taken. A second major concern is whether private providers exist in the area. If these are few, then contracting may prove less appealing. The lack of providers, for example, may be a critical problem for certain social services, especially in small communities (Straussman and Farie, 1981). Third, one study of contracting with private and other public agencies among a large group of southwestern cities finds a primary motive to be the lack of municipal facilities (Morgan et al., 1981). Again, this problem would seem to apply to intergovernmental agreements more than private contracting but, regardless of the ultimate provider chosen, a shortage of city facilities or capacity could be a powerful stimulus to search for an external supplier. For example, if a city lacks its own landfill or incinerator, an outside source for waste disposal is mandatory no matter who collects the garbage and trash. Fourth, the views of municipal employees must be considered. Organized workers, who fear the loss of job or lower pay and benefits, often become a powerful force arrayed against a move toward contracting. Finally, a reluctance on the part of management to give up control over the service represents a major reason for resisting a change from municipal operation (Sonenblum et al., 1977:33).

As noted previously, financial pressures more than anything else are likely to stimulate a search for service delivery alternatives. Yet, there is no unanimity among local officials as to whether contracting saves money. Among a group of 170 city purchasing officers, for instance, 30% said contracting costs less than government provision, whereas 27% believed contracting costs more (34% said the same or gave no answer). But what about quality? Does contracting produce a better service? This same study (Florestano and Gordon, 1981:27) also shows that many of these city officials (35%) thought contracting does lead to improved service quality (8% said quality declines). The largest group (35%), however, indicated that quality remains the same under either arrangement (28% did not answer).

B. Examples of Contracting

Here one might briefly note some interesting or unusual applications of private contracting. Although most has been written about solid waste, one should at least acknowledge one innovative effort in fire protection. The most widely known example of private contracting in the fire service is in Scottsdale, Arizona, where a private company, Rural/Metro, supplies fire protection to about 18% of the state's population from twenty-seven locations in five counties. Two features of this arrangement warrant special attention—the use of a fire auxiliary service (wranglers) and the development and application of new technology (Knight, 1978:60–62). The use of a supplemental fire-fighting force, composed of employees from other city departments (primarily public works and parks) enables Rural/Metro to keep the number of full-time firefighters to a minimum. In addition, the company has pioneered in constructing its own fire trucks and other equipment as a way of saving money. As a result of these innovations, one study (Ahlbrandt, 1974) estimates that Scottsdale receives fire service for about 47% less than from a traditional municipal supplier.

Another creative example of the use of private contracting is found in Minneapolis. This involves the collection of solid waste and pits a private firm against a city department (Savas, 1977a). Prior to 1971, Minneapolis city forces picked up wet garbage from all households, whereas a number of private haulers collected rubbish and trash. A change in state law prompted the city to switch to a combined collection system for all solid waste. The question now was who would provide this combined service. The city ultimately elected to retain the public force at its existing size, but allow it to serve only part of the community. The bulk of the city was then turned over to a single new firm representing many of the old private haulers. Because of the competition between the public and the private sector, the city benefited in several ways. Initially, the private firm provided collection at a lower cost, but the city department began to close the gap before the five-year contract concluded. In fact, the city crews increased their tons collected during this period, and the cost per ton for municipal collection dropped sharply after competition was introduced.

One final illustration involves a decision by Little Rock, Arkansas, to contract for custodial services (Lubin, 1980). By developing and applying engineered work standards, the city was able to make a careful cost comparison between the existing city service and a contract proposal. Examining the time spent on each task, the study showed the city custodial staff to be performing about 45% of "average" efficiency. In effect, the city paid $4.02 for every hour a custodian was on the clock, but it actually cost the city $8.94 for each work unit, or measured hour of work. Even if the city's force could reach 85% of the engineered standard, the cost of the custodial service was estimated to be $58,998. Any bid figure below that would save the city money and would likely improve the quality of service. Thirteen bidders responded to a request for bids, with the lowest figure at $30,360. By contracting out, the city concluded it would not only reap an immediate savings of $28,638 ($58,998 – $30,360), but the contractor would provide an additional 5840 units of work worth some $23,477. The total savings then was about $52,000. The contractor's price was so much lower than the city cost primarily because the company paid its employees, most of whom worked there as a second job, the minimum wage, then $2.30 per hour (compared with the city's $4.02 per hour).

C. Other Empirical Evidence on Contracting

As these examples suggest, most studies show that contracting out reduces costs. Much of this research has been done on solid waste collection. A few years ago a large-scale study was undertaken at Columbia University comparing relative efficiency of the various arrangements by which cities collect solid waste. With efficiency defined as cost to the household (excluding disposal costs), an analysis of 315 cities showed that municipal collection was some 15% more per household than contract collection (Savas, 1977b). But, city crews more often provided rear-of-house service. So taking level of service into account, the results are not so clear-cut. For once-a-week service, contract collection again emerged as less costly than city collection, but for twice-a-week curbside service, municipal provision was slightly less costly. Size of city turns out to be important as well as level of service. Based on the same set of data, Stevens (1978) finds that among large cities (greater than 50,000), private contracting did save over municipal collection, but the cost differences were not significant for smaller communities. The savings achieved by private firms apparently resulted from three things: smaller crews; less absenteeism; and, a much greater use of vehicles that can be driver loaded.

No doubt the element of competition may make a real difference. Based on six fairly large cities, Savas (1981) confirms that intracity competition between public and private providers in solid waste collection yields a more efficient system than an all-municipal arrangement. Phoenix has carried the principle of competition between the public and private sector beyond the area of solid waste. There, city departments have vied with outside contractors in garbage and trash collection, landfill operations, landscape maintenance, public housing maintenance, and street sweeping (Hughes, 1982). The city not only collects bids from private firms, but a municipal department also submits its own price for the job. The department's cost is determined by an independent city auditing agency that submits the bid in a sealed envelope. The city price remains unknown even to the competing city department until bid opening day. Of twenty-two services handled in this competitive way, city forces have bid lowest ten times. Outside vendors have been more successful at winning jobs requiring semiskilled or unskilled labor because they tend to pay minimum wages. Although the city now uses private firms to collect garbage in about half the city, Phoenix does not plan to bid the entire service area because if the city gets out of the sanitation business it would be completely at the mercy of private contractors.

D. Administrative Considerations in Contracting

At least three basic steps are involved if a municipality plans to contract out. First, a precontract study must be made to establish the pros and cons of contracting. As part of this exercise, a decision must be made as to the level of service desired. Then, a careful analysis of in-house costs should be done. One study (Fisk et al., 1978:93) reports that less than 10% of localities switching from government to private provision undertook a comparison of the costs of private and public delivery. Determining municipal costs is no simple matter because few cities keep true cost-accounting records. In fact, using solid waste as an example, Savas (1979) argues that city budgetary figures substantially understate actual service costs. Various items such as fringe benefits, managerial overhead, insurance, billing costs, or even capital outlays may be omitted unless a complete and accurate cost assessment is undertaken.

A second basic step is the actual contract preparation. This will require a decision regarding the type of contract to be let, bid, or negotiated, for example. Also specifications for the work must be drawn (tasks, hours, location, bonding, and so forth) along with the criteria in selecting the contractor (price, ability to perform, experience, and the like) (Fisk, 1982:2). Increasingly, performance specs are included that set time and cost constraints together with quality standards (Florestano, 1982:355). According to the Phoenix assistant public works director, "The whole key is in the specs. They must be very, very clear" (Hughes, 1982:4).

After bids are solicited and the contract awarded, vendor performance must be monitored and evaluated. One of the problems in accurate monitoring lies in the general absence of good municipal performance measures. Data for several indicators of efficiency and effectiveness should be maintained to allow a reasonably careful assessment of service output whether by a public or private provider. Costs per ton collected and complaints received, for example, might be the minimally required information to evaluate collection performance of solid waste. The cost of this essential monitoring and evaluation process must also be explicitly incorporated into any predecision estimates on how much contracting may cost compared with municipal provision.

One final administrative issue should be considered. Once contracting is chosen, it may be difficult to change back to a municipal service. This could leave the city vulnerable to rapidly increasing costs. If this happens, of course, privatization may no longer be a cheaper or more efficient alternative to municipal delivery.

III. INTERLOCAL AGREEMENTS

Intergovernmental agreements among various units of local government constitute the second most common form of alternative service delivery. Many of the reasons municipalities turn to interlocal agreements parallel those often cited in favor of privatizing. Cost savings rank high, for example. But more than with private contracting, interlocal agreements arise to meet a perceived need for a service that the city does not offer and perhaps cannot provide without an inordinate expense. For example, some small suburban communities are land-locked, totally surrounded by the large central city. In such instances, these suburbs may have no sanitary landfill, or they may not have access to a river to permit disposal of sanitary sewage. Likewise, it might be much less expensive to purchase water from the large city as opposed to constructing (or expanding) local treatment facilities. In other cases, municipalities may join together to attack a common problem beyond the reach of a single community. Joint agreements thus might be created to establish a new facility or to pool existing resources to meet an areawide problem. Many of these agreements involve other levels of government, especially the county, and to some extent the state government or special districts.

The most comprehensive study of intergovernmental agreements was performed in the early 1970s by Joseph Zimmerman (1973), based on a large survey for the ICMA. He reports that 61% of the 2248 responding municipalities had entered into formal or informal agreements to provide certain local services. Larger units tended to become involved more with such agreements than small cities, and the county emerged as the most frequent external provider. Nonmetropolitan municipalities were less likely to engage in intergovernmental contracting than central cities and suburban communities. To achieve economies of scale was by far the most common reason offered for using an alternative service arrangement. This was true regardless of whether the service was of a housekeeping nature (assessing, payroll, utility billing, or treasury functions) or a direct public service (health, welfare, police, public works, or library, museum, and school agreements). The major reason given for lack of more agreements was the "limitations placed on independence of action," or loss of control, in other words. Some cities also objected to what they felt were inadequate divisions of service costs.

Intergovernmental contractual agreements are more pervasive in California than anywhere else. Beginning with the now well-known Lakewood Plan, interlocal agreements have proliferated, especially in the Los Angeles area. The Lakewood community (then about 60,000 people) incorporated in 1954 to avoid annexation by Long Beach. The new city immediately contracted with the county of Los Angeles for almost all its municipal services, including police, animal control, engineering, and street maintenance (Bish and Ostrom, 1973:60). Since that time almost all the suburban Los Angeles communities have followed Lakewood's lead and entered into a host of service contracts with the county. Six departments—sheriff, engineering, roads, health, hospitals, and the registrar/recorder—accounted for four-fifths of the service contracts by the mid-1970s (Sonenblum et al., 1977:95). In the area of law enforcement, where the Los Angeles Sheriff's Department has become such a major provider, a uniform level of service has become increasingly common among many suburban cities. This may have both advantages and disadvantages. According to the sheriff, such interlocal contracting brings coordination and integration to the county police function; the county department has become a "binding cohesive force" permeating law enforcement throughout the county (Sonenblum et al., 1977:111). Yet clearly the locality has less chance to influence the type of police service it receives. In fact, most contract cities spend less for police and have fewer patrol officers than noncontract cities. But these reduced expenditures may also be responsible for lowering the quality of service (Mehay, 1979).

The Lakewood Plan in the Los Angeles area is exceptional, but the same pressures that lead to more private contracting will surely compel a growing number of cities to also consider more interlocal agreements. As with purchases of private service, intergovernmental contracting should be easier to achieve if the service is new or noncontroversial. Although interlocal agreements may prove especially attractive to smaller communities searching for economies of scale, we should recognize that large-scale operations may not produce more competition. A large provider, whether public or private, may so dominate a market that competition suffers. If lack of competition results in excessive costs, a municipality may be forced to provide the service with its own employees.

IV. VOLUNTARY PROVISION OF SERVICES

Small communities in particular have always relied on citizen volunteers to provide or assist in supplying local services. Now, even in some large cities, the financial crunch has revived interest in finding ways of inducing citizens to do more for themselves or to assist municipal bureaucrats in providing various services. Traditionally, the citizens' role in service delivery is viewed as essentially passive, to consume and perhaps evaluate service quantity or quality. Citizens may also take part in a limited way by demanding more or better services, from complaining to petitioning or even organizing protest groups. Yet as several scholars (see Whitaker, 1980; Brudney and England, 1983) now remind us, citizens can and do participate in more direct ways by sharing in the production of certain services. Called *coproduction*, this approach contrasts with the dominant model of the passive citizen recipient by emphasizing the way in which citizens interact with public officials to jointly assist in producing the service.

Coproduction is probably easiest to see in the human services area. Rich (1981) notes, for example, that the effectiveness of drug abuse, family planning, nutrition, and similar programs depends as much on the cooperation of clients as it does on the ability of program staff members. But coproduction may function in the "hard" services as well—homeowners carrying their garbage cans to the curb, organizing neighborhood watch groups, or even becoming involved with a police auxiliary or volunteer fire department. The city manager of Killeen, Texas, for example, reports that the largest single savings of tax money achieved to stretch resources has been the use of a combination paid and volunteer fire department (Eastland, 1981). A recent news story also describes an "adopt-a-pothole" program begun in Kingman, Arizona. Members of the North Kingman Merchants Association persuaded Mohave County officials to dump 100 cubic yards of asphalt behind a local bar, which was then made available to anyone who wished to patch a pothole. With only eight road repair employees, the county was unable to provide the necessary maintenance. Within a week, the adopt-a-pothole campaign had resulted in the complete patching of Northern Avenue where most of the members of the merchants group have their businesses.

Coproduction is not limited to small towns. In response to a severe revenue shortage, Detroit Mayor Coleman Young in 1980 unveiled his self-serve city plan (Cheyfitz, 1980). The mayor's proposal included the following:

- Expansion of the Detroit Police reserve, composed of trained citizens who accompany regular officers in many routine cases
- Revival of the Fire Department Auxiliary, a voluntary unit disbanded after a brief existence during the 1950s
- Adopt-a-Park, a program that asks neighborhood groups to cut the grass and pick up litter in the nearest city park
- A directive to those who complain of weeds in vacant lots to get out their lawnmowers (the city has twenty-three workers to cut weeds on some 25,000 vacant lots)

- The *Detroit Christmas Catalogue*, a new catalogue the mayor wants people to use to select gifts for the city (including, for example, a honeysuckle shrub for $15; a picnic table, $120; a swing set for $800; or the ultimate gift, a combination senior citizens center and regional arts complex at $3.5 million)

In the face of continuing revenue shortages, more cities may be forced to follow the lead of Detroit or Kingman, Arizona. Citizens may be called upon to participate in the delivery of urban services in a much more active way than before. Although on the surface more voluntarism sounds good, several questions must be raised. First, urban bureaucrats may not welcome more direct citizen involvement in service delivery. In fact, some evidence suggests the contrary, that police officers, for example, prefer that citizens engage in more passive forms of behavior (such as locking windows) than in the more active role of crime fighting such as joining citizen patrols or carrying weapons (Rosentraub et al., 1982: Ch. 5). Second, equity problems may arise. Rosentraub and Sharp (1981:517) suggest that, "Wealthier, better-educated, or non-minority citizens may be more willing or able to engage in coproduction activities. To the extent that coproduction raises the quality of services received, it may exacerbate gaps between the advantaged and disadvantaged classes."

V. DELIVERY ALTERNATIVES AND EQUITY ISSUES

As should be evident by now, much of the heightened interest in service delivery alternatives has resulted from a slowdown if not decline in municipal resources. Cities are fervently searching for ways of cutting costs without substantial reductions in service quality. Thus, contracting, for example, may be seen as a part of a larger cutback management strategy. Accompanying if not preceding such a move will likely be an adoption or extension of user charges. In fact, charges for specific urban services consumed directly by an individual or family have been growing steadily, especially in the wake of the various tax limitation efforts of the late 1970s. Quite clearly, user charges, such as payments for the use of recreation facilities or health services, tend to hurt the poor more than the well-off. Moreover, contracting refuse collection to the private sector, for example, will assure that the full cost of that service is borne by the user. Perhaps this is as it should be. Nonetheless, making the city more businesslike is apt to result in lower-income groups paying a larger share of the costs of local services.

A second and probably more widely accepted concern associated with privatizing is the effect on affirmative action. City governments historically have been major employers of minority groups, especially in large urban areas. The governments of many large cities have twice the proportion of minorities in their workforce than does the general economy (Pascal, 1981:11). If fewer public jobs are available as a result of a shift to market-oriented service mechanisms, minorities and women are likely to suffer.

A third and related issue involves municipal pay and fringe benefit levels. The evidence is mixed as to whether employees performing similar work for private firms receive less pay than public employees. It would appear, however, that employee benefits are considerably higher in the public than in the private sector. And, of course, unionization is more prevalent at the state and local levels than among private firms. We might ask then which worker is better off? Are lower levels of benefits and less unionization advantageous to a workforce? Many might think not. Conversely, some argue that replacing higher-paid municipal employees with lower-compensated private workers might mean more job opportunities for lower-paid workers (Pascal, 1981:11). This is the same argument, of course, that has been used against the minimum wage for years. One's position on this issue then becomes more a matter of philosophy than objective economic fact. It might be remembered in this context that one of those who most strongly endorsed Savas's book, *Privatizing the Public Sector* (1982), was President Reagan's Director of the Office of Management and Budget, David Stockman.

VI. CONCLUSION

An exploration of municipal service delivery alternatives will undoubtedly expand in the years ahead. And wisely so in many cases. Where economies of scale can be achieved either through the use of a private firm or by joining forces with another local government, city governments should actively pursue those options in hopes of holding down costs and maintaining if not improving service quality. Where competition can be assured, the use of alternative structures seems especially attractive. For example, the use of a mixed public and private solid waste collection system appears to yield very satisfactory results.

The principal advantage of alternative service forms indeed appears to be its potential for cost reductions. The experience in California suggests that cities are not likely to abandon the municipal monopoly unless cost savings are expected. Otherwise, city officials prefer the service control afforded by the traditional approach. In the minds of these officials, public control more than contracting is likely to assure service quality and responsiveness to citizens (Kirlin et al., 1977:124). Does the use of service alternatives save money? In many cases, yes. But does quality suffer? This is harder to answer, but for law enforcement among contracting cities in the Los Angeles area, the answer was also yes. Yet in other instances where, for example, cities switched to private janitorial service, performance improved. Thus, no firm assurances either way can be offered on the matter of service quality.

The use of service options is not without its problems, of course—the most obvious of which is the likely political opposition of municipal employees. The increased potential for corruption and the difficulties in drafting and monitoring contracts are also frequently mentioned. And, finally, the question of equity should not be ignored. The case is far from clear-cut, but some evidence suggests that certain market-oriented mechanisms, such as private contracting, may inhibit or even reverse affirmative action gains and work to the disadvantage of lower-income groups.

In short, as cities strive to do more with less, alternative service mechanisms should certainly be considered. If studied thoroughly beforehand and entered into cautiously and carefully, such arrangements may indeed provide local management with a useful tool for controlling costs without serious erosion of service quality.

REFERENCES

Ahlbrandt, R. S., Jr. (1974). Implications of contracting for a public service. *Urban Affairs Quarterly 9*:337–358.

Bennett, J. T., and Johnson, M. H. (1980). Tax reduction without sacrifice: Private-sector production of public services. *Public Finance Quarterly 8*: 363–396.

Berenyi, E. B. (1981). Contracting out refuse collection: The nature and impact of change. *Urban Interest 3*:30–42.

Bish, R. L. and Ostrom, V. (1973). *Understanding Urban Government*. American Enterprise Institute, Washington, D.C.

Brudney, J. L. and England, R. E. (1983). Toward a definition of the coproduction concept. *Public Administration Review 43*:59–65.

Cheyfitz, K. (November 15, 1980). Self-service. *New Republic*.

Eastland, M. R. (1981). Stretching services to fit available revenue. *Public Management 63*:8–9.

Fisk, D. (1982). Issues in contracting for public services from the private sector. In *Management Information Service Report 14*. International City Management Association, Washington, D.C.

Fisk, D., Kiesling, H., and Muller, T. (1978). *Private Provision of Public Services*. Urban Institute, Washington, D.C.

Florestano, P. S. (1982). Contracting with the private sector. *National Civic Review 71*:350–357.

Florestano, P. S. and Gordon, S. B. (1981). A survey of city and county use of private contracting. *Urban Interest 3*:22–29.

Hughes, M. (1982). Contracting services in Phoenix. *Public Management 64*: 2–4.

Kirlin, J. J., Ries, J. C., and Sonenblum, S. (1977). Alternatives to city departments. In Savas, E. S., ed., *Alternatives for Delivering Public Services*. Westview, Boulder, Col., pp. 111–145.

Knight, F. S. (1978). Fire service productivity: The Scottsdale approach. In Knight, F. and Rancer, M., eds., *Tried and Tested: Case Studies in Municipal Innovation*. International City Management Association, Washington, D.C.

Lubin, R. (1980). Little Rock, Arkansas' make-buy study. In *Management Information Service 4*. International City Management Association, Washington, D.C., pp. 11–15.

Mehay, S. L. (1979). Intergovernmental contracting for municipal police services: An empirical analysis. *Land Economics 55*:59–72.

Morgan, D. R., England, R. E., and Meyer, M. (1981). Alternatives to municipal service delivery: A four-state comparison. *Southern Review of Public Administration 5*:184–198.

Pascal, A. H. (1981). User charges, contracting out, and privatization in an era of fiscal retrenchment. *Urban Interest 3*:6–12.

Rich, R. C. (1981). Interaction of the voluntary and governmental sectors: Toward an understanding of the coproduction of municipal services. *Administration and Society 13*:59–76.

Rosentraub, M. S. and Sharp, E. B. (1981). Consumers as producers of social services: Coproduction and the level of social services. *Southern Review of Public Administration 4*:502–539.

Rosentraub, M. S., Harlow, K., Warren, R., and Card, B. (1982). *Citizen Involvement in the Production of Personal Safety: What Citizens Do and What Police Officers Want Them To Do*. Institute of Urban Studies, University of Texas at Arlington.

Savas, E. S. (1977a). An empirical study of competition in municipal service delivery. *Public Administration Review 37*:717–724.

Savas, E. S. (1977b). Policy analysis for local government: Public vs. private refuse collection. *Policy Analysis 3*:49–74.

Savas, E. S. (1979). How much do government services really cost? *Urban Affairs Quarterly 15*:23–42.

Savas, E. S. (1981). Intracity competition between public and private sector delivery. *Public Administration Review 41*:46–52.

Savas, E. S. (1982). *Privatizing the Public Sector*. Chatham House, Chatham, N.J.

Shulman, M. A. (October, 1982). Alternative approaches for delivering public services. In *Urban Data Service Reports 14*. International City Management Association, Washington, D.C.

Sonenblum, S., Kirlin, J. J., and Ries, J. C. (1977). *How Cities Provide Services*. Ballinger, Cambridge, Mass.

Stevens, B. J. (1978). Scale, market structure, and the cost of refuse collection. *Review of Economics and Statistics 60*:438–448.

Straussman, J. and Farie, J. (1981). Contracting for social services at the local level. *Urban Interest 3*:43–50.

Whitaker, G. P. (1980). Coproduction: Citizen participation in service delivery. *Public Administration Review 40*:240–246.

Zimmerman, J. (1973). Meeting service needs through intergovernmental agreements. In *Municipal Year Book*. International City Management Association, Washington, D.C.

17

Integrating Human Services Management and Delivery Systems*

Beaumont R. Hagebak   United States Public Health Service, Region IV, Atlanta, Georgia

I. HUMAN SERVICES POLICY AND THE CLIENT

When business executives define their bottom line, they are talking about profit—the financial gain to be realized from the sale of goods or services. That margin of profit depends upon many factors, including their understanding of the markets, the availability of resources, the productivity of their employees, sound pricing strategies, and sales. Although there may be predictable fixed costs associated with production and marketing decisions, profit is also strongly influenced by forces over which a company has little control. No business executive can be certain of cause and effect relationships leading to profit or loss. Many variables are involved, their interactions difficult to predict and measure. Even leading economic theorists differ when attempting to predict the impact of recession or in devising cures for inflation. Yet the bottom line for any business is clearly profit.

A. The Human Services Bottom Line

The human services, like business, work with forces over which they have little control. Complex and interrelated variables impact the lives of those they serve,

---

*Disclaimer: The concepts presented in this chapter are those of its author, and are not intended to reflect the official position of the United States Public Health Service or of any agency of the federal government.

making it difficult to assess the specific effects of their services. Client gains in one area of life may, just as in business, be offset by losses in another. Policy-makers are at odds over such basic issues as, "Who shall be served?" "How much service is enough?" and "What treatments are most effective?" Although agency budgets establish service limits in stark fiscal terms, human service profits cannot be measured in dollars and cents. Their bottom line is not so easily defined.

Most agencies report their gains in increased *units of service* provided (hours devoted to direct client care, total number of contacts, or even the number of forms completed each week, month, and year). These figures do not really get at the human services bottom line. When pressed for definition, agency managers will finally respond with words and phrases reflecting the cultural values that support their public programs: "reduce dependency," "increase productivity," "overcome physical or emotional illness," "achieve personal responsibility," through services designed to educate, rehabilitate, support, and encourage the client. The bottom line for any human service agency is client gain in such intangibles as health, happiness, productivity, responsibility, and inde-pendence. The common denominator is the preface used in all such definitions by every agency: "To help our client. . . ."

B. The Human Services Client

And who is the client? The client may be any one of a number of people:

- A black teenager who dropped out of school, has no marketable skills, and who is turning to drugs as a way out of boredom, frustration, and failure
- A retarded man in his early twenties who was sent to prison for the theft of several watches from the display case of a local department store
- A seventy-two-year-old woman whose husband's death left her poverty stricken, severely depressed, and fearful, who spends long days and longer nights behind the locked doors of her small apartment, managing to survive without heat or electricity
- A thirty-two-year-old father of three whose crippling spinal cord injury turned his world upside down, who now lies in his bed unable to work, and equally unable to cope with his growing anger and frustration
- A forty-three-year-old former corporate executive who lost his job, his family, and his future as the result of acute alcoholism
- A twenty-five-year-old unwed mother of two preschool children, without family, friends, or resources, whose futile attempts to find work have left her defeated and apathetic

These are not cardboard cutouts. These are real people, who breathe, sleep, eat, laugh, and cry just as we do. They are people with problems, usually many problems. Helping them to help themselves is the human service worker's bottom line. Their needs are recognized by the public, and form the basis for policy development in all human service programs.

C. The Problem of System

It would seem reasonable, then, to expect that the system created to deliver services at the local level, where people with problems live, would concentrate the attentions of a variety of professional specialties to meet all of the human needs each of these clients presents. That father with the spinal cord injury, for example, would require the simultaneous assistance of a visiting nurse, a psychologist, and a vocational rehabilitation counselor. His wife and children may need the services of a professional social worker as they attempt to cope with this unexpected family crisis. The sudden loss of his regular income might make some temporary financial support necessary. Professional specialists, working together, might be able to restore this father's health and productivity, his family's happiness and independence. If specialized treatment services were not closely coordinated, the bottom line for this man and his family, and for other multiple-problem clients, would be impossible to achieve.

Unfortunately, local service delivery does not work quite that way. Simultaneous and coordinated services on behalf of a particular client or family are highly unusual, despite the underlying logic. In most communities there is no *system*, there are many separate systems. Dozens of local agencies provide their own specialized services, each operating within its own organizational structure and out of its own facility and each treating some special human condition. Cooperation among systems is difficult; coordination is rare. With few exceptions, no community has taken up the challenge of defining policies and creating systems to meet the comprehensive needs of individuals or families. Community-based whole-person treatment has seldom been attempted.

This chapter explores the problem of system in human service delivery by presenting an overview of categorical programs, their developmental history, administrative structures and authorities, and their effects; by reviewing the essential elements in each of three organizational approaches that form a continuum of specialty-program linkage between categorical and integrated systems; and, by describing the philosophy, structural components, and procedures that form a different model for public caring—human service integration. The potential of integrated systems is discussed in the new context for public administration emerging in the 1980s.

II. CATEGORICAL SERVICE SYSTEMS

Prior to 1900, public caring was left in the uncertain hands of private charity. There were few exceptions. Although state and local governments did assume some responsibility for controlling epidemics of smallpox, yellow fever, and cholera, little attention was given to other social problems emerging in the wake of America's transition from an agrarian culture to a complex technological society of huge cities and roaring factories. By the turn of the century some 10 million persons—the dregs of a newly industrialized nation—were ". . . failing to obtain sufficient necessities for maintaining physical efficiency" (Hunter, 1904).

A. Categorical Program Development

The hands-off policy of government came to an abrupt end in the Great Depression of the 1930s, as Americans were shocked into recognition of their economic and social interdependence. The people demanded a "New Deal," and government responded with an unprecedented array of public programs to assist the unemployed, the aged, and dependent children. By the end of World War II, constituency groups formed in support of these public programs had grown in strength and number. America's new affluence, the problem-solving character of her people, and the dedicated efforts of countless special-interest organizations concerned with yet-unsolved and equally special human problems, combined to bear abundant fruit in the 1960s as Americans sought a "Great Society" and fought a "War on Poverty." In 1965 alone, Congress enacted twenty-five major pieces of legislation affecting health care, education, and welfare.

Between 1960 and 1983, human services spending grew from $27.3 billion to $372 billion, an increase of 1217% (Sugarman and Bass, 1982). Congressional legislation had spawned hundreds of new programs, each earmarked to meet a specific social ill with its own funding, law, policies, regulations, delivery system, and organizational structure. Over one-third of the entire federal budget was being funneled through 10 major federal agencies managing over 100 special-purpose human service programs, to hundreds of state-level organizations, to 28,000 units of local government, and to an estimated 140,000 nongovernmental agencies directly involved in service delivery. The development of each categorical program represented the culmination of a political process similar for all:

- A problem or condition was identified that demanded remediation.
- Advocacy groups were formed among people afflicted with the problem, their families, friends, and associates, building grass-roots support at local, state, and national levels.
- The support of public and private professional persons who worked with the problem was enlisted or, over time, a cadre of specialists particularly concerned with the condition was created.
- These groups worked to personalize the problem, to illustrate that those afflicted were worthy of public support, and to lobby Congress for special-purpose funding.

- When funding was provided, congressional appropriations were accompanied by controlling legislation that established a special program to treat the problem and policies to guide that program.
- With no coherent national plan, state and local planning was geared to compliance with separate federal program mandates and to full draw-down of dollars available from each, duplicating the patchwork of federal programs at these levels.
- Although some programs became part of larger organizations, most retained their special identity and funding (e.g., mental retardation as a special program of services within a mental health system, family planning as a special program of services within a public health system).
- Specialized personnel were employed to provide special treatments and to manage state and local systems.
- Dedicated special-interest groups, specialized care givers supported by their own powerful professional associations, and program managers responsible for preserving the organizational integrity of their single-purpose agencies formed a well-intentioned but self-serving and politically powerful "iron triangle" that then became self-perpetuating.

The very fact that all categorical human service programs have gone through this laborious process, waging successful battles for recognition and resources, contributes to their firm resolve to remain separate and apart.

B. Categorical Program Structure and Authority

Any discussion of service delivery structure is certain to be an oversimplification, because each system develops organizational charts that take into account such unique characteristics as political power, funding levels and sources, organizational history and traditions, and even, perhaps, the abilities of an incumbent who happens to occupy a particular box on the chart. At the local level, chain-of-command structures become particularly difficult to define. Most local agencies are funded through counterpart state organizations, but some may report only to federal agencies that fund them directly; some may receive funding support only from local sources, whereas others may enjoy a multiplicity of funding sources and charge fees for their services as well. Yet one basic key to structure is constant: whoever controls the flow of program dollars will have a significant impact on organizational structure.

Each categorical program maintains its own top-down structure, a vertical organization that may extend from Washington to semiautonomous state-level program administrators, possibly through substate regional specialty directors, then to counterpart local program managers. Each state specialty organization employs a staff that performs its fiscal management, planning, public information, personnel, training, program management, and program evaluation functions. Each conducts its own legislative liaison and funding development activities in direct competition with all others. At the local level, each categorical program manager is responsible to the state program administrator for implementing plans and directives, and for assuring the provision of special services at a prescribed level and of a defined quality. Performance is evaluated primarily on the local program's success in meeting these standards. Each local program is likely to be housed in its own facility, employ its own fiscal officer, maintain its own personnel records and, depending on size, may duplicate other functions also performed at the state level.

The authority exercised by categorical program administrators at any level is firmly established in public law. Enabling legislation is likely to be extremely specific, accompanied by detailed administrative regulations and by program policy manuals that define precise eligibility requirements to be met by the client. Most categorical programs are creatures of the executive branch of government. The governor may have span-of-control problems, but also has the authority to convene meetings of two or more agency heads to resolve common problems. That resolution, however, is likely to be heavily influenced by the amount of political support each special interest is able to muster on a given issue, leading to charges that categorical systems are often unresponsive to public policy-makers. Although the elected chief executive officer may control the flow of dollars earmarked for each special-purpose state program, state agency administrators are likely to enjoy great flexibility when determining local levels of funding support. Executive authority is further eroded by the proliferation of legislatively created policy-making boards whose members are prominent in the specialty as professional representatives or as citizen advocates, by the political power that can be generated through professional specialty associations with national affiliation, and by well-organized and highly vocal special-interest lobbies whose efforts led to the creation of each single-purpose program. These political interests merge with bureaucratic interests at the highest appointed and elected levels of public administration, where short-term leadership demands acceptance of minimal gain in most efforts to reorganize whole systems of service delivery. At the local level, then, when issues arise that require the joint attention of two or more programs, representatives of each program meet as equals, if at all. There is no formal, unifying, policy-making authority at the local level.

C. Categorical Program Goals and Treatments

Categorical systems represent the functional theory of organization: the management of specialized services by specialists who possess doctrinal orientations and professional expertise in the function (service) to be performed by those they manage. As a result, categorical service goals are limited to the provision of specialized treatments and rely heavily on the term *professional*. Client treatment in a categorical agency takes on the character of agency structure.

Typically, a particular treatment is provided through a single agency staff member whose independent professional judgment determines the treatment plan. The work of that staff member may be reviewed by a professional supervisor or by a team of like-type professionals responsible for quality control; the counsel of peers may be sought as unique problems are encountered, but treatment decisions rest with the individual care giver. Occasionally, referral may be made to other staff members who have subspecialty training or specialized skills. Occasionally, too, the professional care giver may suggest that the client seek help for other pressing problems through different community agencies, and may go so far as to contact intake workers in other agencies to complete a referral. Some agencies may even schedule a particular day to be devoted to the treatment of a specific type of problem, requesting that the client exhibiting those symptoms attend on that day. The medical model of specialized treatment provided through a single professional staff member is the treatment model used most often in categorical service organizations, whatever the nature of the service provided.

D. The Effects of Categorical Service Systems

With public funding sufficient to support a host of single-purpose programs at every level of government, the nation tackled physical and emotional illness, poverty, delinquency and crime, disability, hunger, inadequate housing, and child abuse as problems to be solved. Problems *were* solved, and their negative effects were minimized in the lives of many individuals and families. The nation moved services for the elderly, the retarded, and the mentally ill out of large institutional settings, establishing community-based care as a matter of public policy. Colleges and universities matriculated thousands of highly trained specialists into local public programs with demonstrable needs for their services and with the funding and positions to absorb them. Such gains could not have been made without the determined special-interest advocacy groups that heightened American awareness of special needs and provided needs-based information to legislators equally concerned with road construction and bridge building. Human service lobbyists, professional specialists, and categorical program managers who understand their own delivery systems from the perspective of the service worker have contributed greatly to the awareness of, and support for, people with problems.

But there have been negative effects as well. Public caring has been translated into an inconsistent, fragmented, and costly maze of specialized community programs, each treating part-problems. The impact of this haphazard growth on the administration of public programs was well defined by the then-Secretary of the U.S. Department of Health and Human Services in 1981 (Schweiker, 1981):

Each of these [categorical] programs, however, has carried with it costly administrative and other restrictive requirements. As a result of the fragmented and overlapping nature of the current system of federal assistance, spending frequently does not reflect community priorities and often persons in need are not served effectively. The categorical programs and their requirements have also led to substantial inefficiencies in the way services are provided and to burdensome administrative costs that waste scarce resources.

State-level policy-makers attempt to cope with span-of-control problems, limited accountability for program effectiveness and cost control, and low levels of responsiveness to policy direction initiated by elected officials. Caseworkers, counselors, nurses, and other service providers whose daily client contacts make them painfully aware of the multiplicity of human service needs find that their offices have become "revolving doors" for those who regress because the weight of other untreated problems pulls them down. But the individual client in need of several simultaneous services may feel most directly the negative effects of caring delivered in categories.

The multiple-problem client seeking assistance will find program offices located many miles apart. Lacking coordinated transportation systems, access to those services is limited at best. Complicated and similar application forms must be completed for each agency, but no agency is likely to assess all of that client's needs because each views the client from its own problem-solving perspective. No comprehensive plan is developed to meet all of the client's needs; no opportunity exists to fill gaps in locally available services. Proper referral is difficult because the totality of client needs is not understood, and accurate information about services provided through other community agencies does not exist. No one person is responsible for helping the client through the maze; no one coordinates the efforts of service providers. Categorical restrictions may even prevent specialists in one agency from discussing the client's problems with staff in another agency also providing treatment. The results are conflicting treatments, confusing counsel, duplicated effort, and a structural inability to achieve the human services bottom line.

III. THE LINKAGE-BUILDING CONTINUUM

To solve the problems inherent in categorical systems of human service organization, those concerned have engaged in the development of linkage-building activities between programs. Three basic approaches have been most frequently employed. Together, they form an authority-based relationship continuum between categorical and integrated systems.

A. Cooperation

A recently published text on interagency cooperation begins by stating: "Agencies don't cooperate, *people* do. When they *want* to" (Hagebak, 1982). The decision to cooperate is a voluntary and highly personal decision. An agency director may or may not choose to cooperate with others. That decision may be reflected through active participation in joint activities, overt hostility, or subtle passive resistance. Whatever the decision, it's not likely to affect salary and promotion decisions made about the agency director at higher levels in the categorical program. Those decisions are based almost entirely on success in achieving specific single-purpose performance targets. Cooperation depends upon personal contact, interpersonal trust, and mutual concerns. When agency heads meet over a cup of coffee to discuss and solve some community issue of interest to all, any movement toward joint resolution is a function of cooperation.

One of the primary advantages of cooperation is that those involved know that the others have a personal investment in the hoped-for outcome, because no one is under a mandate to act. Cooperation is the least threatening and most familiar method of interagency linkage building. However, cooperation suffers from one major structural flaw. It is a horizontal effort between equals that permits the least-willing agency director to set the limits on what can be accomplished. Cooperation has no centralizing authority beyond the informal persuasive power produced by the people involved.

B. Coordination

Coordination represents the beginning of structured linkage building among agencies. Like cooperation, coordination depends heavily on the good will of its participants, but with two important differences: some organization has been created to support it; and, someone is attempting to manage it. Coordination may be best illustrated by the voluntary affiliation of several agencies in a Community Council of Social Service Agencies, created by local program directors who see some need for a centralizing focal point. Authority is delegated by the several vertical special-purpose agencies involved, but is limited by the degree of autonomy each may have in its own categorical structure. Delegated powers are carefully circumscribed, and may be rescinded by any member agency if conflicts develop, or if its special-purpose resources are threatened. The coordinator may guide, but the group decides. Faced, perhaps, with community concerns that might require the creation of multidisciplinary treatment teams to meet multiple-service needs, the coordinator's actual authority may only assure some representation from each participating agency at interagency meetings.

Coordinated systems do have two key advantages over informal inter-personal cooperation: some individual or group has accepted interagency linkage building as a primary objective, and a structure has been created to provide order while participants share information and deliberate over issues of mutual concern. Its major weakness lies in the fact that, once again, the lowest common denominator controls the level of activity and the sharing of resources. Gains are still made through the powers of persuasion rather than as the result of enforce-able mandates. Any member agency can pick up its marbles and go home.

C. Consolidation

Consolidation involves the merger of previously autonomous human service administrative systems under a single statutory authority. Although each special-purpose program may retain its separate identity, continuing to direct and evaluate the delivery of its own specialized services, personnel who formerly performed administrative support functions (planning, budgeting, personnel, and training) in each system are combined into discrete units accountable to the centralized authority. Because categorical funding requirements often restricted the creation of consolidated systems at the service delivery level, and because decentralized mandates for consolidation would arouse the greater ire of special interests seeking to maintain distinct specialty services, consolidation is a linkage-building technique employed primarily by state governments interested in achieving economies of scale, in reducing span-of-control problems, in eliminating duplication of management functions, and in developing greater capacity for policy management—all at the state level. During the 1970s some thirty-seven states moved to consolidate two or more independent human services organizations. These state-level "umbrella systems" serve as the best examples of the consolidated model in human services organization. The consoli-dated systems have produced mixed results because they only affected the ways in which once-separate systems related to one another at the state level.

Consolidation offers the advantages available to any legally empowered system: control over all essential administrative support functions of the program divisions and the authority to appoint and remove program adminis-trators. Consolidation can resolve many of the organizational concerns posed by policy-makers, while it overcomes most special-interest objections by maintain-ing separate single-purpose service identity. But consolidated systems also exhibit several areas of weakness. Consolidation does not necessarily engender cooperation between specialty programs; rather, it refocuses their competition for service resources on the new decision-maker. Because their specialty programs remain intact, consolidated systems may face repeated threats to organizational integrity as the result of political pressures applied by special-interest advocates displeased with their particular program's status or funding.

The greatest weakness, however, occurs because consolidation does not extend its linkages to the local level where direct services are delivered and where the bulk of an organization's resources are expended through still-separate programs. As a result, the client continues to cope with a fragmented patchwork of programs, opportunities for cost-effective resource sharing are minimized, and the taxpaying public perceives little change in program operations that their tax dollars support.

IV. INTEGRATED SERVICE SYSTEMS

Working together in the solution of common problems is anything but new. Efforts to bring people together in cooperative ventures form a rich part of our folk heritage: covered wagon trains to the West, old-fashioned barn raisings and, more recently, class-action lawsuits. Efforts to link the people, professions, and systems that deliver public human services, though, are of more recent vintage. The fact that research (Council of State Governments, 1974) and a major conference (Agranoff, 1977) on that topic conducted as recently as the mid-1970s produced publications now widely viewed as classics in the field illustrates the point. Service integration is a relatively new organizational strategy for the human services. Its undergirding philosophy and goals and its structure and its treatment methods constitute a significant departure from past practice.

A. Integrated Service Philosophy and Goals

All human service organizations operate on a series of "shoulds"—program goals that may be formalized in writing or simply understood. They describe what the organization *should* be attempting to achieve and what the nature and outcomes of client treatment *should* be. All human service organizations share the intangible goals of client gain in health and happiness, responsibility, and productivity. All seek to reduce dependency. Service integration represents a way of thinking about people and their problems that leads to nontraditional methods for helping them meet these goals.

The cornerstone of integrated services and systems is a holistic philosophy of life. People share basic similarities in their problems of living. For any individual these problems are likely to be complex, multidimensional, and interlocking. The client is more than a diagnostic label. The client is a whole person in need.

1. Basic Client Treatment Goals

Service integration makes use of client treatment methods that are based on four key assumptions:

- The care giver should be accountable for the effectiveness of treatment, not only to professional colleagues, but to the client and to the public.
- A universal concern for client well-being should transcend the boundaries of professional discipline.
- Barriers of an administrative and geographic nature that limit client access to needed services should be eliminated.
- Specialized services should be coordinated and simultaneously delivered to assure whole-person treatment.

2.   Basic Organizational Goals

State legislatures mandating merger of human service organizations define goals for reorganization that are always essentially the same: to increase organizational efficiency; to reduce costly duplication of support services; to reduce span of control; to enhance organizational responsiveness; and, to more effectively utilize resources. These expectations are reflected in the concerns for efficiency that led to integration of the human services delivery system in the State of Florida (Shute and Lunt, 1977). The new organization was expected to:

- Resolve span of control problems.
- Strengthen administrative support capability.
- Eliminate duplication of effort and overlapping jurisdictions.
- Provide greater accountability for program effectiveness evaluation and for cost control.
- Ensure organizational responsiveness to policy direction from the governor and legislature.

In Florida's policy planning, concerns for efficiency also extended to local systems and to recipients of service. Most statements of organizational "shoulds" reflect only the hopes of their framers that costs will be reduced and responsiveness will be enhanced. Few address local management and service delivery methods, and most mention the client only in passing. As a result, structures created to achieve the policy-maker's goals seldom meet their expectations.

To attain the level of efficiency anticipated in public policy statements, service integration requires structures and systems that are developed on the basis of five additional assumptions:

- Strategic action plans should be based on the provision of holistic treatment services rather than on short-term problem-solving or categorical regulatory compliance.
- Strategic planning should take into account the implications of well-intentioned but antagonistic special-interest reaction, and other barriers of organization, attitude, and vision.

- Integrated organizations should be the result of well-formulated public policy translated into clear legal mandates that define and empower each dimension of the new system at state, local, and client treatment levels, and that specifically countermand all prior legislation in the field.
- Authority should be decentralized on area rather than functional lines, to assure generalist multispecialty program direction and treatment coordination within the boundaries of geographic service areas common to all specialties.
- Generalist managers at state, local, and treatment levels should be carefully selected to assure that each possesses those personal characteristics necessary to create an atmosphere of cooperation among people working in the new system at every level.

Translated into systems, the "shoulds" of integrated treatment and structure lead naturally into the development of teamed approaches for comprehensive case planning, case management, and treatment that serve clients residing in the same geographic area, with facilities housing multiple specialties, assuring ease of access and continuity of care. Goals for client treatment and goals for the organization, when policy is properly conceived, are inseparable. The efficiencies sought through organizational change are not incompatible with improved client services.

B. Integrated Program Structure and Authority

Integrated organizations, like categorical programs, make use of vertical structures. The chain of command extends from the state-level commissioner or administrator to a local or multicounty counterpart. Here the similarity ends. At the state level, previously independent organizations have been merged and their administrative functions have been consolidated. Fiscal management is centralized under a single authority, as is the personnel function. Planners from each discipline are brought together in a unified planning unit charged with the development of compatible goals, objectives, and implementation designs. Training staff may even be consolidated, with some continuing to perform professional training in specialized fields whereas others become responsible for broadly based training in intake, team casework, the use of volunteers, and multispecialty management techniques. The legislative liaison activities of each specialty program have been curtailed to allow the integrated system to unify its funding development efforts and to address policy and political issues more systematically. For similar reasons, specialty councils and boards have been disbanded in favor, perhaps, of a single-policy review board made up of people representing a variety of professions and advocacy groups. Categorical specialty directors have become key technical consultants on program issues, each reporting to the single state commissioner (as do the heads of each administrative unit), and their specialized staff members perform similar consultative functions for local care givers. Program evaluation is performed by multidisciplinary teams that also contain generalist experts in finance and management. Local program administration has been delegated, not to the specialty programs, but to a multi-agency manager responsible for all human services in a particular geographic area.

Locally, once-autonomous agencies have also been merged into a single unifying administrative system. A number of geographic areas have been created throughout the state, each headed by a generalist manager who reports to the state commissioner and who has been delegated administrative authority to employ and remove local agency directors. In the new system, these agency heads become senior program consultants to the local generalist manager, bringing the benefits of their professional expertise to bear on the work of an area administrative team that also includes those people selected to manage consolidated fiscal, personnel, and planning functions. A geographically representative human services citizen board composed of local providers, special-interest advocates, and recipients of service may also be established to advise the administrative team as it jointly defines area service needs and allocates resources to meet them. Structural changes extend well beyond the local administrative system, to include:

- Common service areas: Specialty services are restructured so that all provide their services within the same geographic boundaries and relate to the same potential client population, making possible the joint assessment of multiple-service needs and jointly delivered services.
- Collocation: Facilities that once housed separate services become human service centers, as specialized staff is relocated to assure that a variety of services are offered under one roof in neighborhoods and communities. Outreach staff working in hard-to-serve areas are brought together into a single neighborhood service site to reduce costs, improve accessibility, and enhance opportunities for interspecialty referral and teamed care giving.
- Transportation: Vehicles formerly used by separate agencies to transport only their special clients are combined into an areawide transportation network, eliminating duplicated routes, reducing costs of operation and maintenance, and permitting greater flexibility for emergency and demand/response transportation.
- Management services: Management services are consolidated to maximize cost savings in the purchase of equipment and supplies, to permit correction of imbalances in compensation and benefits created by separate systems, to assure the shared use of clerical staff and other support personnel, to permit strategic planning for coordinated service delivery, and to identify unencumbered resources that can be used to fill gaps in the service delivery system.

- Core services: Agency intake services are merged. Intake workers are trained in the identification of multiple needs and in the use of a standardized application form that the client must complete only once to access all necessary services. These workers orient the client to the range of available services and relate those services to individual needs. Generalist intake staff located in each service site become the first point of contact for the client, and the only contact necessary to establish basic eligibility and access the system.
- Case planning: The hard-core multiple-problem client or family in need of a variety of specialized services would be the focus of a care-planning team composed of specialists representing a number of professional disciplines. This team would design a comprehensive treatment plan to simultaneously involve the variety of specialized personnel needed, and would "contract" with the client for implementation of the plan.
- Case management: Each client is assigned to a case manager who coordinates the flow of specialty services and becomes the primary contact person for the client during the process. The case manager conducts follow-up activities to assure that all needed services are being obtained, works out problems of transportation and scheduling, and remains aware of changes in the client's life that might alter the treatment plan.
- Treatment teams: Hands-on treatment methods depend upon the nature and number of client needs. In some cases a single specialist may be capable of providing all necessary treatment. In most instances, however, a treatment team is formed to work with the case manager in carrying out the treatment plan. These specialists, representing different professional disciplines, work as equals, their efforts coordinated by the case manager.

Local models of service integration that employ all of the structural components described in the list are rare. Yet most human service theorists would agree that the structure of a fully integrated local delivery system should contain, at the very least, these elements.

The program authority delegated to generalist managers at the local level resolves the age-old competition between administrative theories of area and function. Both camps seek to divide the universe of human services, but in strikingly different ways. Categorical systems are organized on functional authority lines, each managed by specialists trained in that functional specialty. Integrated systems are based in area theory, linking functional specialties under a generalist manager with geographic responsibilities and with closer ties to elected policy-makers than to any one of several special interests. Integrated systems are empowered systems that use their authorities to build linkages, from the lofty offices of the state human services commissioner to the multidisciplinary client treatment team where the real service work is done.

C. Integrated Client Treatments

Integrated organizations may offer treatment through a single specialized care giver when assessments of client need identify that as appropriate. The typical approach to treatment, though, is based on the multidimensional concerns of holistic philosophy, with services delivered through teams of selected professional specialists and generalist case managers who guide the client and the process. Comprehensive evaluation of the physical, psychological, social, rehabilitative, and life-support needs presented by each client is undertaken by a multidisciplinary assessment team. Specialized assessments may be separately performed, of course, but the results of each evaluation are shared in joint treatment planning. Treatment plans may be developed for individual clients or for entire families, and may even involve members of the client's social network. A generalist case manager coordinates the assessments and the treatment planning, then will coordinate the formation of a multispecialty treatment team that provides each needed professional service according to the client's treatment plan or contract. The client is not a passive recipient of services, but is involved directly in decisions made during plan development. The treatment teams are not static entities; their members are brought together on the basis of a given client's service needs. Actual treatments may be separately performed, but the case manager tracks and monitors the overall process, calling the team together as needed to assure treatment continuity. The case manager becomes a bridge between whole-person client needs and the specialty orientation of each professional team member. In a sense, the generalist case manager's role relieves specialists of the burden of whole-person concern while assuring that the system and treatments respond to that concern, close gaps in available services, and avoid duplication of effort.

D. The Potential of Integrated Service Systems

Performance is the ultimate test of the worth of any service system. The concepts and components that are basic elements of integrated service systems have what statisticians would term *face validity*. They hold the promise of improved performance in achieving goals important to the policy-maker and to the client. But there have been few opportunities to test the performance of integrated human service systems at any level of government, despite a potential that makes service integration the logical imperative for public program administration.

Many models of interpersonal cooperation, interagency coordination, and state-level program consolidation do exist, and the strengths and weaknesses in each are well known. Less well known are the scattered models that illustrate gains to be achieved through integration, although a growing number of generalist publications (*New England Journal of Human Services*, for example) are beginning to describe key concepts and real-world results for subscribers concerned with generic aspects of public administration in the human services. And, there is an increasing body of evidence supporting the performance potential of integrated systems at several organizational levels:

- With the passage of permissive legislation in Minnesota, a unified human services management system was developed to serve a two-county area with headquarters in the City of Mankato. Administrative consolidation, collocation, shared core services, and joint case management resulted in overhead costs of only 5% for the new organization, as compared with similar costs of more than 30% in some of the previously independent agencies (Fuller, 1979).
- In Texarkana, Arkansas, community agencies voluntarily integrated just one component—transportation—overcoming barriers of categorical funding and regulation, to serve clients in a seven-county area that included two cities and the boundaries of two states. The integrated, radio-based client transportation system has been described as "cost-effective and efficient" (Ruyle, 1978).
- Florida's Department of Health and Rehabilitative Services manages the most comprehensive statewide human services integration model in the nation, with decentralized authority in the hands of generalist district managers, collocated service sites, common intake, cross-program training, and case management teams. After eight years the system remains incomplete, but researchers have now been able to report positive effects on the perceived quality of services, increased communication and coordinated activity among service workers, and favorable reaction to the decentralization of administrative authority (Povlika et al., 1981).

In many communities, however, barriers have been raised to bar the development of equally promising integrated service systems. The affluence of separate service organizations has inhibited partnership building among them. Powerful special interests, fearing that the needs of their special client populations will not be adequately addressed if their special programs are merged with others, have forged political alliances to block the creation of essential components (particularly treatment components) at local levels. They have even occasionally been successful in dismantling existing programs. Substate generalist multiagency program managers in Georgia, for example, were first stripped of their line authority over specialty services, then were reduced in number, and finally were abolished entirely over a four-year period, largely as the result of internal and external special-interest pressures. These barriers, which continue to limit the potential of integrated administrative and treatment systems, are beginning to lose their political credibility. Social and economic forces emerging in the 1980s carry with them a new context for caring, and the potential for massive change in the structures and methods we employ to deliver human services.

V. HUMAN SERVICES POLICY IN A NEW CONTEXT

The decade of the 1970s witnessed a fantastic growth in dollars spent for human services. Categorical program budgets expanded rapidly as deinstitutionalization brought more services to the community. But inflation had also begun to grow, emerging from the dry writings of economic theorists to become a double-digit household word. Organized middle-class resistance to spiraling costs and increasing taxation struck first in California, where voters overwhelmingly approved Proposition 13, placing a cap on public spending. Similarly, popular tax referendum efforts were then begun in at least twenty-seven other states. The continued growth of human service budgets and programs was on a collision course with a changing public mood.

Prestigious national policy planning groups such as the President's Commission on Mental Health (1978) began to issue urgent appeals for partnership building in the human services. These appeals went largely unheeded. Congressional human services legislation continued to allocate funds for categorical programs, but each new law made reference to the desirability of interagency coordination. The references lacked clear definition and firm mandates, and were ignored. A majority of the states did move to consolidate independent state-level agencies, but hoped-for cost savings were seldom realized. The consolidated systems did not extend to the local level where their effects would have been more obvious to the public. Reorganization efforts created organizational charts illustrating their confused authorities and accountabilities: each chart became a maze of solid and dotted lines. As public policy-makers attempted to simultaneously address public insistence on greater cost-saving efficiencies and special-interest demands that their functional specialty programs remain intact, they validated the conclusion reached by one of our nation's leading organizational theorists, James W. Fesler: the conflict between area and function is "irreconcilable" (Curtis, 1982).

By 1980, our national economy had become the overriding issue for most Americans, who elected a new president intent on reordering spending priorities. Once in office, the Reagan administration immediately embarked on an economic recovery program that involved reduced taxes, reduced federal spending for human services, reduced federal regulation, and increased state and local responsibility for managing and financing their many long-established categorical service organizations. The speed with which this program was enacted left competitive special-interest groups in disarray. Profound changes in the way tax dollars were allocated for human services, in the amount of funding available, and in public policy affecting human service delivery systems had been set into motion.

A. Barriers and Opportunities

Barriers to the development of more efficient, effective, and humane service delivery systems have been obvious for decades. They include:

- Barriers of organization, created by categorical legislation usually initiated at the federal level, which established in each state and in most communities a host of categorical programs, each supported by its own body of law, policies, regulations, funding, structure, procedures, and service areas.
- Barriers of attitude, created by well-intentioned special-purpose advocacy, which led to isolationist standards, "turf" guarding, professional status considerations, specialty jargon, and which reinforced the tendency of some providers to preselect their clients to avoid dealing with the hard-core multiple problem cases.
- Barriers of vision, created by the blinders of existing organizations and protectionist attitudes, which make it difficult even to conceptualize policies that result in comprehensive services at the local level.

Barriers of attitude can be overcome in time. They are personal, and people change. Barriers of vision can be removed as new ways of doing things eventually become commonplace. Barriers of organization—those formidable barriers grounded in law—have seemed most difficult to deal with in the past. Now, even those impenetrable barriers to service integration have been breached.

In 1981, Congress passed legislation that merged twenty-five categorical health and human service programs under seven Block Grants, eliminating many of their restrictive special-purpose mandates and allocating service dollars in lump-sum amounts directly to the states. Out of that process, a new context for decision-making about human service systems and treatments is emerging, a context that now, more than ever before, involves state and local government.

Policy-makers at these levels face a variety of fascinating challenges and opportunities. Huge federal deficits have led to significant reductions in federal funding for human services, but state policy-makers have greater flexibility in determining how those fewer dollars will be used. Economic recession had impacted the anticipated revenues of state and local governments, and these shortfalls increased the pressure for more efficient systems and procedures. Unemployment forces its newly disadvantaged into a fragmented public service delivery system that frustrates and angers them. Categorical providers, struggling to make the shift from expansionist planning to organizational retrenchment and reductions in services, but still greatly concerned about unmet need, are searching for new ways to assure that their clients continue to receive treatment. Advocacy groups are refocusing their attentions away from the halls of Congress to state capitols, where decisions affecting their special interests are now most likely to be made. Their credibility weakened by growing public resentment for any claim of special privilege in an economic climate that demands sacrifice from all (though disproportionate sacrifice from public service clients), professional associations and citizen lobbies have become less strident and more amenable to organizational change.

The economic forces that have so negatively affected funding and support for categorical human services are likely to persist, at diminishing levels, throughout the decade. Policy-makers and public administrators in state and local government who are concerned with human service issues can find opportunity for positive change in the new decision-making context of the 1980s. They will respond in different ways to this new context. Those that move to integrate their categorical service systems must recognize the need for clear mandates, promulgated at the highest levels and extended to local structures and treatment methods. But organizations restructured on the basis of authority alone will continue to face subtle and not-so-subtle resistance by specialty advocates and by the very people who will be expected to manage and provide needed services, unless their cooperation has been consciously developed and creatively rewarded. Their overriding concerns for their special clients are, from their perspective, legitimate. Those concerns must be positively addressed. The creation of integrated human service delivery systems requires a simultaneous top-down and bottom-up effort.

B. Back to the Bottom Line

If profit is the bottom line for business, then the policies of any corporation can ultimately be evaluated on a single performance criterion: financial gain. Business ventures that do not result in profit fail. Obviously, though, rapidly changing market demands lead most companies into modifications of policy, services, and products, based on their best assessments of potentially profitable performance. Corporate policy-makers who cannot evaluate the potential of a new product line or revised service may survive for a time, but their inability to adapt will eventually be reflected in their ledger books.

The American people have always demanded a high level of excellence from their public services. Any failure becomes a media event. Today, insistence on excellence is joined by equally strong demands for greater efficiency and effectiveness. The marketplace is changing, and human service programs are engaged in a struggle for survival. As always, their ledger books are open to public scrutiny.

Integrated human service management and delivery systems have the potential to resolve dysfunctional aspects of functional organization. Extended to the local level, service integration holds potential for maintaining excellence through greater efficiency in the uses made of diminishing program resources. Of even greater value, though, is the potential afforded by integrated human services to more effectively treat the multiple-problem client. A new context for public policy-making may, finally, permit that potential to be tested at the human services bottom line.

REFERENCES

Agranoff, R., ed. (1977). *Coping With the Demands for Change Within Human Services Administration.* Section on Human Resources, American Society for Public Administration, Washington, D.C.

Council of State Governments. (1974). *Human Services Integration: State Functions in Implementation.* Council of State Governments, Lexington, Ky.

Curtis, W. R. (Fall, 1982). The editors interview James W. Fesler. *New England Journal of Human Services 2*(4):11.

Fuller, G. W. (July 2, 1979). Personal communication. Mankato, Minn.

Hagebak, B. R. (1982). *Getting Local Agencies to Cooperate.* University Park Press, Baltimore, p. 2.

Hunter, R. (1904). *Poverty.* Garrett Press, New York, reprinted 1970.

Povlika, L. , Imershein, A. W., White, J. W., and Stivers, L. E. (May–June, 1981). Human service reorganization and its effects: A preliminary assessment of Florida's services integration "experiment." *Public Administration Review 41*(3):359–365.

President's Commission on Mental Health. (1978). *Report to the President.* U.S. Government Printing Office, Washington, D.C.

Ruyle, J. (October, 1978). *Catalogue of Innovations in Human Services Management and Administration.* No. .085. Southern Institute for Human Resources, Atlanta.

Schweiker, R. S. (April 16, 1981). Block grants to the states for health services. *Fact Sheet.* Office of the Secretary, U.S. Department of Health and Human Services, Washington, D.C.

Shute, R. E. and Lunt, R. W. (1977). Florida: An example of an integrated model for human services administration, adopted after the failure of a consolidated model. In Agranoff, R., ed., *Coping With the Demands for Change Within Human Services Administration.* Section on Human Resources, American Society for Public Administration, Washington, D.C., pp. 52–59.

Sugarman, J. M. and Bass, G. D. (1982). *Human Services in the 1980's: President Reagan's 1982 Proposals.* White Paper No. IV. Human Services Information Center, Arlington, Va., p. 33.

Unit Four

PERSONNEL ADMINISTRATION IN STATES AND LOCALITIES

Part A   Processes and Techniques
Chapters 18-20

Part B   Public Employee Unionism and Collective Bargaining
Chapters 21-22

18

Performance Appraisal in State Government

Arthur L. Finkle   Division of Appellate Practices and Labor Relations, New Jersey Department of Civil Service, Trenton, New Jersey

Performance appraisal in state government tugs and pulls at two values in government—accountability and merit. Because these ideas are often at odds with one another, the performance appraisal system falls short of achieving either objective. For example, the process of a performance appraisal system satisfies the middle manager that employees are performing. But the policy manager asks for what objective the employees are performing. Thus, while the employees are busy earning the taxpayer's money, it is all too likely that their output (delivery of services) is not evaluated. This chapter will describe the current performance appraisal system used in government, its implications, and its use in New Jersey. We will evaluate the system under a theoretical and practical framework. Then we will recite the benefits and detriments of such a system.

I. DEFINITION

Performance appraisal is the review and rating of all factors relevant to an employee's effectiveness on the job. Performance appraisal potentially can influence employee performance by linking performance to such rewards and punishments as pay increases, promotion, pay cuts, and demotion. Performance appraisal can be used in three different manners:

1. Management approach: to achieve organizational objectives (MBO)
2. Development tool: to assess an employee's strengths and weaknesses to develop competence to the fullest
3. Basis for personnel actions: base personnel actions on measurable performance criteria

Performance appraisal requires the supervisor and employee to work together to find the means by which the employee's abilities can best be strengthened and directed. Performance appraisal must be a continuous process to be of significant benefit to all parties involved.

II. SURVEY OF STATE GOVERNMENTS

The Urban Institute completed a study of American state performance appraisal systems (PASs) in 1978. Of these states, twenty-three had traditional systems (narrative-based nonspecific performance factors, performance traits such as attitude, appearance not tailored to specific jobs); thirteen had appraisal-by-objectives (point employee-supervisor standard setting and results-oriented appraisal); one had a behaviorally anchored rating scale (checklists tailored to specific jobs); and thirteen states had no formal system. A trend did appear to favor the performance-by-objectives technique. Of those states which instituted PASs in the 1970s, eleven were appraisal-by-objectives (ABB). And of the twelve states planning new systems, four definitely intended to use the ABB approach, whereas six were considering this approach.

A. Frequency of Appraisals

In those states with formal appraisals, all require at least annual appraisals; some require more frequent appraisals, particularly in the employee's probationary period.

B. Appraisal Interviews

Twenty-seven of the thirty-seven formal PAS states had formal face-to-face interviews. Nine left the option to the supervisor; one, the employee. Many states had PAS manuals. In two states, employee assistance programs (employee counseling, drug and alcoholism programs) were an integral part of the PAS.

C. Coverage

All formal PASs covered both line and management employees, although some used different procedures for managers. Some policy-making, unclassified personnel were exempt from the PAS.

D. Reported Uses

The states utilizing formalized PASs were more likely to punish rather than reward. Thus, 80% indicated they would withhold pay increments for a less than satisfactory performance rating; 68% would withhold promoting; 72% would discharge a probationary employee; and 64% would demote.

On the other hand, the state government would reward 54% by increasing pay beyond the normal increment, and 62% would promote if an employee received a superior performance appraisal.

E. Legal Constraints

There were no legal constraints to modify the PAS. Four states had civil service regulations that provided for some substantial PAS content. And one state had a collective bargaining provision concerning the type of PAS to be used.

F. State Evaluations

There were only three states that had evaluated their PASs. One report recorded (New Jersey Legislature, 1975:159–163):

> The general response was that the basic concept of [the PAS] was beneficial. . . . However, a majority of officials felt that present [PAS] requirements and procedures were unnecessarily complex and time-consuming, and consequently, not properly and uniformly utilized throughout the State. This situation was believed to stem from a lack of uniform, established performance descriptions and performance standards on which evaluations can be used.

G. Productivity

None of the states had any hard evidence that a PAS led to increased productivity. They felt this to be true, but none presented any data to support their claim.

1. Legal Implication

PASs have come under legal scrutiny because the Equal Employment Opportunity Commission (EEOC) Selection Guidelines consider PASs to be a personnel practice, if implementation results in reward or penalty. Therefore, PASs must be valid and must be reliable (Kass et al., 1978:18):

> At a minimum, instruments must meet standards of "content" validity which include a job analysis, coverage of the principal factors identified in the job analysis as necessary for satisfactory job performance, standardized administration sufficient to provide equitable review and a design which will provide statistical reliability.

Indeed there is evidence of state governments losing cases because "no data were presented to demonstrate that the evaluation instrument was a valid predictor of employee job performance" (Halley and Field, 1975:427).

Of all the facets of PASs, psychometrics have been researched more than most other areas. Graphic rating scales have been criticized as being subjective, with low reliability. Checklists have low validity because they are not designed for specific job performances, and even if they were, they would be suspect because of the rater's subjectivity. Force-choice instruments do not have face validity, are unpopular with raters, and might be a deterrent for different jobs. Comparative ranking instruments may be subject to personal biases. Critical incident techniques reflect exceptional incidents and neglect routine performance. They are also subject to personal bias.

There is also a problem of consistency of rating because of different supervisors' rating scales. Behaviorally anchored rating scales (BARS) define performances in behavioral terms and conceptually present the most valid instrument; but the effort and money expended seem to be outrageous to accomplish the goal desired. Furthermore, reliability problems arise similar to those of the checklist instrument.

III. PERFORMANCE APPRAISAL IN NEW JERSEY: EMPLOYEE PERFORMANCE AND IMPROVEMENT SYSTEM (EPEIS)

A. Description

The employee performance and improvement system (EPEIS) can be classified as an *appraisal-by-objectives* process that includes the following components:

1. Joint supervisor-employee job analysis and setting of objectives: This provides an explicit "contract" as to what specific work behaviors and results are to be judged.
2. Progress reviews: These allow for timely reinforcement and reclarification of objectives.
3. Annual or semiannual evaluation of whether objectives were met and setting of new objectives for the next period.

EPEIS was developed in 1971 by the Department of Civil Service and had several intended purposes:

1. Improve employee productivity.
2. Develop employee skills.
3. Provide a means for the identification and remedy of problems that prevent the employee from achieving successful job performance.

4. Provide a means of motivating employees to improve job performance.
5. Reward the more productive employees.
6. Improve morale.

The EPEIS evaluation period extends over a one-year period determined by one's anniversary date. The process starts with the development of a performance agreement between the supervisor and employee.

The first step in developing the performance agreement is listing the tasks and objectives to be performed on the job. These should contribute to the attainment of organizational objectives. The next step is developing several standards for each task or objective, including considerations of quantity, quality, and timeliness.

If the employee is successfully meeting the standards of performance, the supervisor holds an evaluation conference with the employee *at least* twice during the year at approximately six-month intervals. As soon as the supervisor recognizes that standards are not being met and performance is less than satisfactory, the supervisor holds an evaluation conference with the employee to identify the problem areas and to develop with the employee a plan for improvement. As long as the performance remains below a satisfactory level, the supervisor meets with the employee *at least* once every three months and more, if necessary, until improvement is achieved.

The supervisor gives the employee an interim evaluation for the evaluation period. The interim evaluation for a satisfactory performance is made at the end of the first six months of the evaluation period. The interim evaluation for an unsatisfactory performer is made *as soon as performance is recognized as unsatisfactory*. At the end of the evaluation period, the supervisor provides the employee with the final rating that is for the entire evaluation period. The supervisor is responsible for providing each employee with a copy of the EPEIS report.

The graphic representation of this system is shown in Fig. 1.

Employees may appeal their rating through a grievance procedure when:

1. Agreement cannot be reached with the immediate supervisor over the development of performance standards or improvement plans.
2. The employee is rated as "unsatisfactory" at the end of the rating period.

The Department of Civil Service also conducts an audit of the employee performance evaluation and improvement system in each agency at least once each year. The purpose of the audit is to provide appointing authorities with detailed information concerning the administration of the system within the agency.

This seemingly rational management system, however, is under attack. Under critical analysis, two glaring deficiencies arise, one theoretical and one practical.

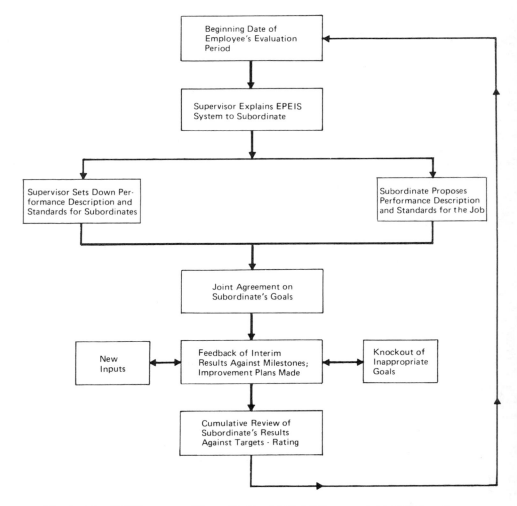

Fig. 1 The EPEIS system. (From Finkle, 1980–1981; copyright 1981 by *The Bureaucrat, Inc.* All rights reserved.)

IV. THEORETICAL DEFICIENCIES

In the EPEIS cycle an employee is directed to set individual performance descriptions, the achievement of which will hopefully help the overall organization (the state) attain its goals. However, no provision has been made in the EPEIS cycle to: (a) include the organization's goals, so the employee may know what the appropriate EPEIS objectives should be, and (b) measure and demonstrate to each employee that the accomplishment of individual objectives is an integral part of the accomplishment of the larger organizational objectives.

A. Goal Ignorance

The nub of this problem is the faulty assumption that supervisors know what the goals of their overall organizational unit are, and therefore can aid their employees in the formulation of the appropriate EPEIS objectives. In virtually all instances this is not true, and, as a result, the EPEIS begins to break down.

Because the EPEIS system is organizationally oriented, most managers view the system as another meaningless addition to a manager's job. It must be emphasized that management by objectives *cannot* be viewed as an additional chore or solely a method of evaluation; *MBO is a method of managing.*

The EPEIS cycle needs to be restructured to include: (a) the formulation and statement of the organization's common goals and measures of performance, and (b) a review of the individual contributions to the overall organization's goals. In effect, it is necessary to tell the employees that they are part of the team. Without the inclusion of these two additional steps, an effective MBO system of management cannot begin or end. A graphic depiction of the revised, complete EPEIS cycle would appear as shown in Fig. 2.

B. Elusive Goals

At the heart of the system is the belief that reasonably specific performance targets can be identified by managers (raters). Ideally, of course, it would be desirable to set these targets in quantifiable terms. It is easy to tell an employee who was committed to the production of 100 units of service that he or she failed to meet the target if he or she produced only 90 by the end of the rating period.

Realistically, of course, we know that not all public services have yet been refined to the point that they can be rated so objectively. Even if they can, many agencies lack the data management systems that would produce this information. Some lack the data because of the different political values attached to a program. Others lack the data because of poor business practices that fail to measure anything. Further, policy-making bodies reflect the differing values of what their constituencies want accomplished.

Thus, public management is presented with unique measurement problems. Walter Balk has indicated that 15–30% of government work can be measured by engineered work standards depending on the size of the operation, the routine of the work, and the level of government. For example, a typist should be able to type at least twenty-five words per minute. He indicates further that another 15–30% can be measured by efficiency ratios (amount of

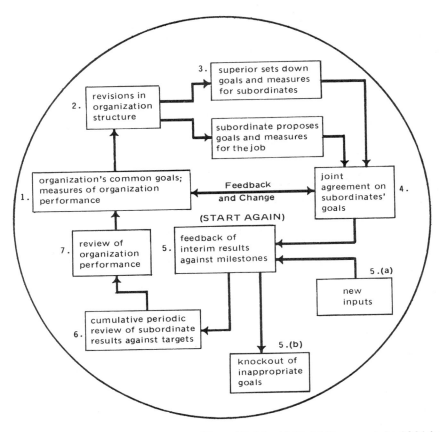

Fig. 2 The revised EPEIS system. (From Finkle, 1980–1981; copyright 1981 by *The Bureaucrat, Inc.* All rights reserved.)

work done historically evaluated). For example, a motor vehicle clerk, by using previous workload trends, produces a tangible output—so many inches of file cards per day. The difficulty comes with the remaining 40% of output to be measured because the concepts of productivity and work are not understood well enough and commonly enough. The remedy lies in defining the nature of work, particularly something called task ambiguity. Work is divided into routine tasks (that can easily be measured) and ambiguous tasks. When there is low ambiguity, there is a high routine of work and this result can be measured by engineered (scientifically derived) work standards. When there is moderate ambiguity, there is a moderate routine of work. This result is measured by workload criteria. And when there is a high-task ambiguity, there is a low routine of work. This result is measured by program elements and schedules. Indeed, the long-term measurement answer seems to lie in the similarities of how organizations attempt to deal with information and the workings of the mind in terms of information perception, processing, and iterative routines. The short-run solution lies in attitudinal testing for psychological qualities reflective of output (what the program produces) or outcome (what the results are). For example, the output of a police force may be to increase patrol officers by 5%; the outcome may be to increase arrests by 2%. On the other hand, the society completely rid of crime will have zero arrests. What we have to do is to reach agreement on programmatic objectives and then apply these objectives, however psychologically subjective they may be, to valid and reliable psychometric techniques (Balk, 1975:178-183).

To cope with the barriers to measurement we have to make a concerted effort to overcome the philosophical inertia: that social services cannot be measured; that there is a lack of power to force compliance; and, that there is an inability to monetarily reward differential levels of performance. In addition, it is important to determine appropriate evaluative criteria in terms of what to measure, securing relevant data, and designing criteria (Applin and Schoderbeck, 1976:88-95).

> In some instances, direct measures . . . may not be available or appropriate, but indirect measures might do the job. For example, policy work is extremely difficult to measure directly. The number of arrests or citations issued can be directly influenced by departmental policy; give a patrolman a quota and he will meet it. Crime victimization studies can be useful, but are too expensive to use routinely. An indirect measure might therefore be the number of citizen complaints about crime conditions in a given area or neighborhood, compared with complaints from other areas; or a change in the rate of complaints from the same area, over time.
>
> These examples are not intended as an exhaustive analysis of the difficult problem of setting objectives. Rather, its purpose is to suggest that we need not stand around wringing our hands over the difficulties, but instead some progress can be made through the use of what might be called "satisfycing" techniques—those which, under the time and data constraints, are satisfactory to utilize. Indeed, whether or not we rate supervisors on the basis of accomplishments, managements make ratings of programs whenever budget decisions are made. And these decisions are made on the basis of whatever evidence is available. The previous suggestions constitute a plea to use the best available information, rather than to make seat-of-pants judgments (Heisel, 1977).

C. Rational Person

Even if the EPEIS cycle is restructured to include organizational goals, an additional difficulty can be anticipated. A basic assumption in MBO is that human behavior is rational. However, it is quite possible that this is a faulty assumption, based on the following: (a) Work is frequently allocated to the public sector that is too risky for performance in the private sector because of lack of knowledge or uncertainty. Many services, such as the cure and prevention of communicable diseases, must be provided to the public irrespective of cost. Thus, the rationality of the private market mechanism breaks down. (b) The stated objective may not be the real objective. In the political arena there is a tendency to emphasize the obvious in stating objectives. When forced to formulate precise, quantifiable objectives that will be publicly scrutinized, there is a tendency to formulate objectives that one is sure to meet. Also, in the public arena there is a tendency to conceal real objectives when the legitimacy of an objective is subject to question.

> Objectives of process, as distinct from substance, tend to be particularly resistant to precision, quantification, and valuation of results. How can one measure the value of the societal maintenance service provided to the public by the police, in terms of the maintenance of law and order and the prevention of crime. But really what do these terms mean? How does one measure them? Is it the number of arrests made, the enforcement of all laws in the book or the objective of ridding the police department of internal corruption. There really are no commonly accepted standards (Finkle, 1980–1981:62).

D. No Rewards Linked to Performance

The rewards to employees include salary, promotion, training opportunities, transfers, temporary work assignments, preferred shifts, as well as other tangible and intangible items. Too often the performance appraisal system and productivity gains both for individuals and work groups are not coterminous. In New Jersey, the original EPEIS system did have a bonus system for one year. On the one hand, there were problems of favoritism. On the other hand, the department heads divided the bonus money evenly and distributed it to each of the employees. Neither practice worked to the satisfaction of either management or its employees. In part it was dysfunctional. It caused morale problems and, in some instances, permanent hard feelings that materially lowered morale. It did, however, prompt the rise of public unionism that much faster.

E. Summary

In short, it may be succinctly stated that from a theoretical perspective the EPEIS system is deficient. Before EPEIS or any MBO system can begin to function effectively, officials must realize that organizational objectives must exist. Moreover, even if a distinct effort is made to formulate these objectives, additional difficulties can be anticipated because of the unique character of public sector work. However, without a clear statement of organizational objectives, individual EPEIS objectives become ineffectual, with no purpose other than work for work's sake. Work only becomes meaningful when rational individuals understand they are a vital, contributing part of their organization. And rational individuals are motivated to achieve these objectives when they are rewarded for their achievement.

V. PRACTICAL PROBLEMS

In addition, several practical problems can be identified in implementing the EPEIS system. The practical problems concern the EPEIS system process, the operational objectives, and the plan of attack.

A. Process

The EPEIS system is an MBO system. As such, notions of *power with* rather than *power over* joint responsibility and multiple leadership are developed. Unless the organization has changed, from a high-threat, low-participation, to a collegial, democratic format,

> . . . the EPEIS system is doomed to failure. Traditionalist Theory X oriented managers are sporadically forced to utilize a participative management style. Conferences with employees will be artificial, one-sided, and counterproductive. Employees will be suspect of managerial motives and will become hostile to the system (Finkle, 1980–1981:62).

Consequently, it is imperative to emphasize that the EPEIS system is a style of management and not exclusively a method of performance evaluation. The central personnel agency has to underscore the concept that EPEIS is a system of management that must coincide with the timely formulation of organizational objectives. In fact, if the EPEIS system is to be successful, two sets of organizational objectives (one long-range set prior to budgeting and the second, short-range, cast after the budget is decided) need to be developed by each department in conjunction with the budgetary agency.

If this process is accomplished, managers will no longer perceive the system as an additional chore but will accept the system as a style of managing. This acceptance will essentially force top management to formulate organizational objectives that will be handed down for allocation and accomplishment to subordinates. In effect, top management support of the program will be automatic.

On the other hand, employee hostility to the program should be reduced because the setting of objectives will take on a meaningful nature. Employees should no longer feel that the setting of objectives is an artificial process designed to exploit their productivity. Instead, employees should view this process as being contributory to the organizational goals, as well as serving to formally include them on their organization's team. The reward that was previously missing should now be the knowledge that they indeed know how they contribute to their organization's output.

B. Operational Objectives

The next major practical problem inherent in the EPEIS system is that the program itself may be evaluated. Although the EPEIS program advocates the establishment of objectives for employees, no statement of goals or objectives for the EPEIS program itself has been articulated. It is fair to conclude that the EPEIS system is a program without a purpose.

> Immediate ameliorative action must be taken. Goals and objectives of the EPEIS program must be set. A method for measuring the progress toward achieving these objectives must be developed. In this way it can be empirically determined whether or not the EPEIS system is accomplishing its stated purpose. If it is not, the appropriate corrective action can be taken. In short, an MBO approach should be utilized to implement an MBO system. In this way, all criticisms of the system can either be sustained as valid or dismissed after being proven empirically inaccurate (Finkle, 1980–1981:62).

C. Plan of Attack

The last practical problem is actually an extension of the lack of EPEIS— program objectives. A plan should be developed after the program objectives are set. Thus, it becomes necessary to formulate the objectives so a plan of attack may be constructed. Once the objectives are set, the central personnel agency should determine what resources are at its disposal to implement the program and then choose the most cost-effective plan. This plan should make some provision for periodic evaluation of progress made toward program goals. It should reflect a causal relationship between a good EPEIS and a salary increase or some other preferment. Indeed, it was not happenstance that federal top and middle management receive their preferments on the basis of their performance appraisal. There should also be a fail-safe system that ensures that a performance appraisal has actually been accomplished. In some departments, the design of the form for a salary increase may actually be part of the EPEIS form so that a person may receive a salary increase only if that person's performance has been evaluated. Another technique is to deny salary increments to those supervisors who do not rate their subordinates. This radical approach is nothing more than communicating that top management supports the performance appraisal system.

D. Limitations of the System

The proposed system is not put forth as the answer to the rating problem. It has a number of limitations:

1. As previously indicated, the emphasis on employee/rater conferences, both at the beginning and at the end of the rating period, inhibits the use of this system in rating persons in a supervisory capacity. However, this is not a serious flaw because a supervisory rating system could be designed.
2. The system relies heavily on competent raters. Raters must be willing to face the persons being rated. Hopefully, the emphasis in this system on objective rating outputs may make it easier for raters to face up to personal contacts. Nevertheless, unless supervisors are willing to use the system properly, it is bound to fail.
3. This system cannot provide objective, quantified performance standards that do not otherwise exist. It might encourage management to give more attention to such standards, by providing them with an additional use; but we know of no automatic way to produce such standards. Nevertheless, we have to crawl before we walk, and hope for results to eventually come with experience.
4. This system will not provide a score of performance that can be mathematically averaged with other tests often used in civil service promotional examinations. How serious a flaw this is will depend on the law in a given jurisdiction. The low weight usually attached to performance evaluations in the typical civil service promotional process would suggest this is not a serious loss.
5. Finally, this system is limited in that research has not been undertaken to establish its value.

E. Benefits

Without attempting to demean these limitations, they can be evaluated only in relation to potential payoffs. Until these payoffs are refuted by empirical evidence, this proposed system offers some benefits not heretofore attainable in a rating system:

1. Focus on outputs instead of inputs not only directs management attention to where it should be, but also it is more likely to be accepted by persons being rated. Many employees want to know where they stand with their bosses (What are my duties, what is my authority, and how am I to be evaluated?) But existing systems rarely tell them. If this system increases their confidence in the rating process by focusing on output, the persons being rated might help to make the system work.

2. As previously indicated, raters may be more comfortable in face-to-face situations, with the focus on outputs rather than on personal qualities. Looked at from the "what-can-you-contribute" perspective, the process takes on a positive and action-oriented managerial perspective.
3. The trend toward objective program standards may be furthered by having an additional use for the process. Evaluation of supervisors is one such additional use. Thus, supervisors will be accountable to policy-makers.

VI. THE FUTURE OF THE EPEIS SYSTEM

Assuming that all or some of these criticisms of the EPEIS system are valid and assuming that the current implementation of the EPEIS system is less than satisfactory, the question to be answered becomes: Can the EPEIS system produce positive results in the future?

The answer to this question largely depends upon the degree to which the practical and theoretical deficiencies are rectified. The introduction of EPEIS in New Jersey State government is certainly a step designed to increase the effectiveness of the public sector. However, it is only the first step. What was introduced thus far has been, for the most part, only a procedure. Most departments and agencies have all the procedures they need—performance is the bottom line.

REFERENCES

Applin, J. C. and Schoderbeck, P. H. (March–April, 1976). How measure MBO. *Public Personnel Management*: 88–95.

Balk, W. L. (March–April, 1975). Technological trends in productivity measurement. *Public Personnel Management*: 178–183.

Finkle, A. L. (Winter, 1980–1981). Avoiding pitfalls in performance appraisal systems. *The Bureaucrat*: 62.

Halley, W. H. and Field, H. S. (July, 1975). Performance appraisal and the law. *Labor Law Journal 26*(7):427.

Heisel, W. D. A new try at performance evaluation. Unpublished, 1977.

Kass, M. P., Woodward, J. P., and Hatry, H. P. (April, 1978). Do employee performance appraisal systems in state and local governments contribute to productivity improvement? Can they? *IPA Project No. H-2162R*. The Urban Institute, Washington, D.C., p. 18.

19

Organizational Training in the 1980s: Refocusing on Building the Capacity of Human Resources

Lyle J. Sumek   Sumek Associates, Inc., Boulder, Colorado

I. INTRODUCTION

With the push for tax limitations on state and local governments, a common response of managers has been that training can no longer be afforded. There have been questions over the commitment of time, diverting of resources from services, and expenditures on training programs. As a result, training programs have been postponed and no new programs initiated in many state and local governments.

Out of this challenge, the training function (including purposes, outcomes, and activities) has been severely questioned and future direction clarified. Training has the potential to be one of the most critical functions within an organization. Organizational training can be defined as an orderly program of activities, focused on developing human resources, resulting in increased capacity of the organization to reach its goals and objectives.

The remainder of this chapter is divided into the following sections: Training Environment in the 1980s; Organization Effectiveness Model: A Guide for Training; Learning Model: A Guide for Adult Development; Manager As Trainer; Traditional Training: Redirection; and, Training: New Frontiers for the 1980s and 1990s.

II. TRAINING ENVIRONMENT IN THE 1980s

In most state and local governments, the training functions in organizations have undergone review and evaluation over the past five years. These activities responded to the changing organizational training environment. Three primary forces appear to be shaping the environment of the 1980s: legacy of cutback management, societal value shifts, and research on organization effectiveness.

A. Legacy of Cutback Management

In response to tax limitation efforts, state and local governments began a process of cutback commonly known as *cutback management* (Kellar, 1979). As public managers searched for areas to cut, training became an obvious choice. As a result, many training programs were reduced or eliminated. The reasons behind the decision to reduce training activities were:

- Training activities were seen as a frivolous expense by many citizens.
- Cutbacks would have a positive symbolic impact with the public.
- The short-term consequences would be minimal—services would continue to be delivered.
- Positive reaction of employees, since training may be perceived as a personal threat.

Beyond the immediate cutbacks, many state and local governments continue with minimal training programs without understanding the consequences. The attitude toward training has gone from cutback management to "anorexia" management. Hence, state and local governments are reducing their internal capacity to provide a well-managed organization that effectively provides public services and programs.

B. Societal Value Shifts

Within the United States, there appears to be a significant shift in societal values (Yankelovich, 1981; Naisbitt, 1982). Five prominent value shifts appear to have a direct impact on training.

1. Decline in Work Ethic

No longer do employees believe that if they work harder they will be rewarded. Thus, there is an emerging attitude among many employees to perform in a minimal manner to survive in the organization. There is no longer the belief that "hard work always pays off."

2. Definition of Success

In the past, success has been associated with one's work life. However, today individuals are placing more emphasis on success in their whole life, including roles as spouse and parent. This has drastic effects on what individuals may want out of their career or what they define as success.

3. "I" Centered

Within our culture there appears to be significant emphasis placed on self-fulfillment. In an organization, this means that an individual may place personal needs and goals above the organization's goals. This can result in less loyalty and commitment to the organization.

4. Need for Commitment

Individuals appear to be demonstrating a need for connectedness within their world. Increased emphasis is placed on building commitments among each other. These commitments are likely to endure over time. This can conflict with the "I" orientation.

5. Need for Participation

There is growing evidence of the desire for increased influence in organizational decision-making.

These value shifts have been a contributing force in redefining organizational training in most state and local governments. More emphasis on training is being placed on the total human resources of the organization, not just concern about the work life of an employee.

C. Research on Organization Effectiveness

During the recent past, a number of researchers have written on organizational effectiveness (Deal and Kennedy, 1982; Pascale and Anthos, 1980; Peters and Waterman, 1982). Many studies have been completed comparing United States with Japanese corporations, and effective with ineffective corporations. Several key ideas from this research were presented that directly affect training.

1. Importance of Invisible

In *The Art of Japanese Management: Applications for American Executives*, Richard Pascale and Anthony Anthos (1981) presented a "Seven S's" framework for organizational effectiveness. They identified seven basic factors.

Strategy. Emphasis is placed on planning a course of action leading to the allocation of an organization's resources over time to reach an identified goal, tactics, and competitiveness.

Structure. Emphasis is placed on the development of an organization chart that reflects the linkages among the organizational actors and functions.

Systems. Emphasis is placed upon predictability and control that provides a framework for individual responsibilities within an organization, and on procedure and policy manuals.

Style. Emphasis is placed upon the management symbols and rewards.

Skills. Emphasis is placed upon distinctive abilities of key organizational personnel and learning change.

Staffing. Emphasis is placed upon the development and use of human resources within an organization, stressing the linkage of the individual and the organization.

Superordinate Goal. The driving force in the organization that provides meaning, distinguishes the organization, and provides concepts that guide the future direction.

Most state and local governments place emphasis on structure, systems, and strategies. These are the most visible and tangible evidence of organizational activities ties. Little emphasis is placed on style, skills, and staffing, which are more spiritually oriented. Many organizations have failed due to the lack of a superordinate goal or the integration of all seven S's.

2. Importance of Culture

Every organization has a culture that reflects a set of managerial values and presents expectations to employees (Deal and Kennedy, 1982). In most organizations, these values and the culture are not written down, but are reflected in the norms developed by individual employees through their observations of managers' behaviors and actions. These behaviors and actions become the foundation for managerial values expectations and form the overall organization philosophy. An individual or an organization will benefit from developing a written statement that will serve as a guidepost for future management and operations. This written statement becomes the organization's philosophy statement.

The characteristics of an effective organization philosophy statement are that it be brief, understood by all, focus on important areas, link management and daily operations, lay a foundation for creating and modifying norms, and provide guidance to individual supervisors.

The importance of an organization philosophy statement is based upon the following ideas:

- The organization philosophy statement sets forth values, thus creating an organization culture and set of norms.
- Values and beliefs are the foundation for an organization culture.
- Strong organization cultures improve organization effectiveness.
- Cultures set norms and informal rules guiding employee behaviors and actions.
- Cultures enable people to feel better about what they are doing.

- Processes in developing an organization's philosophy statement provide an opportunity for management to create norms and build consensus regarding individual actions within the organization.
- Values provide future direction.
- The organization philosophy statement provides the foundation for individual choice.

The training function is critical for developing a strong organizational culture. As a result, the definition of organization training has been expanded in many state and local governments to include imprinting of organizational values.

These value shifts call for a new foundation for training in state and local governments. It can be seen as a combination of organization effectiveness and a learning model.

III. ORGANIZATION EFFECTIVENESS MODEL: A GUIDE FOR TRAINING

In the past, training has focused on meeting the organization's needs. The process begins with an assessment of knowledge and skill needs and the provision of programs to address these needs. In general, state and local governments placed no emphasis on the organization values of culture. In light of the changing environment, there is a need for a more thorough integration of training and organizational effectiveness.

To better understand the concept of organization effectiveness, a visual diagram is presented in Fig. 1. The model consists of five elements (Pascale and Anthos, 1982):

- *Management values and expectations*: the fundamental beliefs about how the organization should be managed
- *Organization philosophy*: the integration of the management values and expectations into a set of norms that guide individual behavior on a daily basis and become management processes
- *Management processes*: the processes of communication, decision-making, leadership, planning, evaluation, monitoring and controlling, and employee development that support and assist in the translating of the management values and philosophy into reality
- *Management skills*: those skills necessary to get the management processes working consistently with the underlying values and philosophy
- *Management evaluation*: links individual manager's actions and behavior to the organization philosophy

As a result of this model, the driving force in guiding the training program will be the organization philosophy. Training becomes a process for translating the values into reality.

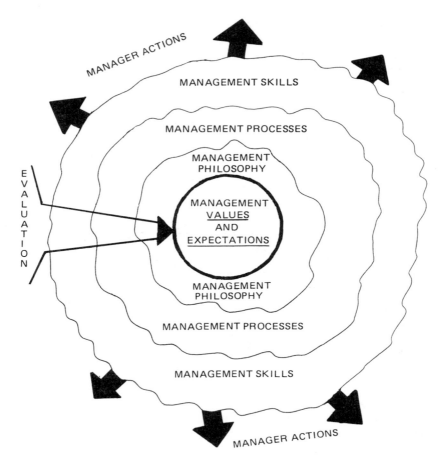

Fig. 1 Organization effectiveness model.

The following guiding principles are based upon this model:

- Every manager serves as trainer, building the capacity of the organization to be guided by the organization values.
- Importance of strong values focused in an organization philosophy statement.
- Importance of evaluation, assessing behavior in light of values.
- Hiring individuals for their capacity, not for their current skill level.
- Emphasis on each individual as a human resource rather than with needs and expectations.
- Importance of process—how things get done.

If state and local governments do not have a strong organization philosophy, the training programs are not likely to have a strong direction.

IV. LEARNING MODEL: A GUIDE FOR ADULT DEVELOPMENT

Learning is changing an individual's behavior as a result of an experience. This definition of learning carries with it a number of implications.

- Knowing a new concept, one that was not known
- Being able to do something, behavior or skill, that one was unable to do before
- Being able to use or apply a combination of skills, knowledge, concepts, or behavior
- Being able to understand and apply skill, knowledge, or behavior

The conditions for effective adult learning are characterized by the following:

- Acceptance that all human beings can learn: individuals of all ages are capable of learning.
- Individual's must be motivated to learn. The learner must be self-motivated, and the trainer must motivate the learner through an effective learning climate.
- Learning is an active process, not a passive one.
- Learner must have guidance, an ongoing process of feedback.
- Time must be provided to practice the learning. Linkages must be made between training and daily operations.
- Learning methods should be varied to avoid boredom. Individuals have different learning styles.
- Learner must gain personal satisfaction from the learning experience.
- Learner must receive reinforcement of correct behavior.

There are four basic realities of adult learning that will affect any training process. First, every individual has a choice of whether to belong to an organization and pursue a specific career. This choice is tested on a daily basis through the individual's every decision and action. Today, most individuals are faced with multiple options regarding their careers.

Second, individuals create their own lives daily by their decisions and actions. Each individual lays a foundation of his or her future life. As a manager, decisions and actions affect the lives of others.

Third, individuals structure their own lives around a key set of values and beliefs. Most of the time, an individual does not reflect and focus on what those value choices are. How individuals spend their time provides a reflection of personal values.

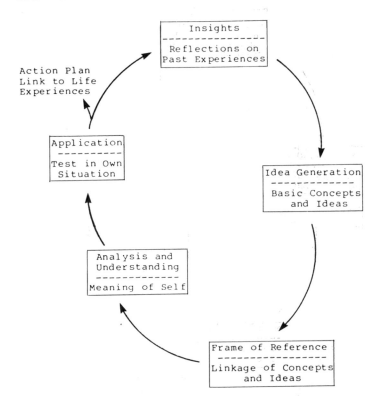

Fig. 2 Training model.

Finally, individuals can only control their own behaviors and actions. Managers cannot control the behaviors of others, but serve only as an influencing force.

In reviewing the literature on adult learning, there appears to be an integrating learning model that can provide insights into training. A summary of this model can be found as Fig. 2. The five steps to the model can best be described in the following sections.

A. Step 1: Insights

The past experiences of an individual provide the foundation for effective adult learning. The initial learning experience should provide an opportunity for individuals to reflect on their past experiences, past performances, and the experiences of others. It is aimed at trying to provide a new perspective for looking at one's own life experiences.

B. Step 2: Idea Generation

The insights and reflections of an individual are linked together to generate new ideas. In addition, the trainer may provide additional new concepts, linking the concepts to the individual insights. The learning process begins by having individuals generate their own ideas based on their insights, followed by presentation of new, alternative concepts.

C. Step 3: Framework for Understanding

The ideas and concepts are linked into an overall conceptual framework. The framework links the various concepts based upon individual insights. An integrated, systematic model is provided for understanding the frustrations and providing a basis for improving personal effectiveness. The framework needs to link to the individual insights, as well as the ideas and concepts.

D. Step 4: Analysis and Understanding

The concepts and framework are analyzed with emphasis on, "What does it mean for me?" It provides linkage of the concepts to real-life situations currently encountered by the individual. The learning experience provides an opportunity to link the new framework to current life situations.

E. Step 5: Application

The individual is provided an opportunity to use the conceptual framework and skills in daily situations. The key idea is to test out the concept, skill, or frame of reference in one's own situation. The learning experience may focus on development of action plans for increasing personal effectiveness through the application of the concepts, skills, and framework.

In summary, the learning model integrates personal experiences with the development of actions for increasing personal effectiveness as an individual. For effective adult learning, there must be an understanding of the concepts, applications of the concepts, and demonstrated use of the concepts.

Another way of looking at adult learning is to identify three common elements: acquisition of knowledge; development of skills; and, understanding values and ideas (Adler, 1982). Each goal element can be linked with different learning modes.

1. Acquisition of knowledge is most effectively accomplished through lecture and reading.
2. Development of skills is most effectively accomplished through experiential learning, mentoring and coaching, and problem-solving exercises.
3. Understanding values and ideas is most effectively accomplished through questioning, participation, and demonstration.

The implications of the learning model for training in state and local governments are:

- Adult learning is a continuous, recurring cycle in which people continually test concepts and experiences and modify them as a result of their observations of those experiences.
- All learning is relearning; all education is reeducation.
- The direction for learning is governed by one's felt needs and goals.
- The learning process is erratic and inefficient when objectives and values are not clear.
- Individual learning styles may vary from individual to individual.

The manager plays a key role in facilitating a learning process for every employee.

V. MANAGER AS TRAINER

Every manager in a state or local government is a trainer. Management is getting a task done through others, and is aimed at achieving the organization's goal. Organization training is building the capacity of the human resources to meet organization goals. Therefore, through deductive reasoning, management becomes organization training. However, most managers do not see themselves as trainers, but prefer training be done by the personnel department. If a training program is to be successful, it is critical for each manager to recognize the strong linkage between the role of manager and that of trainer.

Most managers have not thoroughly thought about what it means to be an effective manager or trainer. In reviewing the literature on managerial effectiveness, there appear to be ten critical factors.

First, the managers must ask if they want to manage others. Managing others entails the following characteristics:

- Desire to influence the performance of other individuals
- Desire to get the job done through others rather than own personal performance
- Desire to develop and stimulate actions in others
- Desire to take responsibility for actions of self and others

Managing entails building the capacity of others to accomplish their job task and contributing to the achievement of organizational goals.

Second, managers must desire power. Power involves the act of influencing. An effective manager is also one who is willing to share power. Power also includes inspiring others toward a common goal and set of values.

Third, managers must have the capacity for empathy. Managing means caring for others, dealing with emotions and feelings, building effective work relationships, being sensitive to others, and a willingness to look at the process (i.e., how things are done).

Fourth, managers must have knowledge of self. The critical factors here are:

- An understanding of one's management style and values
- Consistency of behavioral actions and words
- Desire for feedback from others
- Understanding of own readiness to become a manager
- Understanding of personal strengths and weaknesses

Fifth, managers must be willing to learn. Learning does not just come from a teacher; in fact, managers may learn as much from subordinates. An effective manager is one who has a strong desire to learn, a willingness to learn from others regardless of position in the organization, a desire to develop self as a whole person, and a willingness to view problems not as crisis but as learning opportunities. As a result, the manager will promote learning of others.

Sixth, managers must have a vision of the future. To provide leadership, managers must provide direction not only in organizational goals, but also organization values guiding individual behaviors. This, at times, may mean mobilizing resources to achieve a goal.

Seventh, managers must be willing to ask for help. If a manager is to be effective, he must be willing to recognize his or her own weaknesses and seek help from others. If a manager is unwilling to seek help from others, subordinates are less likely to seek help from their managers. The personal effectiveness of the manager is dependent upon the actions of others.

Eighth, managers must have a tolerance for ambiguity. Not all situations will have well-defined answers or problems. As a result, an effective manager is one who has flexibility, a willingness to deal with uncertain situations, and a willingness to tolerate ambiguity.

Ninth, managers must recognize they imprint values on others. The key definer of organization values for an employee is the immediate supervisor. Managers create organizational norms and shape the behavior of others.

Tenth, managers must recognize the interdependence of their actions and the actions of others. If a task is going to be accomplished within a state or local government, it will require the teamwork of a variety of individuals with differing skills and perspectives. A key role of the manager is to build a sense of "we" (i.e., togetherness). This may mean promoting the interrelationships between individual activities. If an organization is to be effective as a team, it will only be as strong as its weakest link.

As we look to training in the 1980s, managers play a critical role in determining the success of these activities. For every state and local government, the immediate challenge is building the capacity of each manager as a trainer.

VI. TRADITIONAL TRAINING: REDIRECTION

Within state and local governments, training has traditionally focused on developing and refining individuals' skills in their current job. The training function has focused on identifying training resources, assessing organization and individual needs, and, brokering of training programs throughout the organization, assessing organization and individual needs. Training was approached by larger organizations through in-house programs, whereas smaller public agencies relied on community or technical colleges, professional associations, municipal leagues, colleges and universities, and private consultants.

In light of the organization effectiveness model, many state and local governments are redirecting their traditional training programs. The redirected training programs are characterized by:

- *Evaluation of training impact*: The impact of traditional training programs is being evaluated in light of the organizational values, program effectiveness, and changes in participants.
- *Blending of cognitive and affective learning*: The training programs focus not only on the cognitive understanding of individuals, but on the feelings generated by the individual and behavioral change.
- *Variety of training methods*:   Training programs utilize a greater range of learning methods, including lecture, experiential exercises, modeling, and application through problem-solving.
- *Building in-house capacity*: Instead of relying on other institutions to provide training resources, state and local agencies are adapting training resources for direct application in their organizations, increasing the likelihood of direction relevance for participants.

There are five key traditional areas of training: Orientation programs, technical training, management and supervisor training, team building, and personal growth.

A. Orientation Programs

When employees first enter a state or local government, they have a strong need to become acclimated to the organization. The primary objectives of an orientation program are to acquaint employees with the organization's policies and procedures and to provide understanding of the expectations for all employees. The traditional approach tends to focus on the following topics:

- Organizational goals and objectives
- Organization rules and regulations
- Organization programs and activities
- Historical background on governmental body
- Initial skills in dealing with public

In addition to the entry orientation program, state and local governments hold orientation or briefing sessions for employees on specific topics. For example, if the budgeting process is being modified, a common practice is for all employees involved in the budgeting process to go through a program orienting them on the desired outcomes of the new budgeting process, reviewing the budgeting procedures, and building skills in the new process.

Orientation programs are now being redirected, with greater emphasis being placed on the values and beliefs of the organization. Initial orientation programs now include a review of the organization philosophy that guides all employees in their daily activities. Follow-up sessions are usually held within a particular department, focusing on the meaning of the organization philosophy for departmental programs, activities, and employee behavior.

B. Technical Training

As might be expected, the primary objective of technical training is developing employee technical skills. Professional organizations and community colleges have played a significant role in developing courses in technical areas. For example, the American Public Works Association provides a number of regional seminars aimed at developing skills in such areas as waste water management, street maintenance, and traffic flow analysis.

The traditional focus of technical training begins with providing knowledge and understanding of the concepts. Specific skills are then developed within a classroom setting and tested through on-the-job training, linking the training to the assigned job duties of the employee.

As technologies change, greater emphasis has been placed on on-the-job training. Traditionally, a manager or supervisor would conduct the training through films, video cassettes, programmed instruction, and problem-solving exercises.

Due to technological change, the technical skills for many employees have a very limited life span. For example, in the clerical area during the last five years, offices have shifted emphasis from typing to word processing.

The redirection of technical training is on continued retraining of employees as technology changes. Training programs then become an ongoing process within the organization, emphasizing the upgrading of employee skills. In most positions, employees can no longer say that they will be doing the same tasks and using the same skills ten years in the future.

C. Management and Supervisory Training

The traditional focus of management and supervisory training is on building the generic skills in management and supervision. The focus has been on the following topics:

- Leadership skills
- Communications
- Planning and work scheduling
- Monitoring employee performance
- Personnel practices
- Budgeting skills
- Meaning of supervision and management

For many managers in state and local governments, becoming a manager involves a transition from technician to manager.

The redirection of management supervisory training places greater emphasis on individual choice: Do I really want to be a manager? Individual managers, through training sessions and individual counseling, explore the meaning and consequences of being a manager. The focus is on the expectations, changes in relationships with employees, and individual accountability.

The redirected training programs include the following topics:

- Employee counseling
- Career and life planning
- Personal management philosophy
- Team skills
- Evaluation and feedback skills

Because every state and local government has its own culture, there is no one program for management and supervisory training that can be brought into the agency. These governments are building their own in-house capacity through developing training resources that reflect the organization's values and direction, and also through building the capacity of individual managers as trainers.

D. Team Building

Traditionally, team building has been considered part of an organization development program. Most state and local governments have undergone some type of team-building program since the mid-1960s. The primary objective of such programs was to increase understanding of self and build work relationships with others. These programs tended to rely on outside consultants. The primary approaches for team building were:

- Diagnosis of organizational health
- Use of personal style inventories such as the FIRO-B, Thomas-Kilmann Conflict Mode Instrument, and others
- Retreats aimed at building relations and addressing organizational problems
- Intervention sessions aimed at building relationships between individual employees

For many governments, the primary pitfall of these programs was the limited impact on the organization.

The redirected team-building programs emphasize developing a process to support the organization's philosophy. The organization philosophy provides the direction for the team-building activities. Many of the same approaches are included, but the outcomes have changed as well as the focus.

E. Personal Growth Seminars

Within our society, emphasis has been placed on personal growth seminars. The primary purposes of these seminars are increasing understanding of self and building interpersonal skills. The primary focus is on enhancing abilities as an individual and as an employee of a state or local government.

Personal growth seminars are generally offered by nonprofit foundations and private consultants. One of the most popular seminars is offered by the Menninger Foundation. Titled "Toward Understanding Human Behavior and Motivation," it has been offered for government executives at the state and local level for many years.

In addition, a number of organizations offer seminars on specific topics, including conflict management, assertiveness training, time management, and other topics aimed at improving personal effectiveness. Traditionally, a state or local government would send their employees to the session off site. The primary pitfall has been the weak linkage back to daily personal activities and to their immediate supervisor. As a result, expectations were developed during the seminars that cannot be fulfilled by the organization.

The redirected personal growth seminars place greater emphasis on a holistic approach, which involves career and life planning as well as the linkage of the individual with the employing agency. State and local governments are expanding their use of seminars such as the one offered by the Menninger Foundation by allowing not only managers to attend, but other employees.

A brief summary of traditional training programs and approaches has been done by Gerald Brown (1974). State and local governments appear to be refining their use of traditional approaches and adapting these programs to meet their own individual needs.

VII. TRAINING: NEW FRONTIERS FOR THE 1980s AND 1990s

State and local governments are now building their training capacity to meet the challenges of the 1980s and 1990s. To respond to the public demands for services and programs, greater emphasis is being placed on building the total capacity of the organization and translating the organization philosophy into a reality for every employee.

Six new training frontiers provide opportunities for state and local governments including: elected officials training; value clarification of the organization philosophy; mentoring and coaching; career and life planning; wellness programs; and, involvement and participation programs for employees.

A. Elected Officials Training

Today, the job of an elected official is an extremely difficult one. In the past, the governance processes were simple, problems could be addressed by the governmental body, and officials received positive recognition. However, times are changing. The job of an elected official is an extremely difficult one requiring improved governance process, teamwork between elected officials and staff, a reexamination of roles and relationships, and quality leadership with a vision of the future. Few resources were expended to train elected officials. Thus, most elected officials in state and local government have not taken the necessary steps to build their understanding and skills of the governance process.

Theodore Lowi and others have concluded that most state and local governments are well managed, but poorly governed (Lowi, 1969).

Governance is a process for (Neu and Sumek, 1982):

- Developing a vision of the future
- Setting direction and goals
- Anticipating issues
- Focusing and solving problems
- Providing a policy framework and guidelines for services and programs
- Monitoring staff performance in carrying out programs
- Mobilizing support for the governmental body
- Inspiring others to become part of government

Thus, the first new training frontier is to include elected officials in training activities which build their capacity in handling the governance process. The primary objectives are: To build a frame of reference for understanding governance, negotiate roles and relationships between the governing body and staff; develop a vision of the future providing direction for the governmental body; build specific skills necessary for effective governance, and to address specific issues hampering the governance process.

At the state level, the Conference of State Legislatures has developed a series of programs for building the skills of state legislators. Within the state of Colorado there are training programs for committee chairs as well as for new legislators.

At the local level, the Kettering Foundation funded two projects for evaluating the training of local elected officials. These studies showed the primary barriers to effectiveness were:

- Lack of understanding of what it means to govern a city
- Tendency to avoid controversial issues and conflict
- Lack of small group decision-making skills
- Unwillingness to commit time to develop own skills as a governing body
- Confusion of leadership (a vision of the future) with management (implementation of programs)
- Emphasis on responsiveness (responding to individual pressures) versus responsibility (a sense of what is "best" for the community)
- Failure to distinguish the process (how an issue is handled) from results (what happened to the issue) (Burks and Wolf, 1981; Neu and Sumek, 1982)

As a result, many council meetings are characterized by the press as the "best show in town," or "Monday night at the fights."

Municipal leagues in Maryland, Florida, Kansas, Michigan, Texas, Minnesota, Oregon, Colorado, and California have begun to devote some energy to the development of local elected officials. In addition, a number of cities and counties are responding to this opportunity for using consultants in developing programs to meet their individual needs. The Government Leadership Institute has developed a series of programs using videotapes, experiential learning tools, and slide sound presentations for use by counties and cities. The best time for training of an elected body is during its infancy. This is generally six months after the election. Training is not likely to have a positive impact if it is done during the survival period (prior to the election) or during the legacy period (after the election).

The primary topics for the training programs are:

- Goal setting
- Elected official-staff relations
- Roles and relationships
- Leadership: vision of the future
- Meeting effectiveness
- Conflict resolution
- Performance evaluation of our government

B. Value Clarification of the Organization Philosophy

In most state and local governments, the organization philosophy may reflect value shifts within the organizations. Managers have a key role of imprinting the organization values with all employees. The new training frontier is to clarify the organization values and to provide an opportunity for value shifts.

Over the centuries, philosophers have been searching for a definition of values. Values can be defined as beliefs that individuals hold dear to their hearts. As Morrie Smith pointed out: "We are not born with values, but we are born into cultures and societies that promote, teach, and impart their values to us" (Smith, 1977). Throughout life, individuals' values are a process of continual change. For example, an employee may value security at one point in time during his career and retirement at another point. Within most organizations, there is no organization philosophy statement. As a result, employees may see value changes occurring rapidly and become confused about the validity of any particular set of values. Values are formed by a process that integrates one's feelings, thoughts, desires, actions, and needs.

In guiding the value clarification of the organization philosophy, there are eight underlying assumptions. These are that a value:

- must be freely chosen
- must be chosen from alternatives
- must be chosen after considering the consequences
- must be performed
- becomes a pattern of life
- is cherished
- is publicly affirmed
- enhances the person's total growth

Reading and understanding of an organization philosophy statement is not sufficient for the values must be translated into behavioral actions of every employee.

The value clarification process begins with each individual manager preparing a personal philosophy statement. The individual philosophies are then integrated into an organizational philosophy that is shared throughout. Depending upon the values, managers and supervisors need to develop skills and refine organizational processes that support the fundamental values. Their behavior will imprint values on employees. The training activities are likely to be done in individual and small group sessions and not as part of a formalized training program. As a result of the activities, the desired outcome of the value clarification is the development of a consistent set of values as reflected in the employee actions throughout the state or local government. As the organization size increases, the difficulty in this training program increases.

C. Mentoring and Coaching

The capacity-building process is dependent upon the coaching and mentoring done by managers.

The frontier is building managers as coaches and mentors, but most organizations do not effectively distinguish between the two processes.

Mentoring is defined as shaping another individual's behavior through personal influence and power. The mentoring process is characterized by the following:

1. Informality in the relations: The mentoring process is a formally structured set of experiences.
2. Taking advantage of the moment: Builds off the daily experiences of an individual.
3. Based on personal relationships: Effective personal relationships exist between individuals.
4. Sexual bias: Mentors are usually along sexual lines (a man to a man; a woman to a woman).
5. Modeling values and behavior: Mentors provide models to individuals regarding linkages of values and behavior.
6. Transitional mentors versus permanent mentors: Many mentors may be a transitional figure in an individual's life and may serve for only a limited amount of time. Other individuals may be long-term or permanent mentors, in which a relationship is sustained over a number of years.
7. Supports independence, not dependence: Mentors enhance a feeling of self-confidence in others.
8. Voluntary: Mentoring process is a voluntary one. An individual cannot say "I am going to be your mentor."
9. Dependent upon life cycle: Depending on your life cycle, mentors may vary according to your personal needs.
10. Respond to individual needs: Mentoring relationships are based upon the needs of the individual not of the mentor.

Mentors serve the following functions:

- Imprint values
- Enhance skills
- Use influence to facilitate growth in others
- Provide moral support in time of stress
- Set examples to be emulated
- Facilitate entry into an organization
- Support and facilitate realization of "dreams"
- Help others define self

An effective mentor is going to be seen by the individual as:

- Admired
- Respected
- Appreciated
- Loved

An effective mentor is one who recognizes the evolutionary process of mentoring.

In linking the mentoring process to power styles, certain power styles are more conducive to a mentoring approach. An individual who emphasizes information power, expert power, and goodwill power is inclined toward a mentoring approach in dealing with subordinates.

Coaching is defined as the desire to help and improve the performance of others. The basis for coaching is to assess the performance of individuals and work with them in developing a program for removing any deficiencies. At the end of the learning experience, rewards or discipline may occur. The coaching process is characterized by the following:

1. Formality: Structured experiences are provided to build an individual's understanding of concepts or skills. It is based upon the relationships within the organization.
2. Structured program: A game plan is developed for coaching the individual.
3. Job related: The coaching activities are related to job performance and not to an individual as a whole.
4. Use of discipline and rewards: Effective coaching will involve the use of both discipline and reward.
5. Guidance-advice-direction: A coach will provide specific guidance to an individual, provide advice on specific activities, and provide direction for overcoming any performance deficiencies.
6. Task oriented: Coaching is oriented at specific tasks within the organization.
7. Cognitive orientation: Coaching is aimed at building an understanding of the concepts by individuals. Importance is placed on developing a frame of reference.
8. Coaching cycle: There is a cycle in coaching in which the individual is initially dependent upon the coach, moves to rejecting the coach's advice (counterdependence), and recognizes the interdependence of the coach and the individual (interdependence).
9. Involuntary: A coaching relationship is not necessarily a voluntary one. If there are performance deficiencies, the manager may assume the responsibilities of coaching the individual to overcome the deficiencies.
10. Temporary coaches: All coaching relationships are temporary. As an individual grows and develops, he may have a series of coaches.

The primary functions of a coach are:

- To assess performance of others
- Develop a game plan for overcoming deficiencies
- Participate in the various activities in the game plan
- Monitor the personal actions of the individual in carrying out the game plan
- Provide help and support to the individual as he or she develops as an individual

An effective coach is one who:

- Listens to the emotions as well as the facts of others
- Expects and is prepared to hear negative comments
- Develops understanding of others
- Provides meaningful feedback to the others
- Encourages release of pressure
- Provides a supportive atmosphere to the individual

The frontier becomes the turning of managers into mentors or coaches. Some individuals are better coaches, while others are better mentors. It would be difficult to imagine Bobby Knight, basketball coach for Indiana University as a mentor, although he is an extremely effective coach.

D. Career and Life Planning

In the past, state and local governments have placed little emphasis on career planning for employees, a fourth frontier. If any planning was done, it was at the initiative of the employee. Outside seminars have been provided to assist in the career and life planning process. However, in most organizations, there has been minimal success in integrating career and life planning processes into the organizational setting.

Career and life planning places emphasis on integrating the various elements of an individual's life. From Richard Bolles' perspective, there are three basic boxes to life: A work life, an organization life, and a personal life. An effective career and life planning process attempts to integrate all three life boxes (Bolles, 1978).

Career and life planning is aimed at focusing the expectations of the individual and the development of plans for realizing those expectations. The process consists of the following steps:

- Reflection on life and organizational experiences
- Clarification of individual values
- Assessing individual's knowledge areas and skills
- Focusing of expectations from the organization, family, and self
- Development of specific action steps to fulfill expectations

The key problems associated with career and life planning are (Montana and Higginson, 1978):

- Unfocused personal expectations
- Unrealistic assessment of self
- Lack of opportunities for personal growth
- Ineffective support systems from other individuals, including supervisor
- Mismanagement of our lives
- Personal resistance to change

The key to success in overcoming these obstacles is the counseling and training provided by managers and supervisors. The training activities focus more on one-on-one interactions with the individual, rather than on a formal training session.

Integrating individual career and life plans can provide a basis for traditional training activities. For example, if a common need has been identified, a formal training program can be developed. In addition, an experiment in the Portland Fire Bureau has resulted in the development of master career path charts. The career paths of individuals are linked to the Comprehensive Training Program (Marshall et al., 1983). Other organizations are finding ways of using the career and life planning process to link human resources to the organization's programs and activities.

D. Wellness Program

Over the last several years, increased emphasis has been placed on the organization's responsibilities for the whole individual. In the past, state and local governments have focused most of their training attention on the work life of the employees, neglecting the other 128 hours in a week.

Wellness programs have resulted from the accumulation of research on executive health and stress. The initial focus of this new frontier was on burnout. Burnout has been defined by Veninga and Spradley (1981) as the debilitating psychological condition brought about by unrelieved work stress. The primary factors creating burnout are (Veninga and Spradley (1981):

- Ineffective career planning
- Ineffective measurements of success
- Unfulfilled promises or commitments
- No time for self and others
- Lack of understanding of self-limitations
- Family pressures
- No support systems
- No relaxation

The most effective way of dealing with burnout is to take a preventive approach.

State and local governments have placed increased emphasis on wellness. The primary objectives of a wellness program are (Plymann and Perkins, 1983):

- To document personal health and fitness
- To prevent rather than cure illness
- To convince people they are in control of their own lives
- To foster positive lifestyle changes

For people in public safety professions such as fire and police, a number of cities are initiating wellness programs. These include physicals as well as courses that support the objectives of wellness. Within the organization, the training strategies may include:

- Physical fitness training
- Training on nutrition
- Personal counseling

The primary training activities focus on changing behaviors to prevent illness. In a survey conducted by HRI, a nonprofit organization in California, it found that, in 1981, companies had an average annual expenditure for annual health-care cost per employee of $1015. Companies with wellness programs, however, had an average cost of $806, a savings of $209 per employee. These figures do not include the benefits from reduced use of sick leave and increased employee productivity.

E. Involvement in Participation Programs for Employees

Within organizations today, employees are placing greater emphasis on involvement and participation. However, in attempting to cope with this change, many state and local governments have gone to using quality circles as a strategy for meaningful involvement and participation. Other organizations have increased their use of employee task forces for providing opportunities for meaningful participation.

The primary goal of increased involvement and participation is to tap the resources of the organization in solving problems and to develop and enhance commitment to the organization by generating a feeling of importance. Employees begin to feel that their actions really do make a difference. In most organizations, employees are given a problem and asked to analyze the problem and present recommendations. However, efforts at increasing employee involvement and participation have encountered significant obstacles. The primary obstacles appear to be:

- Lack of receptive attitude by management
- Unclear expectations of managers and employees
- Lack of employee skills in group problem-solving and conflict resolution
- Ineffective evaluation of activities
- Lack of participatory value by managers

The new training frontier is two-pronged. First, there is a need to develop the skills of employees in conflict resolution, group decision-making, and group problem-solving. The training activities could be simultaneous, with the work group's activity or task completed prior to being given a problem.

Second, managers need to develop skills in allowing employee participation. At a personal level, it may mean building their personal security as a manager, increasing receptivity to employees' ideas and the value of participation. It also may mean developing the interpersonal skills necessary to develop trusting relationships between employees. If state and local governments have an emphasis on participation, there is a need to develop a frame of reference and the skills necessary to ensure the effectiveness of involvement and participation.

In summary, there are a number of opportunities for new training frontiers in state and local governments. This chapter attempts to highlight six current frontiers. No single state or local government is likely to address all six areas. In addition, there are no well-defined programs or activities, but rather individual agencies experimenting with alternative training approaches.

ACKNOWLEDGMENTS

I am deeply indebted to the discussions and stimulation from two colleagues, Carl Neu of Neu and Company (and The Government Leadership Institute) and Gary Pokorny, City Manager, Corvallis, Oregon.

REFERENCES

Adler, M. J. (1982). *The Paideia Proposal: An Educational Manifesto*. Macmillan, New York.

Blake, R. R. and Mouton, J. S. (1981). *Productivity: The Human Side*. Amacom, New York.

Bolles, R. N. (1978). *The Three Boxes of Life*. Ten Speed Press, Berkeley.

Bolles, R. N. (1978). *What Color Is Your Parachute?* Ten Speed Press, Berkeley.

Brown, F. (1974). Training. In Powers, S. P., Brown, F. G., and D. S. Arnold, eds., *Developing the Municipal Organization*. International City Management Association, New York, pp. 160–173.

Burdick, G. R. (1983). Wellness: A holistic approach to well being. *Public Management 65*:13–16.

Burks, S. W. and Wolf, J. R. (1981). *Building City Council Leadership Skills*. National League of Cities, Washington, D.C.

Deal, T. E. and Kennedy, A. A. (1982). *Corporate Cultures: The Rites and Rituals of Corporate Life*. Addison-Wesley, Reading, Mass.

Dolgoff, T. (1975). *Towards Understanding Morale*. Menninger Foundation, Topeka, Kan.

Dyer, W. G. (1972). *Team Building: Issues and Alternatives*. Addison-Wesley, Reading, Mass.

Fitzgerald, L. and Murphy, J. (1982). *Installing Quality Circles: A Strategic Approach*. University Associates, San Diego.

Fournies, F. F. (1978). *Coaching for Improved Work Performance*. Van Nostrand Reinhold, New York.

Kellar, E., ed. (1979). *Managing with Less*. International City Management Association, Washington, D.C.

Kirkpatrick, D. L. (1982). *How to Improve Performance Through Appraisal and Coaching*. Amacom, New York.

Levinson, D. J. (1978). *The Seasons of a Man's Life*. Ballantine, New York.

Lowi, T. J. (1969). *The End of Liberation*. W. W. Norton, New York.

Marshall, J., O'Toole, D. E., and Sargant, F. (1983). A visual approach to training plan development. *Public Administration Review 43*:166–175.

Montana, P. J. and Higginson, M. V. (1978). *Career Planning for Americans*. Amacom, New York.

Naisbitt, J. (1982). *Megatrends*. Warner, New York.

Neu, C. H. and Sumek, L. J. (1981). *Goal Setting for Municipal Leadership*. The Government Leadership Institute, Boulder, Colo.

Neu, C. H. and Sumek, L. J. (1982). *Governance Challenge of the 1980's*. Copyrighted by The Government Leadership Institute, Boulder, Colo., Various municipal league publications.

Neu, C. H. and Sumek, L. J. (1982). *Governance Crisis: The Collapse of Urban America*. Manuscript. Report prepared for Kettering Foundation.

Neu, C. H. and Sumek, L. J. (1982). *Municipal Leadership: Current Trends and Implications*. Copyrighted by The Government Leadership Institute, Boulder, Colo. Various municipal league publications.

Pascale, R. T. and Anthos, A. G. (1981). *The Art of Japanese Management: Applications for American Executives*. Warner, New York.

Peters, T. J. and Waterman, Jr., R. H. (1982). *In Search of Excellence*. Harper & Row, New York.

Plyman, J. S. and Perkins, L. D. (1983). Fitness monitoring. *Public Management 65*:6–9.

Pokorny, G. F. (1981). Training—why bother in an environment of increasing demands and drastically reduced resources? *State and Local Government Review 13*:47–51.

Rogers, C. R. (1969). *Freedom to Learn*. Charles E. Merrill, Columbus, Oh.

Schein, E. H. (1969). *Process Consultation*. Addison-Wesley, Reading, Mass.

Schon, D. A. (1971). *Beyond the Stable State*. Random House, New York.

Selye, H. (1974). *Stress without Distress*. J. B. Lippincott, Philadelphia.

Souerwine, A. H. (1978). *Career Strategies: Planning for Personal Achievement*. Amacom, New York.

Smith, M. (1977). *A Practical Guide to Value Clarification*. University Associates, San Diego.

Sumek, L. J. (1980). Human resource management in the future. In Johnston, R. V., ed., *Training for the 1980's and Beyond*. International Personnel Management Association, Denver.

Sumek, L. J. (1978). Organization development: A process of managing change. *Public Management 60*:8–10.

Veninga, R. L. and Spradley, J. P. (1981). *The Work Stress Connection*. Ballantine, New York.

Yankelovich, D. (1981). *New Rules*. Random House, New York.

20

State and Local Government Pension Systems

Donald E. Klingner   Department of Public Administration, Florida
International University, North Miami, Florida

Randy L. Nutter*   Institute for Public Management and Community
Services, School of Public Affairs and Services, Florida International University,
North Miami, Florida

I. INTRODUCTION

Over the years, state and local government retirement systems have existed relatively unnoticed by the general public. There has been a lack of interest and
clear understanding on the part of public officials, plan participants, and
citizens. Pensions have been viewed as fringe benefits provided to public
servants, yet they have often been ignored as a public policy concern.

Despite this lack of recognition, state and local public employee retirement systems have a dynamic impact. Their number and assets have grown at a
phenomenal rate. As a result, a number of groups or persons—unions, elected
officials, and taxpayers—have begun to raise serious questions concerning
disclosure, benefits, investment, and funding of these systems. As to disclosure
and funding, a recent report by the Advisory Commission on Intergovernmental
Relations (ACIR) indicated that 56% of seventy-two public pension systems
studied were not funded on an actuarially sound basis—in other words, their
projected benefits were greater than their projected receipts (ACIR, 1980:33).
Although some states (such as Massachusetts, Minnesota, and Pennsylvania) have
taken the lead in introducing reporting, disclosure, and fiduciary requirements,
most of the remaining states have failed to enact legislation to resolve the
disclosure problem.

An example of the public policy consequences of the investment potential
of public pension funds occurred in August, 1976, when Governor Milton Shapp

*Present affiliation: Village of Miami Shores, Miami Shores, Florida

of Pennsylvania announced that he had convinced the German automaker, Volkswagen, to locate an assembly plant in his state. To accomplish this feat, he persuaded two of the state's largest public pension funds to lend $135 million to aid the company in establishing its operation (Rifkin and Barber, 1978:170–172).

II. HISTORICAL OVERVIEW

A public pension plan is established and maintained by a public employer or employee organization, or both, to provide retirement and/or disability income to employees (U.S. Department of Labor, 1979:2). Its central benefit, and the one usually most costly, is the benefit payable to retirees (Jump, 1981:242).

A majority of public plans are classified as some type of defined-benefit plan. The benefit payable is based on the employee's years of service, a measure of gross income, and a maximum benefit reflected as a percentage of total salary (U.S. General Accounting Office, 1980:1). There are varying degrees to which the employee's years of service and final average total salary may be fixed, depending on the particular pension plan.

Historically, public employee pensions have been justified because they implement personnel policies that provide benefits for the disabled and retirees (March, 1980:382, 383). Employee retirement systems first emerged in the public sector. Prior to the 1900s, police, firefighters, and teachers had secured coverage under retirement-benefit systems in Boston, New York, and several other cities. Approximately 12% of state and local retirement systems currently functioning were established before 1930 (U.S. Congress. Senate. Joint Committee on Taxation, 1982:6). Public pension systems continued to grow rapidly, particularly since Social Security system coverage was not extended to state and local government employees when enacted in 1935.

State and local pension plans are created through the legislative process. Laws are needed to establish funds, prescribe their provisions and benefits, and appropriate any funds necessary for their operation. The administration of the plan is usually assigned to an independent board of trustees. State law often requires that local governments have pension plans, or that local governments join the state system. If local governments elect to administer their own systems, state laws often set forth standards, including the method of funding (U.S. General Accounting Office, 1979:2).

Over 90% of those employed full-time in state and local government are covered by some pension plan. Most of these plans are administered by state and local governments. Although the exact number of such plans is not precisely known, estimates range from 3075 (U.S. Department of Commerce. Census Bureau, 1978:11) to 5000. These plans represent future retirement income for over 9 million state and local government employees (U.S. Congress. Senate. Joint Committee on Taxation, 1982:3). In the fiscal year ending between July,

1980 and June, 1981, these retirement systems had receipts of $43.3 *billion*, and held financial assets totaling $210.4 *billion*.

III. CHARACTERISTICS OF PUBLIC PENSION FUNDS

The high numbers of plans, plan participants, and fund receipts and balances are indicative of the vast economic, social, and political implications of state and local government employee retirement systems. Yet the diversity of these plans, and the fact that standards of disclosure and actuarial soundness are not regulated by national standards, makes the task of assessing these systems difficult. The Advisory Commission on Intergovernmental Relations reported (1980:28, 29) 90% of the membership in these systems is concentrated in 120 large systems, each with more than 10,000 employees and most administered at the state level. The diversity of these systems in finances, membership, and benefits makes public officials' search for simple uniform solutions to problems an exceedingly difficult and complex task.

There is lack of agreement among governmental officials concerning what uniform standards should be implemented to regulate public pension systems. The standards set by the Employee Retirement Income Security Act (ERISA) for private plans were designed to protect pension plan participants from employer neglect and possible bankruptcy, thus ensuring future benefits for beneficiaries. Public plans are different from private plans in their conception, historical development, and functions. State and local governments are generally viewed as permanent, economically secure institutions with strong moral, contractual, and (sometimes) constitutional obligations supporting their pension plans.

A basic difference in public and private pension systems from a benefits standpoint relates to the funding method. Private plans are funded by a corporation's earnings or profits. These organizations have the flexibility to increase or decrease their contributions based on earnings. Public plans, however, are funded through the general revenue funds of state and local governments. They therefore do not have the same flexibility afforded private plans. Increases are gained by taxing the general public (Wilson, 1982:185). For these reasons, public employee pension systems were excluded from coverage under ERISA.

IV. PROBLEMS WITH ADMINISTRATION OF PUBLIC PENSION FUNDS

Professional organizations concerned with pension administration cite two recurring problems in the history of state and local government employee systems—a temptation to engage in "financial chauvinism" (local investment at any cost, regardless of the economic sensibility) and a vulnerability to "fiscal plunder" (helping one's self or one's friend to some of the assets) (Coltman and Metzenbaum, 1979:3). These problems impose major costs on the security of retirement revenues that pension systems rules are designed to protect, violate the professional integrity of government officials, and restrict fund administration. Administrators of pension funds have succeeded in alleviating some of the unethical activities, but the general public remains somewhat suspect of investment proposals that do not adhere to the chief goal of maximizing return at minimal risk.

Attempts to evaluate state and local retirement plans have been difficult because of the difference of opinion concerning the proper standards governing funding, disclosure, and benefits that should apply to the variety of retirement systems. Nevertheless, several major studies in recent years have agreed on some basic problems. The U.S. Congress House Committee on Education and Labor (1978, 1982) summarized these problems as: inadequate disclosure, inadequate funding, and unsatisfactory investment policies.

In many cases, plan participants, public officials, and taxpayers are not informed about the financial status and operations of public pension plans. Inadequate disclosure affects the financial stability of the plans, along with that of their sponsoring government. It violates the rights of participants and limits the ability of taxpayers to comprehend the financial responsibility of their government. This limits the effectiveness of utilizing a prudent management approach in the overall administration of public pension plans.

V. PROBLEMS WITH INADEQUATE FUNDING

A second widely publicized problem associated with public pension funds is inadequate funding. This problem has many causes, among them political realities, changing economic conditions, changing social conditions, and the recent decline in public employment.

Political realities make it easier for elected officials to agree to changes in pension plan provisions that have great long-term financial consequences, in preference to approving wage increases that have a greater short-term impact. This is because pension benefit increases are less visible, and will become due when the official is no longer in office. Under these conditions, little attention is directed toward the long-range implications of commitments made to resolve an immediate political crisis.

Changing economic conditions, particularly the rate of inflation, affect the assumptions under which a pension system is administered. Most pension plans provide for cost-of-living adjustments in benefits. Several years of double-digit inflation, such as the United States experienced between 1976 and 1981, have contributed to automatic benefit increases for retirees that place an additional strain on the retirement system.

The declining birth rate since 1960 has been widely publicized as a contributing factor to the crisis with Social Security. Less widely recognized, but no less important, is its general effect on all pension systems. It increases the ratio of retirees to active employees, thereby increasing pressure for benefits at the same time employee contributions are decreasing (Fritz, 1981:406, 407).

Last, reductions in government spending, particularly those occurring at the state and local government level since 1978, have placed pressure on pension systems. Not only is the public increasingly concerned about the costs of public pensions, but the number of employees contributing into the system may actually be reduced because of layoffs or hiring freezes.

Under these circumstances, angry taxpayers have pressured states and localities to cut back on some of the most costly benefits—generous pension and disability plans that pay retirees more than they made when they worked. Liberal pensions of this type are the result of special bills passed by state legislatures. Others have come about as a result of collective bargaining, overlapping pension plans, "double-dipping" (the practice of drawing several pensions from a variety of government jobs), and administrative confusion (Weissler, 1983:59).

Yet, this is a reaction to the problem, rather than a rational solution. Although the problem is caused by some of these factors, a more general cause is the lack of uniform financial standards governing public pension plans. There is no federal requirement that public pension funds be operated with generally accepted accounting principles applicable to private pension plans as set forth in ERISA. Therefore, the assessment of pension costs is incomplete and inaccurate. This lack of uniform accounting, auditing, and actuarial standards impairs the credability of these funds. The U.S. General Accounting Office (GAO) reported (1980), for example, that about 56% of the seventy-two pension plans it reviewed were not actuarially funded.

The most controversial issue relating to public pension funding is underfunding. This can be interpreted in various ways. It can refer to the inability of public employers to meet the increasing costs associated with pension plans. This problem is caused by lack of uniform, sound actuarial methods. The purpose of an actuarial procedure is to predict accurate assumptions concerning probable future frequencies of death rates, retirement rates, and wage increases. Underfunding can also refer to unfunded accrued liabilities. According to pension terminology, an accrued liability is the amount of pension fund liability in excess of the pension plan assets. It can occur either when invested benefits are given to employees for years of service prior to the pension plan being established, or when a pension plan is revised to pay higher benefits (Wilson, 1982: 186).

Most states and localities fund pensions on a full-funding and/or pay-as-you-go basis. With full funding, the government sets aside an actuarily predetermined sum for future pensions as the obligations are incurred. Under a pay-as-you-go system, pensions are financed as they come due. Bacon (1980:266) summarizes the advantages of each system. Full funding is preferable because:

1. It is a cheaper method of financing public pension plans because investment returns act to reduce the amount of contributions made by government to the plans over a period of time.
2. Employees' rights gain better protection in regard to earned pension benefits.
3. Full funding is not as susceptible to being a hidden cost in pension funding and becoming exploited as a tactic by management to avoid wage increases in collective bargaining negotiations.
4. Financing a full-funding system allows taxpayers who receive the services of public employees to pay the wage costs incurred rather than shifting the current employees' pension costs to future taxpayers.

On the other hand, pay-as-you-go funding also has advantages:

1. Administrative costs of funded systems are higher than in pay-as-you-go due to the need for administrative specialists.
2. Pay-as-you-go financing start-up costs are less expensive.
3. The financial conservatism of actuarial standards causes the presence of unnecessary cost "cushions" in funded systems.
4. Pay-as-you-go financing is more resistant to inflationary pressures.

Perhaps one answer to the problem of underfunded retirement systems in state and local government is to change budgetary practices by converting defined benefit plans into defined contribution plans. As mentioned earlier, most state and local government retirement systems are set up under defined benefit plans. Defined benefit plans pay retirement benefits based on projected costs unrelated to available funds. This leads to government officials' trading pension increases for wage hikes. A defined contribution plan derives its fully vested funding through contributions of a fixed amount from plan participants and employers. The funds are invested, and when the participants retire, they receive a return on the money invested.

There are several advantages to a defined contribution plan. First, all associated costs are in plain view, and are reflected accurately by the contributions. Second, if the pension benefits are bargained for by unions, the costs become readily recognizable by the general public. Third, the system also provides an individual account for the employee, who then knows how much money has been allocated to him. Fourth, it allows for the easy transfer of funds into an employee's individual retirement account (IRA) plan. Last, the employee has flexibility in contributing by a variety of different payment methods.

Given the problems associated with establishing national standards for state and local public pension systems, it is not likely that these issues will be resolved quickly. However, there are indications that some states are grappling with the problem. In Florida, for example, legislation was passed in 1979 that requires that all governmental retirement systems in the state are properly funded and administered and that sets minimum requirements to accomplish this goal. In brief, this law mandated that: an actuarial valuation be conducted on each system at least every three years; the fund assets be based on current market value; these actuarial reports be filed within 60 days; and, the auditor general has the authority to investigate any pension plan not meeting these requirements.

VI. PUBLIC PENSIONS AS A STRATEGIC INVESTMENT TOOL

The management and administration of state and local public pension system assets is unsatisfactory. At the one extreme, public pension plans have been administered without common standards to follow, thus allowing for mismanagement. At the other extreme, the system is so overburdened by laws that require that investments be extremely secure. Historically, public administrators have failed to understand and even neglected the socioeconomic consequences of pension plans (March, 1980:382). Traditionally, public pension funds have been administered by boards of trustees who have stressed safety and rate of return rather than *strategic investment*.

Strategic investment of pension monies means an investment policy that incorporates the investment goals of maintaining security and return while directing investments to benefit the general public. A strategic investment program will avoid investing in companies that adversely affect the social and economic interests of the fund participants and general public. It should be emphasized that strategic investment does not specify that the security of the fund and return must be sacrificed to achieve other goals. For example, public pension fund assets have traditionally been invested in corporate bonds and common stock of blue-chip companies, with smaller increments allocated to federal securities and mortgages. A strategic investment policy would suggest an investment that created jobs, provided housing, and so on, in a situation where the criteria of security and return were relatively equal (Triplett, 1980:117). If corporations have an inadequate performance record in the area of occupational health and safety, have failed to follow affirmative action guidelines, or tended to export capital, jobs, and technology abroad, public pension funds would withhold investments from such companies (Webb and Schweke, 1979:1, 2).

Public awareness of the magnitude of state and local pension systems has led to increased recognition of their potential impact, through investment, on social and economic conditions. This awareness has been spearheaded by interest groups and union representatives, who have typically emphasized the potential effect of pension investments on state-local economies, or the potential influence investors can have in changing socially harmful business practices

(Coltman and Metzenbaum, 1979:2). Generally, their efforts have led to increased concern with the following key issues:

Identifying the social effects of public pension investments
Determining the costs of investment, both economic and social
Formulating a response in investment strategy that incorporates socioeconomic
    and political variables to achieve optimal results

Several examples of strategic investment will show how this strategy can be applied. The Ohio legislature enacted a law requiring the state's five public employee pension funds to give "consideration" to investments that benefit citizens of Ohio. The law allows up to 5% of the funds' assets to be invested in small businesses and "nontraditional" ventures such as corporate partnerships, proprietorships, or other investments previously prohibited by state legal restrictions (Legislatures, 1981:8).

One innovative strategic investment technique was used in the state of Minnesota. The $300 million Minneapolis Employees' Retirement Fund (MERF) and a Minnesota-based private company fund combined forces to help finance new, high-technology businesses to create future jobs. This effort represents one of the first times that a public employee pension fund and a privately controlled pension fund have joined together to target pension investment toward economic development.

A model among public employee pension fund loan programs is the Hawaii Employees' Retirement System home loan program. The program offers loans to its membership for mortgages at 1–2.5% below current market rates. Many state and local retirement systems are seeking new ways to target their mortgage programs, creating ". . . neighborhood-specific secondary mortgage markets, and designing mortgages to meet the needs of moderate- to low-income buyers" (LaFollette, 1982:1468).

Investment strategy plays a decisive role in determining how public employee pension systems can best use their pension funds to meet desired objectives. Laws, financial requirements, and administrative rules act to enhance and at the same time restrict the investment method. Administrators of public pension funds must validate investment input surrounding public retirement systems to develop an effective investment strategy.

VII. THE POLITICAL SIGNIFICANCE OF PENSIONS

Inevitably, decisions concerning the investment criteria for public pension systems will be the subject of public policy. At the very least, it is likely that conflict may arise between the beneficiaries' objective of maximizing investment earnings, and interest groups' objectives of attaining socioeconomic benefits. In addition, the growth of public pension plans has caused political debate as state legislatures and special-interest groups maneuver to gain control of the assets for their own purposes (Rohrer, 1982:165). This raises basic questions about how public pension funds should be managed so as to permit the equitable resolution of these issues, particularly since consensus on them is not likely to occur (Coltman and Metzenbaum, 1979:3).

State pension commissions have developed in many states to address these concerns. These commissions serve as an advisory group to administrators and government officials on specific matters governing public pension policy. Ideally, pension commissions are composed of state and local government officials, taxpayers, and employees who are current or past participants in a retirement plan. The makeup of the commission determines to a large extent how successful it can avoid undue political influences.

These commissions are created by state legislatures. Members are appointed by either the governor or state legislature. Their basic functions are to formulate principles of operation for public employee pension systems, identify problems, review proposed legislation, predict future pension costs, and develop pension reform programs. Their most important function is reporting to the legislature on the costs and funding of proposed benefit changes.

The authority and structure of pension commissions are dependent upon the enabling legislation passed by state legislatures. Some state legislatures grant pension commissions more power than do others. For example, North Dakota's Committee on Public Employees' Retirement Programs previously had little authority to determine its functions. In 1981, the state legislature passed an amendment that assigned the committee the authority to: decide which pension proposals warrant introduction to the legislature; determine which legislation affects the public employees' retirement systems; specify that amendments to these bills be returned to the committee with actuarial notes; and, designate its own chair and establish its own rules of operation (Ryan, 1982:11).

By contrast, Nevada's Interim Retirement Committee, whose main function is to review legislation proposed by the Nevada State Retirement Board, met only twice in 1981, *after* the state legislature had adjourned. These meetings aimed to study the salaries of exempt management employees of the state's public retirement system.

State public pension commissions are desirable because they can provide the kind of ongoing independent analysis of retirement costs and related matters required to control such a complex and costly budget item. These commissions act as a watchdog for unwise investment practices. The success of pension commissions has been positive enough to gain the support of most pension experts.

VIII. COLLECTIVE BARGAINING

Public employee organizations, through the collective bargaining process, have begun to play a crucial role in influencing the outcome of public policy disputes involving pension issues. In those cases where they administer a pension fund, they exert this influence directly. Where the pension plan is jointly or solely administered by the government, they exert influence through the collective bargaining and legislative lobbying process. Collective bargaining, therefore, offers a means by which state and local government employees can become influential in the formulation of public policy as it relates to public pension plans.

A great many of the problems confronting public pension systems can be attributed to ineffective collective bargaining. Due to budgetary restraints, negotiators have often agreed to pay higher future benefits to offset the payment of immediate wage increases. Elected officials are frequently willing to ratify such contracts because public interest is focused on *wage* increases, and because they do not plan on being in office when the future pension benefits come due.

The role of unions in the regulation of public pensions has not been clearly defined because of differences in state law. A 1976 case (*National League of Cities et al. v. Usery*, 96 S.Ct. 2465 [1976]) established that state and local governments are not subject to federal regulation of their wage and hour practices, in that extensions of the 1938 Fair Labor Standards Act to this area were an unconstitutional use of the Interstate Commerce Clause of the Constitution (*National League of Cities et al. v. Usery*, 96 S.Ct. 2465 [1976]). One of the effects of this decision was to limit an attempt by the federal government to bring uniformity to the scope of collective bargaining at the state and local level. As a result, some states allow collective bargaining over pensions, and some exclude bargaining. Each state government has the authority to regulate the scope of bargaining for local governments within the state. Therefore, those states that exclude pensions from bargaining for state employees also exclude bargaining over pensions for local government employees.

In those states where pensions are included in bargaining, public employee unions have sometimes been able to gain increased control over pension plans. In one instance, a union representing Wisconsin public employees advanced several investment proposals as part of its bargaining demands with the state. One proposal advocated was that the retirement funds be invested in-state by providing mortgage loans to participants. In another example, through the bargaining efforts of six unions, 28,000 Connecticut employees were able to achieve joint, equal control of the administration and investment of their pension funds. The pension coordinating committee, a joint bargaining unit, negotiated a contract for equal labor-management representation on the Connecticut State Employees Retirement Commission and the Connecticut

Teachers Retirement Board. Prior to the agreement, management representatives controlled these boards ("Connecticut," 1982:1-10).

In those states that exclude pensions from bargaining, public employee organizations still have tremendous influence through the legislative process. In numerous states, public employee unions are using their lobbying abilities to ease legal restrictions that inhibit pension investment. The American Federation of State, County, and Municipal Employees (AFSCME), for example, supports collective bargaining activities that endorse state legislation permitting flexibility in public pension investments as well as other fringe benefits.

One problem with the increased role of collective bargaining in state and local pension plan administration is that collective bargaining agreements are, of necessity, based on assumptions about the future. Changing economic conditions, particularly rates of inflation and public employment, contribute to uncertainty that complicates the bargaining process (Klay, 1981:521).

Management has used this uncertainty factor to its advantage by underestimating future revenues. One of the techniques used is to conservatively estimate the future rate of inflation, which acts to reduce the overall dollar amount of fringe benefits contained in the provisions of a negotiated agreement. As to pension plans, it can mean that future beneficiaries will receive less retirement income.

Public sector unions are countering this tactic by developing forecasts that can be used to check management's revenue forecasts. Their experience has led unions to become reluctant to bargain for long-term contracts over economic issues and to attach cost-of-living adjustments to negotiated compensation packages.

The concealment of possible reserve funds through methods such as underestimating future revenues, and the greater willingness to agree to long-term pension increases in preference to short-term wage increases, may be viewed as rational and necessary strategies for state and local officials. However, they do also tend to enhance feelings of mistrust in collective bargaining, and they may also contribute to the development of financially unsound pension systems.

IX. THE CONTROVERSY OVER REGULATION

Since the early 1970s, the intergovernmental aspects of state and local public pension problems have drawn increasing public interest. The ability of states to regulate their retirement systems (and those of local governments) effectively has become questionable. Congress took responsibility for regulating private pension plans through the passage of ERISA. As mentioned earlier, public pension systems were excluded from the ERISA legislative provisions. Two reasons Congress did not include public retirement systems, in addition to those discussed previously, were that they have received relatively few complaints from participants in these systems, and there existed no reliable information about these plans.

Current trends reflect that the federal government is at least considering the regulation of state and local government pension plans through standards similar to ERISA. A debate has been developing over which level of government should determine the standards of administration and control for state and local government pension plans. At the federal level, Congress has considered the enactment of the Public Employee Retirement Income Security Act (PERISA). PERISA would cover all public plans except those that are unfunded and maintained by public employers as a means for providing deferred compensation to management employees. This legislation would require that state and local governments implement reporting and disclosure procedures to inform plan participants, retirees, employee organizations, and the general public of the status of their public pension plans (Wilson, 1982:184).

To counter federal initiatives, state and local governments are beginning to undertake major reform modifications to improve their public pension plans. Political and economic forces are the primary reasons contributing to state-local pension reform activity. The threat of PERISA has caused many states to seek more comprehensive pension plan regulation. The tax increases associated with rising pension costs are prompting many state and local governments to examine their own systems more carefully, particularly if these systems are subject to collective bargaining. The third force leading to pension reforms, as always, is a financial emergency. Massachusetts, for example, faced severe funding problems in the 1970s. These were caused when a pay-as-you-go system encountered problems caused by high tax rates, an older workforce, a declining population, and increasing benefits. Widespread public concern with the financial stability of the system led to the adoption of a more aggressive funding program (ACIR, 1980:36).

In conclusion, state and local public pension systems face problems caused by inadequate disclosure, funding, and management policies. These problems can be corrected by the state or federal enactment of laws providing minimum standards for disclosure and actuarial soundness, and by the adoption of strategic investment techniques to more fully use this tremendous financial resource for the achievement of social and economic objectives.

REFERENCES

Advisory Commission on Intergovernmental Relations. (1980). *State and Local Pension Systems*. U.S. Government Printing Office, Washington, D.C.

Bacon, A. R. (May/June, 1980). A note on selecting the appropriate pension funding method for localities. *Public Administration Review 40*:265–269.

Coltman, E. and Metzenbaum, S. (1979). *A Report to the Task Force on Public Pension Investments of the Massachusetts Social and Economic Opportunity Council.* Union Printers, Washington, D.C.

Connecticut public employee unions win voice in pension fund investment. (July/August 1982). *Labor & Investments*, pp. 1-10.

Fritz, D. (1981). The growing challenges of providing pensions to state and local civil servants in an aging society. *International Journal of Public Administration 3*(4):405-422.

Jump, B., Jr. (1981). Compensating city government employees: Pension benefit objectives, cost measurement and financing. In Klingner, D. E., ed., *Public Personnel Management, Readings in Contexts and Strategies.* Mayfield, Palo Alto, pp. 293-313.

Klay, W. E. (September–October, 1981). Combating inflation through wage negotiations: A strategy for public administration. *Public Administration Review 41*:520-526.

La Follette, C. (August 21, 1982). Public pension funds being channeled into local economic development. *National Journal 14*:1466-1469.

Legislatures expand investments for public funds. (September, 1981). *Labor & Investments*, pp. 1-8.

March, M. S. (July–August, 1980). Pensions for public employees present nationwide problems. *Public Administration Review 40*:382-389.

National League of Cities et al. v. Usery. (1976). 96 S.Ct. 2465.

Public employee contract gains average 8.1 percent. (September, 1982). *Nation's Cities Weekly 5*(37):7.

Rifkin, J. and Barber, R. (1978). *The North Will Rise Again.* Beacon Press, Boston.

Rohrer, J. (October, 1982). The uneasy revolution of public funds. *Institutional Investor*, pp. 165-178.

Ryan, J. M. (1982). *Report on State Pension Commissions–1981.* Pension Commission Clearinghouse, Washington, D.C.

Thompson, W. N. (Winter, 1980). An answer to the public pension funding problem. *Policy Analysis 6*:117-120.

Triplett, T. J. (Autumn, 1980). Investing state moneys: Making every dollar work. *State Government 53*:181-184.

U.S. Congress. House. Committee on Education and Labor. (March 15, 1970). *Pension Task Report on Public Employee Retirement Systems.* 95th Cong., 2d sess.

U.S. Congress. House. Committee on Education and Labor. (1982). *Report on Public Employee Pension Plan Reporting and Accountability Act of 1982.* H.R. 4928, 97th Cong., 2d sess.

U.S. Congress. Senate. Joint Committee on Taxation. (1982). *Description of S. 2105 and S. 2106 Relating to State and Local Public Employee Benefit Plans.* U.S. Government Printing Office, Washington, D.C.

U.S. Department of Commerce. Bureau of Census. (1978). *Census of Governments: 1977.* Vol. 6., *Employee Retirement Systems of State and Local Governments.* U.S. Government Printing Office, Washington, D.C.

U.S. Department of Commerce. Bureau of Census. (1982). *Finances of Employee–Retirement Systems of State and Local Governments in 1980– 1981*. U.S. Government Printing Office, Washington, D.C.

U.S. Department of Labor. Labor-Management Services Administration. (1979). *Often-Asked Questions About the Employee Retirement Income Security Act*, pamphlet.

U.S. General Accounting Office. (February 26, 1980). *An Actuarial and Economic Analysis of State and Local Pension Plans*. PAD-80-1.

᾿ S. General Accounting Office. (August 30, 1979). *Funding of State and Local Government Pension Plans: A National Problem*. HRD-79-66.

Webb, L. and Schweke, W. (1979). *Public Employee Pension Funds: New Strategies for Investment*. Conference on Alternative State and Local Policies, Washington, D.C.

Weissler, D. A. (January 24, 1983). Lush public pensions that anger taxpayers. *U.S. News & World Report*, pp. 59–60.

Wilson, J. W. (1982). Can public pension plans survive under PERISA. *Journal of Collective Negotiations 11*(3):181–189.

21

State Government Unionism

Arthur L. Finkle   Division of Appellate Practices and Labor Relations, New Jersey Department of Civil Service, Trenton, New Jersey

In 1980, forty state governments had a labor-management relations policy covering at least a part of their workforce and, for these states, thirty-three provided for collective bargaining with employee unions or associations. Further, 1,163,000 full-time employees belonged to employee groups, representing 40% of all full-time state workers. In eight states (Alaska, Connecticut, Florida, Hawaii, Maine, Massachusetts, New York, and Rhode Island), more than two-thirds of such employees belonged to an employee group.

During this time frame labor-management contracts between state government and employee organizations existed in twenty-nine of the thirty-three collective bargaining states. "These states had a total of 778 contractural agreements covering 837,628 state employees" (*The Book of the States 1982–1983*:338). Apparently, there is an enormous amount of management union activity in state government. Coupled with similar-type activity in local government, which obtains its authorization from the sovereignty of the state, public sector state and local unionism represents the new personnel management of the 1980s.

This chapter will detail why *unionism* exists at all in state and local government. Then, it will explain unionism's historical and legal moorings and its pattern of evolution amid the existing components of public personnel systems— civil service, equal employment opportunity, affirmative action, and national safety provisions. Next, the chapter will reveal the inner workings of bilateralism, including recognition, unit determination, scope of negotiability, impasse and dispute settlement, grievances and their remedies, unfair management and labor practices, and the public sector strike. The exposition will conclude with a broad economic and sociological explanation of collective bargaining impacts on government, union perceptions on employer and employee and, finally, a look into the future.

I. UNIONS: WHY ARE THEY FORMED

Unions are groupings of workers formed to seek employment that is steady and that provides continuing improvement in working and hiring conditions (Chamberlain, 1965:82). However, unions are not unique. They exist in an inchoate form as an informal group. In addition, managers and employees continually bargain in the process of exchanging favors (Strauss and Sayles, 1980: 138, 139). Nevertheless, in the private sector, the following conditions obtain for forming a union:

1. Desire for better economic and working conditions
2. Desire for control over benefits
3. Desire to be heard

The precipitative causes in such union formation include change in top management, specific problems in incentive payment systems, cutting off of promotional ladders, sudden cutbacks, and layoffs (Strauss and Sayles, 1980:144, 145). Although private sector unionism had progressed steadily since the 1920s, public sector unionism did not begin to make significant strides until the decade of the 1960s.

II. HISTORY OF PUBLIC SECTOR UNIONISM

Although there were stirrings of public sector labor activity in the 1880s and 1890s among the fraternal benefit and some craft organizations, the unsuccessful Boston Police Strike of 1919 reversed whatever labor movement momentum there was. Further, the common law idea of conspiracy existed for those daring enough to organize and conspire against a public employer. Moreover, the legal concepts of sovereignty and its delegation also impeded the labor movement. Thus, the sovereign in a democracy is the people who cannot cede such power unless they freely and openly participate in the process. However, by contracting out services and purchasing consultants' services, the idea of sovereignty lost its pristine values. Stieber (1973:17) sums up the condition best, "Governments, however supreme, make deals." In addition, white-collar female and minority employees are disproportionately represented in government employment, and these groups have traditionally been extremely difficult to organize (Kearney, 1984:70). Finally, the legal environment was highly unfavorable for such union growth; for what little the courts granted, the legislatures passed laws forbidding strikes, collective bargaining, and the like.

However, with a new coalition leading the New Deal of the 1930s, the Wagner Act heralded the Magna Charta for private sector labor and, as has happened throughout American history, the public sector came shortly behind (Umar and Kirk, 1984:314).

The takeoff period for state and local public sector bargaining occurred in the 1960s and was attributable to five significant factors: First, the growth of state and local government personnel increased 277% from 1951 to 1980, whereas the nation's workforce increased 89% for the same period (Kearney, 1984:11). This increase represented the increased emphasis on that sector of the population in the less than twenty-five and more than sixty-five-years-of-age categories—the age categories requiring the most state and local government services. Indeed, the Great Society's programs of filtering funds to state and local governments heralded the new prominence of health, education, social services, medical care, recreation, and housing. Such programs proceeded throughout the decade of the 1960s and 1970s and necessitated an increased cadre of state and local governmental employees. Second, new public employee cadres observed that private sector union members were gaining better wages and working conditions. To keep up with their brothers and sisters, public employees were generally unsuccessful in obtaining such gains with the entrenched, unilateral, and paternal civil service commissions. Thereafter, they aggressively sought the requisite unification, recognition, and strength through the union mechanism. A third factor was the thawing of the inhibiting legal environment. By 1964, the U.S. Supreme Court ordered Congress, through *Baker v. Carr*, 369 U.S. 186 (1962), and then the fifty state legislatures, through *Reynolds v. Simms*, 84 S.Ct. 1362 (1964), to reapportion legislative districts on the basis of one person one vote. The effort of such reapportionment was to curtail the disproportionate rural domination of the national and state legislatures which were usually hostile to the union movement in general and public unionism in particular:

> Unions, which always have found their strongest support among representatives of metropolitan areas soon discovered more sympathetic ears in the legislative bodies of the states (Kearney, 1984:14).

Thereafter, President Kennedy issued Executive Order 10988 which provided for exclusive union recognition, written agreements, fair labor practices, and limited collective bargaining. However, this order was the first federal governmental recognition of the union movement since the 1912 passage of the Lloyd-LaFollette Act. Indeed, many observers consider this (recognition and attention to public unionism) to be the turning point in state and local unionism (Kearney, 1984:14).

The fourth cause for public unionism was the predisposition of the society to accept protest, confrontation, and militancy as a legitimate means of achieving societal goals. Indeed, with the din of the screaming voices of the civil rights movement, the Vietnam war dissent, and the general rebellion against "the establishment" (Shaw and Clark, 1972:902, 903):

> demonstrations and protest rallies of all kinds proliferated, until they finally gained recognition as a legitimate means of expression. Society appeared to accept, though grudgingly, militancy through protest as a basic right of all citizens. . . . Public employees, in particular, saw the potential of organized, militant action through a strong employee organization.

Fifth, and finally, in addition to all of these global reasons for union growth, there were definite economic and psychological needs that drive American workers to organize. Thus, a survey of state government workers found that positive attitudes to unions were associated with "job dissatisfaction, lack of job involvement, lower occupational status, large organizations and negative life experiences (e.g., raised in a poor family, little formal education)" (Kearney, 1984:16).

III. LEGAL BASES

Oftentimes, the legal justification for the existence of a phenomenon manifests itself after the phenomenon comes into existence. So it was with public sector unionism. Initially, the movement was thwarted by the legal concept of sovereignty, which provided that the ultimate governmental power to decide questions of public policy lies in its citizenry.

> In terms of labor relations, a formal application of the concept of sovereignty would seem to preclude collective bargaining. Only the citizenry, speaking through its government, its representative, would have the authority to establish conditions under which public servants would work (Shafritz et al., 1981:270).

Even if sovereignty were ceded to management, then the illegal delegation of power concept impeded the growth of the public labor movement by prohibiting any power to be delegated to a third party, such as a labor union or an arbitrator (Umar and Kirk, 1984:302). Furthermore, the common law doctrine of conspiracy operated against the unionization process which would "transfer the institutional control of affairs from the people to the hands of conspirators, and a new system of government and rights would be placed at the disposal of a voluntary and self-constituted association" (Umar and Kirk, 1983:302).

However, after the rapid rise of public unionism of the 1960s, a U.S. Court of Appeals in *McLaughlin v. Tilendis*, 398 F.2nd 287 (1968), held that regulations prohibiting public employees from joining unions were unconstitutional. Thereafter the courts generally allowed for collective bargaining in the public sector, unless specifically barred by statute (Shafritz et al., 1981:284). The next important step in the legal process was the announcement that certain public employees held a property right in their job (see *Board of Regents v. Roth*, 408 U.S. 564 [1972]) and held de facto tenure in their jobs after being employed a year (see *Perry v. Sindemann*, 408 U.S. 593 [1972]). Once having acquired this interest, such employees may not be deprived of their job without due process of law, which among other things provides for "basic procedural safeguards so that public employees have a reasonable opportunity to rebut the public employer's rationale for depriving the latter of their property interest in their employment" (Lieberman, 1980:50). In 1976, the U.S. Supreme Court held that the Tenth Amendment guarantees the states sovereignty over conditions of their workers (see *National League of Cities v. Usury*, 426 U.S. 833 [1976]). Thus, the highest federal court provided the legitimacy for states in their pristine sovereignty to fashion collective bargaining laws for its state, local, and teaching employees. Finally, the Court held, in *Abood v. Detroit Board of Education*, 430 U.S. 209 (1977) that public employees can be constitutionally required to pay a fee to unions representing them, even though they do not belong (Shafritz et al., 1981: 288). Thus, permission was granted for the agency shop, a type of union security that provides for nonunion employees to pay for the cost of a union representing them in collective bargaining and grievance matters. Usually, the costs are 85% of the full union membership costs.

IV. THE SPECIAL INGREDIENT: THE POLITICAL DIMENSION

During the initial stages of public sector unionization, organizers argued for equity between private unions and public unions. They argued for the same rights at the bargaining table as unions in the private sector; however, we have seen that various sociological and legal constraints curtailed such equity in bargaining. Nevertheless, the most important ingredient in the public union's existence is its political context. Simply stated, government is not another industry. In the private sector, owners and unions are equal before the law. They jockey for economic position and are inhibited only by economic competition. In the public sector, the union is not one of two parties; there is a third party called the people, which represents the sovereign. In essence, anything and everything in the public arena is a political issue.

Robert Dahl describes politics as the authoritative allocation of values and the "normal" American political process as "one in which there is a high probability that an active and legitimate group in the population can make itself heard effectively at some crucial stage in the process of decision" (Dahl, 1956: 145). As such, the public union competes with other political forces to get a piece of the public pie.

With this background in mind, some opponents of existing public unionism strenuously object to what they believe is the best of both worlds. For example, Myron Lieberman, a negotiator and National Educational Association and American Federation of Teachers activist, changed his mind over the proper role of public sector bargaining and asserts five advantages that public employees have over their private contemporaries. First, he claims that unlike private employees, public employees hold a property interest in their jobs, pursuant to *Perry v. Sindemann*. Thus, they have due process of law working for them. Indeed, public employees without bargaining rights frequently have more protection against arbitrary and unjust employee action than do private sector employees with bargaining rights. He argues that some municipal unions wield substantial political power in large cities, and their political influence is accordingly felt at the bargaining table. Further, he asserts that elected state officials seldom affect the control or substance of private sector bargaining, but they do exercise variable influences in the public sector. Finally, Lieberman points to the statutory benefits that public employees receive, and he lists some of California's benefits (Lieberman, 1980:51, 52):

1. Strong protection against dismissal or suspensions
2. Ten days of sick leave, cumulative without limit
3. Right to due process even as probationary employees
4. Substantial notice before termination
5. Layoff rights
6. Military, bereavement, personal necessity, legislative, industrial accident, and illness leaves
7. Sweeping protections in evaluation
8. Limits on district authority to reduce benefits
9. Protection against noncertified employees doing teacher work
10. Duty-free lunch periods
11. Right to dues collection
12. Right to prompt payment of salary
13. Right to notice of school closing
14. Protection from legal actions for acts in the course of employment
15. Protection from being upbraided, insulted, or abused in the presence of pupils
16. Limits on the work day and work year

Moreover, a state, unlike private industry, cannot move to another area. Lieberman concludes (1980:56): "What we have, therefore, is not an economic test between private parties but a battle for public support between public employees on the one hand and public management on the other."

Nevertheless, public unions have persisted and continue to exist; the political reality is that a public sector union does exist within the political process. However, though unions may influence this process, they do not control it. There are many constraining influences on public unions, some of which exist in the private sector, such as occupational safety and health laws and equal employment opportunity laws. Thus, unions do not have unfettered freedom to negotiate without regard to nondiscrimination on the basis of certain substantive and procedural personnel safeguards for protected groups under the Civil Rights Act of 1964, the Age Discrimination in Employment Act of 1967, the Rehabilitation Act of 1973, the Vietnam Veterans Readjustment Act of 1974, the Education Amendments of 1972, the Age Bias Act, laws dealing with receipt of general and special revenue funds, as well as the Equal Employment Opportunity Commission *Uniform Selection Guidelines*. The other particular dimension, of course, is the merit system which, as in New Jersey, generally has statutory responsibility for the following terms and conditions affecting public employees: salaries, position classification, salary adjustments, hours of work, overtime payment, leaves of absence, compensatory time, out of title work, selection, rule of three, promotion, performance appraisal, holidays, vacations, transfer and reassignment, layoff, recall, tuition refund, training. In addition, other New Jersey state statutes preclude negotiability of pension, health benefits, travel reimbursement, and job safety.

The bottom line is that public unionization and its laws exist in a diverse constraining environment, but the political context through which they exist operates as a feedback mechanism to be factored into public decision-making (see Horton, 1973). For example, if the union has enough political muscle, it could win significant concessions at the bargaining table or in the state legislature. On the other hand, if elected representatives perceive the populace to be restive or unhappy with such gains, they will hold the line against a union gain. Furthermore, in states that have the initiative, the populace may make itself immediately felt as it did with California's Proposition 13.

V. BILATERALISM

Although public sector unions coexist with merit system agencies, these unions traditionally have viewed such agencies at best as paternalistic and, at worst, managerial tools. Thus, "the disillusionment of many public employees as to the role of the (Civil Service) commission as their protector cannot be denied, so that a growing number have turned to the unions for protection" (U.S. Department of Labor, 1972:22, 23). One union leader exemplified this attitude (Wurf, 1969:75):

> There is, I submit, a legitimate—and critical—difference between my requesting something of you, but leaving the final determination in

your hands and my insistence that we sit down together at the negotiating table as equals.

In addition, there are needs for bilateral negotiation in the employment context
because management needs to gauge employee interest and opinion on policy
matters beyond the jurisdiction of its executives. Further, management will
benefit from positive ideas. In addition, the whole process of bilateral
negotiation could promote a mutual rapport and understanding (Stahl, 1976:
339).

Thirty-two states have comprehensive collective bargaining coverage that
generally includes all state, local, and teaching employees, and five states provide
for a meet-and-confer approach. A full thirty-six states provide for local
coverage, but eight of these states provide for either firefighters and/or police
officer coverage only. Thirty-three provide coverage for teachers; thirty for a
state administrative body usually modeled after the National Labor Relations
Board and called the Public Employment Relations Board. Thirty states provide
for exclusive recognition. Although there are seven right-to-work states, many of
them provide for some type of meet-and-confer arrangement (Stahl, 1976:
314):

> Policies governing labor relations . . . call for either . . . binding
> collective negotiations and/or nonbinding meet-and-confer discus-
> sion. The binding collective negotiations process assumes roughly
> equal power of the parties, with the resultant being a legal, mutual
> binding contract. The meet-and-confer arrangement permits the
> parties to discuss issues of employment and, if agreement is reached,
> a memorandum of understanding is produced. But there is no legal
> obligation on the part of the employer either to enter into such
> discussions or to comply with any resulting understanding.

According to Levine and Hagburg, 29% of all state and local governments have
entered into meet-and-confer discussions; 33% have collective bargaining only,
and 38% have both (Levine and Hagburg, 1979). Furthermore, only three states
(Mississippi, Ohio, and South Carolina) have no statutes or policies covering
collective bargaining (Umar and Kirk, 1984:314).

The first states to enact comprehensive collective bargaining legislation
tended to be states with a strong two-party tradition: "These early innovators,
such as Michigan, Rhode Island, New York, Massachusetts, Delaware and
Connecticut, patterned their legislation on the National Labor Relations Act for
private sector employees" (Kearney, 1984:65).

Such a negotiation process has certain elements that we shall now
explore—unit determination, scope of negotiability, grievances, impasses and
dispute settlement, unfair labor practices, union security, and management
rights.

A. Unit Determination

When a group of employees want to organize, the state, similar to the National Labor Relations Act, generally certifies collective bargaining agents who present union desire cards of 30% of employees, who held an election and have determined whether the group is appropriate to form a unit. Such a unit determination involves defining a *community of interest* by common occupation or by the same activity performed. The unit can cut across departmental lines or remain in one department. It can also include a range of skills and geographical dispersion and sometimes can reflect the labor history of the agency and convenience of the employer. After this presentation of documents, the state employment relations board certifies that the union now has exclusive recognition in bilateral negotiations (Shafritz et al., 1981:330):

> In recent years, some public employers have opted for larger units. These have the advantage of reducing fragmentation and its concomitant tendencies toward constant, chaotic bargaining and competition among the units.

New Jersey provides a good example of dividing 80,000 employees into twenty-two unit groups (Appendix A).

There is a problem of whether supervisors in the public sector may join such units. The case could be made that because of the necessarily narrower scope of authority of public sector supervisors they have a community of interest and therefore should be eligible to join union groups. Accordingly, the states have reacted in four ways: exclude entirely, permit full collective bargaining rights, provide for meet-and-confer units, or allow to join rank-and-file units (Shafritz et al., 1981:296).

B. Scope of Negotiability

Negotiations are required over wages, hours, and other terms and conditions of employment. Scope of negotiations are segmented into mandated, permissive, and nonnegotiable topics. Mandatory negotiations in New Jersey encompass grievance procedures, including "binding arbitration, changes in duties and responsibilities, disciplinary procedures, a duty free lunch, hospitalization insurance, salary increments, salary holdbacks, evaluation procedures, fair dismissal procedures, holidays, hours of work, personal leave, vacancy posting, promotional procedures, sabbatical leave, employee safety, seniority, subcontracting, job security, tutoring assignments, vacations, the work day, the work year, the workload, and the work schedule" (Tener, 1977–1978:639–640). However, the New Jersey courts have curtailed such mandatory negotiation only to the extent of the public employers' authority or discretion (Tener, 1977–1978:649). However, such topics are not mandatorily negotiable when a preexisting statute

or regulation exists, an inherent managerial presagative is curtailed, or fundamental public policy is touched (Tener, 1977-1978:640). As was previously
mentioned, certain civil service and pension statutes and regulations preclude
negotiability. In addition, subcontracting in New Jersey is viewed as an inherent
managerial prerogative and is therefore nonnegotiable (*State v. State Supervisory Employees Ass'n*, 78 N.J. 60). Occasionally, however, the political
process becomes operative, and nonnegotiable topics are made the subject of
side letters or memoranda of understanding to be referenced in the collective
bargaining process. Accordingly, management politically is held accountable to
produce for the union. Finally, subjects found to be permissively negotiable
include: "selections of administrators, academic calendars, collegiality,
curriculum review, qualification of department chairmen, assignment of duties,
homeroom supervision, bus duty, coaching assignments, evaluation criteria,
qualifications for hiring, criteria for promotions, index for teacher effectiveness,
manning, tables of organization, involuntary transfers, and the decision to carry
weapons" (Tener, 1977-1978:643).

One of the recent permissively negotiable items is productivity bargaining
where *buy-outs* and *gaining-sharing* techniques are employed (Kearney, 1984:
149):

> Buy outs involve a payment of money (for bonuses) or other finan-
> cial inducements by management to the unions in return for union
> acceptance of changes in work rules which hinder productivity.
>
> Gain sharing refers to a financial incentive system in which a
> cash bonus is offered for measurable increases in productivity for
> extra efforts by employees.

Some authors have cited the lack of distinction between production that
actually raises unit costs and productivity that decreases the input/output ratio
(Horton, 1976:407-414).

Nevertheless, for the bargaining process to become successful, Capozzola
(1976:185-186) indicates the following:

1. Define and communicate the goals of the program.
2. Develop reasonably valid and reliable indicators which are acceptable to
   employees.
3. Develop a method of measuring, appraising and monitoring the programs
   and work performance.
4. Effectively utilize personnel, equipment and materials.
5. Institute training programs.
6. Set up incentive systems in which benefits from increased productivity are
   shared with employees.
7. Recognize the importance of employee involvement and morale.

8. Review and analyze the program continuously, not just in an artificial way but in depth.

C. Grievances

Grievances occur when it is revealed that there is a violation of the labor-management contract. The contract's grievance definition can limit such disagreements to the interpretation, application, and enforcement of the provisions of the agreement, or it can extend to complaints concerning the application to employees of any existing laws, rules, procedures, regulations, administrative orders, or work rules (past practices) involving the employees' working conditions (Nigro and Nigro, 1976:254-261). Elaborate procedures are established to resolve these different interpretations in the interests of industrial harmony and the continuity of the enterprise. However, a study of public contracts concluded that the scope of public sector grievance procedures are narrower than in the private sector (Begin, 1969).

In New Jersey, employees are entitled to be represented by the union and can not be coerced, intimidated, or suffer any reprisal as a result. Witnesses may appear and be cross-examined by the appropriate shop steward. The local president or union representative must also be notified of any scheduled grievance hearing, and has time off to pursue the matter. The procedure initially involves an informal discussion. Failing resolution of the problem, the grievance is then presented in writing to the authorized highest operational state representative. If there is still no resolution, the grievance is presented to the department head or his representative. Finally, the unresolved problem goes to an arbitration panel, which provides a nonbinding decision. However, if management or the union does not abide by the decision, experience has taught that distrust and resultant strife is created. In addition, arbitration awards are not appealable to the courts unless fundamental due process was violated or the decision was arbitrary, capricious, or not supported by sufficient credible evidence.

New modalities in grievance handling include an informal grievance mediation process; a more formal but expedited process that curtails certain formalities (prehearing discovery, shortened time frames); and, labor-management committees that may resolve the issue as an act of good faith (Kearney, 1984:303-308). A further explanation of the procedural aspects is discussed in "Labor Relations in Local and County Government" by Ernest Gross (Ch. 22).

D. Impasses and Dispute Settlement

When there is a breakdown in negotiations in which both sides hold fast to their position and do not give, an impasse results. Impasses are usually resolved by arbitration in twenty states. Mediation is a noncoercive process in which an agreed upon neutral party maintains a flow of communication, offers tentative solutions and presses each party to modify its position so a resolution may result. Fact-finding is a process in which a neutral party holds a hearing, makes an inquiry, analyzes the situation, and makes recommendations. In addition, the fact-finder also puts pressure on the parties to accept the critically exposed agreement. Voluntary arbitration is fact-finding with an advance agreement to accept the result. Compulsory arbitration exists when the parties, by law or rule, must submit to a solution; advisory arbitration is not binding on the parties (Stahl, 1976:364, 365). An in-depth study of impasse procedures is presented by Ernest Gross in Ch. 22.

E. Unfair Labor Practices

Borrowed from the private sector, unfair labor practices are lists of labor-management practices that are adjudicated by a state labor relations board. Some unfair practices by the employer are (Stahl, 1976:353):

1. interfering with employee rights guaranteed by statute, order or other source;
2. initiating, dominating, or interfering in any way with creation of an organization of employees;
3. giving financial support to an employee union;
4. discouraging union members;
5. disciplining an employee for filing a grievance;
6. refusing to recognize a qualified union;
7. refusing to negotiate or bargain with a union in good faith; and
8. violating a bargaining agreement.

Forbidden union actions are (Stahl, 1976:353):

1. seeking to induce the employer to coerce an employee for opposing union leadership;
2. coercing an employee into joining the union;
3. refusing to represent a member in exercising his rights under an agreement;
4. refusing to negotiate or bargain with management in good faith;
5. discriminating against an employee on matters of union membership because of race, color, creed, sex, age or national origin;
6. calling or engaging in a strike, work stoppage, or slowdown of work where such actions are forbidden by law; and
7. violating a bargaining agreement.

F. Union Security

There are certain provisions that enhance union security for which unions may trade off other components of a contract. The dynamics of survival of a social organization are such that management may exact a heavy price for the guarantee of such items as mandatory dues deduction, which exists in twenty states, or the agency shop, which guarantees the union that all employees will pay up to 85% of union dues. Such an agency shop provision exists in twelve states.

G. Management Rights

By the same token, public employers usually insist on a management rights contractual provision. The Advisory Commission on Intergovernmental Relations recommends that management rights should be (1969:102):

1. to direct the work of their employees;
2. to hire, promote, demote, transfer, assign and retain employees in positions within the public agency;
3. to suspend or discharge employees for proper cause;
4. to maintain the efficiency of governmental operations;
5. to relieve employees from duties because of lack of work or for other legitimate reasons;
6. to take actions as may be necessary to carry out the mission of the agency in emergencies; and
7. to determine the methods, means, and performance by which operations are to be carried out.

VI. THE STRIKE

The public employment strike has always been the consummate irony for public unions. In the private sector, the strike is the ultimate weapon. But in the public sector the strike is generally forbidden and certainly outlawed where it involves essential services. Table 1 indicates that, although public workers have shown 25-50% lower participation in strikes, the number of work stoppages and days idle have drastically increased since the early 1960s and steadily increased since the mid-1970s. Proponents of public sector strikes argue that the union as a representative of the worker is a little more than a class of serfs and does not even have the threat of the use of the strike. Thus, whatever leverage a union has is taken away when the strike is absent from the arsenal of the union's weaponry. Those against public employee strikes claim that employee strikes have never been used in the United States for political objectives and a "public sector strike constitutes a basic rupture of this tradition" (Lieberman, 1980:69). In addition, Lieberman (1980:78) states:

Table 1 Work Stoppages in Government, by Level, 1960–1980: Workers Involved and Days Idle in Thousands

Year	Federal			State			Local		
	No. stoppages	Workers involved	Days idle	No. stoppages	Workers involved	Days idle	No. stoppages	Workers involved	Days idle
1960	—	—	—	3	1.0	1.2	33	27.6	67.7
1961	—	—	—	—	—	—	28	6.6	15.3
1962	5	4.2	33.8	2	1.7	2.3	21	25.3	43.1
1963	—	—	—	2	0.3	2.2	27	4.6	67.7
1964	—	—	—	4	0.3	3.2	37	22.5	57.7
1965	—	—	—	—	—	1.9b	42	11.9	145.0
1966	—	—	—	9	3.1	6.0	133	102.0	449.0
1967	—	—	—	12	4.7	16.3	169	127.0	1230.0
1968	3	1.7	9.6	16	9.3	42.8	235	190.9	2492.8
1969	2	0.6	1.1	37	20.5	152.4	372	139.0	592.2
1970	3	155.8	648.3	23	8.8	44.6	386	168.9	1330.5
1971	2	1.0	8.1	23	14.5	81.8	304	137.1	811.6
1972	—	—	—	40	27.4	273.7	335	114.7	983.5
1973	1	0.5	4.6	29	12.3	133.0	357	183.7	2166.3
1974	2	0.5	1.4	34	24.7	86.4	348	135.4	1316.3
1975	1	—a	—a	32	66.6	300.5	446	252.0	1903.9
1976	—	—	—	25	33.8	148.2	352	146.8	1542.6
1977	2	0.4	0.5	44	33.7	181.9	367	136.2	1583.3
1978	1	4.8	27.8	45	17.9	180.2	435	171.0	1498.8
1979	—	—	—	57	48.6	515.5	536	205.5	2467.1
1980	1	0.9	7.2	45	10.0	999.0	493	212.7	2240.6

aLess than 100.
bFigures from 1965 result from two stoppages that began in 1964.
Source: U.S. Bureau of Labor Statistics (1981). Annual Report.

The inescapable reality, however, is that collective bargaining is essentially a bilateral process, whereas public policy-making has always been deemed to be a multilateral process, accessible to all on equal terms.

Thus, unions would obtain too much power in relation to other competing groups in the democratic process. Furthermore, some governmental services are monopolistic and are critical to the survival of human beings who have entered the political social contract (e.g., police protection and fire protection).

However, at least ten states authorize limited strikes of nonessential services, usually after internal procedural requirements, such as mediation or fact-finding, are exhausted (Kearney, 1984:220, 221).

VII. COPING WITH STRIKES

Given the fact that there may be strikes, management has designed coping techniques that have minimized the disruption of services. It has developed a contingency system of communication with supervisors. It provides for longer work days to produce the same output with fewer employees. It identifies the critical operations to be performed over functions not so vital. Next, it provides for adequate protection of working personnel and public property. Finally, it keeps the public informed regarding availability of services and keeps its channels open to the union for the possibility to resume work.

Some state statutes provide for sanctions against strikers, such as dismissals, bans on future employment, fines, loss of dues checkoff, demotions, unfair labor practices, injunctions, and private damage actions. Moreover, a recent study found that strong, consistently enforced penalties against strikes tend to decrease strike incidence (Veglahn, 1983:196).

Often, the employer faces strong pressures to avoid penalties once the strike is over in order to restore amity. Otherwise, the chastened and martyred union remains militant (Veglahn, 1983:198).

Alternatives to the strike are lesser job actions, such as work slowdowns, "blue flu," work speedup (traffic-ticket blitz), lobbying, picketing, or refusal to work overtime (Rubin, 1978:343). In addition, there have been various alternatives to the strike: (a) nonstrike stoppages where both sides pay a fine until the dispute is settled; (b) a graduated strike that reduces services to a minimum but adequate floor; and, (c) a minimum guarantee that, as long as the major contractual items are agreed to, then there will be no strike (Stahl, 1976: 373, 374).

VIII. ECONOMIC IMPACTS

Although there is some dispute among researchers, the economic impact of unionization is that the public employee gains. However, such gains are not evenly distributed across occupational groups. For example, most studies show that union firefighters' salaries were 2-28% higher than their nonunion counterparts; transit workers 9-12% higher; however, unionized police officers did not achieve an immediate differential benefit. General municipal employees, such as workers in highways, sewerage, sanitation, parks, recreation, and libraries also did not receive any significant benefit, immediate or future (Methe and Perry, 1980:366). Furthermore, Methe and Perry (1980), in surveying twenty impact studies, claim that collective bargaining has contributed to increased expenditures and fiscal effort.

Fringe benefits generally increase in a unionized environment. Indeed, after 1968, "transit unions placed a higher priority on securing fringe benefits than they had in the preceding two decades" (Methe and Perry, 1980:366). In addition, although employment of essential service personnel (fire and police) has increased, Benechi (1978:216-230) found that unionization significantly reduced overall employment levels, particularly in large cities. In addition, certain environmental factors determined the extent of any economic differential. For example, the city governmental structure and the degree of monopsony (services limited to the buyer) power held by the city were determinants of wage gains. Thus, the more professional the manager or commission forms of government held wages down better than the highly politicized mayor-council form (Methe and Perry, 1980:367).

IX. NONECONOMIC IMPACTS

The noneconomic impacts of unionization are more subtle but just as inconclusive as the economic studies. At this point, the impression is that unions challenge managerial decisions, compete for worker loyalty, make inflexible rules, threaten efficiency, help to centralize personnel decision-making, introduce outside "experts" to the process, and generally politicize the formerly "business-like" environment (Strauss and Sayles, 1980:154-156).

X. UNION'S PERCEPTION

What does the union think of the collective bargaining system? How does it view itself? The union fears the threat of reaction on the part of the rank and file and the possibility of internal opposition; therefore, it tends to become militant. If feels it has to beat the law or the system or it will lose. Therefore, it enthusiastically and orgiastically goes for Samuel Gomper's standard phrase: "We want more" (Shafritz et al., 1981:308-310).

XI. MANAGEMENT'S PERCEPTION

On the other hand, when unionization first occurs, management is generally fragmented and decision-making is diffused, enabling labor to make significant inroads. Thereafter, managerial personnel decision-making becomes more centralized, resulting in less union power. For example, in New Jersey, collective bargaining responsibility was initially fragmented among the Civil Service Commission, the Division of Pensions, the Budget Bureau, and the twenty personnel agencies of the operating departments of the state government. However, after the first enormous settlements favoring the unions, the Governor, by executive order, created the Office of Employee Relations, which had the sole responsibility to negotiate for state government. In addition, it set policy on day-to-day matters such as grievances, minor disciplinary actions, and unfair labor practices. It was also mandated to coordinate the budgetary and merit systems along with the contractual strictures.

The professional manager sees capitulation to political and economic pressure as unprofessional. Alan Saltzstein (1971:333) observed:

> I contend that most city managers meet the challenge of organized employees from a management perspective. The normal posture of most is to resist the organized employee and counter his demands with a strong defense of the interests of the taxpayer. The effect may be the discouragement of employee organizations and settlements that are often favorable to management. Hence the notion that organized employees are accorded disproportionate power in cities employing them is questionable.

For the politician, there is a dilemma. He or she may owe their election to the unions. Therefore, they are weaker on monetary matters and will generally capitulate on long-term economic matters that will not immediately be felt, such as pensions. Recently, however, in the changing political environment of cutback management and Proposition 13, many politicians have attempted to hold the line by surrounding themselves with professional negotiators. They also will leave a path for the union to retreat from impossible dreams in order to save face (Shafritz et al., 1981:311-314).

XII. FUTURE

Where do we go from here? Marvin Meade (1979:94) makes certain penetrating predictions:

1. An "unseen hand" is emerging as a new king of public discipline as service cutbacks, wage freezes, and revenue decreases occur.
2. Public union leaders are exhibiting more self-discipline as they realize that there are limits to "more."

But whatever the predictions, he cautions:

> [W]e . . . may do ourselves less than justice by concluding . . . that collective bargaining is to be accepted as a fact of life and that our concerns ought to focus on the . . . "how to" of management-labor dealings . . . [W]e can ill afford to ignore the complex of causative factors that underlie the bargaining of public unions nor the long-run implications of how we currently respond to the pressures of fast-moving events in the field.

APPENDIX A Employee Groups and Bargaining Units (New Jersey Office of Employee Relations

1. X. Exempt

Personnel in the exempt group include those employees (and their immediate staff) (exclusive of the state police and department of higher education) who have final responsibility for the policies, laws, and regulations of the state, its branches and agencies.

2. M. Managerial

Personnel in the Management group consist of those employees (exclusive of the state police and department of higher education) not at the very top of state service who formulate management policies and practices and/or those who are charged with implementing the aforesaid policies and practices. All of those engaged in supervision above the higher level of supervision are considered to be managerial.

3. D. Managerial and exempt (higher education)

Those titles which, but for their exclusive assignment to the department of higher education would be assigned to the managerial or exempt groups, are in the managerial and exempt (higher education) group.

4. E. Managerial and exempt (state police)

Those titles which, but for their exclusive assignment to the division of state police would be assigned to the managerial or exempt groups, are in the managerial and exempt (state police) group.

5. V. Confidential

V includes those employees without arrest powers, who supervise the work operations and/or functional programs; whose responsibilities or knowledge in connection with labor relations make it inappropriate to be included in a bargaining unit. Such individuals are staff employees who regularly assist or report to those in management responsible for formulating or effectuating labor relations policy. V has responsibility for effectively recommending the hiring, firing, promoting, demoting, and/or disciplining of supervisory and when warranted non-supervisory employees.

6. Z. Confidential

Z consists of those employees without arrest powers, that are engaged in the first or primary level of supervision; whose responsibilities or knowledge in connection with labor relations make it inappropriate to be included in a bargaining unit. Such individuals are staff employees who regularly assist or report tò those in management responsible for formulating or effectuating labor relation policy. Z has responsibility for effectively recommending the hiring, firing, promoting, demoting and/or disciplining of non-supervisory employees.

7. Y. Confidential

Any employee without arrest powers engaged in work (1) predominantly intellectual and varied in character as opposed to routine mental, manual, mechanical or physical work; (2) involving the consistent exercise of discretion and judgment in its performance; (3) of such a character that the output produced or the result accomplished cannot be standardized in relation to a given period of time; (4) requiring knowledge of an advanced type in a field of science or learning customarily acquired by a prolonged course of specialized intellectual instruction and study in an institution of higher learning or a hospital, as distinguished from a general academic education or from training in the performance of routine mental, manual or physical processes; (5) whose responsibilities or knowledge in connection with labor relations or personnel administration make it inappropriate to be included in a bargaining unit. Such individuals are staff employees who regularly assist or report to those in management responsible for formulating or effectuating labor relations policy.

8. W. Confidential

W consists of those employees engaged in the preparing, transcribing, systematizing and maintaining records, reports and communications by manual processes or by operating various office machines and equipment, as well those engaged in related sub-professional activities; whose responsibilities or knowledge in connection with labor relations or personnel administration make it inappropriate to be included in a bargaining unit. Such individuals are staff employees who regularly assist or report to those in management responsible for formulating or effectuating labor relations policy.

9.   S.   Supervisory—2nd level

Supervises the work operations and/or functional programs. Second level has the responsibility for effectively recommending the hiring, firing, promoting, demoting and/or disciplining of employees.

10.   J.   Supervisory—higher level supervisory—law enforcement

This unit includes those employees (exclusive of the state police) who are responsible for the enforcement of the laws and for supervising work operations and/or functional programs and have responsibility for effectively recommending the hiring, firing, promoting, demoting and/or disciplining of supervisory and when warranted non-supervisory employees.

11.   K.   Supervisory—primary level supervisory—law enforcement

This unit includes those employees (exclusive of the state police) who are responsible for the enforcement of laws and have responsibility for effectively recommending the hiring, firing, promoting, demoting and/or disciplining employees in non-supervisory titles.

12.   N.   Supervisory—state police non-commissioned officers

This unit includes those employees below the rank of Lieutenant in the Division of State Police who are responsible for the enforcement of laws and supervising work operations and/or functional programs and have responsibility for effectively recommending the hiring, firing, promoting, demoting, and/or disciplining of employees.

13.   R.   Supervisory—1st level

This unit includes employees who are engaged in the primary or first level of supervision. First level has the responsibility for effectively recommending the hiring, firing, promoting, demoting and/or disciplining of employees.

14.   L.   Law enforcement

   a.   This unit is composed of non-supervisory employees whose main function is the enforcement of laws through customary police activities.

15.   T.   b.   This unit is composed of non-supervisory New Jersey State
             Troopers.

16.   P.   Professional, scientific, and technical services

Any non-law enforcement employee engaged in work (1) predominantly intellectual and varied in character as opposed to routine mental, manual, mechanical, or physical work (2) involving the consistent exercise of discretion and judgment in its performance; (3) of such a character that the output produced or the result accomplished cannot be standardized in relation to a given period of time; (4) requiring knowledge of an advanced type in a field of science or learning customarily acquired by a prolonged course of specialized intellectual instruction and study in an institution of higher learning or a hospital, as distinguished from a general academic education or from an apprenticeship or from training in the performance of routine mental, manual, or physical processes.

17.   U.   State university professionals

All full-time professional employees engaged in teaching, research, administrative support and academic support activities, who are employed by the nine (9) State Colleges or A. Harry Moore School.

18.   H.   Health, care, rehabilitation services

Composed of employees who are engaged in para-medical activities and employees who participate in the support function such as recreational, vocational, and social programs designed to aid in the care, health and rehabilitation of the physically, *mentally ill*, or handicapped.

19.   C.   Crafts

Persons in this unit employed in positions requiring craftsman status are engaged in a manual pursuit, *usually not routine*, for the pursuance of which a long period of training and/or apprenticeship leading to "journeyman" status is required and which, in its pursuance, calls for a high degree of judgment and manual dexterity and for ability to work with a minimum of supervision and to exercise responsibility for valuable product and equipment. Such crafts persons, as such, together with their apprentices and/or helpers, constitute the unit.

20.   O.   Operations, maintenance, and services

This unit is composed of employees engaged in the performance of skilled and/or semi-skilled work in construction, maintenance, repair, and fabrication activities; in the operation of machines, equipment, and vehicles; and in the provision of domestic and institutional services.

21. I. Inspection and security

Employees in this unit are those engaged in inspection or investigation work and in ensuring the compliance with laws, codes, rules and regulations concerned with public health, food, labor, standards, vehicle and highway safety.

22. A. Administrative

Persons engaged in the preparing, transcribing, systematizing and maintaining records, reports and communications by manual processes or by operating various office machines and equipment and also employees engaged in related sub-professional activities.

REFERENCES

Abood v. Detroit Board of Education (1977). 430 U.S. 209.

Advisory Commission on Intergovernmental Relations (1969). *Labor Management Policies for State and Local Government.* U.S. Government Printing Office, Washington, D.C.

AFSCME, AFL-CIO (n.d.) *AFSCME in the Public Service.* AFSCME, Washington, D.C.

Baker v. Carr (1962). 369 U.S. 186.

Begin, J. P. (1969). *The Development and Operation of Grievances Procedures in Public Employment.* Unpublished Ph.D. Thesis. Purdue University, West Lafayette, Ind.

Board of Regents v. Roth (1972). 408 U.S. 564.

Capozzola, J. (1976). Productivity bargaining: Problems and prospects. *National Civil Review 65*:185-186.

Chamberlain, N. W. (1965). *The Labor Sector.* McGraw-Hill, New York.

Council on State Governments (1983). *The Book of the States 1982-1983.* Lexington, Ky.

Dahl, R. (1956). *A Preface to Democratic Theory.* University of Chicago Press, Chicago, Ill.

Horton, R. D. (1973). *Municipal Labor Relations in New York City.* Praeger, New York.

Kearney, R. C. (1984). *Labor Relations in the Public Sector.* Marcel Dekker, New York.

Levine, M. J. and Hagburg, E. C. (1979). *Public Sector Labor Relations.* West, St. Paul, Minn.

Lieberman, M. (1980). *Public Sector Bargaining.* Lexington Books, Lexington, Mass.

McLaughin v. Tilendis (1968). 398 F.2nd 287.

Meade, M. (1979). Public employee unionism revisited—Perspectives of the 1970's. *Public Administration Review 39*:91–94.

Methe, D. T. and Perry, J. L. (1980). The impacts of collective bargaining on local government services: A review of research. *Public Administration Review 40*:359–371.

National League of Cities v. Usury (1976). 426 U.S. 833.

New Jersey Office of Employee Relations, *Employee Groups and Bargaining Units*, n.d.

Newland, C. A. (1972). Personnel concerns in government: Productivity improvements. *Public Administration Review 32*:807–815.

Nigro, F. A. and Nigro, L. G. (1976). *The New Public Personnel Administration*. F. E. Peacock, Itasca, Ill.

Perry v. Sindemann (1972). 408 U.S. 593.

Reynolds v. Simms (1964). 84 S.Ct. 1362.

Rubin, R. S. (September–October, 1978). Labor relations for police and fire: An overview. *Public Personnel Management*, p. 343.

Saltzstein, A. L. (1971). Can management control the organized employee? *Public Personnel Management 1*:333.

Senechi, S. (1978). Municipal expenditure levels and collective bargaining. *Industrial Relations 17*:216–230.

Shafritz, J., Hyde, A., and Rosenbloom, D. (1981). *Personnel Management in Government*. Marcel Dekker, New York.

Shaw, L. and Clark, T., Jr. (1972). Practical differences between public and private sector collective bargaining: Collective bargaining and politics in public employment. *UCLA Law Review 19*:867–903.

Stahl, O. G. (1976). *Public Personnel Administration*, 7th ed. Harper and Row, New York.

State v. State Supervisory Employees Association (1978). 78 N.J. 60.

Stieber, J. (1973). *Public Employee Unionism: Structure, Growth, Policy*. Marcel Dekker, New York.

Strauss, G. and Sayles, L. (1980). *Personnel*. 4th ed. Prentice-Hall, Englewood Cliffs, N.J.

Tener, J. B. (1977–1978). The public employment relations commission: The first decade. *Rutgers Camden Law Journal 9*:639–649.

Umar, F. F. and Kirk, R. V. (1983). Legal context of public sector labor relations. In Rabin, J. et al., eds., *Handbook on Public Personnel Administration and Labor Relations*. Marcel Dekker, New York.

U.S. Bureau of Labor Statistics (1981). *Annual Report*, U.S. Government Printing Office, Washington, D.C.

U.S. Department of Labor (1981). *Summary of Public Sector Labor Relations Policies*. U.S. Government Printing Office, Washington, D.C.

U.S. Department of Labor (1972). *Collective Bargaining in Public Employment and the Merit System*. U.S. Government Printing Office, Washington, D.C.

Veglahn, P. A. (1983). Public sector strike penalties and their appeal. *Public Personnel Management Journal 12*:196–205.

Wurf, J. (1969). Address to mayors, June 19, 1967. *Sorry. . . . No Government Today: Unions vs. City Hall*. Ed. Walsh, Robert E. Beacon Press, Boston.

22
Labor Relations in Local and County Government

Ernest Gross   Industrial Relations and Human Resources Department, Institute of Management and Labor Relations, Rutgers, The State University of New Jersey, New Brunswick, New Jersey

I. OVERVIEW

There has been very little systematic study of local personnel systems for medium and small jurisdictions (Lee, 1982). One often thinks that civil service is the norm in the public service. In fact, civil service systems are found in the federal and state service and in the large cities. In the smaller cities coverage is often limited to police and fire services (Aronson, 1979). Labor relations policy is often taken as another way of talking about collective bargaining. In this chapter personnel function, personnel systems, merit principle, labor negotiations with unions, or meet-and-confer-with union systems are all treated as aspects of human resource administration.

Wherever there is an employment environment there is of necessity some form of labor relations policy. This chapter, therefore, concerns itself with the employment environment in local government units. In some, there are statutes mandating collective negotiations or the obligation to meet and confer with the organized representatives of employees—labor unions. Some local governments function under civil service laws; others have neither mandatory collective negotiations laws nor civil service laws. Some local governments function in environments where accommodation is required between collective negotiations obligations and civil service requirements.[1]

Table 1 Organized Full-Time Employees, by Level
and Type of Government

Level and type of government	Organized full-time employees	
	Number	Percent
Total	5,030,564	48.8
State governments	1,162,878	40.5
Local governments	3,867,686	52.0
Counties	547,169	34.9
Municipalities	1,117,070	53.9
Townships	130,678	58.6
Special districts	143,787	37.8
School districts	1,928,982	60.2

Source: U.S. Bureau of the Census (1980). *Labor Management Relations in State and Local Governments: 1980.* Series GSS No. 120. U.S. Government Printing Office, Washington, D.C.

II. PROFILE OF LOCAL GOVERNMENT EMPLOYEES

Recently published census figures show 3,867,686 full-time local government employees who belong to employee organizations (U.S. Bureau of the Census, 1980). This accounts for 52% of all full-time employees of local government. The more specific breakdown is shown in Table 1.

The fire protection function showed the highest proportion of organized employees: 70.6% of full-time fire protection employees belonged to employee organizations (Table 2).

Translating these figures, it would follow that there are 3,570,171 full-time local government employees who did not belong to employee organizations. These are broken down as follows:

Level and type of government	Unorganized full-time employees
Local governments	3,570,171
Counties	1,020,650
Municipalities	955,416
Townships	92,322
Special districts	236,601
School districts	1,275,307

Table 2 Percent of Full-Time Employees Organized by Function and Level of Government

Function	State and local governments	State governments	Local governments
Total	48.8	40.5	51.9
For selected functions:			
Education	55.4	29.6	61.3
Teachers	64.9	36.1	67.9
Other	38.1	26.4	44.4
Highways	45.0	52.9	37.6
Public welfare	41.8	41.2	42.4
Hospitals	40.0	49.8	29.4
Police protection	52.7	51.8	52.8
Local fire protection	70.6	–	70.6
Sanitation other than sewerage	40.2	–	40.2
All other functions	39.4	41.4	38.3

– Represents zero.
Source: U.S. Bureau of the Census (1980). *Labor Management Relations in State and Local Governments: 1980*. Series GSS No. 120. U.S. Government Printing Office, Washington, D.C.

Table 3 Governments with a Labor Relations Policy, by Level and Type of Government

Level and type of government	Number of governments	Governments reporting a labor relations policy	
		Number	Percent
Total	79,928	14,302	17.9
State governments	50	43	86.0
Local governments	79,878	14,259	17.9
Counties	3040	755	24.8
Municipalities	18,878	2624	13.9
Townships	16,827	1088	6.5
Special districts	26,010	913	3.5
School districts	15,123	8879	58.7

Source: U.S. Bureau of the Census (1980). *Labor Management Relations in State and Local Governments: 1980*. Series GSS No. 120. U.S. Government Printing Office, Washington, D.C.

There were 79,878 local governments in the last published census figures. Of them, 17.9%, or 14,259, reported a labor relations policy. The more detailed breakdown is shown in Table 3.

Labor relations policy describes not only the 6511 units engaged in collective negotiations but 2050 units with a policy of meet-and-confer discussions and 5741 units engaged in both collective negotiations and meet-and-confer discussions.

III. UNION ENVIRONMENT

Collective negotiations, which are usually statutorily mandated, give legal rights to the employees' majority representatives in a unit appropriate for negotiations to meet with representatives of the public employer and through bilateral negotiations enter into agreements. The extent of negotiations depends upon the statute or case law of the states. Most of the statutes are modeled after the National Labor Relations Act. There is usually an administrative agency similar to the National Labor Relations Board.[2] The statutes give public employees the right to organize themselves or to engage in concerted activities more often without the right to strike. The private sector model has been adopted to the extent that the majority representative of the employees in a unit appropriate for collective negotiations is the employees' exclusive representative. This also imposes upon the negotiating representative, union or association as it may be called, a duty of fair representation for all employees in the unit whether they are members of the organization or not.

A. Bargaining Units

North Carolina and Virginia had no governments engaged in collective negotiations or meet-and-confer discussions according to the 1980 census (U.S. Bureau of the Census, 1980).

Where negotiations or meet-and-confer discussions take place, it is in the context of units appropriate for negotiations. The bargaining unit is the arena in which bargaining takes place. Thus, the union is the chosen vessel that employees' rights to concerted action are effectuated. Neither the National Labor Relations Act, which is the model, nor the various state statutes in the public sector refer to unions in the statements on employee rights. The statutes give employees the right to join together to negotiate and for other concerted activities, including the right to join or refrain from joining labor organizations.[2]

Because the end result of negotiations is usually a written agreement spelling out rights and responsibilities, it has to be manageable. Thus, the literature speaks of appropriate units, usually in terms of community of interest between employees. What is meant is simply whether all who ought to be included are included and all who ought to be excluded are excluded.[2,3]

B. Scope of Negotiations

The scope of negotiations in some states follows the private sector model. There are mandatory subjects for bargaining on wages, hours, terms, and other conditions of employment, illegal subjects, and permissive subjects.[3] There are areas of inherent management right or policy that may be subjects of bargaining but are not necessarily required to be; thus they are called permissive. Some states, such as New Jersey, have limited the requirement to negotiate terms and conditions of employment and grievance procedures to either mandatory or illegal subjects. That is, only matters appropriate for negotiation are those not covered by a statute. Where a statute sets the floors and the ceilings, there may be negotiations between the floor and the ceiling but not below or above. Where a statute covers an entire field, that matter is preempted and there can be no negotiation. Meet-and-confer discussions describe a process in which a public employer meets with employee representatives. In form, the public employer is consenting to meet with the employee representatives and seek advice. The public employer is not bound to agree, and although there are often memoranda of agreement or understanding drafted, they are not binding agreements in theory of law. In practice, there is variation in the processes and the outcomes.

The structure of state and local governments excluding special districts that engage in collective negotiations and/or meet-and-confer discussions is shown in Table 4.

IV. CIVIL SERVICE ENVIRONMENT

There are 3,570,171 full-time employees who did not belong to employee organizations in 1980. Some 82.1% of the local governments in the United States in 1980 did not have a labor relations policy: they neither negotiated with unions nor met and conferred with employee representatives. This does not mean that they did not have labor relations policies toward their employees in a broad sense. Since 1883 when the federal civil service act was adopted many state and local governments followed its principles. A 1970 study found comprehensive civil service laws in thirty-four states and in practically all cities with a population of over 100,000 (Aronson, 1979). The National Governors' Conference executive committee defined the merit principle as "the concept that public employees should be selected and retained solely on the basis of merit. Political, religious, or racial consideration should play no part in such employment practices as selection, promotion, wages, career progression, assignment, and discharge."[4]

Aronson (1979) reported:

All of the cities with a population of over 250,000, with the exception of Washington, D.C., which receives some services from the U.S.

Table 4 Number and Percent of State and Local Governments That Engaged in Collective Negotiations and/or Meet and Confer Discussions, by State: October 1980

States	All state and local governments			State and local governments, excluding special districts		
	Total	Governments which engage in CN and/or MC discussions		Total	Governments which engage in CN and/or MC discussions	
		Number	Percent		Number	Percent
United States, total	79,928	14,302	17.9	53,918	13,389	24.8
Alabama	953	37	3.9	614	32	5.2
Alaska	151	30	19.9	151	30	19.9
Arizona	420	103	24.5	314	102	32.5
Arkansas	1347	66	4.9	923	65	7.0
California	3807	1485	39.0	1578	1241	78.6
Colorado	1465	132	9.0	510	120	23.5
Connecticut	435	187	43.0	199	165	82.9
Delaware	211	22	10.4	84	21	25.0
District of Columbia	2	2	100.0	1	1	100.0
Florida	912	212	23.2	551	198	35.9
Georgia	1267	16	1.3	877	8	.9
Hawaii	20	5	25.0	5	5	100.0
Idaho	973	114	11.7	361	104	28.8
Illinois	6619	869	13.1	3872	829	21.4
Indiana	2867	351	12.2	1977	336	17.0
Iowa	1851	491	26.5	1517	489	26.9
Kansas	3726	296	7.9	2507	293	11.7
Kentucky	1185	45	3.8	707	41	5.8
Louisiana	459	24	5.2	429	23	5.4
Maine	782	189	24.2	604	178	29.6
Maryland	427	38	8.9	175	35	20.0

Massachusetts	768	402	52.3	440	377	85.7
Michigan	2627	907	34.5	2460	886	36.0
Minnesota	3439	654	19.0	3176	637	20.1
Mississippi	836	14	1.7	532	14	2.6
Missouri	2938	249	8.5	1927	233	12.1
Montana	950	217	22.8	639	211	33.0
Nebraska	3425	382	11.2	2232	372	16.7
Nevada	183	39	21.3	51	34	66.7
New Hampshire	507	116	22.9	404	115	28.5
New Jersey	1516	882	58.2	1136	828	78.9
New Mexico	315	41	13.0	215	41	19.1
New York	3307	1124	34.0	2342	1110	47.4
North Carolina	875	–	–	573	–	–
North Dakota	2706	193	7.1	2119	192	9.1
Ohio	3333	778	23.3	3018	751	24.9
Oklahoma	1695	198	11.7	1290	196	15.2
Oregon	1449	392	27.1	652	348	53.4
Pennsylvania	5239	1192	22.8	3200	1057	33.0
Rhode Island	120	48	40.0	43	39	90.7
South Carolina	585	9	1.5	403	8	2.0
South Dakota	1729	196	11.3	1581	194	12.3
Tennessee	907	71	7.8	436	66	15.1
Texas	3897	118	3.0	2455	111	4.5
Utah	493	55	11.2	287	52	18.1
Vermont	648	158	24.4	581	158	27.2
Virginia	390	–	–	325	–	–
Washington	1669	476	28.5	607	376	61.9
West Virginia	597	32	5.4	338	27	8.0
Wisconsin	2519	601	23.9	2329	597	25.6
Wyoming	387	44	11.4	171	43	25.1

– Represents zero.

Source: U.S. Bureau of the Census (1980). *Labor Management Relations in State and Local Governments: 1980.* Series GSS No. 120. U.S. Government Printing Office, Washington, D.C.

Civil Service Commission, have provisions for a municipal civil service system. Most cities between 100,000 and 250,000 are under a law, charter, or ordinance for such a system. Many smaller cities also have civil service systems. In a substantial number of them, coverage is limited to the police and fire departments. A few cities have two systems, one general and one for police and fire.

There has been less activity in establishment of civil service systems at the county level. There are various systems in the counties of the following states: New York, Ohio, New Jersey, and California. In other states coverage is limited to the larger metropolitan or suburban counties. Massachusetts has civil service coverage of localities and a few states have a combined city-county civil service system.

In its 1982 personnel program inventory the Center for Personnel Research, International Personnel Management Association (IPMA) found that 63% of the respondents had a merit system by statute or ordinance. Thirty-four percent had personnel policies and procedures manuals, and 50% had the power to modify disciplinary action of appointing authorities. The survey was based upon 519 completed questionnaires.[5]

The data described so far indicate a pattern of three personnel systems or functions that embody labor relations policies in a broad sense. There is the system in those states where municipalities and counties are required or may negotiate or meet and confer with employee organizations. There is a substantial literature describing how collective negotiations function. There is the system where the merit principle applies by statute, charter, or ordinance commonly referred to as the civil service system. There is also the overlapping situation in states such as New Jersey, New York, and others that require collective negotiations with employee representatives where the employees as a matter of statutory right have selected a majority representative in units appropriate for collective negotiations. There is substantial literature about the accommodation of the two and a great deal of soothsaying as to which will wither away and which will flourish. The most recent literature indicates that there is more accommodation than otherwise expected.[1,6] The third area is that a rather substantial portion of the municipalities and counties in the United States and a rather substantial percentage of employees who are in smaller units are neither covered by collective negotiations statutes nor by civil service statutes. Amazingly, there is a scant literature as to how they function. There is not much substantial data as to whether their productivity is measurable and whether the measurements show anything different from employees covered by collective negotiations contracts, civil service, or both. Employees not covered by collective negotiations or civil service are in situations analogous to the employment-at-will relationship known as the common law. That is, in an employment-at-will situation, an employer may terminate the employee at any time with cause or without cause, and the employee may sever the relationship the same way.

V. THE OTHER RELATIONSHIP

The employment-at-will relationship has been eroding. The first and most important aspect that also affects the employees covered by collective negotiations statutes and civil service statutes is the effect of civil rights laws; specifically, Title VII of the Civil Rights Act of 1964 and the Age and Discrimination in Employment Act.[7] There may not by federal law be a discriminatory hiring policy, promotion policy, or dismissal policy. The other development changing the employment-at-will situation is the growing consciousness that employees by and large are entitled to some kind of due process system protecting them against arbitrary discipline and dismissal. The common term for such systems is grievance procedures. In many ways grievance procedures lie at the heart of personnel administration.

VI. GRIEVANCE PROCEDURES

A study by Begin of 304 contracts in federal, state, and local governments concluded that the scope of grievance procedures generally tends to be narrower in the public sector than in the private sector with some variation.[6,8] The breadth and scope of negotiated grievance procedures depends upon the statutory or case definitions of scope of negotiations and the availability of civil service appeals procedures for matters of job evaluation, promotion, classification, discipline, and discharge. Some statutes, such as in New Jersey, require public employers to negotiate grievance procedures but permit either advisory or binding arbitration as a final step. The New Jersey Supreme Court construing the statute has held that a public employer may enter into grievance procedures with various tracks. Not every type of grievance has to go to binding arbitration as a last step. Almost any problem can be raised in a grievance procedure, but every problem is not required to go to binding arbitration. In New Jersey, the collective negotiation law specifically saves individual employee civil service rights. The New Jersey civil service law provides for a due process hearing procedure for all discipline cases or reduction in pay or position of more than five days. It is, therefore, not uncommon to have a two-track system. For example, a negotiated agreement would go through the grievance procedure with a binding arbitration or advisory arbitration terminal step. Employees may elect, if more than a five-day penalty is imposed, to use the grievance procedure or the civil service appeal route. Some agreements, especially in the first few years of experience with the collective negotiations law, did not provide for election or waiver; employees had literally two routes by following the grievance procedure and also the civil service appeal procedure.[7] Of the 304 contracts, 90% contained negotiated grievance procedures; 19% contained agency or civil service procedures, but additional information indicated that a 40–50% range might have been more accurate. Over 61% contained some type of arbitration provision, of which 8% had advisory arbitration, 51% had binding arbitration, and about 2% had both types.

Begin also found that the mechanical structure of the public sector grievance procedure was similar to that in the private sector. The contracts listed successive steps in a dispute. A major difference was the existence of alternate methods of resolving grievance impasses in the public agreements. Mediation and fact-finding, which is not common in private sector agreements, were found in many contracts (especially those without binding or advisory arbitration). Mediation and fact-finding are also provided for in some state statutes, even without provision in collective bargaining agreements. There is no solid evidence of the efficacy or lack of efficacy of mediation and fact-finding. A safe assumption is that where the parties want to solve a problem but don't know how, there is a lot to be said for mediation and fact-finding short of arbitration. The problem—to the extent that it is a problem—is complicated because the parties are not only the union and the public employer but also the grievant. Because the employee representatives have a duty of fair representation sometimes in the settlement of a grievance, there are tripartite pressures. That is, the public employee representative had institutional needs that may or may not be the same as the individual who filed a grievance. As a result, the public employee representative and the individual have to reconcile any differences they may have as to the merits, and then they have to reconcile their joint approach with the public employer position. One of the problem areas in the development of grievance procedures in the public sector, especially those that use binding arbitration as a final step, is the status of supervisory employees and department heads. Status can be upgraded or downgraded depending upon how the grievance procedure is administered. There is a tendency where there is binding arbitration to pass all problems up to the highest level. If such a situation is permitted to develop, then both the employee representative and the lower-level supervisory learn that it is futile to spend much time on problems because they will be appealed anyway. The extent of authority with which supervisory employees on various levels of a grievance procedure are cloaked therefore becomes an important policy decision (Gross, 1980). It is a truism in the private sector that where unions negotiate grievance procedures, management reacts by rationalizing its discipline and administrative policies. A standardization of procedures usually evolves. What happens to the various levels of supervision, therefore, depends upon how the overall management chooses to treat the various levels of supervision. The normal statement is that the best sort of administration is one that settles grievances at the lowest possible level. Sometimes the very people who enunciate such statements ignore it in practice. The same tendencies can be observed in the public sector as experience with grievance procedures shows.

The chief distinction between arbitration as a last step and statutory appeal procedures lies in the unique status of arbitration awards. Generally speaking, arbitrators are the final judges of both law and fact, and their awards are not appealable to the courts. Arbitration awards are attacked by a motion either to vacate (i.e., to set it aside) or to modify. Although there are some variations from state to state, in those states that have adopted arbitration statutes an award can usually be set aside only if:[9]

1. It was procured by corruption, fraud or other undue means or
2. The arbitrator was guilty of evident partiality, corruption or misconduct or
3. The arbitrator refused to postpone the hearing upon sufficient cause, or refused to hear material evidence; or otherwise so conducted the hearing as to prejudice substantially the rights of a party.
4. The arbitrator exceeded his powers or so imperfectly executed them that a mutual and final and definite award upon the subject matter was not made.
5. There was no valid agreement to arbitrate which had not been determined in some previous action to compel or stay arbitration and the objection to that fact was properly raised.

Statutory appeal procedures usually have a direct right of appeal into the courts. Donahue (1975:110-112), in discussing the change in Section 75 of the New York State Civil Service law to use binding arbitration in grievance procedures in place of the traditional appeal procedure, found that employees with shockingly poor job performance were often allowed to stay on the state payroll year after year because of the difficulties associated with removing them or taking action to correct their performance. Cases of discharge or discipline for gross misconduct occurred, but rarely. Apparently the change in the New York State service was considered by the state to be an important improvement in the personnel function.

Graham (1982:112-117), in a 1982 study of arbitration results in the public sector, found that, in the early years of the 1970s, public employers lost more cases than public unions. He postulated that the early employer losses resulted from employers taking weak cases to arbitration to retain authority, but after learning more about the process, the win proportion increased. He found that employers in the public sector prevail in about half of the cases.

In 1978, Miller (September–October, 1978:302-315) made a national study of grievance procedures in a nonunion environment. He found five separate models. In his model A, he found that the entry into the grievance procedure was very broad, but final review and decision were in the hands of the chief administrative officer. In model B, there was provision for advisory or binding arbitration. The procedure was open to any government-related issue. In model C, there was external review, but the categories of issues grievable were restricted. Discipline—that is suspension or discharge—was expedited to reduce redundancy and shorten the time span before a final review. In model D, the employee may initiate any grievance on any employment-related matter for which there is an established policy. The grievance is then considered initially by a committee of peers, that is coemployees who formulate a recommendation to the chief administrative officer. Model E followed traditional collective bargaining grievance procedures where the grievances were qualified and then processed through multisteps for management review and then to final and binding arbitration. The authority of management was conserved by limiting the grievable issues.

The National Civil Service League proposed a model public personnel administration law and recommended a seven-member citizen personnel advisory board to provide advice and counsel on all aspects of public personnel administration including, among other things, employee grievances (A Model Public Personnel Public Administration Law, 1970:10, 11). The citizen personnel advisory board would appoint a hearing officer to represent the public interest by reviewing employee appeals resulting from alleged employer action, including unwarranted demotion, dismissal, or suspension. The hearing officer's recommendations would be sent to the chief executive for appropriate action. Although the proposed model law was not widely adopted, the comment on its proposal for a hearing officer system was the need in any jurisdiction to protect the employee from arbitrary action and for the establishment of a system whereby the restraints, penalties, and policies placed on the employee are sound, understandable, fair, and as a result, employee supported.

Acting under an Intergovernmental Personnel Act of 1970 grant, the Department of Civil Service of New Jersey developed "A Model Personnel System for New Jersey County and Municipal Governments" (1974:176, 177). It recommended a four-step grievance procedure with the comment that unless suspense dates are established, it is probable that too much time will elapse in the processing of grievances and appeals. The reasons, of course, are self-evident including the fact that if a grievance is not resolved in the employee's favor there may have to be remedial action including retroactive pay. The four-step procedure set out in full follows.

A. Step No. 1

Whenever possible, grievances may be resolved informally. That is to say, when efforts to resolve complaints are successful at the supervisory level, no further action is necessary. When, however, employee grievances are not resolved within a reasonable period, not to exceed two weeks at the supervisory level, they must be formalized. Formalized grievances fall into two categories: (a) those pertaining to the application and interpretation of agreements between management and employee organizations, and (b) all other matters.

If an employee's grievance is not acted on within the specified time allowed at any step, the employee can refer the grievance to the next higher level. This ensures that grievances are processed expeditiously.

B. Step No. 2

When employees exhaust their informal attempts to resolve complaints, they must resolve them through formalized grievance procedure. The grieved employee should prepare a written statement setting forth the grievance, including a description of the remedial action being sought and any information available in support of the complaint. The statement should be given to the employee's immediate supervisor.

Upon receipt of a written grievance, the supervisor should make all reasonable efforts to resolve the grievance. If it is not resolved, it should be sent to the head of the department in which the employee works within seven days of receipt, together with a statement of efforts made at the supervisory level to resolve the grievance.

C. Step No. 3

If the departmental chief cannot resolve the grievance, it must be forwarded to the appointing officer for decision within seven days, along with a record of the efforts made to resolve it at the departmental level.

D. Step No. 4

To afford the employee prompt consideration, the appointing officer should render a written decision on the grievance within fifteen days of receipt.

VII. ENTRY INTO THE SYSTEM

One of the areas where change through federal statute and public policy affecting local government lies is in the area of hiring. Traditionally, hiring has always had a close relationship to patronage. Even in those areas where the employees have joined labor organizations, unions have not expressed any special interest in employers who hire on an individual basis that is markedly different from the policies before the advent of public sector unionism. In those local governments functioning under civil service laws, especially those with the rule of three, political patronage was not eliminated. Prior to the Civil Rights Act of 1964, the chief statutory inhibition on hiring was the veterans preference laws. Those laws simply narrowed the available employment pool *some*what. For example, the way the draft operated during World War II, the Korean war and the Vietnam war, there were more eligible men available for public sector positions than women. Title VII of the Civil Rights Act of 1964 prohibits employment decisions for hiring, discharging, and promotion to be made on the basis of race, color, religion, sex, or national origin.[7] The Age Discrimination in Employment Act of 1967 creates a protected category of persons between the ages of forty and seventy who cannot be discriminated against as far as hiring and discharge are concerned.[7]

Civil liberties have been guaranteed by the U.S. Constitution from the very beginning of the nation. The First Amendment to the U.S. Constitution guarantees freedom of religion. The Fifth Amendment protects persons against deprivation of life, liberty, or property without due process of law. The Thirteenth Amendment abolished slavery, and the Fourteenth Amendment prohibited the states from abridging the privileges granted by federal law without equal protection or due process of the laws.

The Civil Rights Acts of 1866, 1870, and 1871, codified as 42 U.S.C. Sections 1981-1983, were to implement the constitutional protection of the Fourteenth Amendment. Section 1983 was to protect persons from deprivation of any rights, privileges, or immunities under color of any statute, ordinance, regulation, custom, or usage by any state or territory.

Effective statutory elimination of the discrimination by reason of race, creed, sex, or national origin, however, starts with Title VII of the Civil Rights Act of 1964.

The 1972 amendment, section 701(a) P.L. 92-261, extended coverage of the law to state and local governments, governmental agencies, and political subdivisions. Discrimination against individuals between forty and seventy years of age in hiring, promotion, and dismissal actions was prohibited by the Age Discrimination in Employment Act of 1967, 29 U.S.C. Section 621-634, amended in 1978. The Act's coverage generally follows that of Title VII of the Civil Rights Act of 1964. The remedies under the Act are generally those under the Fair Labor Standards Act. Therefore, if there is disparity between two people doing the same work and one of them falls within the protected class, it is not permissible as a remedy to lower the pay or status of the one with higher pay, which is the general remedy under the Equal Pay Act Amendment to the Fair Labor Standards Act. Furthermore, where there are two people, one of whom is in the protected class between the ages of forty and seventy and they are equal, it would be a violation of the law to favor the younger one for promotion based solely on youth. The coverage of the Age Discrimination in Employment Act was challenged insofar as state and local governments were concerned with the argument that the Tenth

Amendment to the U.S. Constitution reserved to the states the powers not specifically delegated to the federal government. The U.S. Supreme Court upheld the act, and found that the state's ability to carry out its traditional government function was not impaired (*EEOC v. Wyoming*, 1983). The Civil Rights Law does not mandate affirmative action plans as such. However, the statute does say that where an employee or class of employees has been illegally denied the rights protected by the act they should be made whole. As part of the right granted to remedy violations of the act, affirmative action plans have been generally required. Such plans are instituted to have employment brought more or less into a line with the general proportionate representation that the minority group has in the population.

Another thrust of the civil rights laws is to bring about a complete reevaluation of employment requirements, testing requirements, and promotion criteria. Age-old assumptions as to the desirable height of police and firefighters have been challenged by Hispanic minority groups who were not well represented in such departments in some cities. Certain physical qualifications that denied membership to women in many state trooper and police organizations have also been challenged. Stereotyped views as to "women's work" as distinguished from "men's" have also been challenged. Generally speaking, where there is a bona fide occupational qualification there can be differential impact. One of the most troublesome aspects of the administration of the civil rights laws in 1983 rose from the changed economic climate in which the laws operate. In 1964, the economic outlook was rosy and there was general expansion. In the words of President Kennedy, a rising tide floats all boats and thus the thrust of affirmative action recruiting and hiring was considered a viable method of solving discriminatory employment practices. One of the provisions of Title VII, resulting from a congressional compromise to get the law passed, was a protection of bona fide negotiated seniority clauses. That is, where there was a union representing a majority of the employees in a unit appropriate for collective bargaining and a clause was negotiated that provided for seniority as a governing factor in layoff if there was a reduction in force, such provisions were generally to be protected as exceptions to the Civil Rights Act. As cases began to rise through the court system to the U.S. Supreme Court, a remedy was fashioned as appropriate at the time to award artificial seniority to help make whole the victims of discriminatory practices. Thus, where job opportunities depended upon seniority and if an employer had, through discriminatory practices, failed to hire or refused to hire members of a minority group, after they were hired they would still require help through administrative agency or traditional intervention to overcome the original handicap from discriminatory hiring. As the economy began to shrink and employers faced a reduction in force, a different aspect of the problem surfaced. Seniority clauses usually provide that the employee with the least amount of service is the one who is to be severed first. By and large, employers who had embarked upon affirmative action programs hiring minority group members usually found themselves with seniority lists where the newly hired blacks, Hispanics, or women were the lowest on the seniority list. In recent cases, the U.S. Supreme Court has held that, notwithstanding remedial orders and agreements entered into between employers and the Equal Employment Opportunity Commission (EEOC) requiring that members of minority groups be hired on layoff, where there was a bona fide negotiated seniority system with a labor organization representing employees in the bargaining units of which the minority group members were members, then the seniority system in the labor contract had to be followed, not the civil rights consent agreements (*W. R. Grace and Co. v. Rubber Works Local*, 1983). Another abridgement of the traditional right of employers to hire as they choose is the State and Local Fiscal Assistance Act of 1972, as amended, which requires state and local governments receiving federal revenue-sharing funds not to discriminate in employment on the basis of race, color, national origin, sex, religion, age, and handicapped status. Handicapped status, however, is not one of the rights protected by Title VII of the Civil Rights Act of 1964.

VIII.   CIVIL RIGHTS LAWS AND COLLECTIVE NEGOTIATIONS

The thrust of the federal statute and the comparable state statutes apply equally to local government units in states with bargaining laws or meet-and-confer discussion laws or government units without formal labor relations policies.

An employee who is part of the bargaining unit that is a member of a union with a grievance procedure terminating in binding arbitration who is disciplined and who claims that the disciplinary action violated the federal civil rights laws has an independent course of action.

An employee represented by his union has presented the matter to an arbitrator who having heard all of the aspects of the case then rendered an award upholding the disciplinary action. That employee, assuming that a timely charge was filed with the EEOC or a state civil rights agency, would not be prevented from filing suit under Title VII notwithstanding the arbitrator's award rendered. The U.S. Supreme Court has held that the arbitrator's award would simply be another item of evidence to be presented to a trial judge (*Alexander v. Gardner Denver*, 1974). The same issue appeared in two companion cases decided by the Supreme Court of New Jersey concerning the New Jersey Civil Rights Law. The New Jersey statute is generally the same as Title VII in thrust and administration. The court held that even though the grievance had gone through the entire procedure and through arbitration under the union contract, it did not bar a complaint to the division on civil rights. The arbitrator's award, although not binding on the division of civil rights, should be considered (*Teaneck Board of Education v.*

Teaneck Teacher's Association, 1983; *Thomas Thornton v. Potamkin Chevrolet*, 1982). The division should look into what evidence was considered by the arbitrator, what was done to test credibility, how formal the proceedings were, whether the decision was detailed or cursory, and whether the decision was well reasoned and persuasive. The companion case concerned a grievance by a public school teacher who had a statutory due process procedure under the education law. Under the New Jersey Public Employment Relations Act, the Public Employment Relations Commission may rule on scope of negotiations problems. The discrimination claim was filed. The teachers association sought arbitration under its union contract. The arbitrator held that the issue was arbitrable. The board of education asked the Public Employment Relations Commission (PERC) to decide whether or not in fact the matter was within the scope of negotiations, and the PERC agreed with the arbitrator. The appellate division reversed the PERC and remanded the matter, saying that the law against discrimination had preempted the issue. The appellate division gave the grievant the option of going to the division on civil rights or to the superior court or to use the statutory appeal procedure to the commissioner of education. The matter was certified to the New Jersey Supreme Court which held that the division of civil rights was generally the most appropriate forum for resolving a claim of racial discrimination. Even though the review by the division on civil rights would ordinarily imply an interference with the inherent managerial prerogatives of a public employer in matters of hiring and firing, for example, it was proper. The interference was necessary to fulfill governmental policy. However, binding arbitration was not appropriate under New Jersey law to resolve a decision on hiring in the public sector because the New Jersey public negotiations law did not permit negotiations in statutory matters. Nevertheless, the grievance procedure could be used with advisory arbitration. Regardless of the use or absence of advisory arbitration, an employee had a right to present a statutory claim of discrimination to the division on civil rights.

A. Impasse Procedures and the Right to Strike

Most of the states prohibit or limit public employee right to strike. Table 5 summarizes the state laws.[10]

In the private sector, the right to strike by employees and to lock out by employers creates a backdrop of finality to collective bargaining. In the public sector where the organized employees do not have the right to strike and public employers can hardly threaten to close down until a contract is signed, there has been a continuous search for a technique to bring finality to negotiations. Almost every state that permits collective bargaining requires that the bargaining duty be discharged in good faith. Mediation is provided for impasse, and usually fact-finding recommendations follow mediation.

Table 5   State Laws on Public Employee Strikes

State	
Alabama	Firefighter law prohibits the right to strike.
Alaska	Divides its employees between those who do essential services where there can be no strike at all and those that can have limited strikes but not indefinitely and those services where the public will not be seriously affected. Police and fire protection employees may not engage in strikes. Public utility, snow removal, and sanitation employees may not engage in strikes unless there has been mediation and if a majority of employees in the unit appropriate for bargaining vote by secret ballot to authorize the strike.
California	Firefighter law prohibits the right to strike. The city and county of San Francisco ordinance prohibits strike.
Connecticut	Municipal employee relations act prohibits strikes.
Florida	State and local government employee law prohibits strikes.
Georgia	Firefighter law prohibits the right to strike.
Hawaii	Limits the right to strike to employees in appropriate bargaining units where after impasse and a fact-finding board has made public its findings and any recommendations unless the strike will endanger public health or safety. Firefighters may not strike but use a binding arbitration procedure.
Idaho	Firefighters are prohibited from striking.
Indiana	State and government employees law declared unconstitutional in 1977. The right to strike was prohibited.
Iowa	The right to strike is prohibited.
Kansas	State and local government employee laws prohibit the right to strike.
Kentucky	Firefighter law prohibits the right to strike. The law enforcement officer's law also prohibits the right to strike.
Maine	Municipal and public employee relations act prohibits the right to strike. The law enforcement officer's law also prohibits the right to strike.
Maryland	Baltimore City municipal labor relations ordinance prohibits the right to strike. Prince George County employee law does not prohibit the right to strike, but limits it after an impasse panel

certifies that all of the appropriate impasse procedures have been exhausted and the county council has tried to resolve the dispute and is unable to reach an agreement and an intended notice of strike is given. Allegheny County government employees law prohibits the right to strike. Baltimore County employee relations act prohibits the right to strike.

Massachusetts
Massachusetts state and local government employee law prohibits the right to strike.

Michigan
Public employment relations act prohibits the right to strike. The Michigan police and firefighter law specifically prohibits the right to strike but provides for compulsory arbitration.

Minnesota
Public employment labor relations act limits the right to strike to situations where an employer refuses to comply with the provisions of a valid decision of a binding arbitration panel or arbitrator or to the refusal of the employer to request binding arbitration when it was so requested by the representative of the employees. No other unfair labor practice or violation by public employer permits the right to strike but may be taken into consideration by a court in mitigation of or retraction of any penalties as to employees and employee organizations.

Missouri
State and local government employees and firefighter law prohibits the right to strike.

Montana
State and local government employee law has been construed by the Montana Supreme Court to mean that public employees have the right to strike.

Nebraska
Right to strike is prohibited. Nebraska has a court of industrial relations as a terminal step in its impasse procedures.

Nevada
Local government employee management relations act prohibits the right to strike.

New Hampshire
Prohibits the right to strike.

New Jersey
Statute does not prohibit employees from striking, but the New Jersey Supreme Court has held that public employees are prohibited from striking as a matter of common law. In 1977, the legislature provided for compulsory final offer arbitration in disputes for public fire and police departments, and in its policy statement indicated that public employees do not enjoy the right to strike.

New York
The Taylor Law prohibits strikes by public employees. The New York City collective bargaining law prohibits the right to strike.

Oklahoma
Firefighter and police arbitration law prohibits strikes.

Table 5 (Continued)

Oregon	State and local government employees, firefighters, and police law limits the right to strike. Policemen and firemen may not strike. Other employees who are not involved in health safety may strike on a limited basis after fact-finder's report recommendations on ten-day notice. Eugene city ordinance limits the right of strike if either party refuses to accept a fact-finding panel's final offer selection, then on a ten-day notice there may be a strike.
Pennsylvania	Public employees other than guards and court employees have a limited right to strike, provided mediation and fact-finding procedures are completed and unless the strike is a clear and present danger and threat to the health and safety and welfare of the public.
Rhode Island	Municipal employee arbitration act prohibits the right to strike. The Rhode Island firefighter arbitration act prohibits the right to strike. The Rhode Island police arbitration act prohibits the right to strike.
South Dakota	State and local government employee and teacher law prohibits the right to strike.
Texas	Fire and police employee relations act prohibits the right to strike. Texas state and local government employee law prohibits the right to strike.
Utah	Firefighter negotiation act prohibited the right to strike. In 1977, the law was declared unconstitutional. Salt Lake City government employee regulations ordinance prohibited the right to strike.
Vermont	Municipal employee relations act limits the right to strike unless it occurs sooner than thirty days after delivery of a fact-finders report or if it occurs after both parties have voluntarily submitted a dispute to final binding arbitration or after a decision or award has been issued by the arbitrator or if it will endanger the safety or well-being of the public.
Washington	Public employee collective bargaining act prohibits the right to strike.
Wisconsin	Municipal employment relations act permits a limited strike subject to circumstances. A municipal employee in a labor organization may agree in writing if he chooses to a dispute settlement procedure which includes an authorization for a strike or binding interest arbitration. Or parties have failed to reach voluntary settlement after a reasonable period as determined by the mediator-arbitrator and if either party withdraws its final offer; otherwise if the parties do not withdraw the final offer then the mediator-arbitrator resolves the dispute by a final and binding arbitration. Police and firefighter's law prohibits the right to strike.
District of Columbia	Chapter 25A of the District personnel manual prohibits the right to strike.

B. Mediation

A mediator ordinarily has no power to impose any settlement. The mediator functions as a bridge builder. Through charm, persuasion, charisma, and sometimes bluff, a mediator helps people arrive at a solution. Sometimes simply by letting people talk to a mediator, that is in each other's presence, the parties set out their positions. The sounding board helps put things into perspective. Sometimes a mediator talks to the parties separately and acts as a conduit for messages helping to overcome mistrust and suspicion. Sometimes a mediator, drawing upon experience and insight, helps by suggesting possible formulations to break deadlocks. Mediation also works when people really want to settle but just do not know how and are willing, with help, to compromise positions. Mediation never works if the people either do not want to settle or feel they are dealing in areas of principle where compromise is not possible.

C. Fact-Finding

Fact-finding is a quasi-judicial proceeding where the parties present their positions supported by testimony, briefs, argument, or evidentiary material out of which a fact-finder can prepare recommendations. There is a rather substantial literature on mediation and fact-finding.[11] The questions that are often addressed are whether a fact-finder finds what the facts are as between the positions of the parties and then finds as facts what ought to be a desirable solution. Is the appreciation by the fact-finder of the possibility of acceptance or rejection of a recommendation by either party also a fact that should play a part in his recommendations? In most states the fact-finder's recommendations are not binding and very often simply serve as a basis for further negotiations.

Because there is a duty to bargain in good faith, it could be argued that there is a duty for public employers and public employees to be reasonable and arrive at reasonable compromises. In fact, it happens most of the time. One of the underlying assumptions of most bargaining laws is the idea that public opinion plays a part. When the New Jersey Public Employment Relations Commission promulgated its first rules of practice in 1968, it ordered that fact-finders' reports when first made should be secret. That is, if the parties reached an impasse, a mediator would attempt to help settle it. If mediation failed, a fact-finder would be appointed. The fact-finder would make nonbinding recommendations that would then be given to the parties. If either or both of the parties rejected the fact-finder's recommendations, which legally they could, or did nothing about them, then the rules provided the New Jersey Public Employment Relations Commission would release the fact-finder's report to the public. It cannot be denied that, in some communities where there were active interested citizens' groups, the fact-finding reports were made public, which did help build up some form of pressure, but by and large the threat was empty.

D. Compulsory Arbitration

One of the alternatives that has been proposed to voluntary solutions is compulsory arbitration.[12] Many public employers and, in fact, public employee representatives, object to compulsory arbitration because of its possible chilling effect upon negotiations. Where an arbitrator could make any award based upon the evidence, there is perceived to be no incentive on either party to be moderate in prearbitration negotiations. Indeed, it has been argued that if one knows that the ultimate step will be arbitration, it might be prejudicial to take reasonable positions in negotiations that might be considered as admissions against interest in an arbitration hearing. To alleviate that problem and to create some costs on each side if they were not reasonable, final-offer arbitration has been developed. In final-offer arbitration, the arbitrator has to select one position or the other but may make no compromises. Therefore, the theory is that if a party knows that its position is not reasonable it will force an arbitrator to select the other side of the position even though that position might not be as desirable as one might wish. The term that has come into use is mediation-arbitration (med-arb). It is a flexible procedure that encourages the parties to modify their final offers during arbitration and to negotiate before the ultimate final offer is made.

The New Jersey statute for police and firefighters permits the interest arbitrator to act as a mediator (Tener, 1982:9–12). The same person and in the same proceeding has the power and ultimate authority to take testimony and issue a binding award. At the same time, the same person is encouraged to mediate and to help the parties negotiate. Amazingly, the system works. The statutory language indicates that the final offer should be submitted to the arbitrator before the hearing starts. In practice, the parties modify their positions as the hearing goes on, and between sessions and in a substantial number of cases the final offer is made at or after the closing of hearings.

There are six approvable procedures, but the statute does not intend that those six are the only procedures approvable:

1. Conventional arbitration
2. Final-offer arbitration as a package
3. Final-offer arbitration on an issue-by-issue basis
4. Final-offer arbitration on a package basis with the recommendations of the fact-finder as a third choice
5. Final-offer arbitration on issue-by-issue basis with the recommendations of the fact-finder as a third choice on each issue
6. Final-offer arbitration on a package basis for economic issues and on an issue-by-issue basis for noneconomic issues

In the absence of agreement to one of the six statutory methods or any other one approved by the New Jersey Public Employment Relations Commission, the parties are required to submit their final offers to the arbitrator in two parts: first, with the economic issues as a package, and second, the noneconomic matters set out issue by issue. If there is any question as to whether any matter is economic or noneconomic, it is referred to the New Jersey Public Employment Relations Commission, which has the power to resolve a dispute.

The statute defines an economic issue as "a direct relation to employee income including wages, salaries, hours in relation to earnings, and other forms of compensation such as paid vacation, paid holidays, health and medical insurance, and other economic benefits to employees."

Unless the parties agree to submit permissive subjects to arbitration, only those matters can be arbitrated that are within the scope of negotiations. The New Jersey Public Employment Relations Commission resolves all disputes as to whether a matter is a required or a permissive negotiation subject.

The arbitrator must render his or her decision following statutory criteria; that is, "based on a reasonable determination of the issues, giving due weight to those factors listed below that are judged relevant to the resolution of the specific dispute." The statutory criteria listed are:

1. The interest and welfare of the public.
2. Comparison of the wages, salaries, hours and conditions of employment of the employees involved in the arbitration proceedings with the wages, hours, and conditions of employment of other employees performing the same or similar services and with other employees generally:
   (a) In public employment in the same or similar comparable jurisdictions.
   (b) In comparable private employment.
   (c) In public and private employment in general.
3. The overall compensation presently received by the employees, inclusive of direct wages, salary, vacations, holidays, excused leaves, insurance and pension, medical and hospitalization benefits, and all other economic benefits received.
4. Stipulations of the parties.
5. The lawful authority of the employer.
6. The financial impact on the governing unit, its residents and taxpayers.
7. The cost of living.

There are 567 municipalities in New Jersey and of these about 80 have paid firefighters and about 400 have paid police departments. Because supervisory employees are permitted to negotiate in an appropriate unit in some of the larger cities, the superior officers are in separate bargaining units from their rank and file. In addition, there are uniformed units in twenty-one counties. Potentially, there are 600–700 total bargaining units or potential units covered by the act. Tener (1983) found that the number of petitions over the first four years of the act had been relatively constant. He also found that the number of awards declined sharply from 103 in 1978 to 65 in 1981. The decline between 1980 and 1981 was very slight. The data suggested to him that the statute was not inhibiting negotiations.

Approximately two-thirds of the awards analyzed by Tener during the first four years were in final-offer form, and one-sixth were conventional. The remainder were consent awards, and a very small number of issue-by-issue final-offer-awards.

One of the results of the arbitration procedure has been a reduction, according to Tener, of the use of the prior steps. That is, since the arbitrator performs the mediation function, there has been virtually no fact-finding subsequent to the law's enactment and no independent mediation outside of the final-offer process.

Tener's conclusion is that three of the statutory criteria were the most persuasive: (a) comparability, (b) changes in the cost of living, and (c) ability to pay, with comparability serving as the benchmark or central factor.

The ability to pay or the demonstrated inability to pay was viewed as a limiting factor to support an award less generous than otherwise would be indicated by comparability data.

Tener reported that the New Jersey Public Employment Relations Commission estimated that wage increases (excluding any increased economic fringe benefits) in 1978 and 1979 averaged about 7%. Increases in the cost and the consumer's price index for those years were 7.7% and 11.3%, respectively. Although there are too many variables to state with any degree of assurance, he thought it was safe to say that the increases have not been as high over the past few years as in 1980, when the consumer price index stood at 13.5% and in 1981 when it was 10.4%.

The impression, gained from the analysis of those 1983 awards that have become available, is that the consumer price index (CPI) has fallen much faster than the awards. There were still 7, 8, and 9% awards in 1983 with the CPI at 3.5–4%.

The overall conclusion, however, seems to be that the system is working rather well, and there have been very few work stoppages since the law was enacted. Whether wage settlements have been excessive or not is perhaps beside the point because there has been no serious attempt to repeal or modify the law. There is a certain amount of rhetoric by people pro and con, but the system seems to have been accepted. By and large, the result of the mediation-arbitration process in New Jersey seems to leave a spread most of the time between the position of the public employers and the public employees of less than 2%, more often closer to 1%. And the number of sessions seem, in most cases, to be no more than two, with the first session an informal one and the second session as a formal proceeding more or less with the arbitrator acting as a mediator.

NOTES

1. Burton, Jr., J. F. (1977). Local government bargaining and management structure. In Lewin, D., Feuille, P., Kochan, T. A., eds., *Public Sector Labor Relations*, Horton, pp. 101–112. See also Lewin, D. and Horton, D. The impact of collective bargaining on the merit system in government. pp. 415–425; Seidman, J., The merit principle and collective bargaining in Hawaii. In Najita, J. M., ed., *Symposium Proceedings*. Dept. of Personnel Services, Hawaii, 1977. pp. 5–11.

2. Gibbons, M. K., Helsby, R. D., Lefkowitz, J., and Tener, B. Z., eds. (1979). *Portrait of a Process—Collective Negotiations in Public Employment*. Labor Relations Press, Ft. Washington, Penn. See also Najita, J. M., *Guide to Statutory Provisions in Public Sector Collective Bargaining*. There are some ten separate studies in this series produced by the Industrial Relations Center, College of Business Administration, University of Hawaii. Some such as *Employee Organization and Representation Rights* (1975) were done with Triplett, V. L., *Strike Rights and Prohibitions* 1978) were done with Tanimoto, H. S., and *Status of Managerial, Confidential and Supervisory Employees* (1975) with Ogawa, D. T. The series is as good a background study of the state of the art as can be found.

3. See Note 2. See also Stieber, J., *Bargaining Units*, pp. 78–85 and Hayford, S. L. and Sinicropi, A. V., *Bargaining Rights Status of Public Sector Supervisors*, pp. 86–97. Both articles in *Public Sector Labor Relations, Analysis and Readings*, Note 1. See also the Nagita, J. M. series cited in Note 2, especially Unit Determination, third issue, *The Public Employer and the Duty to Bargain*, and with Triplett, V. L., *Employee Organization and Representation Rights*. Also *Portrait of a Process—Collective Negotiations in Public Employment*, Note 2.

4. Report of Task Force on State and Local Government Labor Relations (1967). Executive Committee, National Governors Conference. Public Personnel Association, Chicago, p. 18, cited in Seidman, J. and Najita, J., *The Merit Principle and Collective Bargaining in Hawaii* (1976). Honolulu, Hawaii, sponsored by Governors I.P.A. State Advisory Committee coordinated by the Hawaii State Dept. of Personnel Services. Although addressed to Hawaii this volume of 107 pages is an excellent treatise on the entire subject covering not only collective bargaining but also the emerging issues focused by the civil rights laws.

5. Survey information was supplied by Kenneth A. Long, Director, Center for Personnel Research, International Personnel Management Association, 1850 K Street, N.W., Suite 870, Washington, D.C. 20006.
6. See Note 1. See also Marmo, M. (1983). Public employee unions—The political imperative. In Kershen, H., ed., *Labor/Management Relations Among Government Employees*, Baywood, Farmingdale, N.Y., pp. 57–67 and Gibbens et al. *Portrait of a Process*, Note 2. Also for a good general study see Stanley, D. F. (1972). *Managing Local Government Under Union Pressure*. The Brookings Institution, Washington, D.C.
7. Title VII, Civil Rights Act of 1964 as amended by Equal Employment Opportunity Act of 1972, P.L. No. 92-261, March 24, 1972; 42 U.S.C. Sec. 2000e et seq. (1970). Age Discrimination in Employment Act of 1967, P.L. No. 90-202, amended 1978 by P.L. No. 95-256 and 1983 by P. L. 97-248. Title VI of the Civil Rights Act of 1964, P. L. #88-352, 42 U.S.C. Sec. 2000d et seq. prohibits discrimination for race, color, or national origin by programs or activities receiving federal financial assistance.
8. Begin, J. P. (1969). The development and operation of grievance procedures in public employment. Ph.D. thesis, Purdue University, Ind. See also Stanley, D. F. (1972). *Managing Local Government Under Pressure*, Note 6, pp. 50–59.
9. Elkouri, F. and Elkouri, E. A. (1979). *How Arbitration Works*, 3rd ed. BNA, Washington, D.C., p. 40. Elkouri is the definitive work on grievance arbitration. The five grounds for setting aside an arbitration award are paragraphed from Elkouri.
10. Material on the right to strike adapted from: Tanimoto, H. S. and Najita, J. M. (1978). Strike rights and prohibitions, part of the *Guide to Statutory Provisions in Public Sector Collective Bargaining* series, see Note 2. Doherty, R. E. Public policy and the right to strike, *Portrait of a Process*, pp. 251–268, Note 2. U.S. Bureau of the Census. (1980). *Labor Management Relations in State and Local Governments: 1980*.
11. Rehmus, C. M. (December, 1982). Varieties of final offer arbitration. *The Arbitration Journal 37*(4):4–6. See also Note 2.
12. R.S. 34: 13A–16A et seq.
13. See Tener, J. B. (December, 1982), in references. See also Gross, E. and Stawnychy, P. (October 18, 1979). Mediation by arbitrators under Chapter 85, Laws of 1977. *104 New Jersey Law Journal*, p. 360. Gross, E. and Stawnychy, P. (February 7, 1980). Interest arbitration: Who's winning in New Jersey? *105 New Jersey Law Journal*, p. 115. See also Gross, E., Information Notes Nos. 22 through 26, Analysis of interest arbitration awards. IMLR, Rutgers, The State University of New Jersey, New Brunswick, N.J.

REFERENCES

Aronson, A. H. (1979). State and local personnel administration. In Thompson, F. J., ed., *Classics of Public Personnel Policy*. Moore Publishing, Oak Park, Ill., pp. 102–111.

Alexander v. Gardner Denver (1974). 415 U.S. 36.

Donahue, R. J. (March–April, 1975). Disciplinary actions in New York State service—A radical change. *Public Personnel Management*, pp. 110–112.

EEOC v. Wyoming (1983). 460 U.S. 226 31 FEP cases 74.

Graham, H. (Summer, 1975). Arbitration results in the public sector. *Public Personnel Management* 2(2):112–117.

Gross, E. (1980). Grievance procedures: A conceptual view. *Journal of Collective Negotiations* 9(1):59–80.

Lee, R. D., Jr. (December, 1982). Participants in the public personnel process. *Policy Studies Journal*, p. 261.

Miller, R. L. (September–October, 1978). Grievance procedures for non-union employees. *Public Personnel Management* 7(5):302–315.

A model public personnel administration law (1970). National Civil Service League 1970, Section 4, pp. 10–11.

A model personnel system for New Jersey county and municipal governments (1974). The Dept. of Civil Service, State of New Jersey, Trenton, N.J., pp. 176–177.

Tener, J. B. (December, 1982). Interest arbitration in New Jersey. *The Arbitration Journal* 37(4):9–12.

Teaneck Board of Education v. Teaneck Teacher's Association (1983). 94 N.J. 9.

Thomas Thornton v. Potamkin Chevrolet (1982). 94 N.J. 1.

U.S. Bureau of the Census (1980). *Labor Management Relations in State and Local Governments: 1980*. Series GSS No. 120. U.S. Government Printing Office, Washington, D.C.

W. R. Grace and Co. v. Rubber Works Local 759 (1983). 461 U.S. 757.

Index